Interpreting the Gospel and Letters of John

Interpreting the Gospel and Letters of John

AN INTRODUCTION

Sherri Brown *&* Francis J. Moloney, SDB

WILLIAM B. EERDMANS PUBLISHING COMPANY

GRAND RAPIDS, MICHIGAN

Wm. B. Eerdmans Publishing Co.
2140 Oak Industrial Drive N.E., Grand Rapids, Michigan 49505
www.eerdmans.com

26 25 24 23 22 21 20 19 18 17   1 2 3 4 5 6 7 8 9 10

ISBN 978-0-8028-7338-5

Library of Congress Cataloging-in-Publication Data

Names: Brown, Sherri, author.
Title: Interpreting the Gospel and the Letters of John : an introduction /
    Sherri Brown & Francis J. Moloney, SDB.
Description: Grand Rapids : Eerdmans Publishing Co., 2017. |
    Includes bibliographical references and index.
Identifiers: LCCN 2017018603 | ISBN 9780802873385 (pbk. : alk. paper)
Subjects: LCSH: Bible. John—Textbooks. | Bible. Epistles of John—Textbooks.
Classification: LCC BS2616 .B76 2017 | DDC 226.5/061—dc23
    LC record available at https://lccn.loc.gov/2017018603

In Memory of Frank Gignac, SJ

Contents

Illustrations

Preface

Interpreting the Gospel and Letters of John is a project that both of the authors have had in mind for years. It has taken a long time to come to fruition. We have decided that one of us would write the Preface, and the other would write a Conclusion. I would like to start by sharing my experience that led to the writing of this book. In my years teaching undergraduates and early graduate students I have been called upon to teach at least one class on the Johannine Literature each semester. Across this time I have struggled to find a suitable textbook to guide the students through the material. There are, of course, many fantastic commentaries and thematic volumes available, written by top-notch scholars. Many undergraduates, however, come to the course with little to no background in the Bible or organized biblical studies. A close analysis of the text alone or sometimes complicated discussions of the historical and theological themes can lie well above their level of preparation. They need the background unfolded and a systematic approach to the entirety of the task at hand in order to make any sense of the text beyond basic Christian teaching. Lists of the required texts for class, then, began to get longer and longer as I wanted to find something that responded to all the questions that an undergraduate class might ask. Then I found that many offerings along the lines of introductions to the Bible or biblical interpretation provided much more information or a different focus than what we really needed to augment our Johannine study. Therefore, I began to consider constructing a textbook of my own.

As any scholar or teacher knows, while pointing out the weaknesses in the book options we have before us is easy enough, developing an alternative that meets all the perceived needs is another matter altogether. Over the years, therefore, this project has gone through different iterations. Every new student I encounter gives me more food for thought. Eventually I determined to compose a "full service" textbook that attempts to provide all the steps needed for a beginning student to approach the biblical literature in general with a focus on the Gospel and Letters of John in particular. This would include discussions of the origins of the Bible, a sound methodology for biblical interpretation, some detail of the overarching biblical narrative, and the introduction to Jesus, his teachings, and his followers. Only when this was in place did I feel that I could begin guiding students through a detailed interpretation of the Johannine Literature. In the meantime, I had to hone my own skills at writing such material for my target level of students.

The task was daunting indeed, and I wondered whether I could manage it alone. Like any good student, therefore, I went to my own teachers for help and guidance. While enjoying the annual meeting of the Catholic Biblical Association at Gonzaga University in the summer of 2013 with my teacher and mentor Francis J. Moloney, I was struck with the notion that we should collaborate. His years of expertise with the literature alongside my recent experience in the undergraduate and early graduate classroom could make a winning combination, I thought. This was a stroke of genius. Frank, however, was not so sure of my sudden revelation. At the same time, we began to talk to Michael Thomson at Eerdmans about the project, and it did not take long for Frank to warm to the idea and then eventually get on board with his customary enthusiasm and work ethic.

The rest, as they say, is history. We have had some ups and downs as we sorted out our partnership and working arrangement, as well as a few starts and stops as we endeavored through other commitments and life changes, not to speak of the difficulty of working together across the thousands of miles that separate Omaha, Nebraska, from Melbourne, Australia. But these difficulties can be overcome, and we were fortunate to be able to work face-to-face on a number of occasions when Frank came to the USA for meetings or other teaching obligations. Now that we have seen it through to completion we are pleased indeed. Frank joins me in thanking Michael Thomson for his limitless trust in us and our vision as he encouraged and supported us along the way. In addition, the final text would not have come together as strongly as it has without the tireless commitment of Trevor Thompson. We are ever grateful. We would also like to thank all the teachers and students with whom we have shared our love of the Gospel and Letters of John over the years. We have learned so much from all of them. One of them deserves special attention. Frank Gignac, SJ, taught the Gospel of John to undergraduates at the Catholic University of America for decades. He did not do this course with us, but he taught each of us many things about the Bible, and about being a good Christian. He passed away while we were working on this book. We send it on its way in memory of all that he gave us.

Sherri Brown
Creighton University
Omaha, Nebraska

Francis J. Moloney, SDB
Catholic Theological College, in the University of Divinity
Melbourne, Victoria

The Gospel and Letters of John

PURPOSE The introduction discusses the Gospel and Letters John in terms of the sacred text of Christianity and the literary approach that will be the foundation for analysis in this textbook.

In order to begin our study of the Gospel and Letters of John, we must explore what these writings are and who this "John" is. These are topics that will be discussed in more detail later in the course, but we will lay out some basic terms here to get us started. The Gospel and Letters of John make up four books of the Christian Sacred Scriptures.

Introduction to Studying the Gospel and Letters of John

The term **scripture** comes from the Latin *scriptura* and literally means "writings." This Latin expression is a translation of the Greek word *graphē*, which also means "writing." Both the Jewish and Christian traditions use the term **Scripture**. When used in the religious sense, the term refers to those writings a community of faith has set apart as holy. Indeed, Christians understand their scriptures to be inspired by God. In our contemporary, multi-cultural world, with its diverse religious faiths and practices, we must be aware that there are other religious traditions that regard writings as sacred, or even written by God by means of a chosen prophet. This is especially true for Islam, as Mohammed is understood as the prophet who communicates the words of Allah; but Buddhists, Hindus, and other religious communities also regard certain writings as sacred, even though most would not regard them with the veneration that Christians have for the Bible and Muslims have for the Qur'an.

Scriptures arise in religious communities to serve their particular needs as they struggle to understand their experiences of God and define themselves in relationship to the rest of their society. This is a very important idea to take to

Calendar Designations and Abbreviations

The Gregorian calendar that is commonly used today divides history into two eras.

Traditionally the eras have been marked as **BC** (Before Christ) and **AD** (Anno Domini [beginning with 1 as the "Year of the Lord"]).

Currently, respect for religious diversity leads to the use of **BCE** (Before the Common Era) and **CE** (Common Era).

The latter is used in this textbook. When exact dates are not available, the abbreviation **ca.** is used. It is derived from the Latin word *circa* meaning "about" or "approximately."

heart in approaching the books that form Christianity's Scripture. They express the experiences of real people in a very real world—however distant from ours in time, geography and culture—in their struggle to tell one another and others what they believe, why they believe, and why they are prepared to live and die for that belief. The earliest Christian scriptures were the letters of Paul. They were the first to be written, as this very early missionary sought to keep in touch with the churches he founded, as he traveled through the eastern region of the Roman Empire. It is even possible that the last of his letters were written in the early 60s CE in the city of Rome, as he faced imprisonment and death. The Gospels began to be composed later, as the first generation of disciples died out and the community faced the uncertainties of the future. Paul's letters take it for granted that the earliest Christians knew of Jesus, his life and teaching, his death and resurrection. But this was not so for second and third generation Christians. With the Gospels, it had become necessary for early Christian authors to inform their contemporaries about the significance of the life, death, and resurrection of Jesus. The Gospel and Letters of John are part of these scriptures. The Gospel of John is a narrative about Jesus and the good news he brings, and the Letters of John are later documents that depend upon John's Gospel story. Both the Gospel and the Letters were written by and for the burgeoning communities of belief in what eventually became Christianity.

The Gospel itself calls attention to an otherwise unnamed disciple whom Jesus loved, the Beloved Disciple, as the eyewitness authority behind its good news (see John 13:23–26; 19:25–27; 20:2–10; 21:20–24). As we will see later in our closer reading of the Johannine story, the Gospel gives evidence that it was written for a particular community undergoing crises that challenged its faith and unity. The same is the case for the Letters of John as they, too, were written into a challenging situation. The early church leader Irenaeus (ca. 180 CE) was the first to identify this Beloved Disciple as John, the son of Zebedee, one of Jesus's inner circle of disciples, who lived in Ephesus until the time of the Roman Emperor Trajan (ca. 98 CE). Jesus had many **disciples**, a word whose Greek and Latin equivalents both mean "learners." In the Gospel of Luke and the Letters of Paul, some of those in his inner circle (known in all the Gospels and Paul as "the Twelve") are also called **apostles**. They are "sent" (the meaning of the Greek word behind "apostles") on missions to spread the good news about Jesus and the kingdom of God and thus eventually founded communities of faith. Some of these apostles eventually either wrote about the good news or had their experiences and teachings written on their behalf.

In these first pages we have already seen several issues that come together in our study: a Gospel and Letters that seem to come from the same background, the figure of "the Beloved Disciple" as a character in the Gospel, identified as its writer (John 21:24), and the later identification of the Beloved Disciple as one of the Apostles: John, the son of Zebedee. This combination of issues has led scholars to write and speak of "the Johannine community," and "the Johannine literature." The community produced a literature: a story of Jesus that we know as the Gospel of John, and three Letters of John. A fifth book, Revelation (also called the Apocalypse, based on a Greek word meaning "revelation"), is traditionally included in this group. This inclusion resulted from it being the only book in the New Testament that explicitly identifies its author as a man named "John" (Rev 1:1–9; 22:8). Most scholars today recognize the book of Revelation as an example of apocalyptic literature. There are a number of similarly written apocalyptic texts in ancient Jewish and Christian literature. Such literature has a very different understanding of the end of time and the role of Jesus Christ than the Gospel and Letters of John. Revelation is thus usually regarded as coming from a different author and situation and is interpreted as something quite distinct from the Gospel and Letters. We will do likewise and restrict our study to the Gospel and Letters of John and trace their role in Christianity's Scriptures, despite the traditional association of Revelation with the Johannine literature.

Citing the Books of the Bible

A list of all the books and their common abbreviations is found at the beginning of Bibles. The books of a modern Bible are divided into chapters and verses.

To cite the Bible, the book name is followed by the chapter number; e.g., Genesis 15. If a specific verse is indicated, the name of the book is often abbreviated and followed by the chapter and the verse number separated by a colon; e.g., Genesis 15:10 or Gen 15:10. If several verses are included, they are separated by an en dash; e.g., Gen 15:1–10.

When a verse or verses of a given chapter are designated, the abbreviation **v.** for one verse or **vv.** for more than one verse is used; e.g., v. 15 or vv. 15–20.

The Sacred Text of Christianity: The Bible and Covenant with God

The sacred text of Christianity is called the **Bible**, a term that comes from the Greek words *ta biblia* that can be translated as "the books." Acknowledging this origin helps us recognize something important about the Bible: even though it may look like a regular book in its contemporary editions, it is more like a library of books than a single book. Like a library, the Bible is a collection of books, written by different authors in several different genres or styles, over a long period of time. Nonetheless, all these different books reveal the interaction between God and humankind in creation, telling multi-layered stories of this relationship that begins with the dawn of history and continues all the way through the first century CE. Therefore, also like a library, we should not expect all these books to tell an identical story or have the same perspective on the complex relationship between God and God's creation, with its highpoint in the relationship between God and human beings (see Gen 1:26–31). Consequently, the Bible gives us many voices through its books and shows the growth and development of this relationship over time.

The library of books in the Christian Bible is made up of two parts: the **Old Testament (OT)** and the **New Testament (NT)**. The use of the adjectives "old" and "new" can sometimes be taken as a suggestion that the "old" is now a thing of the past and is of lesser importance than the "new." To use the terms "old" and "new" in this sense when speaking about the Bible would be seriously mistaken. As we will see, both "testaments" are essential to the Christian Bible, and there would never have been a "new" testament if the earliest Christians had not been inspired by the Jewish Scriptures that Christians call the "old" testament. The expressions merely indicate that the former is "older," written roughly between 1000 BCE and 50 BCE, than the "new" Testament, written between 50 CE and 110 CE. *Together* they form the one Scripture of Christians: the Bible.

The term **testament** means "will." The English word comes from the Latin *testamentum* which was used in the first Latin translation of the Bible, known as the Vulgate and largely the work of Jerome (ca. 347–420 CE). This Latin term translates the Greek word *diathēkē* used in the earliest Christian writings, which itself is a translation of the Hebrew word *berit*, meaning **covenant**. In the Jewish Scriptures, the term "covenant" often refers to agreements initiated and spelled out by God with mutual commitments of promises and obligations. This concept of covenant is the principal means by which the Jewish Scriptures describe the relationship between God and his people Israel. The earliest Christians seem to have understood the Christ Event to be the formation of a new covenant between God and all humankind. However, it is still a long step from the establishment of a new covenant to calling a collection of writings the New Testament. Christians eventually made this step, as we will discuss in chapter one. As we have seen already, we cannot refer to something as "new" without a concept of "old" or understanding another body of literature as the Old Testament. The early church incorporated Jewish Scriptures into the Bible as this Old Testament. This indicates that contemporary Christians understand God's activity recorded in the New Testament to be the fulfillment of God's activity in the previous covenants as recorded in the Old Testament. By including the Old and the New Testaments in their sacred writings, early Christian leaders show their conviction that we can fully understand God's new covenant with creation only by having available, in a collection, the fullness of God's relationship with humankind through history. For this important reason, in chapter three, we survey the Old Testament narrative, including key figures and events that appear in both that long story and the Johannine Literature.

The stories of Jesus Christ in the New Testament are called **Gospels**, a term that means "good news." But what exactly is the news, and why is it good? This is the subject of chapter four, but for the moment we can say that for Christians the good news is that God has fulfilled all his prior covenantal promises in the incarnation, death, and resurrection of his Son, and he has put in place a new covenant relationship available to all humankind. How that takes place is explained in different ways by the various authors whose books appear in the New Testament. We will trace how John understands it. But, in their diverse ways, this is the story all the Gospel writers, whom we call "evangelists," share with their original listeners and all later communities and individuals who hear and read their works. The first three Gospels of the New Testament, Matthew, Mark, and Luke, follow the same general plotlines and are called the Synoptic Gospels. The word "synoptic" comes from Greek and means that these three Gospels can be laid out side by side and seen "with one glance of the eye." But John is so strikingly distinctive that it is singled out and identified as the **Fourth Gospel**. John's unique Gospel also summons his community to live in love and faith in a larger society and culture that was determined by a very different understanding of the world, the gods, and how people should relate to one another. This challenge proved to be difficult, and the New Testament also contains three **letters** from the same perspective as the Gospel, most likely written later than the Gospel to provide both encouragement and warnings for this community. These letters, sometimes referred to as "epistles," from the Greek word for "letter," are titled the First, Second, and Third Letter of John. This book has been written with the explicit purpose of guiding its readers through a contemporary interpretation of the Gospel and Letters of John.

A Literary Approach to the Study of the Johannine Literature

In colleges and universities, biblical scholarship is an academic discipline just like other subjects in the humanities and sciences. Scholars explore the biblical texts like other pieces of world literature for what they can tell us about the history and thought processes of the ancients. However, these particular pieces of literature are also sacred to certain communities of faith. Therefore, most scholars also approach them as texts that nourish the spiritual lives of believers who turn to them as the Word of God that reveals God's plan for humankind. As this is a complex task, scholars make use of all the resources at their disposal, including the findings of historians, archaeologists, sociologists, and a number of other disciplines. The goal of biblical scholarship can be explained as the task of **exegesis**. This term is derived from a Greek verb that means "to draw out." The task of exegesis, then, is to draw out from a book or text as accurately as

Maiestas Domini by
Haregarius of Tours

possible the author's intended meaning of its words and phrases, and eventually to explain the text as a whole. Exegesis is, therefore, a technical term used to describe the academic discipline that commits itself to the scholarly interpretation of the Bible. But in the end, it must not be simply regarded as a scholarly discipline. It is a question of "drawing out" meaning from a text written many years ago to stimulate and nourish faith in a way that continues a nourishing process today. As we move through our exegesis of the Gospels and Letters of John, we must always appreciate both the academic discipline and the tradition of faith these texts serve.

Chapter two of this textbook is devoted to surveying different approaches to the process of interpretation, but here we can say that the task of exegesis is the task of asking relevant questions of the ancient biblical text and seeking answers to those questions through responsible methods. Scholars often regard their method of approaching the biblical text as asking questions about one of three "worlds":

1. The World behind the Text
2. The World in the Text
3. The World in front of the Text

Although responsible interpreters research and analyze all these "worlds," scholars often focus their questions on one of them while building upon the work of scholars who have focused their questions on another. This will be the case with the textbook we are introducing. Our interpretation of the Johannine Literature *primarily* represents a literary approach, but it stands on the shoulders of work of others that will be brought to bear on our final analyses. When an author chooses narrative as the mode of communication, this is itself part of the message. Further, the way in which an author tells his or her story determines its meaning. The author of the Gospel of John says this very clearly at the end of his story of Jesus: "Now Jesus did many other signs in the presence of his disciples, which are not written in this book. But these are written so that you may believe" (20:30–31). Likewise, when an author chooses to write a letter, that is part of the message. As we will see in the Letters of John, the communication becomes personal, and often the author makes various appeals to the recipients of his story. More will be said about literary criticism later, but what we have introduced here is sufficient to indicate the direction that this present study will take in order best to serve our audience, perhaps approaching biblical studies and the Johannine Literature for the first time.

The Course of Our Study of the Gospel and Letters of John

In this introduction we have begun to consider the Gospel and the Letters of John and have given some initial pointers to the fact that we will be approaching the interpretation of these important books from the New Testament as literature. Since many students beginning their reflection upon the Johannine Literature may not have background in the Bible or the study of it academically, the next four chapters provide the necessary background for understanding and interpreting this evangelist's particular belief in and teaching on what God did in and through Jesus of Nazareth. As mentioned above, chapter one discusses the Bible as the Scripture of Christianity by introducing the concept of "canon" and surveying the history of "canonization," and chapter two will discuss in more detail contemporary methods of biblical interpretation. Chapter three presents an overview of the story of Israel as it is preserved in the OT. In this way, both the world of the evangelist and the scriptural history he used in composing his Gospel story for his community of readers are also introduced. Chapter four concludes our provision of necessary background material by outlining the story of Jesus of Nazareth and introducing the birth and development of Christianity as the new covenant through the Jesus movement, and the subsequent writing of the Gospels.

The rest of the book focuses on the Johannine Literature. Chapter five studies the world behind these texts in order to provide the historical context of the Gospel and Letters of John. We do this by posing and suggesting answers to the basic questions of authorship, genre, location and period of the writing community, the purpose of the evangelist, and the literary and historical background of the text. Chapter six discusses the author as a storyteller and evangelist by studying the world in the text through the literary characteristics, themes, and plot structure of the narrative that communicates John's understanding of the good news. Chapters seven through fifteen show the interplay of the world in the text with the world in front of the text as we make our way step by step through the Gospel. The Johannine Literature then extends into the world of the Letters of John, written after the Gospel appeared. These letters are the subject of chapter sixteen. The letters enable us to catch a glimpse of the Gospel community and its eventual history as it interpreted and tried to live the message of the Gospel. The Conclusion of the course of study discusses the community produced by the Johannine Literature in the first century and into the present world.

What Have We Learned So Far?

The Gospel and Letters of John are part of the Scripture of both the early Christians and Christians today. They are ancient texts that reveal the religious experiences of real people who lived almost two thousand years ago, at the beginnings of Christianity. But, as we will see in the next chapter introducing the development of what is called a "canon," this collection of sacred books has provided and continues to provide authority and guidance for millions of Christians across time, into today and the future. They may have come into existence almost 2000 years ago, but they remain a life-giving Word of God for many people in our own time. These people form the world in front of the text, the people whose understanding of God, the world, the Christ, and their place in relationship with all of these is at least partially formed by the Johannine Literature. We say "partially" because the Johannine

Literature is only "part" of Scripture. However, it is the literature that will concern us throughout this book. Thus, each chapter will conclude by asking "what have we learned so far?" In answering this question, we will explore what the sacred texts in general and the Fourth Evangelist in particular teach audiences about what is known as theology and its various aspects, including cosmology, anthropology, Christology, ethics, ecclesiology, soteriology, and eschatology. Therefore, in this initial section, we will conclude not so much by drawing together what we have learned so far in *this* chapter, since we have largely introduced what is to come, but by presenting these concepts in general so that we can explore them in the context of the texts studied in later chapters.

Let us explain further. **Theology** is the study of God. As an intellectual discipline, theology explores reality from the perspective that God is its origin, its basis, and its goal. More generally, a person's theology is his or her understanding of who God is and how God works in the world. **Cosmology** is the study of the nature and structure of the universe (the *cosmos*)—how it came to be and how it is ordered. The biblical text, especially Genesis, the first book of the Jewish scriptures and Christian Old Testament, contains a number of stories that are generally called "etiologies." An etiological story explains origins or the causes of how things are as we know them. Beginning with what actually exists, and how things are ordered (or where there is sin and failure—are *dis*ordered), authors speculate about how it all began. A person's cosmology is related to his or her theology and understanding of God's role in creation. Today's environmental crisis leads many to ponder the future of the threatened creation. The choices we make are driven by our cosmology.

Anthropology is the study of human beings and culture. In relation to the study of religion, it refers to the relationship between God, humankind, and creation. Are humans intrinsically good or bad or somewhere in between? How do they relate to God? How do they relate to the rest of creation? In the Johannine Literature, anthropology is intimately related to Christology. **Christology** is the study of the Christ. The term "Christ" (from a Greek word) is synonymous with the word "messiah" (from the Hebrew), and both words mean "the Anointed One." Some religions have a notion of their God (or gods) sending an anointed one (or a prophet) to do something on behalf of humankind. But these religions, and even contrasting voices within the same religion, can have very different ideas about the nature of this anointed one, his role, and his relationship to God and creation. Continuing a theological tradition that can be found in the Old Testament, and in Judaism of the time of Jesus, the early Christians believed that Jesus of Nazareth was the "anointed one" of God, a so-called "Christ." Already in the New Testament he is quickly known as "Jesus Christ," incorporating this title with his name. Given the very name "Christianity," it is easy to see that Christology is central to its belief system and the formation of the community of believers.

The study of **ethics** is the inquiry into the nature of the good, or "right," life in such communities. In this same field, **morality** refers to ways of thinking, feeling, and acting that address considerations of human welfare. On the basis of traditions about right and wrong, the foundation for ethical actions is, therefore, where religious faith and moral decision-making intersect. The biblical texts, including the Johannine Literature, both directly and indirectly offer ethical guidelines for Christian living. This leads us to **ecclesiology**, which refers to the study of the church. The Greek word *ekklēsia* refers to any assembly of people. The early Christians adopted this term to refer to the gathering of the faithful. The concept of "church," therefore, refers first and foremost to the people and their relationship to each other and to God through Christ. It was only much later in the history of Christianity that buildings dedicated to worship also began to be identified as "churches." We will see that John, like the other biblical authors, presents a particular understanding of the people of God through his narrative.

John also has a goal or purpose in mind for the people of God. This leads us to our final two components. **Eschatology** is the study of the last things or end times. These ideas are often associated with beliefs concerning life after death, judgment, and the end of the world as we know it. We will see that, although not alone, John has a very original idea of when and how "end time" is understood. **Soteriology** is the study of salvation. One's soteriology is often closely connected to Christology and eschatology. In Christianity, soteriology focuses upon the saving action of God in and through Jesus Christ and subsequently affects what Christians think about the meaning and goal of life.

John has much to teach through his Gospel and Letters about his understanding of God, the world God created, Jesus Christ, the human condition, how we are to relate to one another, and our search for meaning in this life and in the next. Each chapter of this textbook explores and interprets the Johannine writings, and we will conclude by seeking an answer to the question: "so what?" What does the subject matter of the chapter tell us about what John teaches audiences about life, and the human response to the God who is the primary actor in the story that is reflected in these writings? The Gospel of John, like all the early Christian writings, attempts to *persuade* its readers about God, his Son Jesus Christ, and what God has done for human beings and all creation in and through his Son. Therefore, this book is not only about ancient Christian texts, but also about what we can learn from them about God, humankind, our world, and the way we relate to one another.

Key Terms and Concepts

anthropology
apostles
BC/AD, BCE/CE
Bible
ca.
Christology
cosmology
covenant
disciples
ecclesiology
eschatology
ethics and morality

exegesis
Fourth Gospel
Gospels
letters
New Testament
Old Testament
Scripture
soteriology
testament
theology
v./vv.

Questions for Review

1. What is Scripture and how does it arise in communities of faith?
2. Why is the Bible more like a library than a regular book?
3. What group of books makes up the Johannine Literature? Why are they given this title?
4. What is the relationship between the Old and New Testaments?
5. Why is it important to discuss theology and all that makes up theology when studying the Johannine Literature?

Bibliography and Further Reading

Brown, Raymond E. *An Introduction to the Gospel of John*. Edited by Francis J. Moloney. Anchor Bible Reference Library. New York: Doubleday, 2003.

Lennan, Richard, *An Introduction to Catholic Theology*. Mahwah, NJ: Paulist, 1998.

Moloney, Francis J. *Reading the New Testament in the Church. A Primer for Pastors, Religious Educators, and Believers*. Grand Rapids: Baker Academic, 2015.

Powell, Mark A. *What Is Narrative Criticism?* Guides to Biblical Scholarship: New Testament Series. Minneapolis: Fortress, 1990.

The Origins and Development of the Bible

PURPOSE Chapter one discusses the Bible as the Scripture of Christianity by introducing the concept of canon and surveying the history and development of the Jewish and Christian canons. Understanding the complexity of the biblical text will allow for a more detailed discussion of its contents and their interpretation.

ASSIGNMENT Skim the Table of Contents of your Bible, and then thumb through the books to get a sense of the overall format and organization.

As we noted in the Introduction, both the Jewish and Christian traditions use the term Scripture to refer to those writings the community of faith has set apart as holy. Scriptures arise in religious communities to serve their particular needs as they struggle to understand their experiences of God and define themselves in relationship to the rest of their society. Since the Christian Scriptures are made up of both the Old and the New Testaments, we can discuss the composition of each part as well as how they came together to form the Bible.

Scripture, Canon, and the World That Gave Us the Bible

In the ancient world, where 90 percent of the people could neither read nor write, their shared history in relationship with God was passed down through the generations by word of mouth. Only particular forces, either internal, external, or both, compelled these communities to find the resources to record and preserve their oral traditions in more permanent written forms. As we will see in this chapter, the Jewish people began to pull their traditions together into a written narrative around 1000 BCE during the reign of King David. This time of peace and prosperity in the kingdom of Israel allowed for reflection and collection of traditions as part of court records. Some 500 years later, however, the external forces of the Babylonian Empire imposed upon the kingdom, over-running the land and sending the people into exile from 587 to 538 BCE. This dark period in the history of the Jewish people was a key factor in solidifying the composition of their Scripture. To keep the hope of their religion alive, the people told stories and recorded them in written form for posterity. Across the next 500 years, as the people restored their homeland and developed their particular religious sensibility, they continued to preserve their experiences in written form.

Likewise, as Christianity developed, the disciples and leaders of the early movement, called apostles, passed on their experiences of Jesus Christ and his teachings by word of mouth as they moved from town to town sharing the good news and founding Christian communities. As we discussed in the Introduction, Paul created the earliest extant writings of the Christian faith with his letters to communities as he traveled through the Roman Empire on his missionary journeys. The Gospels, however, were not composed as fully developed narratives until the community felt the need to preserve them. We will discuss this in more detail in chapter four, but we can note here that by 70 CE, about 40 years after the crucifixion of Jesus, the community of believers was experiencing the death of their first generation of disciples and leaders. This internal force of loss was compounded by the devastating external consequences of the First Jewish Revolt against Rome, which occurred ca. 65–70 CE. Although the Jews led a valiant strike against the empire, the Romans eventually surrounded Jerusalem and, after an extended siege, broke through the city walls and burned everything in their path. The Jewish temple was destroyed, and both Judaism and the burgeoning Christian movement were in danger of fading into the shadows of history. The Jewish people dealt with this blow in their own way, which we will discuss in the next section, while the Christians began to compose their stories about the life and teachings of Jesus in written form. The Gospels were written across ca. 70–110 CE and circulated throughout the Christian community to share the message and affirm the faith of believers.

> **Josephus and His Writings**
>
> Flavius Josephus (37–100 CE), a Jewish scholar and eventual militant leader who was forced to surrender to the Romans, recorded the many events of the First Jewish Revolt against Rome (65–70 CE). The book is called *The Jewish War* and is a striking record, even though it is written in support of the Roman offensive. He also wrote a long history of Israel, called *Jewish Antiquities*. These works aid scholars in studying ancient Judaism.

The World of the Text and the Canon It Produces

The question of how an authorized collection of these writings known as Scripture developed is a question of the **canon**. In the end, a canon is a list of books that have authority for a given community. The word "canon" comes from a

Greek word that means "rod," or "reed." Such canons were used for measuring. When the word is applied to a list of books, the implication is that these books are the "standard of measure" for the community. The term "canon" also indicates a plumb line, a weight on a string used to make sure a wall is straight. A canon of Scripture, therefore, also ensures that the life and thought of the community are directed by the Word of God to be correct, or "straight."

So-called canons of scripture develop on the basis of a perceived need for authority. It is sometimes thought that the Christian canon was imposed by authorities such as bishops or emperors. As we will see below, it worked the other way: the Christians gave authority to the books that made most sense of their attempt to live and believe in a Christian way. As we discussed with the writing of Scripture, factors, sometimes internal to the group and sometimes external to it, generated questions in the Christian communities that had to be answered. They eventually became so important that leaders across early Christian communities reflected upon which books were to be "in" the canon, and which books would be excluded. This section discusses the formation of the Christian canon by surveying the history of the development of the books as well as the process that led to the selection of some books to be regarded as "inspired Scripture" and the rejection of others. This is called the process of **canonization**. It has nothing to do with declaring people "saints" by canonization, but it means the establishment of a small library of books that the early Christians call their canon of Scripture.

Chapters three and four will present the narrative history preserved in the Old and New Testaments in more detail. Our task here is to give a rapid overview of the pertinent history and development of the books that became the Christian Bible. The first step in the canonization process in the Jewish and Christian traditions is the grassroots perception of certain writings as sacred—as inspired by God and thus set apart as Scripture. Because of this "grassroots perception," as the starting point of the process of canonization, the idea that the canon was imposed on believers is incorrect. Over time, however, this "grassroots perception" was followed by the felt need to set boundaries on authority. Internal or external factors, such as dissension within the community or pressure or persecution from outside the community, compelled community leaders to determine which texts had authority for the community, which texts may have been helpful but did not determine the teachings of the community or status in the community, and which texts were to be rejected as potentially destructive, or at least, not helpful to the community's well-being and belief system. For an overview of the process of canonization of the Bible into the volume well-known today, we will begin with the sacred texts of Judaism and then follow with the development of the specifically Christian component of the biblical canon.

The Jewish Scriptures and the Old Testament

The biblical narrative begins in the book of Genesis with the story of God's act of creating the cosmos and everything in it. The first eleven chapters of Genesis deal with what is sometimes described as the "pre-history" of Israel. But in Gen 11, the figure of Abraham appears. Thus the story narrates the development of the world as we know it, first following the expansion of humankind and the society it forms, then more narrowly focusing on God's choice of Abraham as the righteous man through whom God will form a covenant and through whose descendants a faithful people will form. The faithful descendants of Abraham are traced through their patriarchs and matriarchs, then through prophets, leaders, and judges like Moses, Joshua, and Samuel, until the people call for a king and the nation of Israel is formed.

These early traditions reflect the people's understanding of God and how the world came to be, as well as their own history and development as a distinctive ethnic group, were preserved by the Israelites through word-of-mouth storytelling as one generation passed on its wisdom to the next. It was likely not until Israel settled into a nation under Kings David and Solomon (ca. 1000 BCE) that its elders and scholars had the luxury and wherewithal to keep a written record. Peace, prosperity, and the construction of a temple as the house of God and the focus of worship allowed for and necessitated Israel's entry into the literary world. In addition to the court records, the initial thread of the story of Israel's ancient history and self-understanding as God's chosen people began to be written. The semi-nomadic people from the time of Abraham (ca. 1800 BCE) through to the time of Moses and the Exodus (ca. 1280 BCE) lived in an oral culture and had little time or resources for the written word. A lively memory of this early history, called **oral tradition**, developed; and the scholars of the kingdom incorporated these ancient songs and traditions, during and after the time of King David, into their literary productions.

After a very brief period under David and Solomon as a unified nation, Israel divided into the northern kingdom of Israel (initially ruled by one of Solomon's servants: Jeroboam) and the southern kingdom of Judah (initially ruled over by one of Solomon's sons: Rehoboam) ca. 920 BCE. From this point, over the succeeding centuries, Judaism traces its heritage through the southern kingdom. Over time, both of these small kingdoms were threatened by enemies from all sides. These political developments also led to the rise of a new type of literature in Israel. By

---

Literacy and Orality in the Ancient World

Most people in the ancient world were not able to read or write. A current estimate is that about five percent of the people in the cities could read and write, but it may have been a bit higher. Almost no country or village person, as in many civilizations today, was literate. It was also very expensive to acquire writing materials and books (scrolls). This led to a great deal of "oral" communication: important messages were "spoken" or even "performed" and passed down through the generations by word of mouth.

the eighth century BCE, prophets, spokespeople for God, began to have their pronouncements and teachings collected and edited into books bearing their names. Prophets like Isaiah and Jeremiah among others called the people and their kings back to covenant with God and warned of the consequences of breaching this covenant. Nonetheless, the northern kingdom fell to the invading Assyrian Empire in 721 BCE, and its inhabitants were deported to all parts of that empire's domain. The southern kingdom withstood this onslaught and even prospered for a time during the seventh century BCE, but eventually it, too, fell to an invading empire. This time it was the Babylonian Empire that overran Judah and destroyed both Jerusalem and the temple, where the worship of God had been centralized. In 587 BCE, the majority of the inhabitants of Judah were deported to the regions of Babylon, and this began the period in Israel's history known as the **exile**.

This dark historical period led to prolific literary production as the Israelites kept their faith alive by committing their story to writing, solidifying their identity and their religious tradition in the face of foreign lands and peoples. This community building that took place during the exile also kept hope alive for an eventual return to their land, a restoration of the holy city of Jerusalem, and a rebuilding of the temple for the worship of God. By 539 BCE, the empire of Persia became the dominant force in the region, and its king, Cyrus, became the focus of Israel's hope. In 538 BCE, Cyrus issued an edict that allowed the Judeans to return to their land and rebuild both their holy city and its temple. The new temple was completed in ca. 515 BCE, and through struggle and perseverance, the people rededicated their temple to God and rededicated themselves to covenant relationship with that same God. However, the 50 years of the exile meant that two generations of Judeans had lived, and some even prospered, outside their homeland. Therefore, not everyone returned. This phenomenon of Jewish people populating the larger world is known as the **diaspora**, from a Greek word that means "dispersion" or "scattering." God's chosen people were now scattered across the known world and remained connected to their homeland and their temple through prayer, pilgrimage, and financial support. From this time on, Jewish people living in the diaspora have been an important part of the literary and political history of Israel.

The new interaction of the Judeans with the larger world affected how they understood God, the world, and the literature they produced. Thus, in addition to the historical narratives and prophetic literature discussed above, the last centuries before the Common Era saw the rise first of **wisdom literature**, then

---

Ancient Empires as They Affect Israel and the Jewish People

Egypt	ca. 3000–1000 BCE
Assyria	ca. 900–605 BCE
Babylon	ca. 605–539 BCE
Persia	ca. 539–332 BCE
Greece	ca. 332–141 BCE
Rome	ca. 63 BCE–600 CE

apocalyptic literature in Israel. Wisdom literature and the sages who contemplated wisdom focus on the individual. They were typically unconcerned with history, or even God's action in history. The major interest of the wisdom writers was the problem of human existence and the lived experiences that are common to all human beings. As with those of many other ancient cultures, Jewish families created ways of passing on the collective wisdom of the ancients about life, from generation to generation. Examples of this literature from the Jewish Scriptures include Proverbs and Job. Apocalyptic literature finds its classic expression in the Jewish Scriptures in the book of Daniel. Contrary to popular usage, the term "apocalypse" means *revelation*; and in Judaism, the genre of Apocalyptic literature refers to the belief that God *reveals* to certain faithful individuals truths that transcend the immediate experience of suffering and hardship and tell of God's ultimate victory over evil. These individuals then share this information in literary form in order to comfort those who are suffering and give them hope to endure until God's eventual victory. This type of literature appeared regularly and remained dominant in Judaism into the Common Era, such that it also became a popular component of early Christian literature.

Over time, all this literature began to be regarded as Scripture and collected in groups for use in teaching and worship. By 400 BCE, the material that became the first five books of the Bible was published together and was accepted in Judaism as the written word of God. The Hebrew word for this collection is **Torah**, a word that means "instruction." These early books, believed to contain the teaching of Moses and the record of the self-understanding of the formation of Israel as God's chosen people, gained their place as the primary Scriptures of Judaism. To this day, *Torah* lies at the heart of the Jewish understanding of its Scriptures. Meanwhile, the later stories of Israel as a people and a nation with a king grew in stature as the definitive record of Israel's history, and the collection of books that bear the names of God's prophets began to appear. By about 200 BCE, these books came to be accepted as the part of the Jewish Scriptures known as the Prophets. The Hebrew word for **Prophets** is *Nevi'im*. We should note here that this group of books included narratives of the history of Israel as well as the sayings of the prophets, which is different from the way these books were eventually collected by Christians. By the turn of the era, the wisdom literature and other writings from the post-exilic period were being referred to with the catch-all term "Writings." The Hebrew word for **Writings** is *Khetubim*. The authority of this last group of books was still in dispute at the time of Jesus and the development of Christianity across the first century CE. This collection of books in the Bible continues to be accepted somewhat differently among Jews and various Christian traditions today. We will return to this issue. For the moment, we can see how these groups of books came to make up the three parts of the Jewish canon. The name of the Jewish Scripture is formed by the first letters of the names of each of these segments in Hebrew: **TaNaKh** *(Torah, Nevi'im, Khetubim).*

Returning to a discussion of the broader process of canonization, we should first note the differences in the Christian Old Testament (OT) canons. The Christian OT is not identical to the three-part Jewish canon, and in fact, there is more than one Christian OT canon. In addition to the thirty-nine books in the Tanakh revered as inspired in Judaism and by the Protestant Christian tradition, the Catholic tradition includes seven other books. Thus, a Catholic Bible will contain forty-six books in its OT canon. The additional books are 1 and 2 Maccabees, Tobit, Judith, Sirach (also known as ben Sira and Ecclesiasticus), Wisdom, and Baruch. As well as these extra books, the Catholic OT canon contains expanded versions of the books of Daniel and Esther. These books are known in the Catholic tradition as the **Deuterocanon** or "Deuterocanonical" books, which means "second canon," to acknowledge their absence from the Tanakh. In the Protestant tradition, these books are part of the **Apocrypha** or "Apocryphal" books, terms indicating that their authority is "hidden" and that they are absent from the Jewish canon.

The mention of the Jewish canon reminds us that this was not originally a Christian debate. The differences we have today stem from the unsettled state of the Jewish canon until the second century CE. This is not to say that the Jews did not have Scriptures at the time: the Law was revered as the Torah of God by ca. 400 BCE, and the Prophets were in place as Scripture by ca. 200 BCE, but the authority of the Writings remained unsettled for many years, even into the period after Jesus and the earliest church. They were widely used in teaching, worship, and writing for years, but for a long time there was no urgency within Jewish life and practice to rank them beside the Torah and the Prophets as Scripture. The **rabbis**, or teachers, began to do so late in the first century CE, not only because they came to their own internal convictions that these books should be regarded as Scripture, but also because they were being used by the early Christians. The early Christian movement had begun quoting these texts as Scripture, and the relationship between Judaism and the burgeoning Christian movement had deteriorated to the point of separation.

At this stage, we can look back over what we have discussed to better understand how this separation took place. Here we will delve deeper into some of the later post-exilic political and historical world events and how they affected Judaism. Linguistic, cultural, and political developments in world history had given rise to various distinctions within Jewish practice. By the time

---

Extra-Canonical Jewish and Christian Literature

In addition to the books found in Bibles, there were many other interesting texts written about the same time, or slightly later, that provide information about the history and thought of the time. Some of them come from Judaism, and others come from Christian authors. Examples of the former include the Letter of Aristeas, mentioned in the text as emerging in the Greek period, as well as the Mishnah, which emerged after the First Jewish Revolt against Rome (65–70 CE). Examples of the latter are the many Gospels that appeared, including the Gospel of Thomas and the Gospel of Mary Magdalene, that were not included in the NT canon.

of the exile in the sixth century BCE, the Israelites began to lose their common language and culture. During the period of the Persian Empire (547–333 BCE), Aramaic, a Semitic dialect related to Hebrew, became the common language of the people of the empire. Indeed, Aramaic remained the native language of the people of Judea for some 500 years, into the Common Era.

Alexander the Great ended Persian rule in 333 BCE by means of a stunning military campaign that took him and his conquering armies as far as the western reaches of today's India. He established Greek rule and cultural influence by setting up military colonies and scholastic academies and founding Greek-style cities, the most important of which was Alexandria in Egypt. This process is known as **Hellenization**, from the Greek word *hellenismos*, meaning "Greek." Hellenization, the political, social, and religious practice of imposing Greek ways on all the conquered countries and civilizations, and its resulting phenomenon, **Hellenism**, were extremely successful and pervaded the ancient world. The Greek language became the common language for most people of the empire, and the language of literature and commerce for all. This process produced a cultural and linguistic unity that had never been known before this time. For the Jewish people, the Hebrew Scriptures became inaccessible to many in the now Greek-speaking world. Therefore, a Greek translation of the Hebrew Scriptures began to appear in Alexandria in the late second century BCE. First the Torah, then all the books circulating in the Alexandrian community as Scripture, were translated into Greek and collected. This work eventually become known as the **Septuagint**, a term derived from the Latin word for "seventy." This name came from the legend preserved in an extra-canonical Jewish work known as the Letter of Aristeas. That so-called "letter" claimed that separate translations from the Hebrew were made by seventy-two scholars—six from each of the twelve tribes of Israel—and all the translations proved to be identical. This legend sought to give a divine authority to the Greek translation of the Hebrew Scriptures. When discussing the Septuagint, scholars often abbreviate this somewhat difficult word with the Roman numeral for 70: LXX.

This Greek translation, the Septuagint (from now on: LXX), moved away from the three-part division of the Jewish Tanakh into a four-part division that saw the Scriptures from a different perspective: the *Pentateuch*, the *Historical Books*, the *Wisdom Literature*, and the *Prophets*. The LXX became the authoritative edition of the Scriptures for the Greek-speaking Jews in the diaspora. It was later adopted by the early Christians who took the good news of Jesus Christ, based in God's covenant with Israel, into the larger Greek-speaking world. As we can see, the LXX was formed during the period when the inclusion of the Writings into the canon of Scripture was still being debated. This meant that the LXX included books and expanded versions of books that were not in circulation in Hebrew. It was used freely by both Jews and Christians in the Greek-speaking world, side-by-side with the use of the Hebrew Scriptures in Judea. It is generally thought that the Hebrew collection in Judea did not contain these books. Although all the Writings were considered sacred, they were not given the same reverence as Torah, and there was initially no felt need to authorize their canonicity.

As history moved forward, the Jewish people eventually gained independence from the remnants of the Greek Empire as a result of the Maccabean Revolt in 167–163 BCE. Although a key moment in Jewish history, this period had little effect on the canonization process. Nonetheless, several books now found in the LXX were produced in this era, for example, the two books of the Maccabees. Over time, the Roman Empire came to power in the Mediterranean world. The Roman general Pompey marched south along the east coast of the Mediterranean Sea, and Judea and its surrounding regions fell under the iron fist of Roman control. The region remained a part of the Roman Empire until its fall centuries later. The *Pax Romana*, or Roman Peace, facilitated a great deal of travel and communication, but the simultaneous suppression of autonomy also facilitated a rebellious spirit, and hopes for a messiah who would throw off the yoke of Roman control became stronger.

The Jewish canon did not take final form until the early second century CE, but the process began in the late first century CE with both the rise of Christianity and the destruction of the temple in Jerusalem as a result of the rise and failure of the First Jewish Revolt against Rome (65–70 CE). The first Christians were observant Jews, and as the books of the NT attest, initially one of several Jewish sects that formed in the Judaism of the time, including the **Pharisees**, **Sadducees**, **Essenes**, and **Zealots**. After the destruction of the temple and the fall of Jerusalem to the Romans in 70 CE, this diversity in both belief and practice began to be a cause of concern. The Sadducees, Essenes, and Zealots did not survive these tumultuous decades as distinctive groups, although there were no doubt still priests and angry revolutionaries present in Jewish society. The rabbis, the heirs of the Pharisees, arose as the new leaders of Judaism, since there was no longer a centralized worship in the temple. They eventually gathered at Jamnia, a city west of Jerusalem near the Mediterranean Sea, slightly south of the present-day International Airport in Israel, to establish a center for rebuilding the battered Jewish religion and people. The diversity, or heterodoxy, of the previous generations was no longer understood as helpful, or even possible, and a stricter orthodoxy ("right thinking or belief") and orthopraxy ("right practice") was sought to unify the people and their religion.

The Septuagint

Many myths surround the origins of Greek translations of the Jewish Scriptures, indicated by the Latin for "seventy" (LXX). The Letter of Aristeas, a document from the middle of the second century BCE, claims a miraculous origin for the Greek translation. The Septuagint was most likely produced in various stages—and in various versions—in Egypt around 280 CE. As many Jewish people living and worshiping in Egypt—and especially Alexandria—no longer knew Hebrew, a Greek translation gradually emerged. Early Christian authors, including the writers of the Gospels, used the Septuagint as the Word of God when they cited Jewish Scriptures in their writings.

The rabbis began to put in place a clearer system of belief, based in a canon of Hebrew Scripture. What emerged over time was Judaism as a religion oriented toward the written "word of God" and the Jewish people as a "people of the book." Therefore, the Tanakh introduced above was formed as canon. In addition, the **synagogues**, community centers that developed in the diaspora, were reoriented as houses of worship for the practice of the Jewish faith. Jewish Christians, those who understood the long-awaited messiah of Israel had come in the person of Jesus, were identified as unorthodox, and their place within Judaism was eventually no longer possible, since mainstream Judaism held the position that God's messiah had not yet come.

By the end of the Second Jewish Revolt against Rome in the mid-130s CE, the two groups, Judaism and Christianity, began to develop their distinct identities and characteristics along separate paths. The newly formed Christians did not initially establish their OT canon. Their attention was more focused on the canon of specifically Christian Scriptures that would eventually form the New Testament, but they made use of the Septuagint they inherited from Greek-speaking Judaism. In this way, the first generation of Christians used the LXX version of the Jewish Scriptures as their "Old Testament" to understand the story of God working in history through Israel and the promises of a messiah. When the eventual books of the Christian NT were written, their authors generally used the text of the LXX and referred to it as "Scripture."

As the Roman Empire flourished, Latin replaced Greek as the language of the Mediterranean world. The fourth century CE church leader and scholar

---

Jewish Groups: Sadducees, Pharisees, Essenes, Zealots, Jesus Movement

Prior to the First Jewish Revolt against Rome, there were several ways of living as a Jew. The Jewish author Josephus describes four:

The **Sadducees** are the more traditional priestly group who adhered strictly to the first five books of the Bible (the Torah). They were closely allied to the Temple, its organization, and influence.

The **Pharisees** are a more recent Jewish movement that was broader in its acceptance of Scripture, looking beyond Torah. They were teachers and scholars who survived the Revolt because they were more dynamic in adapting to the changed conditions and were not bound to the Temple, as were the Sadducees.

The **Essenes**, closely associated with the Dead Sea Scrolls found at Qumran, sought to live an uncontaminated Jewish life. They largely withdrew from society, which they saw as corrupt, and lived a more ascetic life.

The **Zealots** were a revolutionary group that struggled against Rome, sometimes violently, for the liberation of Israel as God's land and people.

Alongside these four, the **Jesus Movement**, before it became universally inclusive, was also a Jewish group who believed Jesus of Nazareth to be the long-awaited messiah through whom God put in place a new covenant. They eventually became known as Christians for these beliefs.

The Jewish Canon and the Two Western Christian Old Testament Canons

Jewish Canon: The Tanakh	Roman Catholic OT Canon	Protestant OT Canon
Law: Torah	**Pentateuch**	**Pentateuch**
Genesis	Genesis	Genesis
Exodus	Exodus	Exodus
Leviticus	Leviticus	Leviticus
Numbers	Numbers	Numbers
Deuteronomy	Deuteronomy	Deuteronomy
Prophets: Nevi'im	**Historical Books**	**Historical Books**
Former Prophets	Joshua	Joshua
Joshua	Judges	Judges
Judges	Ruth	Ruth
1 Samuel	1 Samuel	1 Samuel
2 Samuel	2 Samuel	2 Samuel
1 Kings	1 Kings	1 Kings
2 Kings	2 Kings	2 Kings
	1 Chronicles	1 Chronicles
	2 Chronicles	2 Chronicles
Latter Prophets	Ezra	Ezra
Major Isaiah	Nehemiah	Nehemiah
Jeremiah	Tobit	Esther
Ezekiel	Judith	
Minor Hosea	Esther	
Joel	1 Maccabees	
Amos	2 Maccabees	
Obadiah	**Wisdom/Poetic Books**	**Wisdom/Poetic Books**
Jonah	Job	Job
Micah	Psalms	Psalms
Nahum	Proverbs	Proverbs
Habakkuk	Ecclesiastes	Ecclesiastes
Zephaniah	Song of Songs	Song of Songs
Haggai	The Book of Wisdom	
Zechariah	The Book of Sirach	
Malachi		
Writings: Khetubim	**Prophets**	**Prophets**
Psalms	Isaiah	Isaiah
Proverbs	Jeremiah	Jeremiah
Job	Lamentations	Lamentations
Song of Songs	Baruch	Ezekiel
Ruth	Ezekiel	Daniel
Lamentations	Daniel	Hosea
Ecclesiastes	Hosea	Joel
Esther	Joel	Amos
Daniel	Amos	Obadiah
Ezra	Obadiah	Jonah
Nehemiah	Jonah	Micah
1 Chronicles	Micah	Nahum
2 Chronicles	Nahum	Habakkuk
	Habakkuk	Zephaniah
	Zephaniah	Haggai
	Haggai	Zechariah
	Zechariah	Malachi
	Malachi	

Jerome was commissioned to translate all of Scripture—what the Christian church by then called the Old and New Testaments, into Latin. Jerome's translation, popularly called the Vulgate (from the Latin *vulgata*, meaning "vulgar" or "common" with regard to the language), became the standard for Christianity, and its version of the OT contained all the books, and the expanded versions of books, that were present in the Septuagint. Without ever taking an explicit "vote" on the matter, the question of the OT canon was hardly discussed in the Christian church for some one thousand years, until the era of the Protestant Reformation when the reformers raised it again in the sixteenth century. In his translation of the Bible into German in 1534, Martin Luther grouped the seven books and expansions found in the Christian OT but not in the Jewish Hebrew canon at the end of his version of the OT. He called this group "Apocrypha," as mentioned earlier. He claimed they were "not held equal to the Scriptures and yet are useful and good for reading." It seems Luther mistakenly understood the Jewish canon to have been solidly in place in the time of the first Christians, and he wanted to get back to those origins. The OT canon he formed contains the same books as the Tanakh but still follows the four-part structure of the Septuagint/Catholic OT. In the counter-reformation response, the Roman Catholic Church defined their existing OT as officially part of its canon at the Council of Trent in 1546. The result of these reformation issues is the existence of different Christian OT canons. Debates over the "correctness" of these canons have raged at various points in Christian history since the Reformation, but in today's more collaborative climate they have faded. Scholars, clergy, and lay people alike are more interested in learning from all the ancient texts available to us.

> ### The Vulgate
>
> The Jewish Scriptures were available in Hebrew (with some Aramaic) and Greek (the Septuagint) long before Christianity emerged. As the Mediterranean world was increasingly dominated by Rome and the Christian Church became more focused upon Rome, Latin became an important language. The Jewish and Christian Scriptures were available in a number of Latin translations, known as the Old Latin versions. In 382 CE, Pope Damasus commissioned Jerome to produce a unified Latin translation. A great linguist, Jerome produced a Latin version known as the Vulgate (for the masses) in 405 CE. For many centuries, the Roman Catholic Church regarded the Latin Vulgate as a Sacred Text.

The Christian Scriptures and the New Testament

The process of the formation of the New Testament (NT) is comparable to that of the OT, although it took place across a much briefer timeline. To the best of our knowledge, Jesus of Nazareth left no written records. He lived from ca. 4 BCE to 30 CE and was an itinerant teacher, not a writer or a historian. The Scriptures that he and his disciples lived by and quoted as the basis for their teaching were the Jewish Scriptures we have just been discussing. These Jewish Scriptures that formed part of the life of Jesus would have been passed on to him orally. Instead of reading and quoting from a written text, he would have used the Scriptures on the basis of his memory of what he had been taught. Even though Jesus would have spoken Aramaic and likely was familiar with the Hebrew Scriptures read in the synagogue (see Luke 4:16–20), once the Christians began to write, they wrote in Greek and almost always used the LXX as their "Scripture."

It was some years before written Christian documents appeared. The first complete Christian document has been dated some twenty years after Jesus's lifetime. Scholars suggest the Apostle Paul's first letter to the churches in Thessalonica (1 Thessalonians) has this distinction. Paul was not a disciple of Jesus and did not become a believer in Jesus as the Christ until several years after Jesus's death by crucifixion. It was another decade before he became a prominent apostle and leading voice of early Christianity. Therefore, most interpreters agree that 1 Thessalonians was written about 50–51 CE. It was another twenty years before a Gospel appeared. By that time, all the letters that we can certainly claim that Paul wrote had been completed, and Paul had most likely been martyred, or executed for testifying to his faith (ca. 64–65 CE). Although church tradition has long regarded the Gospel of Matthew as the first and the fullest expression of the Gospel, and placed it as the first of the Gospels in the Christian canon, there is a general scholarly consensus today that the Gospel of Mark was the first full narrative of the good news of Jesus Christ, composed sometime between 65 and 70 CE. The remaining books that eventually became the NT emerged over the course of the next thirty years or so. These books include three more Gospels, one example of a type of historical narrative called an "Acts" (The Acts of the Apostles), a total of twenty-one letters, and one example of apocalyptic literature (Revelation). All the writings of the New Testament were written by the turn of the first century of the Common Era, or ca. 100–110 CE.

The NT literature, like that of the OT, emerged within the community of believers. There were many Christian writings that appeared across the first hundred years of the existence of the Christian community, but some seem to respond more immediately to their understanding of Jesus, and to their own need to understand and live by what he had left them. Under the perceived guidance of the Holy Spirit, they reflected upon and responded to what they understood to have been made available by God as salvation in Jesus Christ, the long-awaited messiah of God for Israel. Of course, these twenty-seven books

The Luther Bible

Prior to the sixteenth-century Reformation of the Christian Church, many people wished to have the Bible in their native language, rather than in Latin. The greatest of the Reformation Bibles came from Martin Luther (1483–1546). He published his translation of the New Testament in 1522 and, along with others, translated the Old Testament. Luther published a complete German Bible in 1534. He continued to work on this translation. It eventually became an important work of literature that played a role in the formation of German religion and culture, widely available because of the invention of the printing machine in the 1450s by Johannes Gutenberg.

are by no means the only early Christian works, and the writing did not stop after the turn of the century. In fact, it is still going on as Christians continue to interpret and write books about how God has worked and is still working in the world throughout history. However, Christians believe that the life, death, and resurrection of Jesus, the Christ and Son of God, was the final public revelation of God to the world, and thus the early records of this event and the church it formed have a particular significance for Christian faith and teachings.

In the first years after the life and death of Jesus, even though the early believers were convinced of the resurrection of Jesus from the dead as an action of God, little thought was given to the production of Christian writings, no doubt because Jesus himself, like the rabbis of the time, taught solely by the spoken word. This teaching was remembered and discussed by his disciples, who in turn passed them on by word of mouth. In this way, the disciples' recollection of these teachings and the memories of the events of Jesus's life were communicated to new audiences and second generation disciples. This is the reason why all the early Christian writings are in Greek, the language understood by everyone in the Mediterranean world and beyond. As this teaching and community building by spoken word carried on, an early "Jesus movement" or loose network of believers formed, and an "oral tradition" developed. Again, as with the OT, there was most likely some writing going on from the earliest years: the developing Christian liturgy, or worship service, included hymns (songs of praise), creeds (statements of belief), and prayers. Some of these early snippets of worship were eventually incorporated into the written texts, as was the case with the inclusion of the hymn about Jesus found in Paul's letter to the community in Philippi (see Phil 2:6–11).

As we have already seen, the first Christian writings to come to us are the letters of Paul. They were attempts to bridge distances as the apostle traveled from town to town in Asia Minor (modern-day Turkey), Greece, and eventually modern-day Europe. He founded and instructed communities in the good news of Christ and then moved on to new areas to do the same. In fact, Paul is the first to call this message "gospel." Once he left his communities, he would stay in touch, mediate disputes, continue the teaching process, and affirm his authority by way of these letters, which were treasured and preserved by their recipients. From these beginnings, the letters of Paul have been part of Christian literature through the ages. Although most scholars today do not think that the Apostle Paul wrote all the letters attributed to him, those who eventually established the NT canon understood all thirteen to be authentic reflections of this early church figure. In addition, the canon includes the so-called letter to the Hebrews, which is not really a letter at all but a sermon or religious treatise. Although this text does not claim to be written by Paul, early tradition collected it with the rest of Paul's letters for a total of fourteen.

Near the end of Paul's ministry, scholars suggest that the writing of the Gospels began. The memory of Jesus's life and ministry had been kept alive in the intervening decades by Paul and the other early preachers, teachers, and storytellers in the various Christian communities. We will discuss the genre of Gospel in greater detail in later chapters, but for now we can note that the First Jewish Revolt against Rome that began to rage across Judea in 65 CE and climaxed with the burning of Jerusalem and the destruction of the temple in 70 CE must have been part of the impetus behind some early Christians feeling compelled to commit their understanding of the good news of God's action in Jesus Christ to the written word in story form. In addition, the first generation of apostles and disciples had largely disappeared off the scene, martyred for their faith, by the late 60s. This would certainly have been another factor in the felt-need to capture both the story and the authority in its telling in literary form. A new generation of Christians was emerging that no longer retained the experiences and the memories that were so closely associated with Jesus of Nazareth and the beginnings of the community. The Gospel accounts differed slightly as the story was told with a different emphasis or theological agenda in Rome, in Jerusalem, or in Ephesus. Thus, from among the many stories of Jesus, and most likely collections of his sayings, we have the four distinct Gospels of Matthew, Mark, Luke, and John that made their way into the Christian canon in the second and third century.

The New Testament Letters outside the Paul collection are often grouped together as the "Catholic" or "General Epistles," because they are addressed to various forms of the universal church body instead of a particular community and are thus known by their authors. These letters include the three letters attributed to the apostle John, known as 1, 2, and 3 John, alongside a letter of James, a letter of Jude, and two attributed to Peter. Finally, we have the book of Revelation, the one NT piece of apocalyptic literature.

For the early Christians, like the Jews, the process of canonizing, or giving official authority to these writings and rejecting the many others of the new movement, came about due to conflict. In the middle of the second century CE a Christian leader by the name of Marcion began to advocate a particular way of being Christian, and he favored writings that supported that way of life. Marcion was the first to indicate "books" that should be regarded as Scripture, but some of his "books" were very different from the books that we have just described. Marcion's teachings were more like a popular Greek philosophy called Gnosticism than Paul's understanding of the new covenant and God's

---

Muratorian Canon Fragment

In the eighteenth century, Ludovico Antonio Muratori was studying an eighth-century manuscript in the Ambrosian Library in Milan, Italy, when he discovered another document between the pages. Upon further investigation, he determined it to be a kind of catalogue of books for a New Testament canon. He published the text in 1740, naming it for himself: *Canon Muratori*. The text itself was written in Latin, but scholars believe it comes from a Greek original. The composition has been dated to the end of the second century CE. Although the beginning and likely the ending of the document are missing, it preserves important information about the development of the New Testament canon.

union of all Israel. Therefore, other church leaders began to advocate a clearer idea of what Christianity was and what writings represented that way of life and faith practice. One of the most important figures from the second century in this quest to establish a canon that best represented the heart of Christianity was the church leader Irenaeus. He was the Bishop of Lyons, in modern-day France, and we single him out because he was a strong defender of the place of the Gospel of John in the canon. His role will be discussed in coming chapters. This process took a long time and did not reach a final consensus for another two hundred years. It appears to have been finalized about the middle of the fourth century. A document known as the Muratorian Canon fragment was discovered in the nineteenth century and has been dated to the late second or early third century. It shows the extensive conflict and debates that arose over this process of canonization. For our purposes, it is sufficient to note three major criteria for inclusion in the canon that developed and led to the acceptance and establishment of the twenty-seven books that now make up the NT canon. They are:

1) Apostolic authority (a book is connected to the authority of an apostle);
2) Usefulness for moral and spiritual encouragement and instruction in the faith; and
3) Popularity and extent of use in the early communities and in their worship services.

The year 367 CE seems to be a milestone for publication of a "final draft" of the canon. In his Easter letter of that year, a very significant and influential early church leader, Athanasius (296–373 CE), included the list of twenty-seven books that was eventually accepted by the whole church and became the New Testament canon. This letter can still be found in its original Greek, and in Syriac and Coptic translations. The existence of this letter in the languages that came from dominant churches *in the East* at that time (Syriac came from Palestine and parts of Asia Minor, and Coptic from Egypt) is an indication of the authority of Athanasius, and the widespread acceptance of his list. He includes the four Gospels, followed by Acts and the Catholic Epistles (James, 1–2 Peter, 1–3 John, Jude), then fourteen Pauline epistles (Hebrews is listed after 2 Thessalonians, before

> **Athanasius**
>
> Saint Athanasius of Alexandria (296–373 CE) was an influential figure in the fourth century CE. He stood for what eventually became accepted Christian doctrine, articulating in his many works and homilies what became the orthodox teaching of the Church on the Trinity and the role of Jesus Christ. Despite much suffering, he was highly respected. For that reason, his list of the books that should be accepted as Christian Scriptures, named in an Easter Letter of 367, was quickly accepted as the authoritative word on a discussion that had been unresolved since late in the second century.

the Pastorals and Philemon) and Revelation at the end. In the Latin tradition *in the West*, Pope Innocent I (pope from 401 to 417), in response to a question from the Gallic bishops concerning the canon, named the list of Athanasius in 405. He was most likely under the influence of the authority of the great fathers of the Latin-speaking church, Jerome (ca. 347–420) and Augustine (354–430), who had already accepted the Athanasian canon. This is the canon that was finally and universally adopted by the early Christian church. It remains the authoritative NT canon for all Christians around the world today.

The Christian New Testament Canon

Gospels	Letters of Paul	Catholic Epistles
Matthew	Romans	James
Mark	1 Corinthians	1 Peter
Luke	2 Corinthians	2 Peter
John	Galatians	1 John
	Ephesians	2 John
Acts	Philippians	3 John
Acts of the Apostles	Colossians	Jude
	1 Thessalonians	
	2 Thessalonians	**Apocalypse**
	1 Timothy	Revelation
	2 Timothy	
	Titus	
	Philemon	
	Hebrews	

What Have We Learned So Far?
The Canon of Scripture

As we first discussed in the introduction, this section of each chapter will reflect upon the ground we have covered and explore the theological components that have risen to the surface. Since this chapter has provided a rapid historical overview of the development of the Bible as the canon of Scripture of Christianity, there has been little focus on theology. However, we must remember that in the ancient world there was no separation between the religious, political, social, and literary worlds. The hand of God (or the gods, depending upon one's religious system) was understood to be involved in every natural and human-created phenomenon. Further, as the people of faith reflected upon the story of their relationship with God and God's action in the world in relationship to them, they understood the traditions they developed and the texts their authors composed as inspired by that God. The formation of the canon of Christian Scripture is thus theological from beginning to end, as well as historical and literary. Therefore, although our task in this course is largely historical and literary, it is also by nature theological as we seek answers that the Christian faithful have been seeking and will continue to ask of the Gospel and Letters of John. The succeeding chapters will have much more to add to this component of our study.

Key Terms and Concepts

apocalyptic literature

Apocrypha

canon/canonization

Deuterocanon

diaspora

Essenes

exile

Hellenism/Hellenization

Jesus movement

oral tradition

Pharisees

Prophets

rabbis

Sadducees

Septuagint (LXX)

synagogues

TaNaKh

Torah

wisdom literature

Writings

Zealots

Questions for Review

1. What is generally meant by the expression Scripture?
2. What is meant by the expression "canon"?
3. What were the most important factors that led to the development of the Jewish canon known as the Tanakh? When did that development come to an end?
4. What role did "oral" transmission of stories and teachings play in formation of both the OT and the NT?
5. Who was the first Christian author? Why is understanding the role of this Apostle, as well as the texts he did (or did not) write, important to understanding early Christianity and its canon?
6. What were the important factors that led to the development of the NT canon?

Bibliography and Further Reading

Dawes, Gregory. *Introduction to the Bible.* New Collegeville Bible Commentary: Old Testament. Vol. 1. Collegeville, MN: Liturgical, 2007.

Frigge, Marielle. *Beginning Biblcal Studies.* Rev. ed. Winona: Anselm Academic, 2013.

Miller, John W. *How the Bible Came to Be: Exploring the Narrative and Message.* Mahwah, NJ: Paulist, 2004.

Moloney, Francis J. *Reading the New Testament in the Church. A Primer for Pastors, Religious Educators, and Believers.* Grand Rapids: Baker Academic, 2015.

Methodology for Biblical Interpretation

PURPOSE Chapter two presents the basis for biblical interpretation as well as a brief overview of the development of contemporary methodologies. We will focus attention on approaching interpretation through the "worlds" of the biblical text.

ASSIGNMENT Have your Bible at hand to read the passages from the Gospel of John as they are discussed in this chapter to get a better sense of the methods for biblical interpretation being introduced.

As we pointed out in the introduction, the goal of biblical scholarship can be explained as the task of **exegesis**. This term is derived from a Greek verb which means "to draw out." From that primary meaning, it thus also denotes "to explain," or even "to unfold the story" in the sense of interpreting its meaning. The verb form of this word is "to exegete." However, the word "exegete" is also sometimes used as a noun to indicate the one who exegetes the text. For example, we might say that Dr. Jones is an exegete of the biblical text. One of the tasks of exegesis, then, is to draw out from a book or text the author's intended meaning of its words or phrases and to explain the text as a whole. As we will see, it is not the only task for the biblical interpreter, or exegete, as this activity includes not only the *textual* meaning (the sense of its words and phrases), but also its *contextual* meaning (the sense of its words or phrases in the framework of the given passage or book around it), and its *relational* meaning (their sense in relation to the body of works and faith as a whole). Therefore, we might say that once we have exegeted the text, we then have to answer the question, "so what"? So what does this text mean, and how is it relevant to people's lives?

Methods for Interpreting the Bible: The Worlds of the Text

The mode of interpretation that has been dominant in the twentieth and twenty-first centuries is called the **Historical-Critical Method**. This exegetical method seeks to establish the original meaning of the text by using techniques of historical and literary criticism to trace the ancient foundations of the people of God and of the Christian church. It is called a *critical* method not because it criticizes the Bible in the sense of fault-finding or seeks to be skeptical about the ancient text, but because it compares and analyzes the details of the text in an effort to arrive at a historical and literary judgment about it. The method recognizes that the Bible, though it is considered by Christians to be the inspired written word of God, is an ancient record, composed by many human authors over a long period of time. As such, it should be read, studied, and analyzed as other ancient records of history. The Historical-Critical Method attempts to reach back into the past to understand the meaning of the ancient records of God's dealing with his people and of the ministry of Jesus of Nazareth and of the emerging communities that believed they continued his ministry and presence "in the Spirit." These critical techniques are geared to one end: to determine the meaning of the sacred text as it was intended by the human author, understood by the Christian faithful to be inspired by God, who composed it long ago. Traditionally, this is where historical criticism ceased, but more recent times have seen a demand from scholars, and from Christian believers, for exegetes also to attempt to ascertain what the text is saying to readers today.

At present, again as we indicated in the introduction, it is common for biblical interpreters to speak of investigating the "worlds" of scriptural texts in an effort to form a more complete picture of their meaning. These worlds include the historical background, which is often identified as the **World behind the Text**. This is the world of the author, his or her social and belief systems, the larger political, cultural, and economic systems around the author, as well as any needs in this regard that the author's intended audience might have. When approaching the world behind the text, scholars attempt to discover the ancient foundations for a people of God, and to understand what was meant by the ancient records of God's dealing with that people. What is most important is the reconstruction and the interpretation of *the past*, including the events, people, places, and time that produced the composition. This task is very important to ensure that we approach the real-life experiences and possibilities of both the biblical authors and the people and events portrayed by these authors. A book written hundreds of years ago must be read on its own terms, and not as if it were written in the twenty-first century. In other words, we must seek to understand *their* world and how *they* experienced God in that world in order to make sense of how *they* expressed those experiences in their writings. Only then can we begin to apply what they teach to our contemporary world. All these elements come together for the author to conceive and compose the content of the text.

The latter half of the twentieth century, however, also began to look more closely at the way the text itself has been assembled by the author, i.e., to analyze its literary characteristics and style. This approach attends to the **World**

in the Text. This is the world of literary genres and forms, of the symbols and metaphors the author uses, and of how the author develops and orders all of these elements into the plot of the narrative, the direction of the letter, or the imperatives of the essay. In this approach, the interpreter explores the content, literary characteristics, and themes present within the final composition—the writing as a whole. With narratives, this includes all the storytelling techniques the author may employ, such as plot, setting, the passing of time, places where events take place, and characterization, to mention just some of the important elements that can be found in any "story." When it comes to letters, the approach must be different. The interpreter must trace rhetorical devices the author uses to communicate a message and to persuade readers. The Letters of John, as with most of the letters that are found in the New Testament (and many letters throughout history), were written to "persuade." Many interpreters claim that what they must discover is the author's "rhetoric of persuasion."

In addition, more recently, interpreters have begun to ask about the effect that a biblical text makes upon audiences and readers. While they must never ignore the historical and literary interpretations of the text, interpreters who follow these more audience-focused methods attend to the **World in Front of the Text**. They focus on the emotional and intellectual effect that compositions have upon their audiences, be they readers or watchers and hearers of oral performances of written texts. All authors have agendas, or reasons for putting pen to paper (or quill to parchment in the case of the ancients), and the task of interpretation is discovering what authors want their audiences to take away from their encounter with these writings. This approach to a text can have a number of objectives. For example, the interpreter can use parallel documents from the past to try to understand how the original author may or may not have perceived his text to impact original readers. However, there is now an increasing interest in how these ancient texts make an impact upon an audience (reader/hearer, etc.) literally sitting *in front of the text* then and now. This, in many ways, is the world the text produces as it persuades people who read or hear it and leads them to live accordingly, either in agreement with or in reaction against it.

As we also indicated in the introduction, our primary focus in this book will be literary. We will be interested in uncovering what the Gospel of John says to readers and listeners of today. However, as you will see, we cannot ignore the other worlds. The brief historical background and the description of how we came to have a biblical canon, as provided in the previous chapter, already indicate that we want our readers to understand from where all these texts came. Therefore, we will inquire about all the worlds of the text. We introduced this chapter by saying that the goal of biblical scholarship is the task of exegesis. In that same vein, the process of exegesis is the task of asking questions of the ancient biblical text and seeking answers to those questions through responsible methods. When we analyze the text by asking and answering these ques-

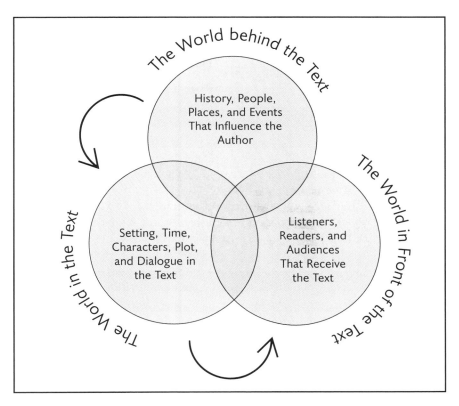

THE WORLDS OF THE TEXT

tions, this is **criticism**. The term "criticism" in this context means a systematic analysis of data (in our case ancient texts) with the aim of making decisions and drawing conclusions. In popular language, criticism often indicates tearing down or finding fault, but this is not necessarily the case and never the goal of a good biblical scholar. Rather, the focus here is on analysis and decision-making about meaning. What type of criticism we are doing depends upon what type of questions we are asking. Although there are a number of sometimes complex types of criticism, in the sections that follow we will introduce several basic areas of criticism within their respective worlds of the text. We will utilize these approaches later on as we exegete the Gospel and Letters of John.

The World behind the Text

In order to begin interpreting any biblical text, we must understand its context in the world from which it came. The world behind the text is the world of its author and the writing he or she produced. If we establish as best as we can how the text was composed and preserved and what was important in those communities in the ancient world, then we can move forward on solid ground as we explore how it is important in our own time. **Textual criticism** is a fundamental step in asking and answering questions about the world behind any biblical text. Textual criticism is concerned with the transmission of the biblical text in its original language (and also in ancient translations through the many copies made over the years) and attempts to establish the best-preserved text. Scholars of the early Jewish and Christian eras were called "scribes," and part of their role was to transmit the early texts by hand. They had no printing presses or copy machines or any other way to distribute the Gospels, letters, and other important texts to the widespread communities. These scribes were very good at their jobs, and this hand-copying was done remarkably well, with precision and care. Nonetheless, changes in the text seeped in, sometimes by mistake and other times as a result of the scribes trying to clarify what they perceived to be unclear thoughts or poor grammar on the part of authors. Therefore, although there are no originals of any of our biblical texts, we have thousands of ancient copies in the form of scrolls, papyrus fragments, and parchment codexes, and few of these copies are identical. So, the task of the textual critic is to determine, as a result of studying all the possible options, what the best or most original text is. By "best" or "most original," scholars indicate the text most likely written by the author.

Fortunately for us, this work has already been done, and we read the Bible in English based on the work of skilled textual critics and translators. Nonetheless, textual criticism is a crucial component of biblical interpretation. Some of these discrepancies are still a matter of debate. Very often, English study Bibles will indicate serious textual issues (places where the ancient manuscripts have conflicting readings of the text) by retaining the word or phrases in question

---

Example of Textual Criticism

The basis of English-language New Testaments is a Greek text that has been constructed into a printed edition from thousands of manuscripts and ancient translations, some of which come from the second century and others from the early Middle Ages. Textual Criticism is a branch of New Testament studies that attempts to establish the most original text possible from these many sources. A good example of Textual Criticism is found in John 20:30–31, where scholars ask whether John wishes to call people to faith when he ends his Gospel claiming that he wrote "so that you may believe" (*pisteusēte*) or to exhort them to continue and deepen their faith: "so that you may go on believing" (*pisteuēte*). Only the Greek letter for "s" differs between these two texts, and they are both found in ancient manuscripts. The Text Critic assesses which one represents the earliest text, and issues like this are found on every page of the New Testament.

in the final text, but enclosing them in square brackets. Other study Bibles may indicate potential alternate texts in a footnote. This practice allows readers to identify the scholarly concern while continuing to read a smooth translation of the text. We will discuss the relevant examples as they arise in our study of the Gospel of John.

Once we have completed textual criticism and decided what the best form of our text is, we turn to **historical criticism** to attempt to reconstruct the world the texts relate to us. We use all the resources at our disposal, including archaeology, anthropology, and numerous other academic disciplines to learn as much as possible about the world in which the authors and audiences of our text lived. We have already begun to do this in chapter one of this textbook and will continue to delve into that history in the next three chapters. We must always remember that the biblical world is very different from our own, and we must respect that world and its culture. This includes the geography and climate, but also the ruling people and their governments alongside subjected peoples and their ideals, as well as religious beliefs, cultural norms, and societal standards. All of this helps us understand the events that take place, the concerns people have, the symbols and images the writer uses, as well as the expectations those writers place on both people in the texts and audiences of them.

Regardless of the historical reality that produced a text, however, we must also take seriously that the author has chosen to transmit the message in a literary form. Just like authors today, ancient authors sometimes wrote from their own experiences, sometimes wrote from the shared wisdom of their community, identified as oral tradition, and sometimes used other literary sources. **source criticism**, therefore, seeks to determine the literary prehistory of a biblical book. Exegetes ask the question, what sources did the author use in composing the book? This type of criticism, therefore, tries to construct a bibliography

---

Example of Source Criticism

The term Source Criticism is classically applied to the search for the sources used by biblical authors in composing their books. With regard to John, Rudolf Bultmann famously suggested that behind the prologue to the Gospel (1:1–18), and many of Jesus's lengthy discourses, he could trace original discourses that came from early gnostic literature. Similarly, many scholars claim that behind the series of events in John 6 (multiplication of the loaves and fishes, boat journey, Peter's confession) lies Mark 6:31–8:29. Others claim that John is using Luke's passion account. Source critics attempt to discover "sources" for the text they are analyzing and explain it in terms of a "reworking" of an original source. Although not unanimous, most critics think that John is using his own sources, much of which are oral tradition that certainly has contacts with the Synoptic Tradition; but he does not use them as, for example, Matthew and Luke used Mark.

of sorts after the fact for a text that did not originally cite its sources. Answering this question can tell us a great deal about why the author included some information but omitted other events or data. Source Criticism can also tell us what was important for the author as he shaped his own telling of the tradition.

Textual, Historical, and Source Criticism are three basic types of questions and answers that help exegetes construct the world behind the text. There are others, but these will be most useful for our purposes in this textbook. We will highlight their uses in the coming chapters.

The World in the Text

The notion of addressing the situation of John's first readers and hearers is the driving principle behind the analysis of the "world in the text." The task of exegesis does not come to an end once we have identified the final form of the text and the possible historical background of its component parts. Next we must ask and answer questions about how these component parts are woven together to form the text as we now have it. The fundamental approach to reconstructing this world is **literary criticism**. Literary Criticism analyzes the form and stylistic character of the text. We ask questions about genre, word choice, symbolism, and style of writing. The answers to these questions are crucial because they can set parameters for a judgment on the historical aspects of a text. If we see that the writer has employed poetry for a certain effect or used certain persuasive techniques to make a point, then we may realize that the historicity of the writing may not have been the writer's primary concern. We can also make decisions about the author's background and theological concerns as well as those of his intended audiences. With the Johannine Literature, we know we are working with a

---

Example of Literary Criticism

Several different things are indicated by Literary Criticism. For many early critics, it meant source criticism as scholars debated the literary origins of each tradition in the Gospels. At present, it is often used by scholars to refer to the parallels that exist between the literary style and unity of a particular passage, in comparison with great literature. For example, the Johannine prologue (1:1–18) has the same literary function as the prologues used in Greek dramas, to inform the audience of the central features of the drama that they were about to witness, before the action began. For others, it refers to the literary techniques used to analyze a passage. For example, this book has traced a chiasm behind John 1:1–18. Another of John's literary traits is his tendency to state and restate the same message (John 6:25–51; 14:1–16:33). The recognition of these "literary features" is also called Literary Criticism.

Gospel and three letters. Both of these genres of literature have conventions of form and content. The author adopts these generic customs and adapts them to his own personal style. Literary critics then explore these stylistic characteristics to learn more about the author and what he is trying to teach through this medium.

We will discuss genre and the literary characteristics of the Johannine Literature in more detail in chapters four and six. In addition, we will say more about the literary approach later on in this chapter, as it is our primary area of inquiry in this textbook.

Form criticism is a further step in Literary Criticism, as it seeks to specify the literary form or sub-form of a given biblical passage. The questions an exegete asks in this type of criticism include whether the text is, for example, a hymn or psalm. If so, what kind? Is the text prophetic? Apocalyptic? Is a given Gospel episode a parable? A miracle story? A pronouncement story? A historical narrative? The answers to all these questions set boundaries for the text and allow exegetes to make use of the customs and conventions of those forms to help them make sense of and interpret the text. Forms in the Gospel of John include poetry, narratives, miracles (called "signs" in the Gospel of John), discourses where Jesus gives extended teachings, and prayers, among others.

Redaction criticism is the final type of interaction with the world in the text that we will

---

The Development of Form Criticism

Late in the nineteenth and early in the twentieth century, Gospel scholars attempted to situate various literary forms into particular situations both in the life of Jesus and in Christian communities. One of these was Rudolf Bultmann who wrote a major handbook, heavily used to this day, *The History of the Synoptic Tradition* (1921). His focus was upon the history that produced the Gospel texts. Bultmann also wrote a significant commentary on the Gospel of John, claiming to have identified its original sources.

Example of Form Criticism

A major development in biblical scholarship was to recognize that the material in the New Testament, and especially in the Gospels, repeated well-known "forms" of literature: miracle stories, parables, discourses, prayers, farewell speeches, and hymns, to give a few examples. John uses a number of these (miracle stories, discourses, a farewell speech), but other "forms" are absent. For example, there are no parables in the Gospel of John. However much John may be using literary forms, he often uses these forms in an unexpected fashion. For example, the miracle stories of 2:1–12 and 4:46–54 feature Jesus's refusal to respond to the request from his mother and the royal official. John uses the miracle form in his own way. Forms are also called "genres." An important contemporary Johannine scholar, Harold Attridge, argues that the author regularly practices "genre bending." He may use a "farewell discourse," but he uses it in a unique fashion, determined by his unique theology and rhetoric.

discuss in our course. The verb "to redact" means to put into a suitable literary form for the author's purposes. The terms we may use more commonly include "to revise" or "to edit." Redaction criticism, therefore, seeks to determine how biblical writers have shaped, modified, developed, or "redacted" the source material they have inherited from other writers or from community traditions before them in the interest of their own literary or theological goals. If we have a strong sense of the sources writers used, we can ask questions about how they revised those sources and traditions and why they may have left some information in, taken some out, or tweaked other aspects. The answers to these questions can shed light on the authors' concerns about the theological, political, or social situations that have compelled them to write in the first place. We can then suggest how these concerns might be relevant to our own times and situations.

Literary, Form, and Redaction Criticism are three basic approaches to the world in the text. These techniques help exegetes know how and why the Johannine community and the author of the Johannine Literature generated the unified texts as they have been preserved for us. There are a number of features *within the text* that indicate why John gathered the material in this way. These are the elements that guide an interpreter attempting to uncover the world in the text. We will make use of these critical methods and note these features as we explore the Gospel and Letters.

The Development of Redaction Criticism

A number of earlier interpreters suggested that each Gospel was driven by a unified theological point of view. However, the use of so-called Redaction Criticism became a part of the interpreter's trade after the work on the Gospel of Luke by Hans Conzelmann, *Die Mitte der Zeit* in 1954 (English: *The Midpoint of Time*). He asked scholars to trace the traditions that formed the Gospels, but focus their attention upon how an Evangelist uses those traditions, placing them side by side in a deliberate sequence. What does the story as a whole proclaim?

Example of Redaction Criticism

Redaction critics classically trace the original source of any given passage (e.g., Mark 8:27–30) and examine how a later author has "redacted" the source, giving new meaning (e.g., how Matt 16:13–20 reshapes that passage from Mark). This is not easy for the Gospel of John, as we are not certain about the sources he worked with. However, as we have seen, the narrative is shaped in a very obvious way, with its prologue, Book of Signs, Book of Glory, and its necessary epilogue. The audience may not be able to discover his sources, but he has told a story that resulted from a deliberate choice of only some of the "signs that Jesus did in the presence of his disciples" (20:30). He used this collection to tell a story that might lead his audience to ever greater faith (v. 31).

The World in Front of the Text

As we approach our final "world," it is important that we recognize that the interpreter should always be aware that she or he depends upon all the different methods of approach. No one method should be regarded as the only way to understand the biblical text. We stand on the shoulders of those who went before us. This is very much the case as we turn our focus to the world in front of the text. This textbook's main concern will be the presentation of the Gospel and Letters of John from this perspective. But at no stage will we neglect the fact that our understanding of the Johannine Literature depends upon the historical and literary studies that have been pursued for centuries by many great and hard-working scholars. Nor should we ignore the fact that the Gospel of John has been the source of reflection and commentary in the life of the Christian churches for almost two thousand years. What follows as an introduction to learning about the world in front of the text builds upon what we have seen in the worlds behind and in the text. But it transposes them into another key. Now this message is not only in a printed text, but in the eyes, ears, and hearts of people who are reading this text, hearing it read, or even seeing it performed.

As we work our way through the story of Jesus recorded in the Gospel of John, we will find that it makes a strong impression upon its readers and hearers because of patterns of repetition. We read or hear the central message of the Gospel of John articulated in various ways, and by means of different literary forms, over and over again. It has often been said that the message of the Johannine Literature is very simple, but very deep. Its simplicity comes from the fact that it is the same message, stated and restated throughout the telling of the story and the commentary of the letters. Building upon what we have seen in our reflections upon the worlds behind and in the text, we can suggest that the world in front of the text can be discovered through Narrative Criticism, Rhetorical Criticism, and what we will call Audience-Response Criticism.

Narrative criticism concentrates on the communicative power of stories as a means of transmitting the Word of God. Throughout history people have often passed on messages or made argumentative points by telling a story. When an author chooses narrative as the mode of communication, this is itself part of the message. Telling a story resonates with the lived experience of readers and allows these readers to identify with but

---

The Development of Narrative Criticism

R. Alan Culpepper's *Anatomy of the Fourth Gospel: A Study in Literary Design* was a significant development in the appreciation of the Gospel of John as a unique literary contribution. Culpepper drew upon the work of Frank Kermode, a renowned literary critic, to analyze such elements as the use of plot, time, and characters in the Gospel of John, using the methods of contemporary literary criticism. This approach to the text—similar to Redaction Criticism in focusing upon the whole of the narrative as a single utterance; different from Redaction Criticism in hesitating to identify sources—has led to Narrative Criticism. Interpretation does not depend upon sources, but on the narrative appeal of the story itself to audiences.

Example of Narrative Criticism

Narrative critics devote great attention to the inner workings, the flow, and the communication process that goes on *inside the narrative*. Although not without interest in the historical setting that generated the narrative, the workings of the narrative itself are most important. In John 20, for example, the (implied) author leads the audience from one episode to another, as people respond to the empty tomb, the message that Jesus has been raised, and the appearances of Jesus. Tension mounts as Mary Magdalene, Simon Peter, and the Beloved Disciple from the Gospel demonstrate no faith, partial faith, and true faith. The (implied) reader is being led from one episode to another, until Jesus issues his final words to the characters in the story: "Blessed are those who have not seen, and yet have come to believe" (v. 29). The reader recalls that the Beloved Disciple believed (v. 8) but did not see the risen Jesus. The stage is now set for the author to tell the reader why he wrote his Gospel: "that you may go on believing" (AT: v. 31). By means of this narrative, the implied author has persuaded the implied reader about the need for strong faith to have life in the name of Jesus.

---

also distance themselves from various aspects of and characters in the story. Further, within the narrative, authors select from among so many events that could be shared, how they will be narrated, and in what order. This selection is made so that an author can best communicate the message as he or she intends it to be received. Thus the way in which an author tells his or her story determines its meaning. When we ask questions that approach the biblical texts only as compilations of data, we fail to take seriously the power of storytelling and the agency of the authors who chose to share their messages as narratives. Interpreters who use this technique, therefore, seek to reckon with the Bible's narrative accounts: stories with plots, characters, and climaxes. The Gospels are stories about Jesus that are intended to be read from beginning to end. Narrative critics, therefore, ask questions about plot and storylines as well as how the author shapes characters and develops the story to achieve a certain outcome by the conclusion.

Similarly, **rhetorical criticism** analyzes the persuasive character of the text. The term "rhetoric" refers to using language effectively through word choice and figures of speech in order to influence an audience. These techniques, sometimes called "rhetorical devices," are used by authors and speakers to affect audiences and to arouse in them certain reactions, emotions, values, and interests. Rhetorical critics ask questions in an effort to uncover the author's agenda and determine the message of the writing as a whole. While Narrative Criticism is particularly helpful with biblical books like the Gospels, Rhetorical Criticism is largely used with the letters and more essay-oriented texts. For example, when an author chooses to write a letter, that is part of the message. As

Example of Rhetorical Criticism

The side-bar on Narrative Criticism indicates that the Gospel of John has its own "rhetoric." It is written to "persuade" readers to accept truths about God, Jesus Christ, and what it means to have life from faith in him. Thus, one of its rhetorical aims is to "communicate truths of faith." There are other "rhetorics," and many elements in a written document are rhetorical, that is, written in order to have a desired effect (e.g., a letter written to a loved one is always rhetorical). This is especially clear in 1 John. This Letter is written to confirm early Christians in the correct understanding of what God has done in Jesus, and in the fact that the human person of Jesus was indeed the Christ and the Son of God. It is clear that the community has divided (see 1 John 2:19). There are now other understandings of God and Jesus Christ.

A good example of the rhetoric used by the author of 1 John can be found at the beginning of the Letter. After affirming the truth of what the community learned "from the beginning" of their lives as Johannine Christians, in a series of accusations, he points out that there are now some who have a different opinion. They are pointedly described: "If we say that we have fellowship with him while we are walking in darkness . . ." (1:6); "If we say that we have no sin . . ." (1:8); "Whoever says, 'I have come to know him,' and does not obey his commandments . . ." (2:4); "Whoever says, 'I am in the light,' while hating a brother and sister . . ." (2:9). They are wrong! The author is rhetorically indicating that certain people have strayed from the truth. Their teaching must not be accepted, while that of the author continues what they learned "in the beginning." Rhetoric is a way of writing (and speaking) that makes a point strongly and clearly by means of different techniques.

we will see in the Letters of John, the communication often becomes personal as the author makes various appeals to the recipients of his story. Nonetheless, the techniques of both of these types of criticism can be used across genres to great benefit. Further, these critical approaches also cross the worlds in and in front of the text. We gather our data about the narrative and its rhetoric from the texts; this information has its most profound effect on the world in front of the text as audiences respond to its influence.

What we are calling **audience-response criticism** is really a combination of two other types of analysis that have developed in recent years: Reader-Response Criticism and Performance Criticism. Which type of Audience-Response Criticism one is investigating depends upon whether the interpreter envisions the audience of the text as an individual reader or a group who are seeing and hearing a storyteller share the text orally. Both types of transmission certainly occur in our world that includes individual silent readings as well as multi-media productions on stage and screen. Scholars have also shown that both types of transmission occurred in the ancient world as well. **Reader-response criticism** focuses on the act of reading itself. Different readers and groups of readers will have different responses to a given text. This approach asks what those might be and how the author may have been envisioning and using potential responses in the construction of his story.

In recent years, some scholars have also begun to argue for the centrality of performance in the early life of the church. Therefore, **performance criticism** has emerged as a discipline to inquire about the impact of this oral and aural culture. Performance Critics ask questions about the multifaceted sensory experience that develops between storytellers and audiences in the oral culture of formal and informal story and letter sharing that sustained the early Christian traditions. Realizing that authors knew their works would be seen and heard as well as read, performance critical techniques focus on the cues they may have embedded in their texts as "stage directions" or how seeing and hearing the spoken text may affect how it is received by audiences and how they may live in response to it.

Narrative, Rhetorical, and Audience-Response Criticism are three widely used approaches to discovering the world in front of the text. This world is expansive and marked by great diversity. Engaging this world can, in many ways, be the most creative and satisfying aspect of biblical scholarship. This means, however, that these types of criticism can also lead to irresponsible methods and unfounded, even dangerous conclusions. We must caution one more time, then, to use the techniques of exploring all the worlds of the text in conjunction with each other in order to preserve the ancient meanings while also answering the questions of inquiring audiences today.

Example of Audience-Response Criticism

In recent years, critics have become more aware that most early Christians could not read—they either heard these texts read or saw them performed. There are often signs that a narrative was deliberately constructed for oral communication and for performance. The text, as we have it written, was to make an impact in an oral world, drawing an intellectual and emotional response from the audience. A fine example of this is found in John 18:28–19:16a: Jesus's trial before Pilate. After setting the scene (very dramatically, as the light of day opens, in v. 28), the so-called trial takes place "outside" and "inside" the praetorium. Pilate comes out, Pilate and Jesus go in, Pilate and Jesus come out, Pilate and Jesus go in, etc. Verbs of motion mark changes of location. Outside, Pilate presents Jesus as innocent and the King of the Jews. Inside, Pilate becomes increasingly under the impact of Jesus, finally asking the key Johannine question: "Where are you from?" (19:9). At the center of this dramatic change of location, associated with the gradual recognition of a rejected king, Jesus is ironically and mockingly crowned and dressed as a king (19:1–3). An audience follows the movement, the different voices, abuse, ironic confessions of the truth, and the rejection of that truth. This audience is both intellectually and emotionally involved as it responds to a story that ends: "Then he handed him over to them to be crucified" (19:16a).

As we bring this foray into the worlds of biblical interpretation—exegesis—to a conclusion, we can suggest that these critical techniques are all geared to one end: to determine the meaning of the sacred text as it was intended by the human author moved long ago to compose it and to ascertain what it is saying to readers today. A story about Jesus, written almost two thousand years ago, made sense to its readers and listeners *then* (the world behind and in the text). It continues to make sense to believing readers and listeners *today* (the world in front of the text). We will ask a variety of questions of these sorts across the rest of the course as we uncover the complexity and beauty of the Johannine Literature.

Exegeting Biblical Texts

When biblical scholars discuss using different critical approaches to the text, the concept of **hermeneutics** often arises. The term "hermeneutics" comes from the Greek word for "interpretation" and is used in biblical scholarship to refer to a particular interpretive approach. Although, as we discussed above, it is crucial for exegetes to incorporate critical techniques from all the worlds of the text, it is difficult—if not impossible—for a single interpreter to responsibly address every angle a complex text presents. Indeed, a scholar may not be interested in answering every possible question that may arise when studying a text. Therefore, biblical scholars often have a particular hermeneutic, that is, specific concerns when inquiring into a text. Various important hermeneutics have developed in biblical scholarship that have added a great deal to the discussion and brought to light many important components of this literature, including Feminist, Liberation, and Cultural Criticisms.

Feminist Criticism seeks the historical and literary recovery of the role of women in the ancient world in general and the biblical story in particular; and it tries to point out the dangers of interpretation. Liberation Criticism approaches the text from the perspective that God opposes all aspects of human oppression and seeks to realize here on earth the reality that all people are created equally. Cultural Criticism approaches the text with the desire to undercut the monopolization of culture by the elite in community and makes room for cultural expressions of the masses. These hermeneutics allow more emphasis on subjectivity, that is, how a given text affects the interpreter as well as specific groups and periods of time with which the interpreter is familiar. These approaches add many more important voices to the discussion of the exegesis of the biblical literature—voices that have often been ignored or even suppressed in the past. For the Bible and biblical study to remain relevant in our contemporary world and into the future, these voices must have a place at the table and be heard.

In addition to what it adds to the exegesis of a text, the key in taking any hermeneutical stance is for the interpreter to be self-aware of his or her position. This will allow a more responsible, balanced approach to the text. Whether one has a feminist, a historic, a literary, or any other hermeneutic, acknowledging this interest and focus will further the discussion in an open and explicit manner. As we have indicated already in this chapter, the hermeneutic of this textbook and its authors is primarily literary. We find questions about genre, plot, narrative structure, symbolism, language choice, themes, and characteristics more important to explore and answer than questions about historical facticity, sources, layers of composition, or the like. We build upon the world behind the text in order to explore the worlds in and in front of it.

This literary-critical hermeneutic results in a continuous two-level reading of the text. We will say more about two-level readings from a different perspective when we discuss the world in the text of the Gospel of John in chapter six, but at this stage we are still focused on the process of exegesis. Again, as exegetes, we are always asking questions of the text. We can introduce these two levels in terms of (1) asking questions about the author and (2) inquiring as to what the author is trying to do. We can ask, what does the author say, and what is the author trying to teach? When we are working with narratives, these are two distinct questions. In our study of the Gospel of John we will make both types of inquiry. When, however, we are working with letters, the distinction is not so strong. Often what the authors say and what they are trying to teach are the same. Indeed, they may not be trying to teach anything. Instead they are simply giving travel plans or personal health wishes. Therefore, we will not make this distinction in our questions so often when we study the Letters of John. That said, even letter-writers sometimes tell stories to make a point, or quote scripture or some other source to teach a lesson. In those cases, we attend to both levels of the text.

In terms of narratives in general and the Gospel of John in particular, we can note that storytellers create plots, characters, and setting. They reveal information about the world of their story while they entertain or inform. Characters move from place to place, encounter other characters, are faced with crises and decisions, etc., all as the plot unfolds to a climax and eventual resolution. This is what we can call the **narrative level of the text**. In the Gospel of John, for example, Jesus, his disciples, and potential opponents are introduced early on, they move through the regions of Galilee, Judea, and Samaria in the eastern Roman Empire along the Mediterranean coast, meet new people, face opposition, etc., all leading to the climax of Jesus's passion, death, and resurrection. This narrative level of the text tells us something about Jesus and his disciples, as well as Judaism and the Greco-Roman world in the first half of the first century CE. However, the Gospel does not and cannot tell us everything about these people or their world. It is also not an objective telling in the sense of a camera following these people around simply showing what happens without comment. In fact, what we have is an author who himself does not know everything about the life of Jesus who further selects from what he does know to shape the story he wants to tell. He further inserts himself as the narrator to shape and comment upon what he does tell.

All storytellers shape their traditions and information in such a way as to evoke responses from their intended audiences. This is certainly true for fictional narratives that derive largely from an author's imagination, but it is also the case for stories that render actual historical events and people. Whether an author is telling a bedtime story to a small child or sharing the news of the day, that author shapes the story or events to give a message, to teach a lesson, or to evoke a response. We can call this message sharing on the part of authors through the stories they tell the **discourse level of the text**. The term "discourse" can mean different things in different contexts, but its basic definition refers to written or spoken communication. Through the discourse level of the text, therefore, the author is communicating something beyond the content of the story. In the Gospel of John, the author, in addition to telling us something about Jesus and his mission (the narrative level) is also continually teaching us what all this means and how we should or should not act accordingly. This discourse level is strongly determined by the world of the author and the events and crises he or she may be facing. The evangelist writes his story of Jesus several decades after the events of Jesus's life and several decades into the Christian movement spawned by Jesus's mission. We will discuss this world of the evangelist in more detail in chapter five, but for now we can say that he writes from his *particular* perspective for a community that needs to be told a *particular* story in a *particular* way. He infuses his messages to his intended audience throughout the narrative. Therefore, we can also call this discourse level the teaching level of the text. And we must attend to what the evangelist is trying to *teach* us about what Jesus and the life that results from his mission mean right alongside our attention to what he *tells* us about who Jesus was, where he went, and what happened to him, etc.

> **Narrative and Discourse Levels of the Text**
>
> It is important to distinguish between what is said as the story (the narrative) unfolds and the overall message that the author wants to communicate (discourse) by telling the story in a particular fashion. Although this has long been recognized, the work of Seymour Chatman, *Story and Discourse: Narrative Structure in Fiction and Film* (1978), is very influential. As the title of the book indicates, Chatman does not focus upon New Testament narratives. However, his theoretical understanding of how narratives work remains important for biblical scholars today.

The narrative level of the text is the story that the evangelist tells, and the discourse level of the text is the meaning of these people and events that the evangelist teaches. Thorough exegesis draws out both levels of any text. What this means for our project in this textbook is that, as we move into a close exegesis of the Gospel and Letters beginning in chapter seven, we will both *summarize* what happens in each narrative unit (the narrative level) and *analyze* the meaning of each passage. We will, therefore, ask both what the evangelist is saying and what he is teaching by saying it *this way*.

The methodology of exegesis provides a fairly standard process for exegeting a text along these lines. We begin with a broad knowledge of the world behind the text. We enter into this process in the next chapter (chapter three and on into chapter four) and eventually carry it through to the more specific historical context of the evangelist (chapter five). We then turn to the world in the text. The first step here has to do with structure and literary flow of the narrative. By establishing a broad outline of the narrative, we are respecting the fact that the author chose to write a story as opposed to a letter, a sermon, or any other genre of literature. Stories unfold in certain manners, and knowing where we are in the story helps us exegete any particular passage. We will discuss the structure and flow of the Gospel of John in chapter six. Thereafter, we will explore and exegete the text along this structure. In this way we can make sense of what happens, and why it happens when it does. Each chapter beginning with chapter seven will exegete a narrative unit in the overall flow established in this structure. In each chapter, once we discuss and develop the literary context of a given passage or narrative unit, we will then explore in great detail what occurs in it (the narrative level). This will lead us to suggest what it reveals about the world behind the text and what the author may intend audiences to do as a result (the discourse level and the world in front of the text). In the end we will draw all this together to answer what we might call the "so what?" question. So what have we learned, and what does it all mean? This, of course, is the goal of exegesis.

This process is customary in exegeting any passage. A "to-do" list of the exegesis of a given passage could, therefore, look like this:

1. **Introduction and Thesis**: Here an exegete might introduce the overall text and context as well as establish the thesis for this particular exegetical project. The questions this thesis might want to answer are, "Why does the author tell this story in this way? Why is this passage important in the overall narrative? And what is the author teaching audiences by narrating this passage in this manner?

2. **Context and Structure**: Here an exegete might establish where audiences are in the larger plot and what this means for interpretation. In other words, are we at the beginning of the story? The middle? The end? How might establishing this location in the flow of the narrative help us interpret it? The exegete could provide a detailed structure for the outline of the text in question. Again, how we understand the way authors structure passages helps us understand what they intend to narrate and teach.

3. **Exegetical Analysis**: Here an exegete might take on each component of the outline established in the previous section to provide a close analysis of the constituent parts of the overall passage. Exegetes gather data from all the worlds of the text and bring them to bear from their particular hermeneutics in order to draw out the author's intended meaning.

4. **Conclusion**: Here an exegete brings it all together to answer that "so what?" question. The thesis that was introduced and has been threaded through the exegesis is concluded in terms of what the passage means for people of both the first century and today.

The content of this to-do list is not a novel idea. Rather, it reflects a process that will allow for a strong, responsible exegesis from our particular hermeneutic. The succeeding chapters in this textbook will exegete the Gospel and Letters of John following this pattern through a literary-critical hermeneutic. In this way we hope to bring to life the texts in terms of their meaning for both first-century and twenty-first-century audiences.

What Have We Learned So Far?
The Worlds That Created and Are Created by the Text

Much like the previous chapter, this chapter has not focused on new information regarding the components of theology as expressed in the Johannine Literature. Since this chapter has provided a brief overview of the methodology for scholarly exegesis of that Bible, there has been little focus on theology. We mentioned in the previous chapter that in the ancient world there was no separation between the religious, political, social, and literary worlds. In this same vein, the endeavor of biblical interpretation was first engaged by people of faith inquiring about God's message to them and interaction with their lives and the lives of their community. This continues to be the case today. The succeeding chapters will, therefore, have much more to add to this component of our study.

Key Terms and Concepts

audience-response criticism

criticism

discourse level of the text

exegesis

form criticism

hermeneutics

historical-critical method

historical criticism

literary criticism

narrative criticism

narrative level of the text

performance criticism

reader-response criticism

redaction criticism

rhetorical criticism

source criticism

textual criticism

world behind the text

world in front of the text

world in the text

Questions for Review

1. What is meant by the term "exegesis"?
2. Briefly describe what is meant by the approaches of biblical interpretation that consider "the world behind the text," "the world in the text," and "the world in front of the text."
3. What is textual criticism, and why is it important in establishing the text of the Bible?
4. What is literary criticism, and why is understanding genres and literary forms so important in interpreting the Bible?
5. How do audiences shape and how are they shaped by the biblical text? Why might understanding these potential responses aid in biblical interpretation?
6. What is meant by the narrative and discourse levels of a biblical text? Why must an exegete always keep an eye on each of these levels?

Bibliography and Further Reading

Attridge, Harold W. "Genre Bending in the Fourth Gopel." *Journal for Biblical Literature* 121 (2002): 3–21.

Carvalho, Corrine. *Primer on Biblical Methods.* Winona, MN: Anselm Academic, 2009.

Dawes, Gregory. *Introduction to the Bible.* New Collegeville Bible Commentary: Old Testament. Vol. 1. Collegeville, MN: Liturgical, 2007.

Fitzmyer, Joseph A. *Scripture, the Soul of Theology.* New York: Paulist, 1994.

Rhoads, David. "Performance Criticism: An Emerging Methodology in Second Testament Studies." *Biblical Theological Bulletin* 36 (2006): 118–40, 164–88.

CHAPTER THREE

The Old Testament Story:
Israel and Covenant with God

PURPOSE Chapter three presents an overview of the story of Israel as it is preserved in the Christian Old Testament. In this way both the world of the evangelist and the world behind the text of the literature he composed on behalf of his community are also introduced.

ASSIGNMENT Skim the key texts in your Bible as indicated in the subheadings of the story of Israel below alongside the brief analyses provided.

In this chapter we will thread the narrative of the history and development of Judaism as it is woven through the Jewish Scriptures. The many books that tell the history of Israel were written at different times and places and by authors who sometimes report events in different ways. That need not bother us, as the final product of this complex history of writing tells its own story. The biblical story of Israel can be traced by following the accounts in the OT books in the way they have come down to us. Indeed, this was the way that Jesus, the early church, John, and his readers understood the history of God's people. Therefore, we will not overly concern ourselves with the world behind these texts, but focus on the worlds in and in front of them so that we can get a sense of how Jewish people in the first century CE might have understood their history in relationship with God, with each other, and with the rest of the world. We can also begin to form a picture of how some Jewish people, including John and his community, might have understood God to be acting in and through Jesus to offer a new development in that relationship. What follows is thus not close, technical exegesis of the Old Testament—that is an entire course in its own right!—but a broad overview of the story, highlighting key figures and their roles in the history and theology of Judaism. As a result, when we come across these people and concepts in the Johannine Literature, we will have a better understanding of who and what they are and why they are important in these NT texts.

The Story of Israel

As we read through the OT, a basic component of the narrative history that emerges is that a single God is creator and ruler of all. This is known as "monotheism." Further, this God interacts with the created world in a relationship that is described as a covenant. The Jewish people trace their story to the beginning of creation and come to understand themselves as having a unique covenant relationship with God. As this story develops, some basic characteristics of what is meant by a covenant relationship also materialize: one party of the covenant (God) is vastly more knowledgeable, more powerful, and more "sighted" than the other (humans). In every instance, then, God *knows*, can *do*, and can *see* things in creation and history that the human parties do not and cannot know, do, or see. This constant feature of the relationship between God and humankind means God is always the initiating agent of these covenants. This gives God encompassing *authority* in this relationship, while the human participants are always called to some form of *obedience*. There are always binding promises and obligations at play. In the first century CE when the earliest Christians—who were Jewish people—described their experience of Jesus, they understood God to be acting in and through Jesus in this same fashion. When John the Evangelist set out to compose his Gospel story, he saw it as the continuation of this same story of God's relationship with humankind. To prepare ourselves for John's story, therefore, we must begin at the beginning—the *genesis*—of his people Israel's story as he would have understood it.

> **Monotheism**
>
> The belief in only one deity is called monotheism. In the ancient world, the major religions were polytheistic, meaning they had several, and often many, deities. Ancient Israelites were devoted to one primary God, sovereign and creator. This was still the case as Judaism developed in the first century CE. Today the world's major monotheistic religions—Judaism, Christianity, and Islam—profess belief in the same God.

The Beginnings of God's Work in Creation as Preserved in Genesis 1–11 (Primeval History)

The Old Testament narrative begins with the book of Genesis, which, as its name indicates, tells the story of the creation of the world by the one sovereign creator God and then the story of the birth of Judaism. The text can be divided in the broadest sense into two parts. Gen 1–11 is an account of the primordial history of the known world. The text then moves into the more specific account of the ancestry of the people of Israel in Gen 12–50. Even though Israel did not yet exist as God's people, the first part narrates several key episodes in how the Jewish people understand who God is and how God works in the world in relationship to creation and all humankind. These and other narratives across

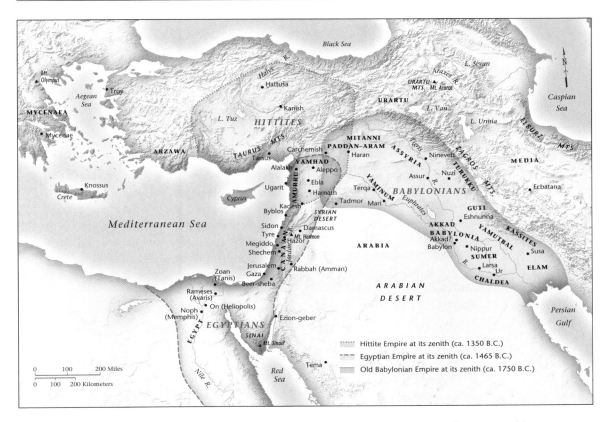

REGION OF MESOPOTAMIA

the Old Testament give what are called **etiologies**. An etiology is a study of causes or origins. Therefore, an **etiological story** explains in narrative form how something or some custom or practice came to be in the world or in a particular community. Genesis 1–3 tells the story of creation itself as well as the story of the first human beings and their relationship with God. These first chapters of Genesis are a very good example of an "etiological story." Writing during difficult times in Israel's history, the authors want to show that in the *beginning* everything was good, and that the evil and division experienced by the people did not *begin* with God's creation. It came about because of the disobedience of human beings. After a lengthy genealogy in Gen 5 that moves us several centuries forward in history, Gen 6–9 tells the story of Noah, his ark, and the flood that God sends over the earth. Another genealogy in Gen 10 is sometimes called the Table of Nations and lays out the diversity of peoples who have developed over the millennia and leads to the story of the Tower of Babel in Gen 11. This event becomes a catalyst in God's choosing of Abraham as the eventual father of the Jewish people. The following paragraphs will give

Literary Forms in the OT

In addition to **etiologies** (short narratives that serve to explain the origin or meaning of elements of daily life such as customs, names, or rituals) several other literary forms are prominent in the OT. Examples include:

Myth: A narrative that explains profound human truths through the interaction of the divine with the earthly or human. Myths typically express a group's self-understanding of identity and serve to bond the community members together. Scholars speak of the Creation Myth or the Exodus Myth in the OT without judgment about their historicity.

Legend: A narrative, typically of exaggerated history from a core historical event. Legends usually develop around larger-than-life community heroes and tend to magnify their accomplishments. Scholars can speak of legends of the patriarchs or the legend of David.

Law Code: A series of behavioral precepts concerning interpersonal ethics or ritual worship life in the community. In this vein, Exod 20:19–23:33 is often referred to as the Covenant Code, while Deut 12–26 is called the Deuteronomic Code.

Call Story: These brief narratives portray the call of important people by God. Typically 1) God appears in some form, 2) God commissions a person to a task, 3) the person then responds, often offering an objection, and 4) then God insists and reassures the one called. Call stories are typical in the prophets but occur across Scriptures.

Psalms: Brief songs or hymns that typically fall into one of several categories: praise, laments, thanksgiving, repentance, royal celebration, wisdom, or historical memory.

Proverbs: A short popular saying that communicates a practical truth, observation, or guide to good living in a pithy, easily remembered form.

a bit more detail on these initial chapters of Jewish Scripture as they set the pattern for how God works in the world, how the world itself works, and how humankind is created to respond to God.

The beginning of Israel's story tells of God's word of creation. God literally spoke creation into being (1:1–2:4a). Communication thus becomes the basis of relationship, and relationship becomes the basis of God's interaction with creation. God creates the world as we know it in a pattern of days that systematically expands the creative act until God can rest and reflect on its goodness on the seventh day. God gives **Adam**, the first human and pinnacle of creation, life and food and shelter, then culminates this relationship in the gift of community with the creation of Adam's partner, the woman Eve. The promise of this relationship is Eden, the garden that represents the ideal dwelling place in peace with the created order. In return, God demands obedience. Living in harmony with God and the rest of creation is dependent upon their refraining from eating from the Tree of the Knowledge of Good and Evil. In short order, however, Adam and Eve fail: they disobey when Eve is seduced by the serpent, the cleverest of all creatures, into eating from the fruit of the tree. The lesson

Adam and Eve by
Albrecht Dürer

here has to do not with serpents and apples but with forgoing immediate gratification and looking to long-term rewards and taking responsibility for one's
own decisions. As a result of Adam and Eve's disobedience, the perfect union of
their relationship with God is broken. The re-establishment of right relationship
with God becomes the guiding force of the rest of the Jewish Scriptures.

Sin and death enter the world through this disobedience and quickly spread
as humankind grows. The story of Adam and Eve's first children, Cain and
Abel, and Cain's falling to sin in killing his brother out of jealousy, establishes
how quickly disorder takes root in creation (Gen 4). The narrative is careful
to illustrate, however, that God never breaks fidelity to his promises. Even as

Adam and Eve lose their right to Eden, God clothes and prepares them for the life they have chosen (Gen 3:21). Likewise, God protects Cain even as Cain has to live out his life in the consequences of his actions. Further, God gives Adam and Eve a third son, Seth, to continue the line of humankind in creation, which leads to the founding of Judaism. God begins to rectify this relationship with creation by offering a covenant to Noah.

The story about **Noah** and his experience of covenant with God makes up Gen 6–9. The sixth chapter of Genesis opens with a strange and provocative story of the spread of humankind, which is consonant with the multiplication of evil across the earth. Humankind, to whom the earth was given and whose inclination was to be for God, is focused only on evil. God's heart was aggrieved, and he determined to "un-create" through the flood. But Noah found favor in the eyes of God (Gen 6:8), ensuring that "re-creation" would follow. Noah is characterized immediately as a father who is "righteous," "blameless," and who "walked with God" (Gen 6:9–10). Because of these attributes, God chooses Noah and through him and his obedient action saves the best of what was already created. God gives Noah his reasoning for re-creation through a coming flood and then instructs Noah to build an ark—a boat in the middle of the desert. This command emphasizes the obedience that is demanded of Noah, and Noah's unyielding response in action confirms his integrity. In response, God establishes a covenant with Noah.

Genesis 7–8 details the flood itself as God does as promised, allowing the waters of the deep and the heavens to burst forth. God then begins to speak to Noah again and once more opens with another command, this time "Go out." Noah again responds in full obedience to God's call. This second act of response-in-action is followed by Noah's first initiating action as he builds an altar and offers a burnt sacrifice. God gives his blessing to Noah and affirms the sanctity of life, particularly human life, however limited and transient. Genesis 9 then turns to God's covenant with Noah. What was promised before the flood comes to fruition as part of the re-creative communication. God makes his covenant with Noah and his offspring as well as with all of the re-created order. The covenant is eternal and creation will never again be destroyed. Noah, the primary human character of this account, is silent throughout. God initiates all the action and does all the speaking. Noah's response is in his action, and by his obedient action he accepts God's word of covenant and lives his life in accord with that relationship, thus facilitating God's covenant with all creation.

Genesis 6–9, therefore, tells the story of God's work in creation, beginning anew through Noah. God's relationship with humankind, however, needs more story, as the early chapters of Genesis close with the confusion and scattering of humankind following the attempted construction of the **Tower of Babel** (Gen 11). The people of God's creation continue to show that although they have an innate desire to live in right relationship with God they also have tendencies to look for other means of fulfillment. They often follow human authority and the

desires of this world. The culmination of these latter tendencies is narrated as the people determine to build a tower to get to the heavens and God and "make a name" for themselves. The narrative of Genesis thus far has shown us that the people are meant to be "calling on the name" of God. God, therefore, thwarts these attempts by "confusing" their language and "scattering" the people over the face of the earth. This scattering symbolizes the radical break in the relationship between God and humankind as the opposite of the unity for which it was created. This entire episode also becomes an etiological story for the many languages of humankind as well as how people came to populate the entire earth.

The narrative then moves forward several hundred years by way of a genealogy, further symbolizing this breakdown in the relationship. From this point forward, God will never again walk with his creation in the garden, or anywhere else for that matter. The distance between God and his creation only grows. The characterization of the fearsome and awesome power of God also expands. From what we have shared from Gen 1–11, we can see how this profound story

The Tower of Babel by Pieter Bruegel the Elder

informs Israel about God, creation, sin, blessing and protection from God, and the divisions among peoples, nations, and languages. This is how it all began.

Abraham and the Jewish Ancestors as Preserved in Genesis 12–50 (ca. 1800 BCE)

The second part of the book of Genesis, chs. 12–50, covers the ancestral period of the history of Israel. It begins with a man called Abram, whom God eventually renames **Abraham** (Gen 17:5). We will devote several pages to this portion of the story since it is fundamental to the story that follows. The Abraham cycle of stories begins at Gen 12 and runs through Gen 25. Scholars tend to call these stories of the patriarchs—a term that means something like "father-leader"— cycles. They are called cycles because they are repetitive and spiral from one to the next. Genesis 12 is traditionally understood to recount the call of Abraham. After several centuries of apparent silence, God calls out to one person: "Now God said to Abram, 'Go . . .'" (v. 1). And that one person responds, taking his family and all that he owns with him: "So Abram went . . ." (v. 4). Once again the narrative recounts God's call in terms of command and the chosen one's response-in-action in terms of precise obedience. And for his obedience Abram receives the assurance of blessing—a great nation and a great name—along with the covenantal obligation of invoking the name of the Lord in blessing or cursing those he encounters (vv. 2–3). After the radical break with all creation at Gen 11, God chooses to work in terms of one man—of individual faith and practice. From this action, we find the new basis for a people of God. In response to God's call at Gen 12, Abram moves his wife, Sarai (eventually renamed Sarah), and his nephew, Lot, to Canaan.

Crucial for our study is not only God's covenant with Abraham, but also the journey, of both body and spirit, that is integral to the content and the purpose of that relationship. In the narrative, God's relationship with Abraham grows as Abraham grows. Abraham's movement, therefore, is not only physical but spiritual as well, as he moves from pure response in action accompanied by a faith riddled with doubt to a response in action that is grounded in the fullness of faith. Doubt overtakes Abraham almost immediately as he endangers Sarah, the promised matriarch, to the hands of Pharaoh (12:10–20). This doubt continues to hinder Abraham's faith even as he continues to respond in action. Thus, his is a move from strict obedience to obedience in faith. And this is what is eventually credited as righteousness (15:6).

In Genesis 13, God once again commands Abraham to go, and Abraham complies. This new act of obedience is followed by Abraham's overwhelming success in rescuing Lot from eastern kings, exemplifying his ability to protect his people and overcome his enemies (14:1–24). The proof of this blessing, and Abraham's acknowledgment of it, brings him to the first full expression of God's covenantal action: the promise of descendants (15:1–6) and land (15:7–21). For the first time in the biblical narrative, the human party responds to God verbally (vv. 2–3). Further, Abraham enters into full dialogue with God by expressing his doubt about God's ability to carry out his promise, given the reality of his aging situation. Even more remarkably, God responds not in anger, but in the openness of relationship in communication, bringing Abraham outside and giving the visual confirmation of the stars as the gauge by which his offspring will be numbered (vv. 4–5). Abraham then takes the first step from mere obedience in action to active obedience in faith when "he believed" God. And here God first credits his faith (v. 6).

This is not the end of Abraham's journey, however. The very next chapter describes the doubt that persists when Abraham "listened to the voice" of another human being, in this case Sarah (16:2), when he has been called time and again to "listen to the voice" of God. This leads to strife in the family and the endangerment of Abraham's own child Ishmael by his concubine Hagar (16:3–6). God must intervene, rectifying the wrong done to Hagar, saving the unborn child, and presenting the child Ishmael with a divine commitment of his own (vv. 7–16). God then goes to Abraham and recommits them both to the covenanted promises. Scholars generally consider Genesis 15 and 17 to be varying traditions of the same event told from different perspectives. On reading the final form of the narrative, however, we see the ups and downs of Abraham's journey of faith. In Gen 17, Abraham is renamed in the process to represent this divine commitment. The eternal nature of the covenant is clarified and the promise of land is once again brought to bear. Distinctive in this episode is the sign of the covenant that God introduces. Circumcision will henceforth mark God's covenant with Abraham and all that are his. Sarai, too, is renamed Sarah, and the child from her womb is identified as Isaac. Thus, as the story progresses, the covenant develops further. Its sheer magnitude comes to the fore. When God finishes speaking, he departs. Abraham's agency as a participant is reduced; he simply receives the promise in silent awe. His ensuing action, however, is once again full obedience as he takes his entire house to be circumcised (vv. 23–27).

Abraham's agency is then reasserted in the following chapters, and his journey comes to its climax at Gen 22. His winding path of growth and development over the last ten chapters of narrative has been building to this ultimate point of decision where "God puts Abraham to the test," and Abraham must confront not only his own true nature but also that of the God with whom he is covenanted. In this encounter, God, for the first time in their relationship, calls Abraham by name. In fact, Abraham is called three times by three different characters, denoting the crucial nature of his role: first by God ("Abraham!" v. 1), then by Isaac ("my Father!" v. 7), and finally by the angel of God ("Abraham!" v. 11). Each time Abraham answers in the same fundamental manner. With this simple particle of existence, best translated as "Here I am," Abraham places himself before God in a direct way. This episode thus embodies a profound

Sacrifice of Isaac
by Rembrandt

personal experience with God. The command to sacrifice his "only son," the
beloved son of the promise, puts Abraham, who has been so obedient in action,
to the ultimate test of faith. For his part, Abraham responds in word as well
as deed, exemplifying that his faith in God's promise has finally matured with
his obedience. By raising his hand to kill his son, Abraham's journey of faith
reaches its goal, and he is rewarded. Isaac is spared (as is Abraham), and a ram

is given for the sacrifice. It is this sacrifice—the result of Abraham passing God's test—which ultimately seals his covenant with God. Abraham's story quickly comes to a close, his place in God's covenantal action in history assured. The remainder of Genesis details the fruition of God's promises as the descendants of Abraham eventually become the Israelites, a great clan that eventually makes its way down into Egypt. Abraham thus becomes the father of Judaism and the model of faith for his descendants across history.

Abraham's son Isaac marries Rebekah, and they have two sons, Jacob and Esau (Gen 24:67; 25:25–26). Jacob becomes the son of God's promise over a lengthy cycle of stories that show that he is manipulative and a bit duplicitous in his efforts to get his father's blessing and the wife he desires (Gen 25–47). Nonetheless, Jacob proves his mettle with God and is renamed **Israel**, which means "he strives with God" (Gen 32:29). Jacob eventually becomes the father of many sons who develop into the twelve tribes of Israel. One of these sons is Joseph, with whom many are familiar because of the "coat of many colors" given to him by his father (Gen 37:3). Joseph becomes very successful in the Pharaoh's court in Egypt and eventually brings his entire family there to escape famine in the land promised to them by God (Genesis 41–50). This "Joseph story" is one of the most beautiful stories in the Bible, especially when we recognize that it was written more than three thousand years ago. The book of Genesis ends with the "twelve tribes of Israel" successful and content in Egypt. They have received the blessing of their covenant with God, but they are outside the land promised to them by God's covenant with Abraham. This situation becomes the setting for the book of Exodus and the next major narrative episode in Israel's history.

Moses and the Sinai Covenant as Preserved in Exodus, Leviticus, Numbers, and Deuteronomy (ca. 1280 BCE)

The book of Exodus opens by narrating the passing of a number of generations. The Israelites, as they are now identified, are successful for some time in Egypt. However, once a new Pharaoh comes to power, they fall out of favor and are forced into labor camps for the royal building projects. This situation sets the stage for the next major events in Israel's history, the Exodus and the Sinai covenant that is forged in its aftermath. We are also introduced to arguably the most important figure in Israel's history, **Moses**. The magnitude of this period in Israelite history

---

Israel

The name Israel comes from the Hebrew "he strives with God" or possibly "may God rule." It was first given to Jacob in Gen 32:28. The name is later extended to the twelve tribes descended from Jacob/Israel. The people come to be called "the children of Israel" or "the Israelites." The earliest occurrence of the name outside Israel is in Egypt ca. 1230 BCE. The name was extended to the nation ca. 1000 BCE. After the division, "Israel" is usually preserved for the northern nation. Over time, the name came to encompass not only an ethnic and political designation but a theological description for the people of God in any age.

is matched by the amount of narrative devoted to its telling. While the early millennia of the history of the world were narrated in the first eleven chapters of Genesis, the period of fifty to a hundred years during the time of Moses, the Exodus, and the Sinai covenant is narrated across the next four books of the Bible: Exodus, Leviticus, Numbers, and Deuteronomy.

Moses is called by God and, despite all of his efforts to get out of God's call, becomes God's greatest prophet. Exodus 3 tells the famous story about Moses tending the flocks of his father-in-law and seeing a bush that is on fire, but one that does not burn up. Once he investigates, he encounters God, who calls him to be both the leader of the Israelites and God's spokesperson. This portion of the narrative also shares the sacred name of God. This name is so revered that it is never spoken aloud. Even today, it is never uttered, and we cannot be sure how it should be spoken. In Exod 3:14 God shares this name. The Hebrew word is derived from this and can be written in English as **YHWH**. Even in Hebrew this is an odd formulation; but scholars agree it

> **The Tetragrammaton**
>
> The sacred name of the God of Israel is written in Hebrew as יהוה and is transliterated into English as YHWH. Scholars sometimes refer to it as the **tetragrammaton**, a term that comes from the Greek and means "the four-letter word." Since it is not to be uttered out of reverence for God, we do not know how it would be pronounced. The ancient Jews developed the practice of saying the title "Lord" when they read the sacred name. Therefore, to indicate where the Jewish Scriptures use the tetragrammaton, many modern Bibles and textbooks use "Lord" with small capital letters.

is some form of the Hebrew verb for "to be," and English translations render it as something like "I am who am." The divine name is, therefore, connected to the very essence of being. Because the Israelites revere this word, they develop the custom of saying "Lord," a more common word of honor, when they see it. The word is so sacred to Jews that they never say it.

For his part, Moses takes this divine name and the authority God gives him as God's **prophet**, or spokesperson, and challenges Pharaoh to let the descendants of Abraham, Isaac, and Jacob (whom we now know as the Israelites) go to worship God in the wilderness. The book of **Exodus** is named for the events of the rest of its first half as Moses proves the wondrous power of God and eventually leads the people out of Egypt from under the Pharaoh's control. Moses continually wields the power of God, and the Israelites make their way into the desert of the Sinai Peninsula, where they encounter God in a new way. The miracles Moses performs are identified as **signs**, because they point to the wonders of God's awesome power.

Exodus 19–24 provides the narrative of the next step in God's relationship with the descendants of Abraham, which scholars generally call the **Sinai covenant**. This new covenantal development is marked by a call and response. Crucial to sealing this covenant is God's promise, ". . . if you will obey my voice and keep my covenant, you shall be my own possession among all the peoples" (19:5). And it is an offer that is not operative until the

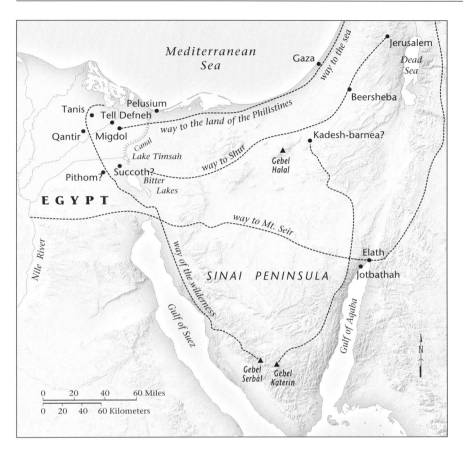

SINAI PENINSULA AND POTENTIAL EXODUS ROUTES

people accept. The Israelites, who had fallen into slavery, have struggled to make their exodus from Egypt under the leadership of Moses and now stand before God in the wilderness of the Sinai Peninsula. The solemn introduction to the Sinai covenant affirms that this covenant is different from those that God has established thus far. God uses Moses as a mediator to offer a conditional covenant to an entire people and has them respond first by word and then, only when the covenant is sealed, by deed. This is a development of the covenantal nature of God's relationship with the children of Israel. The divine commitment remains, but the human obligation in word and deed—in *relationship*—comes to the fore. The people must "obey the voice" of God and "keep the covenant." They must remain in active relationship with God and God alone. Abraham "hearkened to the voice" of another on occasion and caused his own stumbling on his journey, but his covenant was never at stake. In the conditional nature of this covenant, God presents its maintenance as dependent upon this obedience. Moses does as he is commanded, and the people respond positively in full voice, "All that God has said, we will do" (19:8). The people are then instructed to consecrate themselves for two days to prepare themselves, for "on the third day the

Moses by Michelangelo

Lord will come down upon Mount Sinai in the sight of all the people" (19:11). The appearance of God occurs on the third day, as promised (19:16–25).

The purpose of the consecration and appearance, or **theophany**, is so that God may initiate the covenant-making process through the giving of his words. Exodus 20 is devoted to the narration of these **Ten Commandments**, the Decalogue, in covenant form. God is identified as the covenant-giver, and, after a brief history of their relationship, the people are given the obligations of the covenant in the Ten Commandments. Witnessing to the theophany strikes fear in the people, leading them to ask Moses to be the official mediator, thus formalizing his role as God's prophet. Moses agrees and urges the people not to fear but to understand the curses that are integral to the covenant relationship. He then draws near to God to receive further instruction, resulting in the laws that are often called the Covenant Collection or "book of the covenant." Exodus 20:22–23:19 begins and ends with legislation regarding ritual and the worship of God, so that all social interaction as the people of God is framed in worship, while Exodus 24 narrates the completion and ratification of the covenant in two rituals. In order for the covenant to be completed, it seems necessary for the people to give a twofold reiteration of their commitment to exclusive relationship with God through keeping the covenant stipulations laid before them in the Ten Commandments.

Across the rest of Israel's Scriptures, this Sinai covenant is the covenant necessary for the people to understand how to live in right relationship with God. This is also the foundation of the covenant that lies behind the thinking of the early Christians. The rest of these early books are dedicated to God giving his people all the obligations of this covenant (Exod 20–31; Lev 1–27; Num 28–36; Deut 4–30), as well as the events that lead a new generation of Israelites, forged in the wilderness under the direction of Moses and the Sinai covenant, back to the land promised to their ancestor Abraham. For their part, God's chosen people struggle with the covenant's demands, but this Law, the *Torah* in Hebrew, is given as the gift that guides the people into right relationship with God. The book of Deuteronomy closes with the death of the great prophet and leader, Moses; and the people, under the leadership of Joshua, are poised to retake the land they understand to be theirs through this covenantal history.

The Conquest and Settlement of Canaan as Preserved in Joshua and Judges (ca. 1200 BCE)

The book of Joshua describes the conquest of Canaan, the land promised first to Abraham and then to the children of Israel at Sinai, in epic pageantry. The tribal assembly at Shechem is a covenant-making event, in terms of a renewal of the Sinai covenant, to form a twelve-tribe league of crucial importance to the

---

Joshua 24:14–24

"Now therefore revere the LORD, and serve him in sincerity and in faithfulness; put away the gods that your ancestors served beyond the River and in Egypt, and serve the LORD. Now if you are unwilling to serve the LORD, choose this day whom you will serve, whether the gods your ancestors served in the region beyond the River or the gods of the Amorites in whose land you are living; but as for me and my household, we will serve the LORD."

Then the people answered, "Far be it from us that we should forsake the LORD to serve other gods; for it is the LORD our God who brought us and our ancestors up from the land of Egypt, out of the house of slavery, and who did those great signs in our sight. He protected us along all the way that we went, and among all the peoples through whom we passed; and the LORD drove out before us all the peoples, the Amorites who lived in the land. Therefore we also will serve the LORD, for he is our God."

But Joshua said to the people, "You cannot serve the LORD, for he is a holy God. He is a jealous God; he will not forgive your transgressions or your sins. If you forsake the LORD and serve foreign gods, then he will turn and do you harm, and consume you, after having done you good."

And the people said to Joshua, "No, we will serve the LORD!"

Then Joshua said to the people, "You are witnesses against yourselves that you have chosen the LORD, to serve him."

And they said, "We are witnesses."

He said, "Then put away the foreign gods that are among you, and incline your hearts to the LORD, the God of Israel."

The people said to Joshua, "The LORD our God we will serve, and him we will obey."

---

creation of a unified people. By reaffirming the Sinai covenant, this new generation of people render themselves personal participants in that same covenant.

Joshua 23 recounts the farewell speech of Joshua himself. Therefore, bringing the tribes together in covenant renewal to form a confederation is Joshua's final act as prophetic leader of the people of God. The final verses of Joshua 24, and the final verses of the book as a whole, recount Joshua's death and the faithfulness of Israel that he facilitated. When Joshua recites the sacred history of Israel, he dwells on God's action on Israel's behalf in the Exodus and the wilderness, but begins with the divine promises to the patriarchs. The purpose of the recitation comes in the call to decision. Joshua 24:14–24 is marked, as are all the covenant-making passages, by call and response. The first commandment of Sinai is here reiterated in terms of service. God has already chosen Israel; it is now for Israel, in the form of the tribal confederation, to respond with their choice for God. And the people do so, three times. When they give their final response to the call, they affirm their determination to serve God by also vowing their obedience. Therefore, it is the demands of the Sinai covenant that determine the success or failure of both Israel as a whole and the lives of its individual people.

The book of Judges takes us from this ideal period of all the tribes working together to a time when the leaders call for a king and a unified nation. As the story continues, we learn that, despite the magnificent conquest narrated in the book of Joshua, the Israelites continue to contend with peoples such as the Philistines in the land of Canaan. The early leaders of Israel are called judges because they are local military and judicial leaders who are called by God to liberate the people from their enemies. They do not form dynasties, nor do they act as a sovereign leader over all the tribes. The events of this period and the leadership of twelve judges against powerful odds are narrated across this text. Over time, however, the Israelites contend not only with outsiders but with each other, and they begin to clamor for a king who will not only go before them in battle but who will also unite them as a nation.

King David and the Nation as Preserved in the Books of Samuel and Kings (ca. 1000–587 BCE)

The story of **David**, the shepherd who becomes king of Israel, spans the books of Samuel and continues into the first chapters of the books of Kings. If Moses is the ideal prophet of Israel and the primary figure of the Torah, David becomes the ideal king and the figure that looms largest over the books known as the Prophets and much of the remaining Jewish Scriptures. The story of the monarchy does not begin with David, but with Samuel, the last judge, and Saul, the first king anointed by Samuel.

As 1 Samuel opens, the birth and development of Samuel, as a man of God and just judge following the model of Moses, are narrated alongside evidence that this organizational structure for the expanding tribes of Israel is not sustainable. The elders of the tribes come to Samuel and call for a king "like the other nations"; but Samuel gives voice to the potential negative consequences to living under a monarchy, reminding the Israelites that as God's chosen people they are not meant to be "like the other nations." Nonetheless, God accedes to the people's wishes and directs Samuel to anoint Saul, who ruled in the late eleventh century BCE, ca. 1020. Saul seems to have been a more effective military leader than a governor. Even his military expertise faded, however, once he lost God's favor by overstepping the bounds of his role as king. He commanded a citadel at Gibeah, a few miles northwest of Jerusalem, but never controlled all the tribes. He did, however, create some sort of union stable enough to endure the external threat from the Philistines and form a basis for the national developments to come.

David enters the narrative of Israel's history at 1 Samuel 16 as a boy tending his father's flock in Bethlehem, from the tribe of Judah. Even at the first mention of his name, readers begin to understand the powerful role he will have in the national and religious developments to come: "And Samuel took the horn of oil, and anointed him in the midst of his brothers; and the Spirit of God came mightily upon David from that day forward" (1 Sam 16:13). David's rise to power is swift and direct from the moment he enters public life, first as a musician in King Saul's court, then as the king's armor-bearer and the champion who slays the giant Philistine warrior Goliath. His special relationship with God is foreshadowed even in these early verses. By the time David becomes king (2 Samuel 2), and certainly by the time of his death (1 Kings 2),

David by Michelangelo, Galleria dell'Accademia
© Jörg Bittner Unna

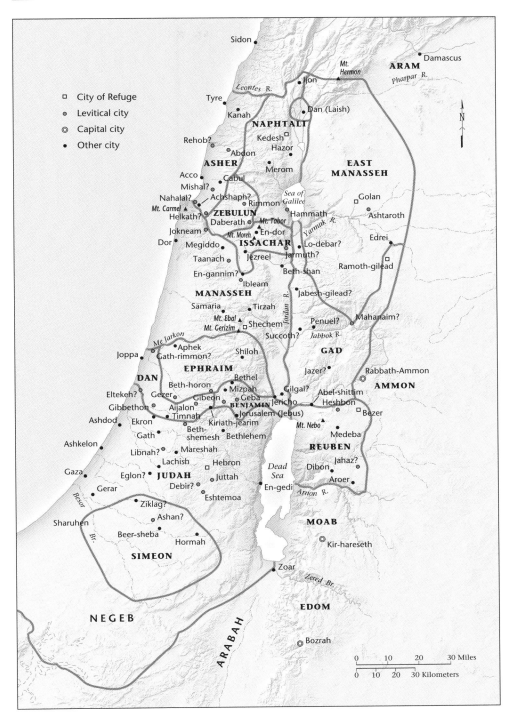

TRIBAL DISTRIBUTION IN THE PROMISED LAND

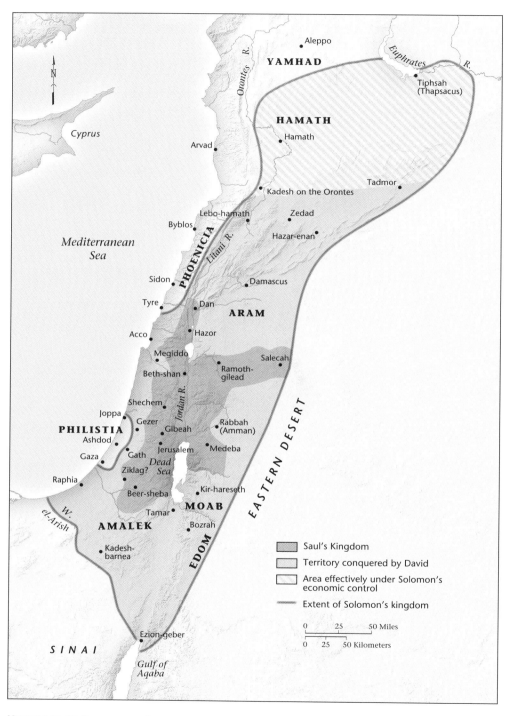

KINGDOM OF DAVID AND SOLOMON

this relationship has become one of the most complex and intricately drawn in all of Israel's Scriptures.

David is anointed king prior to the death of Saul, who is then presented more or less as a tragic character who falls to the growing power of a supposed ally (David) and the rejection of the prophet who anointed him (Samuel). For his part, David becomes a larger than life figure in Israelite tradition, becoming the model for anointed leaders from that point forward. David marries Saul's daughter, Michal, and becomes beloved friends with Saul's heir apparent, Jonathan. Saul's fear and jealousy of David forced the latter into exile among the Philistines. Jonathan eventually dies in battle, and King Saul, tragically, by his own sword. David then moves quickly to solidify his power and establish his kingship of Judah at Hebron. The Philistines see their former accomplice as a new enemy of dangerous proportions and attack in force. David deals them a decisive defeat and further consolidates his power by capturing Jerusalem from the Jebusites. The city was naturally well suited for defense and lay neither in Saul's ancestral land of Benjamin nor David's home of Judah; thus he quickly transferred his capital there. At its greatest extent, David's kingdom possibly stretched as far north as the Lebanon mountain range to deep into the Sinai desert in the south, and from the Mediterranean in the west to the desert in the east. He ruled across the early tenth century BCE, ca 1000–960.

2 Samuel 7–8 provides a crux to the David story that underscores his personal relationship with God and his role as God's king and anointed one, or **messiah**. David's initiative to build a house for God is presented as the impetus for God to make a new covenant with him and through him with the Israelites as a nation. The theme of "dwelling" runs through this passage, such that the concepts of "house" and "dynasty" are interwoven to make up the divine promise and commitment. God's promise of future glory and unmatched greatness in name is given to David, through the prophet Nathan, as a reaffirmation of a land where the people may live in peace and security. God then assures David's dynasty by establishing an everlasting relationship. David is promised offspring who will build a house for God, and God likens their relationship to a father-son kinship of obedience and discipline as well as steadfast love and blessing. For his part, David enters the tent in which the Ark of the Covenant (the container that holds the Ten Commandments from the Sinai Covenant) dwells. In prayer, David extols the greatness and uniqueness of God, who has made the divine presence known, then recounts God's redeeming action on Israel's behalf through the Exodus, when the people were set apart in God's name. With this prayer David accepts God's promise, including the blessing and obedience that it entails.

Through this covenant, God promises that a descendent of David will always be king over God's people. Since kings are anointed in the ancient world, this king would be God's "anointed one." In the Hebrew language, the word for "anointed one" is *mashiach*, which comes into English as messiah. In the Greek language, the word for "anointed one" is *christos*, which comes into English as **Christ**. The words "messiah" and "Christ" are, therefore, synonyms. A messiah, then, is a term used for kings in ancient Israel, and God's messiahs rule the people in God's name. What scholars call "messianic expectations" are now also introduced into the hope of Israel. As a result of God's covenant with King David, whenever they find themselves suffering and oppressed by outsiders, God's people can expect that God will send a messiah, whom they understand to be a descendant of David, to liberate them from this oppression and become king over them as a sovereign nation. This Davidic covenant adds a new component to God's covenantal relationship with Israel. Jerusalem becomes the holy city and a royal component of the nation, and God's anointed one, who will lead it, comes into play.

David's military and governing expertise mark a sharp contrast to his relative weakness in personal and family relations. A lengthy narrative running through the remainder of 2 Samuel and into 1 Kings tells of the darker side of David and the limits of his power. The intrigue that follows over David's successor hints at the problems that would only heighten during his son Solomon's reign and lead to the eventual split of the kingdom. As King Solomon takes the throne, we see the strengths of his character in his wisdom as well as his determination to complete the **temple** as the house of God. Like his father before him, Solomon also shows weaknesses as he marries numerous foreign wives and subjects his people to conscription into his military, forced labor, and a heavy tax burden. Solomon preserved and even further consolidated David's kingdom throughout a long and relatively peaceful reign (ca. 960–920 BCE). In the midst of all this prosperity, however, the solidity of the kingdom was beginning to show signs of wear and tear. Solomon's foreign wives brought with them the religions and cultic worship of their homelands, and the king did little to prevent their influence on the worship of the God of Israel. Solomon's successful commercial ventures were still not enough to fund his bureaucracy, and he divided the nation into twelve administrative districts across tribal lines in an attempt to streamline management as well as break down tribal allegiances. These measures were most successful at producing resentment toward the monarchy, especially in the north, which felt it bore the major burden of supporting the extravagance of the court in the south with little benefit. Although the kingdom remained intact at Solomon's death, the edifice was beginning to shake and would soon crack apart.

Messiah/Christ

The expression "Christ" is the Greek form of the Hebrew/Aramaic expression "messiah." It means "anointed one" and was used to refer to any king who was understood by his subjects to be "anointed" to the role. Israelites referred to all of their kings as messiahs and understood them to be anointed by God. Even the Persian King Cyrus, who allowed the Israelites to return home from Babylon, is called "messiah" for his beneficence to the people (Isa 45:1).

THE DIVIDED KINGDOM

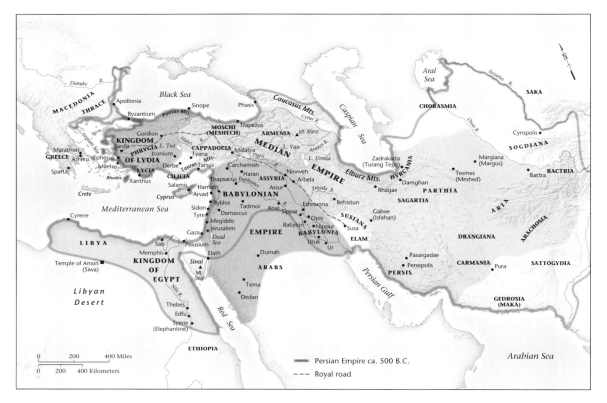

ISRAEL AND BABYLON

....

Rehoboam succeeded Solomon as king ca. 922 BCE and went to Shechem to solidify the allegiance of the northern tribes. Failing to grasp the fragility of the alliance, however, he refused the northern leaders' demand for easing the burdens of taxation and forced labor. This failed summit resulted in a revolt of the northern tribes under Jeroboam I. Therefore, what had been the united kingdom of Israel under David and Solomon was divided into the northern kingdom of Israel (10 tribes) and the southern kingdom of **Judah** (2 tribes). The secession of the northern tribes from the united kingdom is understood by the biblical authors to be a "sin," and the resulting southern kingdom of Judah is presented as maintaining right relationship with God through the covenants with Abraham, Moses, and David, as well as worship at the temple in Jerusalem. It is through Judah that the story will continue, and through this kingdom the people and religion of Judaism eventually develop.

Jeroboam I was the first king of the northern kingdom, and he took measures to divert attention away from Jerusalem and the temple, as the focus of the faith, by establishing sanctuaries at the ancient religious sites at Dan and Bethel. This northern kingdom of Israel eventually established its capital at Samaria and survived for two hundred years, until it fell in 721 BCE to an onslaught by the Assyrian Empire from the east. From the time of the division forward, the narrative of 2 Kings switches back and forth between the two kingdoms, tracing their history until the northern kingdom falls, then focusing solely on the southern kingdom of Judah, which remained more stable under the dynasty of David, such that it withstood the Assyrian aggression. Good, strong kings like Hezekiah and Josiah come to the fore, but many kings struggle under the external pressure of powerful enemies, as well as the internal concerns of a small monotheistic people in a larger polytheistic society.

In the sixth century BCE, a new powerful empire arises centered in Babylon, and like those who came before, the Babylonians set their sights on the key route from the east down into Egypt along the east coast of the Mediterranean Sea. The tiny nation of Judah sat squarely in their path. This time Judah could not withstand the attacks, and the Babylonians captured Jerusalem in 597 BCE. They deported the king and many of the people into Babylon. The Babylonian King Nebuchanezzar placed a weak and vacillating King Zedekiah on the throne in Judah, who staged an ill-fated revolt against Babylon. This time, Nebuchadnezzar destroyed the city completely—razing the temple and deporting most of the remaining people into exile in Babylon by 587–586 BCE. 2 Kings 25 (the last chapter of the book) recounts this tragic event, telling that he left only "some of the country's poor." The beginning of this dark historical period, known as the **Babylonian Exile**, brings us to the end of what the Jewish Scriptures call the Former Prophets. It also brings us to a break in what the Christian OT calls the Historical Books and allows us to take a look at key figures in the story of Israel called prophets, as well as touch upon the many books that bear their names.

The Rise of the Prophets in Judaism (ca. 800–400 BCE)

Since our primary concern in this chapter is to bring to light the theological and historical world behind the text of the Fourth Evangelist, even a brief overview of all the OT prophets is beyond our scope. We can, however, note the rise of this important group in Israel's history known as the "classical prophets," as well as the body of literature their schools produced. In the scriptures of Judaism, a prophet is one who speaks for another, and the term is generally used for one who relates the messages of the divine. A true prophet in Israel, therefore, is one who speaks for God. We already noted that Moses is the figure who encompasses the ideal prophet of God. Moses not only spoke for God, but he led God's people out of bondage in Egypt, through the forging of the Sinai covenant, and to the boundary of the land promised to them by God as their inheritance. Upon his death, the scriptures reveal:

> Since then no prophet has arisen in Israel like Moses, whom the LORD knew face to face. He had no equal in all the signs and wonders the LORD sent him to perform in the land of Egypt against Pharaoh and all his servants and against all his land, and for the might and the terrifying power that Moses exhibited in the sight of all Israel. (Deut 34:10–12)

Once Israel enters the period of the monarchy, the role of the prophet shifts from that of the primary leader to the "right hand man" of the king. For example, the prophet Nathan was integral to David's rule. However, over time the role of the prophet shifted again, and the true prophets more often than not found themselves outside of the circles of power confronting those who rule, calling them back to the covenant and right relationship with God. The earliest example of this sort of prophet is Elijah, whose story is contained within 1–2 Kings. Elijah speaks out against the kings of the north and risks his life in so doing. Once he appoints his successor Elisha, God takes him directly into heaven by way of a fiery chariot. Elijah becomes the only prophet in Israel's biblical history who does not die. Therefore, over time he becomes identified with the people's messianic expectations, and they begin to look to his return as the sign of the advent of the messianic era.

The work of the latter prophets is preserved in books that bear their names. The books of Isaiah, Jeremiah, and Ezekiel are the longest and are thus referred to as the "major prophets." Much less is preserved about the twelve "minor prophets," and their books are briefer. Nonetheless, prophets like Amos, Hosea, Micah, and Zechariah have much to say about social justice, the people's covenantal duty to God and each other, and their hopes for a messiah. The earliest of these literary prophets appear in the eighth century BCE. Amos and Hosea worked in the northern kingdom, while Isaiah and Micah worked in the southern kingdom. The idea of "knowing God" begins to appear in prophetic texts to reflect being in covenant with God, while the concept of "truth" is found throughout the literature to signify the origin and nature of this relationship, as well as the fidelity inherent in maintaining it. For example, the prophet Hosea teaches that the lack of knowledge is tantamount to a breach of covenant with God.

> Hear the word of God, O people of Israel; for God has an indictment against the inhabitants of the land. There is no faithfulness or loyalty, and no knowledge of God in the land. (Hos 4:1)

Biblical and Contemporary Prophets

The contemporary use of the word **prophet** as someone who foretells the future is quite different from the biblical understanding of prophecy. In the Bible, a true prophet is "one who speaks for God," sharing God's message with all who would listen. In this sense, future events are merely the result of acceptance or refusal of the given message. We must bear this in mind as we exegete the biblical texts.

The prophet Isaiah likewise describes life in Israel in breach of covenant as the failure of truth:

> Justice is turned back, and righteousness stands at a distance; for truth stumbles in the public square, and uprightness cannot enter. Truth is lacking, and whoever turns from evil is despoiled. (Isa 59:14–15)

The seventh- and sixth-century prophets Jeremiah and Ezekiel build upon this symbolism and understanding of truth. God's relationship with Israel is intimate, grounded in its Sinai role as God's chosen people and the obligatory response of absolute fidelity. In describing the hope for the future repentance of the people, Jeremiah reports:

> I will give them a heart to know that I am God; and they shall be my people and I will be their God, for they shall return to me with their whole heart. (Jer 24:7)

Jeremiah's famous "new covenant" passage is probably the most telling—and the most beautiful—example of God's desire for the knowledge of the people in terms of their heart:

> See, the days are coming, says God, when I will make a new covenant with the house of Israel and the house of Judah, not like the covenant which . . . they broke, though I was their husband, says God. But this is the covenant which I will make . . . I will put my law within them, and I will write it upon their hearts; and I will be their God, and they shall be my people. And no longer shall each man teach his neighbor and each his brother, saying, "Know God," for they shall all know me, from the least of them to the greatest, says God; for I will forgive their iniquity, and I will remember their sin no more. (Jer 31:31–34)

What is striking about this passage is not just the connection between knowing God and living in covenant, but the promise of a new covenant, built upon the old, which will be expressed and lived in a distinctive way. Like Jeremiah before him, Ezekiel believed the covenant that God will establish with his people in the future will have a distinctive character, yet be built solidly upon the old. This new covenant of peace will encompass both the action and the very being of those counted among God's sheep, yet remain alive intimately in the knowledge of God. Even after the exile, the prophets continue to employ the concept of "truth" to express the essential nature of this relationship. Through Zechariah, God commands the people:

> Render true judgments, show kindness and mercy to one another, do not oppress the widow, the orphan, the alien, or the poor; and do not devise evil in your hearts against one another. (Zech 7:9–10; see also 8:16–17).

Likewise, God commands the people to express their worship with the simple command: "Love truth and peace" (Zech 8:19).

The writing of prophetic literature gradually declined in the fifth and fourth centuries BCE. The oracles of Malachi, Joel, Obadiah, and Jonah are the final works of prophecy to be included in the canon. The body of prophetic books is traditionally understood to come to a close by 400 BCE as they begin to be collected as Scripture. They serve as the moral compass of the people and, alongside Torah, as both the heart of and the guidebook for the preserved relationship between God and the chosen people. The prophets, therefore, are not seers of the future; rather they "look back" to covenant and call God's people to faithfulness.

The Books of Maccabees and the Canon

Remember that the two books of the Maccabees are not found in all Bibles. This is the result of the development of the Septuagint (LXX) alongside the Tanakh in Jewish tradition. These books are found in the LXX and therefore in the Roman Catholic OT. Because they are not found in the Tanakh, they are not in many Protestant editions of the OT. Refer to chapter one for more detail.

The Exile and Post-Exilic Era as Preserved in Ezra and Nehemiah (ca. 538–333 BCE)

We can now take up our overview of the biblical narrative once again. The holy city of Jerusalem was overrun by the Babylonians in 587 BCE. The temple was destroyed, and the people of Judah were exiled across the Babylonian Empire. The return to Jerusalem occurred in 538 BCE under Cyrus, the king of the newly rising Persian Empire. The Books of Ezra and Nehemiah recount the end of the exile and the return and restoration of the land following the Edict of Cyrus. Many faithful Judeans returned to their promised land and the rebuilding of the city and temple commenced, full of hope and tension and conflict. However, after 50 years living outside the land, many faithful Judeans also decided not to return, but to continue to live as God's people outside their homeland, while supporting those who returned however they could. This situation inaugurates the phenomenon in Judaism known as the diaspora, a term that means "dispersion" or "scattering" and refers to the reality that ethnic and religious Jews now live "dispersed" across the known world, gathering and worshiping in synagogues and other communal environments.

The period of the return and restoration through the end of the Persian reign is known as the **Post-Exilic Era**. After much struggle, the people of Judah rebuilt their temple in ca. 515 BCE. Nehemiah 8 records that Ezra read a book of the Law in the hearing of all Jerusalem. This could be the first reading of the Torah as we now have it. Further, Nehemiah 9 recounts that Ezra organized a formal ratification of the covenant of Moses after the feast of Tabernacles. Later Jewish tradition considers Ezra a second Moses, attributing the definitive editing of the Torah to him. The restoration of the exiled people of Judah to

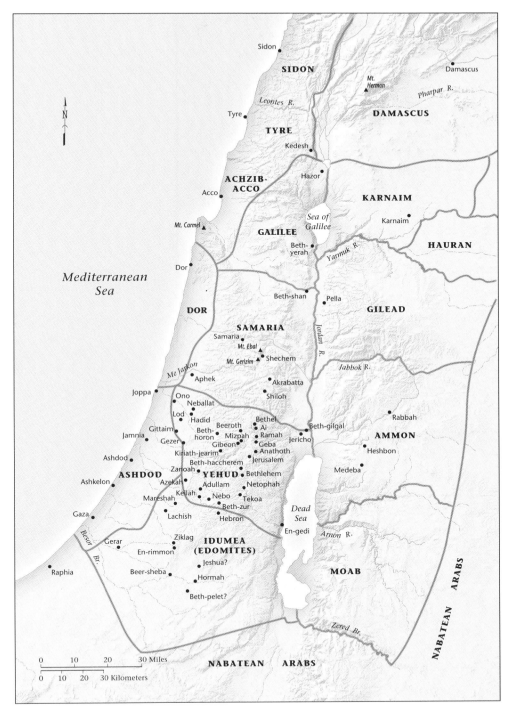

POST-EXILIC JUDEA AND SAMARIA

their land culminates in the momentous event of rededication to Torah, thus paralleling the covenant-making events in the wilderness at Sinai with regard to the formation of the people of God. All the people gather, and their initiative is the impetus behind the reading and renewal. The narrative is careful to assert the people's full understanding of the Torah they heard, as well as their verbal assent to the blessing of God. The Torah is then implemented in the celebration of the festival of Tabernacles as prescribed. The covenant renewal itself is presented in terms of confession and commitment. The people acknowledge the steadfast love of God as the integral component of his covenant-keeping in their final plea for continued protection in relationship. They close in prayer and confirm their commitment to God in writing. The communal pledge of commitment reflects the stipulations of covenantal behavior that the people take upon themselves.

Judah was relatively self-enclosed from the rest of the world during these years, but it was still a part of the Persian Empire and was affected by its policies. It was at this time that Hebrew began to be displaced by Aramaic, a fellow Semitic language that had become normative in the empire. The high priests gave in only reluctantly, and Hebrew was still preserved as the language of worship and study. Those who remained in what had been the northern kingdom of Israel were now known as **Samaritans**, and they were completely excluded from Jewish life and worship. They eventually built a temple of their own on Mount Gerazim in the latter part of the fourth century, and the opposition and hostility between the two former tribal siblings of Judeans and Samaritans grows as they are both confronted by a new era of civilization.

Jews and Samaritans

When the united kingdom of Israel divided, the southern kingdom was known as Judah and maintained its capital at Jerusalem. Judaism traces its story through the happenings in Judah. The northern kingdom takes the name Israel and eventually locates its capital at Samaria with a temple built on Mount Gerizim. They were strict Torah observers and look to Moses as the teacher of the true faith. After the destruction of the northern kingdom of Israel in 722 BCE (see 2 Kgs 17), the conquering Assyrians introduced various other races into the region and deported many originally Israelite people elsewhere. By the time of Judah's restoration in 538 BCE, these were known as Samaritans. The people of Judah understood their northern neighbors to be "apostates" (they had fallen away from the true faith). The feeling was mutual. As often happens with peoples of a shared ancestry who have diverged due to historical events and religious beliefs, anger against each other is often stronger than that for complete outsiders.

The Jewish People and the Greek Empire as Preserved in 1 and 2 Maccabees (333–63 BCE)

In the late fourth century BCE, a new set of influences began to affect the Jewish people. In 336 BCE, Alexander, who would be called the Great, ascended to the throne in Macedonia. After imposing unity on Greece, he turned to the east. In 333 BCE at the decisive battle of Issus (in present-day Turkey), he defeated the Persian army and began the period of Greek domination in the known world. Judea (as the region is now known) thus came under Alexander's control at this time, as he marched down the Mediterranean coast from Syria, through Palestine, and into Egypt. He established the city of Alexandria in Egypt in 332 BCE. As we saw in chapter one, Alexander's strong Hellenizing program began immediately. His practice of infusing conquered lands with Greek language and culture—or Hellenization—became a threat to the worship of God, just as Baal worship had been in the past. The resulting phenomenon of **Hellenism** pervaded the Mediterranean region for centuries thereafter.

A short ten years later, in 323 BCE, Alexander died, and his kingdom divided among his warring generals. Ptolemy seized control of Egypt. Seleucus took Babylon and the regions west to Syria. The region of Judea was thus first controlled by the Ptolemies, who were fairly non-interventionist. In 198 BCE, however, the east coast of the Mediterranean Sea came under Seleucid rule. The Seleucid king, Antiochus III, accorded the inhabitants of Judea the same privileges they had been receiving for some time; but his star began to fade, and he was assassinated by his son, Seleucus IV, who took over (187–175 BCE) and whose subjects began to feel a tax burden. He was eventually assassinated and succeeded by his brother Antiochus IV Epiphanes (175–163 BCE). Antiochus IV determined to crush the worship of Israel's God. This severe religious persecution provoked the **Maccabean Revolt** in 167–164 BCE. Accounts of this event are given in 1 and 2 Maccabees. The book of Daniel was also composed during this time to encourage hope and faithfulness. Here we see the use of apocalyptic language and imagery to concentrate on the last days of judgment and final victory.

According to 1 Maccabees 1, Antiochus IV imposed universal Hellenism in an effort to unify his empire for defense, including emperor worship as well as that of Zeus and the rest of the Greek pantheon. This policy put him on a collision course with Judaism. He appointed high priests supportive of his policies and eventually forbade circumcision and other Jewish observances, using temple funds for his own projects. 2 Maccabees 6 reports that the last straw was the erection of an altar to Zeus in the temple. This is also the "horrible abomination" mentioned in Daniel 9. Rebellion erupted when the head of a faithful Jewish family, Mattathias, refused to offer sacrifice to Zeus and rallied a band of revolutionaries in the Judean hills. When Mattathias died in 166 BCE, leadership fell to his son, known as Judah the Hammer, or the Maccabee. Judah

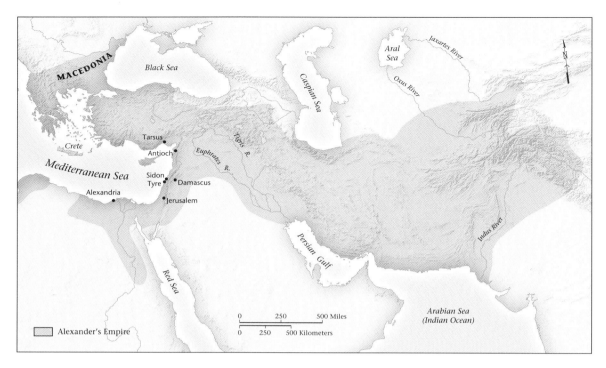

THE GREEK EMPIRE

led a full-scale revolt against the forces of Antiochus, and his group became known as the Maccabees. He was eventually victorious, pushing the Greeks out of Jerusalem and purifying the temple in 164 BCE. These faithful Jews first rededicated the temple to the worship of Israel's God—a celebration that is commemorated every year in the festival of Dedication, more commonly known by its Hebrew name, Hanukkah. Judah continued his campaign for complete independence and finally fell in battle in 160. He was succeeded by his younger brother Jonathan, who was the first of the family to be named high priest by the current Seleucid ruler. Jonathan was succeeded by his brother Simon, who managed to get an official decree of independence from the Seleucid Demetrius II in 142 BCE.

1 Maccabees 14 records that the people decreed that Simon would be accepted as their true ruler and high priest until "a true prophet arises." Nonetheless, the Maccabees, however heroic, were not of the Davidic line of kings, nor of the Zadokite line of high priests, and this angered the purists. The Jewish separatist movement of the Essenes is thought to date from this time. Simon was eventually succeeded by his son John Hyrcanus. This dynasty eventually became known as the Hasmoneans, named after an ancestor of Mattathias. John solidified his rule and expanded north, ultimately destroying the Samaritan

temple at Mount Gerizim. The other Jewish groups known from the NT, the Sadducees and the Pharisees, seem to have emerged during this reign, with the Pharisees eventually breaking with the Hasmoneans in protest over the secular nature of their rule. As political power corrupted the Judean leaders over time, many faithful Jews once again found themselves suffering persecution and the inability to worship effectively. The beleaguered nation found itself in turmoil once again, and messianic expectations began to rise.

The Jewish People and the Roman Empire (ca. 63 BCE into New Testament Times)

The wrangling for rule that arose in the following years eventually brought about the intervention of **Rome**. In 63 BCE, the Roman general Pompey marched on Jerusalem, and the independence won by the Maccabees came to an end. Pompey made Judea part of the Roman province of Syria. The major cities were Antioch and Damascus. When Julius Caesar defeated Pompey and visited Syria in 47 BCE, he appointed a Roman prefect, or governor, and a series of rulers from the resident ethnic groups. Herod governed Judea and remained in Rome's favor during the tumult that followed the assassination of Caesar. Herod was eventually named King of Judea (and later also Samaria) by Marc Antony and Octavian. He solidified his rule in 37 BCE and reigned until his death in 4 BCE. His reign is noted for vicious acts of brutality, as well as for major building projects. He supported Roman emperor worship, which added to the resentment the Jews felt toward him. To curry favor, in 20 BCE he began the restoration of the temple that was completed in 515 BCE. This work continued during the lifetime of Jesus and was not finished until 63 CE, just seven short years before the temple was destroyed forever in 70 CE. Historically this brings us to the tumultuous times of Jesus of Nazareth and the events of the NT, when messianic expectations among faithful Jewish people reached a fever pitch.

The Zadokite Line of High Priests

Zadok served as a priest under King David and was traditionally understood to be a descendant of Moses's brother Aaron. In the succession struggle, Zadok supported Solomon and became his sole priest once Solomon took the throne. His descendants controlled the priesthood in Jerusalem until the exile. Even then the prophet Ezekiel declared that only Zadokite priests should minister in the rebuilt Temple. They continued to serve in the high priesthood until 171 BCE when others—at first Hellenizers, then Hasmoneans—took over the position. Scholars suggest that the Jewish groups known as the Essenes and the Sadducees could have formed during this time in protest over the outsiders usurping this key role in the worship life of the Temple.

What Have We Learned So Far?
The Story of God, Creation, and God's Chosen People

Our relatively brief overview of the story of Israel has presented not only the birth and development of Judaism but has also shed a great deal of light on the people of Israel's relationship with God and therefore on the components of Jewish theology. The most fundamental of these is, of course, theology itself: the Jewish understanding of who God is and how God works in the world. As we introduced earlier in the chapter, Judaism is monotheistic. **Monotheism** is the belief in one sovereign creator God who is both transcendent (exists beyond creation) and immanent (is intimately involved in creation through relationships). The hallmark of this belief is found in the Torah and is known as the Great Shema, or the great call to hear: "Hear O Israel, the Lord is our God, the Lord alone. You shall love the Lord your God with all your heart, and with all your soul, and with all your might" (Deut 6:4–5). Judaism is understood to have invented monotheism in the sense that it is the earliest religion to advocate this theology. Further, the strength and tenacity of the religion was built upon sustaining and developing this faith in a singular God in the midst of polytheistic cultures that often demanded obedience in their own right.

As is typically the case, Jewish cosmology and anthropology are systematic with Jewish theology. In other words, the belief in God is somewhat determinative of the understanding of how the world came to be and the role of humankind within that world and in relationship with God. The book of Genesis narrates the creation of the heavens and the earth in a six-day period of goodness, with rest on the seventh day. In terms of cosmology, the key takeaway from this story is the all-encompassing power, authority, and knowledge of God in this creative act, as well as the inherent goodness of the result. In addition, however, we learn that the world is not how it was intended to be due to an early act of disobedience that results in a *dis*order of the perfectly ordered world. Creation, therefore, is in a constant struggle to live out its true nature in relationship with God in the face of the challenges presented by disorder and chaos. This leads directly into anthropology and the biblical understanding of people. Genesis also shows that humankind is the pinnacle of God's creation in the image of God. Perfect relationship with God is breached by disobedience and breakdown of this relationship, resulting in the ongoing struggle in the human will between good and evil. Nonetheless, God continues to work with all humankind through the period of the flood until the climactic event of the Tower of Babel. From this point forward, God works in relationship only with the descendants of Abraham, who become first the Israelites and then are eventually known as the Jewish people.

By the time we get to the end of the OT narrative, these people understand themselves to be in special relationship with God. This means, of course, that the vast majority of humankind does not enjoy this special relationship. Further, the Jewish people have reason to expect things from God, including the sending of a messiah to redeem them from their current suffering at the hands of these other peoples (the Romans) and rectify their status in the world. This, then, is mainstream Jewish Christology: that God will send a messiah who is a descendant of David and who will become a king like David, a military ruler who will lead the people once again out of bondage and into a sovereign nation.

The story of the Jewish peoples' developing understanding of God, the world, and their role in it leads to a clear position on morality and ethics. The foundation for Jewish values and right actions is based in Torah and the guidelines given in the Sinai covenant. Loving God and humankind as God's creation and living in a socially just society are essential to the Jewish worldview and find their impetus in the Ten Commandments. These commandments, however, are moral ideals, and the reality of life in this disordered world is complex. Therefore, Torah, as a "full service" manual for life in relationship with God, offers a complete set of contingency plans for ethical action in every eventuality. Further, Torah demands **sacrifice** as a means of **atonement** for sin and straying from the right path of relationship with God. When one turns away from God to pursue more immediate gratification, this results in a breakdown of communication, which in turn results in a breakdown of the intended union within relationship. To "atone" means to become "at one" once again. Torah dictates the offering of some sort of sacrifice—something important to one's life and well-being—in order to bring the individual or, at times, the entire people back into union with God.

The final components that we want to bring to the fore here are eschatology and soteriology. As these portions of the theological worldview often overlap, it is helpful to discuss them together. Judaism offers a linear view of history that posits a clear understanding of a beginning, middle, and future end. This, like the other basic beliefs of Judaism, is quite distinctive in the ancient world. Eschatology, by nature, focuses on that future end, and Judaism, through the

---

Sin, Sacrifice, and Atonement

Broadly speaking, **sin** is anything that is in opposition to God's purposes for creation. In Scripture, sin is detailed as missing the mark, conscious rebellious action, and abomination. Sin, then, is any turning away from God. Repentance, or turning back, is often the counter to sin. The Jewish people developed a system of sacrifice to atone for sin. **Sacrifice** is the offering or surrender of something precious for the sake of something else. Ideal sacrificial worship is described in Priestly writings, esp. the Book of Leviticus. Sacrifices could be burnt offerings, peace offerings, sin offerings, guilt offerings, or cereal offerings. The burnt, guilt, and cereal offerings were done to atone for sin. **Atonement** is the means by which the chain of sin is broken resulting in reconciliation. "At-one-ment" indicates the reunification of relationship with God.

particular contributions of the prophetic and apocalyptic texts, developed a belief in a "Day of the Lord," on which God would judge everyone on the basis of the theological and ethical decisions they have made. Apocalyptic literature also provided an additional development of the potential for reward and punishment in a next life. The book of Daniel speaks of a life after death through the resurrection of the body, in which the good will be rewarded with eternal life in perfect union with God and the wicked will be destined to a life of suffering outside the presence of God.

By the first century CE, Judaism was complex and multifaceted. This means that the theological worldview we have just presented took on a variety of expressions. The rabbis and other Jewish leaders and followers take both pleasure and pride in debating the potentialities of God's offerings. The more archaeologists and other scholars unearth about this period and the more we take in from the literature it produced, the more we can appreciate the beauty and profundity of first-century Judaism. We also learn, however, that this complex history and theology has several valid interpretations. The Jewish people have been living and struggling in relationship with God for millennia by the time we find ourselves in the first-century Roman oppression. They have learned to adapt, but they are tenacious and ever hopeful that their God will intervene on their behalf to make right the world and facilitate right relationship. We must take this reality seriously, for the worlds in and in front of the texts of what Christians call the Old Testament form a major portion of the world behind the texts of the Gospel and Letters of John. We can now turn our attention to the events of the life and literature of Jesus of Nazareth.

Key Terms and Concepts

Abraham

Adam

atonement

Babylonian Exile

David

etiology/etiological stories

Exodus

Hellenism

Israel

Judah

Maccabean Revolt

messiah/christ

monotheism

Moses

Noah

Post-Exilic Era

prophet

Rome

sacrifice

Samaritans

signs

Sinai covenant

Ten Commandments

Tetragrammaton

theophany

the temple

Tower of Babel

YHWH

Questions for Review

1. Who are the major figures in Israel's history? Trace a brief chronological overview of the development of this story.
2. What are the major covenantal stories of the Old Testament narrative? Who are the mediators of this developing relationship, and how might they come into play in the Gospel story of the new covenant?
3. What is a messiah? From where does this concept come, and how does it develop in Judaism? How might this affect the development of a religion called Christianity?
4. How do concepts such obedience, knowledge, and truth help us understand the Jewish understanding of the relationship between humankind and God?
5. What are the political, social, and theological elements of Jewish life in the Roman Empire in the first century CE that lead to extreme messianic expectations?

Bibliography and Further Reading

Anderson, Bernhard W., Steven Bishop, and Judith H. Newman. *Understanding the Old Testament.* 5th ed. Upper Saddle River: Pearson, 2007.

Brown, Sherri. *God's Promise: Covenant Relationship in John.* New York: Paulist, 2014.

Carvalho, Corrine. *Encountering Ancient Voices: A Guide to Reading the Old Testament.* Winona, MN: Anselm Academic, 2006.

Green, Barbara. *From Earth's Creation to John's Revelation: The INTERFACES Biblical Storyline Companion.* Collegeville, MN: Liturgical, 2003.

Knight, Douglas A., and Amy-Jill Levine. *The Meaning of the Bible: What the Jewish Scriptures and Christian Old Testament Can Teach Us.* New York: Harper One, 2011.

The New Testament Story: Jesus and the New Covenant

PURPOSE Chapter four outlines the story of Jesus of Nazareth and introduces the birth and development of Christianity through the Jesus movement, as well as the world behind the text of the writing of the Gospels.

ASSIGNMENT Read through any introductory essays on the New Testament that may be in the study Bible.

Now that we have established the "big picture" of the world behind the evangelist and his texts, in terms of Judaism and the Old Testament Story, we can turn our attention to the larger world in which he lived and worked. The world of the Roman Empire is the socio-cultural milieu that was familiar to him. It is also the world in which he understood God to have acted and to continue to act in and through Jesus Christ. This is the contextual background that ultimately compelled him to write his understanding of the good news.

The World of the New Testament Story

Once we arrive in the first century of the Common Era on the east coast of the Mediterranean Sea in the regions of Judea, Samaria, and Galilee, we are in the midst of a complex world indeed. Biblical scholar Luke Timothy Johnson discusses social environments in terms of "**symbolic worlds**." He suggests that we all get along in our cultures by forming symbolic worlds through which we live, learn, work, and pass on wisdom to the next generation. These symbolic worlds influence, but more importantly are influenced by, the larger world around us. Thus, a symbolic world is made up of the social structures in which people live, as well as the symbols attached to and supporting those structures. Johnson also claims that in the case of the eastern Roman Empire in the first century, it might be better to speak of *symbolic worlds*, so complex and pluralistic was this setting. This diverse climate was constituted by the combination of four distinctive elements: Jewish Religion, Mediterranean Culture, Hellenistic civilization, and Roman Rule. It is from these elements in their life setting that first-century Jewish people in general, Jesus and his disciples in particular, as well as the later writers of the New Testament were given symbols with which to develop their worldviews and understand how God was working in their world.

Jewish Religion

We have already said a great deal about the world of **Judaism** in the previous chapter. Here it will serve us well simply to draw some major points together in terms of the Jewish self-understanding of Jesus and those around him. The Judaism of the first century was complex. As we saw in the last chapter, it was the product of a long history that looked back to Abraham as the father of the nation, and Moses as the one who freed Israel from the slavery of Egypt and to whom God gave the law. David was the remembered hero, and the hoped-for messiah, or "anointed one," would be from the house of David who would defeat those who oppress the Jewish people. But the royal line had disappeared over time, and the nation had suffered great losses and exile. The land was no longer theirs. Acts of heroism on the part of the Maccabees and their descendants, a few centuries before the Christian era, led to the re-establishment of Israel, but it soon fell into division and turmoil. In the time of Jesus and the early Christians, there was no independent Israel. It was ruled by Rome through the agency of a puppet royalty. Eventually, Jewish conflict with the Roman occupiers was so intense that it led to the First Jewish Revolt of 65–70 CE. This uprising held on for a surprising length of time, but the Romans eventually broke through the city walls, burning and leaving devastation in their wake, including the destruction of the temple. Judaism has always been marked by people of great holiness and loyalty. However, there were times when the God of Israel and his commandments were remembered only by a remnant.

In the time of Jesus and the earliest Christians there were many ways of being Jewish, just as today there are many ways in which people accept the Christian faith. As we introduced in chapter one, in those days Sadducees, Pharisees, Zealots, Essenes, and Christians, to mention only the best-known groups, lived side by side and practiced a common faith. Belief in the one true God, worshiping him in the temple, and the observance of his commandments stood at the center of this faith. But that observance was understood

---

The North American Symbolic World

The North American symbolic world is diverse and multifaceted. It includes constitutional issues such as freedom of religion and expression and the right to vote and privacy. It also includes more esoteric concerns such as individualism and the pursuit of happiness. The list goes on for the varying race, ethnic, gender, sexual orientation, and familial identities that make up the ever-evolving society. Students should try to cultivate an understanding of their own symbolic make-ups.

in different ways, often shaped by the history that gave birth to those various expressions of Judaism. Nevertheless, Judaism had its history (interpreted and told in its Scriptures), its law, its traditions, and its land. Jesus lived and died at a time when these fundamentals of the Jewish way of life and hope were under threat.

There were different understandings of how God would resolve this threat. One way was known as "messianism," that is, the hope for a messiah. But not everyone expected a messiah. The hopes of a saving figure that God would raise up from among the people fluctuated, depending upon the socio-political situation of Israel at any given time. At the time of Jesus there were hopes for a messiah who might be a soldier messiah of the line of David. But there were also hopes for a messianic Priest. Some hoped for a combination of both. Above all, Jewish hope was based on the unshakeable belief that God would intervene, destroying all evil and restoring the original glory and beauty of his creation, lost because of human sin and evil. In the end, God will reign over all. Keep this in mind when you read or hear the words "the kingdom of God."

Mediterranean Culture

The Jewish world described above did not exist in a vacuum. The larger Mediterranean culture had always served as the backdrop for the development of these religious symbols and beliefs. Although this world was deeply affected by the empires that swept through it, over time the patterns of the **Mediterranean culture** were deeply infused into the Jewish way of life. The larger economy was still primarily agricultural and based in rural villages, but the trade of the sea was booming and the diversity of languages, philosophies, and religions allowed for growth and the development of new ideas. This world of large households,

---

Messianic Expectations

Recall that the expression "Christ" is the Greek form of the Hebrew/Aramaic expression "messiah." It means "anointed one" and was used to refer to an anointed king. The Jewish people believed that God's covenant with David insured that one of his descendants would be their messiah. Historical events, including subjugation by Rome, resulted in conflicting expectations for the Messiah. In the first century CE, some thought he would be a priest; others hoped for a royal and military figure. While not all Jewish people looked for a messiah, many expected a figure who would release Israel from its service to the Roman Empire. Several individuals arose who claimed to be such a messiah. Jesus and the Gospels have a very different, more God-oriented idea of Jesus as the Messiah, or Christ.

run by patriarchs with slaves, facilitated a culture of severe disparities between the elites and the majority of the population. A system of patronage developed, as benefactors and beneficiaries sought honor and avoided shame at all costs. This world of land and sea, food and wine, agriculture and trade, and haves and have-nots also provided the setting for the multifaceted civilization of the Greeks.

Hellenistic Civilization

As we have already discussed, the Jewish people of the first century CE had a history, whether as a nation or as an occupied ethnic group, of being forever under siege and conquered by the Assyrians and the Babylonians. Prior to the Roman occupation of the first century, the people had been subjected to the Persians and were eventually swept into the Hellenistic Empire that had its origins in Alexander the Great. An incredible leader who lived from 356 to only 323 BCE, he conquered almost the whole of the known world before dying at thirty-three years of age. He believed the use of Greek language and culture (known as Hellenism) was so significant that they should be accepted and used by the whole world. After Alexander, his generals fought over the Hellenistic Empire, and Israel passed from the Hellenistic rulers in Egypt (known as the Ptolemies) to the Hellenistic rulers in Syria (known as the Seleucids).

Greek culture, language, and religion permeated Jewish life. Jesus most likely spoke Aramaic (a holdover in Judea and the surrounding region from the time of the Persian Empire) and some Greek. Indeed, Greek would have been the common language even of the Roman Empire—the

> **Alexander the Great**
>
> Born in Macedonia in 356 CE, Alexander was a remarkable figure who extended a form of Greek religion and culture across the whole of the Mediterranean basin, and even into northern India. He achieved stunning military victories and took non-Greek peoples into his armies and court. He died in Babylon in 323 CE, at the age of thirty-three.

language of literature, commerce, and trade. As it does in all cultures, language also provides for symbols and ways of understanding both the natural world and the potential for a supernatural reality. The Jewish people were also affected by these ideas about reality. In the Hellenistic world, the people hungered for a way to God, for salvation. They developed miracle stories and miraculous locations. Most important in this "hunger for God" was the development of the mystery religions and Gnosticism. These forms of faith had captured the hearts and minds of many. They were religions into which specially privileged and illuminated people entered, assured of salvation through contact with, or knowledge of, the gods. Such religious thinking was foreign to Judaism, but very much a part of the world that saw the birth of Christianity and the writing of the New Testament.

Bust of Alexander the
Great, Musei Capitolini
© Livioandronico 2013

Jesus and the people around him would also have been familiar with Hellenistic thinking about philosophy and religion. The time of Greek rule, however, had come and gone. The iron fist of the Roman Empire was now the pervasive entity looming over the Jewish people.

Roman Rule

After a brief period of independence, due to the victory over the Hellenistic Empire of Syria in the Maccabean wars (early in the second century BCE), the growth of the Roman Empire swallowed Israel. The birth and development of Christianity as a world religion owe much to the Roman Empire. Christianity came into existence during the high point of Roman rule, a period referred to as the Roman peace (*pax Romana*). We know that in an act of violence, Jesus was crucified, a Roman form of execution. But peaceful conditions that dominated the Roman system—where local administrations were allowed to continue, as long as the Roman dominion was not threatened—accompanied the beginnings of a new world religion. The books of the New Testament reflect a believing community moving freely into the world beyond Judaism and the Jewish homeland of Judea.

As the Hellenistic powers faded and the Roman Empire took over, new religions emerged. This was a time when the established religions were losing their attraction. The classical Greek religions were fading, helped by the fact that the Romans did not come with new religions of their own. They tended to adapt the fading Greek religions and use them as they saw fit. Alexander the Great eventually declared himself to be a "son of God," and subsequently the Roman emperors had themselves proclaimed as "gods" and demanded emperor worship.

These political and religious components of the Roman Empire were a constant shadow looming over the Jewish people across the world of the New Testament. As we read the Gospel of John, we must try to take in the depth of the tension and conflict of an occupying force that at once allows for security and freedom of movement *and* is seen as the enemy encroaching upon God-given land and liberty, a force that threatens their very survival as a religious people. Such is the complex world of the New Testament and the east coastal regions of the Mediterranean Sea in the first century CE. All four of the elements in this section contribute to this complexity and both the struggle and hope for God's intervention that we have been discussing. This is the world into which Jesus of Nazareth was born.

Jesus of Nazareth

Jesus was a Jew, and so were his first disciples. Scholars give the approximate dates of his lifetime as 4 BCE–30 CE. The Gospel of Matthew narrates Jesus's birth sometime before the death of the puppet king of Judea and the surrounding regions known as Herod the Great, who died in 4 BCE. Further, all four Gospels as well as early Christian tradition affirm that Jesus was arrested, convicted of a capital crime, and crucified under the Roman governor Pontius Pilate. Roman records indicate that Pilate governed Judea and the surrounding regions from 26 to 36 CE. Tradition, coupled with the Gospel accounts, also holds that Jesus took on a public ministry at around age thirty that lasted some three years. Scholars, therefore, posit that Jesus came to trial sometime in the middle of Pilate's ten-year term. The Gospels also indicate that Jesus grew up in Nazareth, a town that likely served as what we today would call a "suburb" of the larger city of Sepphoris in the region of Galilee. These early decades of the first century CE saw the Roman Empire at the height of its power and control of the Mediterranean, and the region of Galilee was populated by people restless in their current political and social situation. Messianic expectations were at a fever pitch. If both Jesus and his disciples grew up in Galilee, they were surrounded by these hopes. Indeed, the name Jesus Christ, so familiar to us as if it were his family name, is really a title that indicates the belief that Jesus of Nazareth was the expected messiah of Israel.

Head of Christ
by Rembrandt

It may come as a surprise to hear that we do not have a life of Jesus as we would understand the "life of" anyone. We will discuss the Gospels in more detail later in the chapter, but for now we can say that each of the four Gospels tells its story of Jesus differently. They were not written to be read as a modern biography, or "life of Jesus." It might also be a surprise to know that the man so commonly known today as "Jesus Christ" was never known by that during his life. He was known as "**Jesus of Nazareth**" (see especially Matt 2:23). He was probably also known as "Jesus son of Joseph" (see John 1:45). These were names given to a person seen to be special, but only human, by all who knew him. Therefore, the best we can do is trace the elements of his life by looking across the Gospels to find the outline of his story.

Jesus's story would look something like this. After his young life in Nazareth, about which we know little or nothing, he appeared on the scene at about thirty years of age. Although very different, the stories of Jesus's birth and beginnings (Matt 1–2 and Luke 1–2) agree that he grew up in Galilee and began his ministry there. However, initially he was most likely a follower of John the Baptist, who may also have been related to him, as we hear in the Gospel of Luke (Luke 1:36). On some occasions John the Baptist speaks of Jesus as one who "comes after him," probably indicating that he was his follower (see Mark 1:7; Matt 3:11; John 1:27). However, as the Baptist disappeared off the scene, arrested and eventually slain by Herod, Jesus began his own ministry, probably in Galilee (see Mark 1:14–15; Matt 4:12–17; Luke 4:14–15; John 3:22–24).

Jesus was a wandering preacher who brought much hope and love into a society that was oppressed by the presence of the Romans and exploited by the wealthy. As he began to preach about the coming of the reigning presence of God into the hearts and lives of all men and women, he quickly gathered many who followed him and placed their hopes in him. He was certainly seen as a prophet like the great prophets of Israel (see Mark 8:28; Matt 16:14; Luke 9:19; John 4:19, 44). He chose an inner circle of twelve to journey with him (see Mark 3:13–14; Matt 10:2–4; Luke 6:12–13; John 6:70). There was probably also a larger group of friends who followed him, including women (see Luke 8:1–3), and many people in the villages and even the towns who looked to him with hope. Indeed, he became so popular that the Romans and even some Jewish authorities became concerned that he might cause trouble—arousing the people to rebellion (see John 11:45–54). They thought he might even be seen as the much-expected messiah of Israel (see Mark 8:29; Matt 16:16; Luke 9:20; John 1:41).

Jesus was unhappy with any popular acclaim that he might be the expected messiah. Throughout the Gospels he is cautious about any such acclamation. This was especially clear as he did not ride into Jerusalem on a war-horse with a sword in his hand to drive out the enemies of the true Israel (see Mark 11:1–10; Matt 21:1–9; Luke 19:28–38; John 12:12–19). If he was the hoped-for messiah, then, his actions and teaching seemed to be redefining these standard messianic expectations. This is symbolized in the title with which he prefers to designate himself and his role, the "Son of Man" (see, e.g., Mark 2:10; Matt 8:20; Luke 5:24; John 1:51; see also Dan 7:13). Indeed, he began to speak of openness to God, the need for unconditional love and obedience, even unto death (see Mark 8:34–9:1; Matt 16:24–28; Luke 9:23–27; John 13:1–21). And yet, Jesus made it clear to his followers that he did not see death as the end of his story. He showed trust and confidence in God, whom he dared to call "father" (see Mark 14:36; John 5:17; 8:16, 49, 54; 10:29–30; 12:27–28; see 17:1–24). God would win through Jesus's death and vindicate his suffering (Mark 8:31; 9:31; 10:32–34). Many of the disciples, and even the Twelve, found this difficult to accept, and the Gospels tell us, in their various ways, that one of them betrayed him, another denied him, and everyone else ran away.

All the Gospels agree in what is commonly known as the passion narrative (Mark 14–15; Matt 26–27; Luke 22–23; John 20:18–19). Jesus was arrested, put through some sort of Jewish trial process, followed by a trial before the Roman governor Pilate. Ultimately Jesus was convicted of the crime of treason—a threat to the *pax Romana*—and for this insurrection was sentenced to death by crucifixion, the Romans' preferred method of capital punishment for its dual purpose as a public warning to others who might have similar ideas. In the end, Jesus was crucified alone, the worst death the Romans could inflict upon anyone.

After three days women (maybe only one, Mary Magdalene [John 20:11–18]) found an empty tomb, and more and more people had an experience of the risen Jesus (1 Cor 15:3–8). He was alive! Now they began to understand that Jesus was the Messiah, but the Messiah that God wanted, not the one expected by popular culture. Now he could be called Jesus Christ. Many of the disciples gathered, their weakness was forgiven, and they were promised they would continue his presence in the world in their meals, their prayers, their love, their hope, and in their imitation of Jesus—prepared to be obedient to God unto death, confident that God would have the last word.

The Birth of Christianity

That is how "the **church**" began. It was not known by that name until much later—indeed, the term simply means "gathering." The death and resurrection of Jesus created a small community of fragile believers. They began to tell stories about his time among them, to celebrate a meal "in memory of him," and they tried to live as he had taught them. Now deeper questions began to emerge. In the light of his death and resurrection, what was Jesus's relationship to the God of Israel, whom he called "father"? What was the gift of the Spirit he had promised would be with them? How had his death and resurrection offered a new life to humankind? It was out of all these thoughts, discussions, prayers, exhortations, and stories that what we now call **Christianity** was born.

As we discuss the claims of the first Christians, we would do better to think and talk in terms of a "**Jesus Movement**" to really get a sense of the atmosphere of these early years. When we think of Christianity in the twenty-first century, we may think of a wide variety of ways of being "church," but we likely always think of a belief system that is well organized with a lot of resources and buildings and is entrenched in the larger society. As this early Jesus movement began to gather—often in secret—to share and discuss their experiences of Jesus and their understanding of how God was working in the world, they were anything but these things. The first task of these early believers was to begin to come to a common understanding of who Jesus was and what he had accomplished through the will of God.

The members of this group within Judaism were eventually called **Christians** because of their belief that Jesus was the Christ (see Acts 11:26; 26:28; 1 Peter 4:15–16). As they affirmed their belief that Jesus was the long-awaited, long-hoped-for Messiah, however, they also had to come to terms with the fact that Jesus did not meet the standard Jewish messianic expectation of God's "Anointed One" who would be a geo-political king like David and would throw off the yoke of Roman oppression. Nonetheless, Jesus's disciples were still convinced he was the Christ, due to their experience of him. In their gatherings, discussions, and storytelling, they looked back into their Scriptures and began to realize that the alternative prophet-messiah—who speaks the word of God and suffers, even sacrifices, on behalf of the people—fit their experience of Jesus's life, ministry, *and* death. What really made the Jesus movement different from other messianic movements of the first century CE, however, is also what allowed them to survive the initial chaos of his arrest and crucifixion: the **resurrection faith**.

The disciples' conviction that Jesus was dead, then alive again, made the Jesus movement different than other messianic movements. Most of these early groups would rally around a figure in which they would put their nationalistic and religious hopes. When the Romans quashed their plans, often killing the leader to set an example, the group would go into hiding and eventually dissipate. This was the desired effect. The Gospels suggest the early Christians experienced just such a panic at Jesus's death, but overcame this early doubt and fear as a result of their experience of the risen Jesus. Therefore, they came to believe the resurrection to be proof that Jesus is God's Anointed One, not bound by death. But if his role as Christ was not to put in place a new sovereign nation like the kingdom of David, what was it?

Resurrection Faith

The fundamental and founding experience of Christianity is the resurrection of Jesus. Without the encounter that the first Christians had with the risen Jesus, there would be no Christianity. This does not mean that Christianity is founded on an empty tomb. It means that Christians believe that Jesus lives on, no longer simply a good man with a powerful message. When Greek Christians greet one another at Easter, one says: "Christ is risen!" To which the other responds: "Christ is truly risen!" This exchange captures the essence of Easter faith.

Again turning to their Scriptures and the long-held understandings of how God works in the world, which we discussed in the previous chapter, the Jesus movement began to recognize new covenantal activity. Paul, the most prolific early Christian theologian and author, was the first to articulate that the faith and sacrifice of Jesus fulfilled the Sinai-covenant stipulation of sacrifice to atone for sin. Further, the remembrance of Jesus's own preferred self-designation as the Son of Man echoed the book of Daniel's vision of one who would come from God to save the people. The basic belief of the developing church, then, was that God had put in place a new covenant through Jesus Christ. Jesus was the Messiah whose death was the sacrifice that atoned for all sin for all time and thereby fulfilled the promises of God's earlier covenants. This new covenant through Jesus was available not only to ethnic Jews, but once again to all humankind, as it was in the covenant with Adam. The determining factor for the potential receivers of God's new-covenant offer was no longer being an ethnic descendant of Abraham who keeps Torah, but being anyone who believes that Jesus is the Christ, sent from God to make relationship with God available to all through his life and death. A term that we can use to encompass the entirety of this story is the **Christ Event**. This term is used as a shorthand of sorts to refer to the entirety of the life, ministry, death, and resurrection of Jesus, as well as this developing belief that Jesus is the long-awaited Messiah who is not bound by death.

The absolute conviction in the resurrection led these early believers to articulate that since the Christ was not bound by death, neither would his followers be. Even in this they were following the recent teaching of the Jewish Scriptures (see Daniel 12), and also the belief of Jesus (see Mark 12:18–27). They began to talk about right relationship with God in this world, leading to eternal union with God in the heavenly realm. Indeed, Jesus Christ's ability to take on death and overcome it allowed for the further articulation of Jesus as the Son of God, one whose divine origins dictated that he now be understood as the risen Lord who returned to his Father and paved the way for all believers to do the same. This is the **good news** of the new covenant.

These developing beliefs, the opening of covenant relationship with God to Jews and Gentiles (non-Jews) alike and the understanding of Jesus as divine, put the early Christians, many of whom were ethnic Jews, at odds with mainstream Judaism by the end of the first century CE. As we indicated in chapter one and again earlier in this chapter, Judaism in the early part of the century was quite di-

---

The Earliest Church

In order to understand the spirit of the first Christians, it is important to set aside modern notions of "the Church" as a large and well-structured organization. Made up of people from various walks of life, the first believers were like Jesus, Jewish. They quickly reached out to non-Jews. Early Christ-believers struggled to understand what God had done for humankind in and through Jesus Christ. Many of these struggles are reflected in the documents of the New Testament. The Gospel of John is a good example of how the early Church adapted its storytelling to speak to the Greco-Roman world.

verse. Belief or, at the very least, hope that one or another was a potential messiah was somewhat commonplace. The First Jewish Revolt against Rome from 65 to 70 CE changed all this. The failure of this revolt resulted in the burning of Jerusalem and the destruction of the temple. Judaism was once again at the brink of dissolution. Many of the groups that were so active during Jesus's life were either wiped out or dispersed in the aftermath. The Sadducees, Essenes, and Zealots were no longer unified, powerful groups. Some would have continued after the war, but they eventually disappeared. The Pharisees were reorganizing as rabbis who were attempting to save Judaism by putting in place a canon of Scripture and an orthodox belief system. The early Christians, once just one more group within Judaism, could no longer be reconciled with the Jewish ethnic identity based in the Abrahamic and Sinai covenants and the continued hope for a messiah to come. Christianity and Judaism began to diverge onto their own trajectories as distinct forms of faith. The First Jewish Revolt and this beginning separation provided the context for the writing of the Gospels and much of the New Testament.

Icon of St. Mark
the Evangelist
(seventeenth century)

The Writing of the Gospel Narratives

For the first Christians, the memory of Jesus's life, teaching, death, and resurrection was still powerfully alive. Paul did not tell it, but with the passing of time, and the gradual spread of the Christian communities beyond Judaism into the larger Greco-Roman world, a question began to emerge: "Who was this man Jesus of Nazareth whom you Christians regard as the Christ, the Son of God?" The best way to answer that question, some believed, was to tell his story. In time, the telling of these stories led to the writing of what are now called Gos-

Icon of St. Matthew the Evangelist (early fourteenth century)

pels. A **gospel** is the literary form of Christian narratives about Jesus. The term is a translation of the Greek noun *euangelion*, which means *good news*, as it is derived from the verb form that means *to announce or proclaim something good*. The term has also come to mean the Christian message in general. Thus, for Paul, the first to use the word "gospel" for the message of the Christ Event, the word referred to the saving effect of Jesus's death and resurrection. The Gospel of Mark is the first to apply it to the good news of the story of Jesus (Mark 1:1). The writer of a Gospel is, thus, the **Evangelist**, from the same Greek root. In modern times this term has also taken on the meaning of one who preaches this good news, but we will use both terms in their narrower senses to refer to the early Christian literary genre and its authors. Indeed, this literary genre as we know it today was in some sense invented by the early Christians. Gospels are narratives—stories—that share the "good news" of the Christ Event. As we have just mentioned, the evangelist Mark, writing about 70 CE, first used this term to identify this type of writing. But notice that this is some forty years after the life of Jesus. As we introduced in chapter one, it was some time before the early Christians saw the need to start telling the story of Jesus's life, teaching, death, and resurrection.

To trace the movement from the life of Jesus of Nazareth to the development of the Gospel as a genre of literature, we can discuss five major developments: 1) the formation of the church as a community of believers; 2) the believers' teaching about their experiences; 3) the development of oral teachings (stories) about Jesus; 4) many uses of the same stories in varying contexts; and finally, 5) the crystallization of this oral tradition into written Gospels. Let's explore these developments in more detail.

1) The Formation of the Church as a Community of Believers

The community Jesus forged tells us much about the character of his ministry and even more about the strength of the bond that existed between those who believed in him as the Christ. We have already said a good deal about the early Jesus movement and the church they eventually formed. We need not say much more here. The Gospels had their beginnings in the life and teaching of Jesus of Nazareth. The birth of Christianity, as the Jesus movement, began as a small association of his disciples in the years that followed his death, meeting at first in secret to reflect upon their experiences. In addition to their conviction that Jesus was the Christ who was resurrected from death, they soon came to understand he left them with a mission to share this good news with any and all who would hear. Across the next years they began to meet regularly, sharing a meal in memory of him, telling stories about him, and opening their community to all those who came to share these beliefs.

2) The Believers' Teaching about Their Experiences

Certainly by the 40s–50s CE, these disciples began to take it upon themselves to seek out opportunities to teach about Christ and their experiences of him. Some early Christians, like Peter and James of Jerusalem, continued their work largely in the Jewish communities, teaching in synagogues and other gatherings. Others hit the road and began to found small communities in cities across the Roman Empire. The apostle Paul eventually turned his attention exclusively to non-Jews, who are known as Gentiles, and met people in the marketplace and organized small communities in the homes of believers. All the early leaders taught by sharing their stories.

3) The Development of Oral Teachings (Stories) about Jesus

From the start, even before Jesus died, those who heard him remembered what he had said. His parables were especially memorable. They also remembered what he did and recalled the incredible authority he had over sickness and evil. They remembered Jesus had told them that he was bringing in a new era, a time when God would reign in their hearts, minds, and lives as their king. They remembered that in both his teaching and in his very personality, there were clear signs that the kingdom of God was at hand. For decades, these "memories" remained unwritten. The early Christians encouraged one another in difficulty, they gathered for prayer and remembered things that Jesus had said and done. But there was no need for any "story" of Jesus. They knew it. They had either been with Jesus (a minority of people, the Twelve, and probably some other followers, including significant women, among them his mother), or had at least known him (the majority of people whose villages and homes he visited). One thing they all knew about was that he had been crucified.

> **Orality**
>
> Scholars of the Gospels recognize that the stories in the Gospels first circulated orally in a world in which very few people were literate. Gospels began as "oral" (i.e., word of mouth) communication. When the Gospels are performed, it is possible to capture some of the story's emotions.

How did they overcome the scandal of the cross? This was the very first problem that the earliest Christians had to handle. So they turned to Jesus's own teaching. Jesus had always trusted in his Father, and his Father entered the story after the crucifixion by raising Jesus from the dead. Jesus had died on a Roman cross, but the cross was now empty. The death and resurrection of Jesus were the heart of the earliest Christian message. As Christians gathered for the celebration of a special meal, they told the story of what Jesus had said and done "on the night before he died." Jesus, crucified and risen, continued to be with his followers, as they "remembered" him in a way that made him present. The "story" of Jesus's celebration of a meal, the beginning of Eucharistic meals that are still the central celebration of the Christian community, must have been told often. Another "story" that was told from the very beginnings of Christianity was the story of Jesus's passion, death, and resurrection. The fact that Jesus was crucified as a criminal was a challenge to all who followed him as the Christ and the Son of God. The narratives of Jesus's final night with his disciples, his prayer in Gethsemane, his arrest, his trial before Jewish and Roman authorities, his crucifixion and death, the discovery of an empty tomb three days after the crucifixion, and a number of encounters between the disciples and the Risen Jesus are very old. Indeed, in one of the oldest passages in the New Testament, Paul writes to the Christians in Corinth, reminding them of the "story" he told them about Jesus's death, burial, resurrection, and appearances (1 Cor 15:1–7). Paul does not tell many stories, so this one was very important to him, and to all early Christians. All the Gospels tell this particular "story" in the same sequence. This does not happen anywhere else in the Gospels. The reporting of the basic story of the passion and resurrection never changes because they were told this way *from the beginning*. The early Christians boldly told this story, along with many others, over and over again, explaining what each event and each moment meant for Jesus, and for them.

4) Many Uses of Same Stories in Varying Contexts

So the community of believers formed around their shared experience of Jesus and his life, death, and resurrection and developed their mission of sharing the good news of God's new covenant available to all through telling stories of this shared experience. This reality quickly led them outside Judea and the surrounding regions to far-flung cities of the Roman Empire and beyond. The early apostles quickly adapted to their new surroundings, absorbing new cultural practices and symbols, sometimes learning new local languages, and always finding new ways to share their stories. These new socio-cultural environments facilitated a certain creativity in the early storytellers as they sought to make the truth of their stories comprehensible in these varying contexts. They became genuine authors in the sense of "tellers of stories" as they shaped their received traditions for these new peoples and places.

We see this development in the traditions about Jesus in the final written Gospels of the New Testament, particularly in the telling of Jesus's miracle working and individual teachings. An account of an encounter between Jesus and a Syro-Phoenician woman recorded in Mark's Gospel becomes the story of Jesus and a Canaanite woman in Matthew's Gospel. One Gospel shares the story of the healing of an unidentified synagogue official's child, while another Gospel shares a name and other details about what seems to be the same event. All four of the Gospels share the story of Jesus miraculously feeding a multitude with a small amount of food, but the details of the scene, the crowd, and the food vary. Likewise, the Gospels record Jesus giving similar teachings using different symbols and metaphors. Jesus himself likely used a variety of images to suit the situation he was in and his later storytellers also did the same. None of this mitigates the "truth" of the stories about Jesus that the early Christians shared and preserved. Indeed, it speaks to the value of the essence of these experiences and teaching that they took the steps necessary to adapt them to fresh and varying contexts so that new audiences could also benefit from their power and wisdom.

5) The Crystallization of This Oral Tradition into Written Gospels

Of course, many stories are found in the Gospels. We cannot be sure whether there were some narratives about the life of Jesus available in written form before the Gospel of Mark appeared in about 70 CE. There were many "stories of Jesus" alive in the early Christian communities. The parables must have rung in the ears, minds, and hearts of the original listeners, and they would have been told over and over again as the generations passed. But there was still no single "story of Jesus" told from beginning to end, existing in written form.

Notice that the movement thus far has all been in terms of **oral tradition**. Very few people could read or write, and what we call "oral tradition," the passing on of stories from the life and teaching of Jesus, would have been a major part of the sharing of faith among those first believers. They would have encouraged one another in times of difficulty, instructed their children, spoken about Jesus to their friends, and told stories to those whom they wanted to draw into their community of faith. These stories about Jesus and his teaching were shared and handed down by word of mouth in increasingly varied contexts. Over time, they began to develop into a more complete oral tradition. The Roman Empire allowed for relative freedom of movement, and the natural gathering places such as markets, town squares, and theaters in the cities and villages around the empire facilitated the media for this sharing and spreading. Thus, the oral culture of the first century provided the forums for early Christian teaching and led to the development of an oral tradition about the life and ministry of Jesus.

These somewhat "fluid" oral traditions became relatively stabilized in the Christian community and were eventually "crystallized" in written form. Both these oral and brief written forms were used and adapted by the NT authors to tell their stories and teach their messages to the Christian community. The question that remains is, why? We noted in chapter one that in the oral culture of the ancient world, traditions moved from oral to written form only for particular purposes, usually to capture the authority of a particular telling, as a result of specific forces, either internal, external, or both. In the case of the writing of the Gospels, the authors no doubt had their own particular reasons for putting pen to paper, but we can point to two events that had great influence in this regard. First, we note a concern internal to the developing community. By the end of the 60s CE, the first generation of apostles was all but dead, and most had been martyred for their beliefs and profession of Jesus as Christ. This situation led to a certain urgency in preserving their first-hand experiences for future generations. Secondly, we bring to bear an event only somewhat external to the burgeoning faith tradition. Again, by the late 60s the Christian community was open to Gentiles, that is, non-Jews, living and worshiping alongside the ethnically Jewish Christians as equals in the new covenant. That said, when the Jewish rebels revolted against the Roman Empire in 65 CE, the Christians were by no means unaffected. And when this First Jewish Revolt against Rome failed in the devastation of Jerusalem and destruction of the temple in 70 CE, all the Christians were in as much fear about what the future held as their Jewish counterparts. This too led to the acute need to solidify their traditions and lay claim to the authority behind their teachings of the good news of Jesus Christ and the new covenant in the written form of complete narratives that we now call Gospels.

Within the New Testament itself we find a wonderful description of the stages of development that eventually led to the Gospels as we now have them. Writing to a person called Theophilus, the evangelist Luke tells him that there were eyewitnesses to the life of Jesus at the beginning, that subsequently many have written narratives about what had been accomplished, and that Luke, who has been observing this development for some time, now wants to tell his version of the story (Luke 1:1–3). He states unequivocally that he is not doing this just to tell Theophilus what happened, but to instruct him on the trustworthy basis upon which the story of Jesus has been constructed. He can be sure that his life of faith is well grounded (Luke 1:4). Eventually, a large number of so-called Gospels came to be written for use in the communities. Those few who could read and write provided a story of Jesus to be read by very few, but listened to by the vast majority. To this day we have many Gospels that are not found in the New Testament. You may have heard of some of them: the Gospel of Philip, the Gospel of Judas, the Gospel of Mary. By the middle of the second century, four of the many Gospels were accepted, continuing the practice of telling stories about the great figures of the past that forms a major part of the Old Testament. They were read in the churches as part of the developing Christian Scriptures. The four Gospels are the Gospel of Mark (written ca. 70 CE), the Gospels of Matthew and Luke (both written ca. 85 CE), and the Gospel of John (written ca. 100 CE).

Studying the Gospels

These four Gospels are divided into two groups. Matthew, Mark, and Luke are called "Synoptic Gospels." This expression comes from the fact that by putting the three Gospels side by side, one can see that they closely compare with one another. They can be seen with one look of the eye. This is what is meant by the Greek word behind "synoptic"—*syn-opsis*: "with the eye." This is not the case for the Gospel of John. The Synoptic Gospels all begin with Jesus's ministry in Galilee and have him eventually journey to Jerusalem. After a brief but intense ministry in Jerusalem, he is eventually arrested, tried, and killed. It is in Jerusalem that he dies and is raised. John, on the other hand, has Jesus moving in, around, and out of Jerusalem, the surrounding Judea, and the region of Galilee across a public ministry lasting more than two years, eventually (like the Synoptics) ending with his arrest and conviction in Jerusalem.

As we introduced above, Mark's Gospel was most likely written first (ca. 70 CE). Matthew and Luke followed sometime in the 80s. These evangelists probably had Mark in front of them, as they depend upon his order and often on his words, but there are also places where they differ. Matthew and Luke did not follow Mark slavishly. Indeed, there are many places where Matthew and Luke have material from Jesus (especially his teaching) that is not found in Mark or John. They appear to have had another "source," independent of Mark. This material has come to be known as "Q," the first letter of the German word for "source" (*Quelle*). As well as this special material from a common source, both Matthew and Luke had their own memories of Jesus, their own stories of Jesus told in their communities. Thus, there are stories and teachings of Jesus found only in Matthew and Luke, and there are stories and teachings of Jesus found *only* in Matthew and *only* in Luke.

The Gospel of John is very different. Jesus is regularly in Jerusalem, especially for the celebrations of the great feasts (Passover [John 2], Sabbath [John 5], Passover [John 6], Tabernacles [John 7:1–10:21] and Dedication [John 10:22–42]). Written at the end of the first Christian century (ca. 100 CE), after more reflection, life in the Spirit and prayer, the understanding of Jesus as the Christ and the Son of God has developed even further. Though some of the stories from the Synoptic Gospels reappear (e.g., the multiplication of the loaves and fishes, the confession of Peter, the passion story), the Jesus of the Gospel of John is also different. He is presented as the pre-existent *logos* (John 1:1–18). He knows all things and leads the believer—both the disciples in the story and the audiences of the story—into an ever greater commitment of faith, so that everyone might believe more deeply that Jesus is the Christ, the Son of God, and have life because of this belief (see 20:30–31).

Despite the overlap from the strong oral tradition that is preserved in written form, each evangelist has his own distinctive voice through which he presents his particular message for his

The Gospel of Mark

Mark's Gospel (old English: god-spel) appeared about 70 CE and focuses on Jesus's vindication through suffering. The author portrays the disciples as good people who struggle to comprehend Jesus's teaching and way of life.

The Gospel of Matthew

This story of Jesus depends heavily upon the Gospel of Mark. It most likely appeared in the 80s of the first century somewhere in Syria, where Jewish Christians were establishing their identity in a new world. As well as the Markan material, Matthew presents Jesus as the perfection of the promises to Israel and Jesus's "church" as the true Israel (Matthew is the only Gospel that uses this term [cf. 16:18]). He instructs his disciples to bring the good news to all the nations.

The Gospel of Luke

The author of Luke used the Gospel of Mark and other sources in creative ways. Also written late in the 80s of the first century, Luke's work is made up of two volumes (the Gospel and the Acts of the Apostles); both directed to Gentile Churches. Universal and compassionate, especially for the marginalized in society, the Gospel of Luke makes radical demands on those who would be disciples of Jesus.

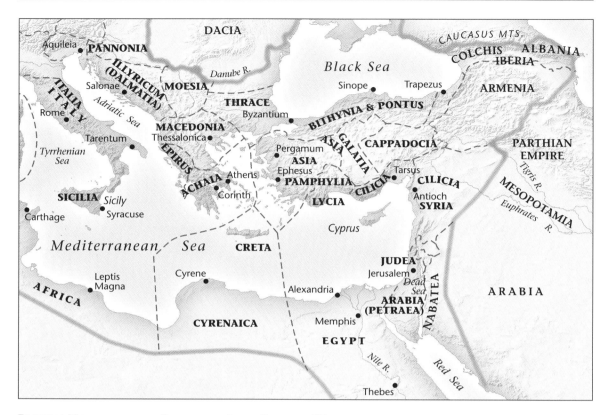

EASTERN MEDITERRANEAN REGION CA. FIRST CENTURY CE

early Christian community. To truly hear these voices as they stretch across the centuries and continue to teach twenty-first-century communities of readers, we must consider once again the tools of exegesis, the art of biblical interpretation, which we have already introduced in this textbook. Therefore, we will begin to bring this chapter to a close by briefly laying out the worlds behind, in, and in front of the texts of the gospel narratives.

The World behind the Text of the Gospels

It could be said that this section is an unnecessary distinction since we have been exploring the world behind the text of the Gospels through this entire chapter. The complex socio-cultural milieu of the New Testament comprised by Jewish religion, Mediterranean culture, Hellenistic civilization, and Roman rule directly influences the perspective and content of the Gospels. The life, ministry, and death of the historical figure Jesus of Nazareth is the focus of the theological reflection that serves as the impetus behind the evangelists putting pen to paper. The birth of Christianity and the steps in the movement from the life of Jesus to the writing of the Gospels provide the historical context of the evangelists and the communities for whom they composed their narratives. Therefore, little more need be said here to sketch a portrait of the world behind the Gospels. We mention this step in the exegetical process at this point largely to remind ourselves how important it is to ask and answer historical questions in order to establish the worldview of the authors in terms of the events that affected their communities and the kinds of issues that concerned them.

The new piece of information that we can present here is to bring together the development of the Jesus movement into the early Christian tradition to establish the world that facilitated the writing of the Gospels. This, in turn, will facilitate exegeting them. We can discuss this as the stages in the development of Christian tradition.

- **Stage 1**: The early Jesus movement can be characterized as Aramaic-speaking and centered in Jerusalem among first-generation ethnically Jewish disciples of Jesus who believed that Jesus was the long-hoped-for messiah sent by God to Israel as promised in the covenant with David. This stage spanned the 30s of the first century CE.
- **Stage 2**: In the subsequent years, Jewish Christianity spread through Judea to Samaria and Antioch and into the Hellenistic Roman Empire through the felt-urgency of missionary preaching. The apostles understood the risen Christ to have given them a mission to share the good news of the new covenant to any and all who would hear. The focus is still primarily among Jews, but the movement out into the larger empire necessitated the beginning of the shift to Greek language and culture in theological reflection and storytelling. This stage crosses the 40s of the first century CE.
- **Stage 3**: In this period, Christian preaching in the Greco-Roman world began to attract larger and larger numbers of non-Jews, whom we typically call Gentiles. This new cultural milieu led to shifts in emphases away from the Jewish roots of Jesus and toward his role as divine Lord. This stage developed primarily, but not only, through the ministry and work of the apostle Paul and his understanding of a new covenant available to all through faith regardless of ethnicity or social status across the 50s and into the 60s of the first century CE. This, in turn, led to the widening gap between Judaism and developing Christianity. What we have just said about the role of Paul in this third stage is most likely not the whole truth. But it is the way the story of the growth of the Christian community is told in the Acts of the Apostles. There were no doubt other missionaries and even martyrs across this period whom we do not know about. Paul is the figure whose story is told, but the rapid growth of Christianity must have been generated alongside him.

- **Stage 4**: The First Jewish Revolt against Rome of 65–70 CE marks the beginning of the fourth stage. The devastating loss of this war and the resulting burning of Jerusalem and destruction of the temple were a watershed moment in the long history of Judaism. In this chapter, we discussed this era and the effects it had on Judaism. By this time, the first generation of Jesus's disciples had also largely passed, many of them martyred for their profession of their newfound or newly oriented faith in Jesus as the Christ. This is the immediate context for the composition of the Gospel of Mark. The other three Gospels followed in the succeeding decades. This stage lasted across the turn of the century and came to a close with the Second Jewish Revolt against Rome (132–135 CE). This second revolt was explicitly messianic in nature, and its loss was even more devastating for the Jewish people. The Romans expelled them from Jerusalem and renamed the entire region Palestine. The year 135 CE can mark the beginning of the full separation of Judaism and Christianity as distinct religious traditions.

The Second Jewish Revolt against Rome

The Second Jewish Revolt against Rome occurred from 132 to 135 CE. It was preceded by years of clashes between Jews and Romans in the area. The misrule of Rufus, the Roman governor of Judea, combined with the emperor Hadrian's intention to found a Roman colony on the site of Jerusalem and his restrictions on Jewish religious freedom and observances provoked Bar Kokhba, who claimed to be the messiah, to lead the uprising. Although initially gaining some traction, his forces proved no match against the methodical and ruthless tactics of the Roman military. Upon the death of Bar Kokhba, the rebellion was crushed in 135 and the Jewish people were banned from Jerusalem.

The world behind the text of the Gospels is, therefore, one of change and turmoil as many people, both Jew and Gentile alike, attempt to understand the world around them and how God is working in it through his larger plan for history. The evangelists compose their Gospels to capture authoritative stories of the Christ Event and assist their communities of believers in negotiating this world.

The World in the Text of the Gospels

As we approach the world in the text of the Gospels, our first task is to ask a question about **genre**. The term "genre" comes to us from the French and refers to a category of artistic endeavor that has a particular form, technique, or content. In literature, genre refers to the type of writing an author chooses to use as the medium for his or her message. The evangelists chose to share their understandings of the good news of the Christ Event in narrative form. As interpreters we must respect that form. Narratives have characters, settings, and plots with beginnings, middles, and ends, among other characteristics. Narratives, even "true" stories of historical figures, are also developed, shaped, and told by their authors through their points of view to tell the stories they believe their readers need to hear. This does not make the stories any less "true." All humans have perspectives, and all potential audiences have needs.

We can take an example from our own lives. Very often when we answer questions, we tell stories to make our points. The simplest question, "how was your day?" can elicit very different responses from us depending upon who the questioner is. Our employers need certain data from such a question, while our parents or grandparents need other information. Children, nieces, nephews, or younger brothers and sisters need still different material. We speak to our friends and other intimates in still different tones with distinct areas of emphasis. Our responses to each and every one of these questioners will be different. And yet every story can be true. We are forthright and sincere with each of these stories that we tell, although they may begin and end in different places, use very different language (it is rarely advisable to speak to grandparents and buddies with the same slang), and focus on entirely different events. Our Gospel writers, by necessity, do the same thing. This is why, with all the overlap in these four different narratives, each has its own unique voice.

Once we settle on the notion of stories and storytellers, we must determine what kind of narrative a Gospel is. As we introduced earlier in this chapter, in one sense, Gospels are like biographies in that they tell the story of the life of a person who really lived in our world. However, Gospels are not biographies in the modern sense. They share little to nothing about Jesus's formative years, associations, education, and they in no way attempt to present the complete life of Jesus or to explain the social, cultural, historical, or political forces that could have influenced who he came to be. They simply relate certain material they deem crucial to the witness of the "good news." Further, in all four Gospels, only the final week of Jesus's human existence is related in any kind of detail. The significance of Jesus's suffering and death is the central concern of each evangelist. Even John, who relates more of Jesus's public life than the others, devotes nearly half his narrative to this Passion and the retelling of the events of Jesus's last few days on earth (John 13–19). Therefore, in the sense that Gospels tell life stories, they are ancient biographies that focus on the events in the life of the protagonist that are key for understanding the *meaning* of the person's life. The Greek term for this ancient genre is *bios*. Ancient biographers could not always check facts and did not necessarily have access to verbatim records of their hero's speeches. They were comfortable in describing the types of things that happened and the sorts of things that would have been said in order to share their messages. Therefore, we are best served by moving away from the idea of the modern biography and toward a new genre created by the earliest evangelists that was related to the ancient biography but focused on sharing the good news of the Christ Event. We call this genre the Gospel.

Gospels are heavily influenced by the narratives of the Jewish Scriptures in their form and content. In addition, they have particular agendas. Gospel authors are overtly evangelistic. They do not want their audiences to finish hear-

Literary Forms in the NT

There are numerous literary forms found in the NT. Indeed, a number of the forms are found across Scripture and are not limited to one testament or the other.

Parable: Typically brief stories that offer a comparison that teaches a lesson. The term comes from the Greek verb that means "to go around." A parable offers a round-about way to evoke an insight resulting in a more profound impact than a direct response.

Pronouncement Story:A brief narrative that culminates in a significant saying, or pronouncement, on the part of Jesus. They are typically structured in three parts: setting, action, and resulting pronouncement.

Miracle Story: Narrative episodes that include the performance of a miracle or, to use John's term, a sign. The basic structure of these stories includes the following: the description of a need, the miraculous act itself, and the consequences of the miracle.

Dominical Sayings: "Sayings of the Lord" are often independent proclamations that have no clear setting or strong narrative framework. These were preserved in the oral tradition and are often clustered together in the final form of the Gospels.

ing or reading their stories and go home or put them away and say, "That was nice; I think I'll take a nap." Rather, they desire their stories to change lives. The goal would be for their audiences to believe that Jesus is the long-awaited messiah and change their lives—even risk their lives—accordingly. Every plotline, character development, and symbol is shaped toward this end. In the coming chapters we will be discussing how the evangelist John takes on this task and shapes his narrative in more literary terms such as structure and characteristics. Therefore, it is crucial to understand that each evangelist, just like every storyteller in history, makes these important choices.

The World in Front of the Text of the Gospels

As we also indicated above, the early Christian community produced many Gospel narratives about Jesus or collections of his sayings, but the four we commonly refer to as Matthew, Mark, Luke, and John are those recognized as authoritative for Christianity. It is appropriate to note here that the authors of the Gospels never identify themselves by name anywhere in their writing. The Gospel titles, e.g. *According to John*, etc., are added to the Gospels late in the second century CE in order to differentiate them from one another as the Christian leaders participated in debates about the canon. These leaders identified the Gospel authors through their strong oral traditions from the first generation of apostles. Even careful study, however, cannot verify these traditional attributions. Nonetheless, we will continue to refer to the Gospels by their traditional authors. More will be said about the authorship of the Gospel of John in the next chapter.

As we have noted, each evangelist has his own unique perspective on the Christ Event and each Gospel presents a distinctive portrait of Jesus and his life and ministry. This means that, try as we might, we cannot reconcile the chronologies and details of each Gospel into one seamless story. The fact that the primitive Christian community did not adopt one official version free from these contradictions is itself significant. Perhaps the early church leaders saw that Jesus and the Christ Event could not be reduced to a single perspective. Recognizing and analyzing the Gospels' discrepancies and inconsistencies, however, can reveal much about their writers' intentions and individual perceptions of Jesus and his significance. This, as we introduced in chapter two, is called redaction criticism. Jesus elicited widely divergent responses in people, so the formers of the canon retained these for the community of faith. The manner in which these distinctive portraits of the good news affected audiences and the responses they elicited is the focus of the world in front of the text.

> **Biography as Proclamation**
>
> Perhaps the greatest challenge a twenty-first century reader of the Gospel faces is recognizing that the Gospels are not primarily a collection of "stories about Jesus." However much actual history might lie behind them, they are written to proclaim the great truths about Jesus and how we should respond to him. As John tells his readers, these things are written "that you may believe, and that through believing you may have life in his name" (20:31). A Gospel has the form of a biography. However, it should not be confused with a modern biography, as its purpose is to proclaim the truth about what the author thinks God has done.

As we discussed in the previous section, the evangelists desired their audiences to respond by believing that Jesus was the Christ and to change their lives accordingly. The questions we must ask each evangelist include what, according to their understanding of the good news and their communities' needs, that believing entails and how exactly they expect lives to change. We cannot answer these questions in this brief space. Indeed, the bulk of this textbook is devoted to exegeting and understanding John's expectations of his audiences. Exploring the answers to such questions about the Synoptic Gospels merits additional textbooks. What we can do here is to reiterate that the belief that Jesus is the Christ necessitated paradigm shifts for both Jews and Gentiles. Ethnically Jewish believers had to redefine their messianic expectations from a military king like David who would establish a sovereign nation to a suffering and vindicated Son of Man who gave himself unconditionally to God's will, even unto death. God's acceptance of Jesus's obedient and loving way of life and death in the resurrection put in place a new covenant open to all humankind. Gentile believers had to let go of their Greco-Roman ideals of gods and heroes to embrace a savior who was a peasant, executed as a common criminal. The apostle Paul described this reality in this way, "For Jews demand signs and

Greeks desire wisdom, but we proclaim Christ crucified, a stumbling block to Jews and foolishness to Gentiles" (1 Cor 1:22–23). Paul goes on to say, however, that "but to those who are the called, both Jews and Greeks, Christ the power of God and the wisdom of God" (1 Cor 1:24). This power and wisdom is what each evangelist sought to instill and inspire in their audiences to meet their needs and speak to their contexts. Now, some two thousand years later audiences are still asking questions in order to interpret these messages and apply their power and wisdom to their own lives.

In the next chapters, we will begin exploring the Gospel of John through the worlds behind, in, and in front of the text. Following this sound method of exegeting the Gospels, we will establish the historical context that facilitated the writing of the Gospel, then explore the literary features the evangelist employs in the text to share his message, so that we can draw some conclusions about what he envisioned for the world in front of his text.

Gospels in the Early Church

Preserving the distinctive perspectives of the Gospels was certainly the mindset of the church leaders late in the second century, when the names Mark, Matthew, Luke and John were attached to the four Gospels of the New Testament. They faced the danger that the four different stories were being collapsed into one coherent story. At that time a person called Tatian developed a document, of which we now have only fragments, called The *Diatesseron*, which did exactly that. Names were thus given to each of the Gospels, so that their uniqueness would be recognized and respected.

What Have We Learned So Far?
Jesus and the Good News

Christianity developed out of Judaism; therefore, we can expect similar theological worldviews in the two religious traditions. Indeed, every aspect of Christian belief finds its foundation in ancient Judaism. The hallmark of Jewish theology is monotheism, the belief in one all-powerful creator and sovereign God. This view of God and how God works in the world was counter-cultural, even subversive, in the Roman Empire. Christianity also maintained this strong belief system. What developed in the early Jesus movement, however, was a Christology that was intimately connected to this theology. The standard Jewish messianic expectations were somewhat diverse, but always understood the expected messiah to be fully human. During his lifetime, Jesus set about redefining those messianic expectations. The early Christians, upon their experience of the resurrection and their reflection on who Jesus really was and what God did in and through Jesus, began to develop a further understanding of Jesus as, yes, fully human, but *also* divine. As the Christ, Jesus was the Son of Man (human) who was also the Son of God (divine). But this understanding did not take away from the oneness of God. Eventually, the early Christians also came to understand a third person in this divine relationship that communicated the fullness of what this relationship could be in God's creation. Still using terminology from the Jewish Scriptures, Christians call this third person the Holy Spirit. Eventually the Christian communities will identify this theological understanding of God as a unity of one in three persons as Trinity. This intimate relationship of theology and Christology will take centuries to fully develop, but we can see the seeds planted across the New Testament books. As the textbook moves forward, we will point out how these seeds are sown in the Gospel and Letters of John. We will also see that what the authors of the books of the New Testament, and especially what John says about Father, Son, and Holy Spirit, sometimes creates more problems than answers. It took the church almost three hundred years of arguing, thinking, praying, and celebrating before it came to state its belief in a Triune God.

The Christian understanding of the new covenant bred many new developments; the aspect that is clearly recognizable around the world in the twenty-first century is ecclesiology. As we discussed in the introduction, this concept comes from the Greek word *ekklēsia*, which means gathering and is related to the Jewish concept of the synagogue. The term *ekklēsia* comes into English as "church" and refers to the community of believers as they gather, reflect, worship, and support one another. Only eventually does this term also come to refer to buildings and the institution of the Christian religion. What we see in the New Testament books is the gathering of believers in Jesus the Christ who found a common theology, Christology, and worldview based on equal footing as human beings before God through Christ. This church is open and inclusive to all who believe; the cultural conditions of race, gender, ethnicity and social class so pervasive in the Roman Empire no longer apply. As we explore the Gospel and Letters of John, we come face to face with this subversive reality and the challenges it often posed for the burgeoning tradition.

The final components of the theological worldview that we have touched upon in this chapter are those of eschatology and soteriology. These two concepts often go hand in hand in religious traditions and are always connected in Christianity. The resurrection faith that we discussed above means that Christians believe that Jesus lived, died, and was resurrected by God to live again. After some time on earth with his disciples, the risen Christ ascended to heaven to dwell with God the Father. Many Christians believed that Jesus would return to earth one day to end the world as we know it and launch a new age of the kingdom of God on earth. This "second coming" is often referred to by its Greek terminology, the *parousia*. This is, broadly speaking, Christian eschatology, that at the end of days Jesus would come again to inaugurate a new reign for the faithful. Further, Jesus's victory over death also conquered death for all the faithful. What exactly this might look like, when it might happen, and where and how it might manifest, vary among the New Testament authors. Again, as we saw above, the New Testament sometimes creates more questions than answers. That is fine, as the history of the church and its faith unfolds around its search for these answers. Regardless, this sort of eternal dwelling in union with God the Father and Jesus the Son and Christ is the essence of eschatology as well as its intersection with soteriology, the Christian understanding of salvation.

New Testament authors write about two kinds of eschatology and soteriology. What we have been discussing so far can be called "end-times" eschatology and looks to the future for the culmination of history and the kingdom of God. At that point, the timing of which no human can know, the faithful will be rewarded with full union with God. Those who have passed will be raised from the dead to this same eternal dwelling. Another perspective is what is called "realized eschatology" and focuses on the present and how salvation can be experienced now. What this means is that union with God in full relationship can be experienced the moment one accepts Jesus as the Christ and believes that God has put in place a new covenant through him. This sort of "present-tense" salvation allows for a reign of God on earth in our own time through the community of believers. Eternal life in communion with God is still promised, but that life begins now.

In the Gospel and Letters of John, we will find both of these kinds of belief systems fully entrenched in the developing theology, Christology, and ecclesiology of first-century Christianity. They can and do often exist together. We will, therefore, develop our understanding of all of these aspects of the theological worldview in more depth as we make our way through them. We can now turn our attention fully to interpretation of these texts in their historical, literary, and theological contexts.

Key Terms and Concepts

Christ Event

Christianity/Christians

church

evangelist

genre

good news

gospel

Hellenistic civilization

Jesus Movement

Jesus of Nazareth

Judaism

Mediterranean culture

new covenant

oral tradition

resurrection faith

Roman rule

symbolic worlds

Questions for Review

1. The New Testament world was complex and diverse. With this in mind, identify and describe the four major elements of this pluralistic cultural milieu.

2. Using information from the Gospels coupled with archaeological and historical evidence from the Roman Empire, scholars sketch the life and ministry of Jesus of Nazareth. How might that portrait look?

3. The birth of Christianity resulted from the early Jesus Movement's conviction of the call to share the good news with the world. What exactly is this news, and why is it so good?

4. Identify and describe the steps in the movement from the life of Jesus of Nazareth to the composition of the written Gospels.

5. Discuss the stages in the development of the Christian tradition as they form the world behind the text of the Gospels.

6. Define what a Gospel as a genre of literature is, and identify several key issues one must bear in mind when studying them.

Bibliography and Further Reading

Hurtado, Larry. *How on Earth Did Jesus Become a God? Historical Questions about Earliest Devotion to Jesus*. Grand Rapids: Eerdmans, 2005.

Johnson, Luke Timothy. *The Writings of the New Testament: An Interpretation*. 3rd ed. Minneapolis: Fortress, 2010.

Moloney, Francis J. *Reading the New Testament in the Church. A Primer for Pastors, Religious Educators, and Believers*. Grand Rapids: Baker Academic, 2015.

Nickle, Keith F. *The Synoptic Gospels: An Introduction*. Revised and expanded edition. Louisville: Westminster John Knox, 2001.

Powell, Mark Allan. *Introducing the New Testament: A Historical, Literary, and Theological Survey*. Ada, MI: Baker Academic, 2009.

Steggemann, Ekkehard W., and Wolfgang Steggemann. *The Jesus Movement: A Social History of Its First Century*. Translated by O. C. Dean. Minneapolis: Fortress, 1999.

John and His Writings

PURPOSE Chapter five provides the historical context of the Gospel and Letters of John by posing and suggesting possible answers to the basic questions of authorship, genre, location and period of the writing community, purpose of the evangelist, and the literary background of the text.

ASSIGNMENT Read any introductory material on the Gospel and Letters of John that may be in the study Bible.

Now that we have presented a portrait of the Jewish background of Jesus and the early Christian movement through a presentation of the Old Testament narrative and the Jesus movement, we can turn our attention to the immediate historical context of the evangelist John and his community. This somewhat difficult situation is what ultimately resulted in the composition of the Gospel and Letters of John.

The World behind the Text: The Historical Background of the Gospel and Letters of John

When biblical scholars use all the evidence available to them, including archaeological discoveries, data from both in and outside the biblical text, music, art, and other artifacts of the period in order to reconstruct the world behind the text, they are seeking to establish **historical context**. We do this because we must understand as best as we can what the world looked like and what was important for the author in question. This, of course, is why we have spent two chapters preparing ourselves to discuss the evangelist and his community before we ever get to his literature that is preserved in the New Testament. Now that we are here, the most succinct way to articulate this historical context is to ask and answer what we will call the "basic questions." Recalling some of the issues we have already discussed, in this chapter we will primarily be historical critics.

We are asking and seeking answers to the questions of who, what, where, when, why, and how of the world of the evangelist, which is, by extension, the world behind the text of the Gospel and Letters of John.

Answering the Question of Authorship

In establishing the world behind the text, when we ask the question "who," we are really asking a question about **authorship**. As we indicated in the last chapter, this is a complicated question when it comes to the Gospels. They, like many texts in the ancient world, were all written anonymously. Issues such as "intellectual property" and "by-lines" are concerns of our world, not theirs. The message of the text was what primarily mattered. Writers of the biblical books are true authors in the sense that they are more than just editors of received oral traditions. Rather, they composed, developed, and shaped their material to share the message their audiences needed to hear. That said, self-interest and notoriety were not part of their perceived mission. What did matter, how-

John the Evangelist,
early nineteenth-
century Russian icon

ever, was credibility. For their message to be received and responded to as they hoped, their compositions had to carry the weight of authority. The kind of authority necessary depended upon the audience and what it held sacred. For the early Christian communities, the apostles—the first generation of disciples that Jesus sent out to spread the good news—had this authority. These were the authors whose messages they held dear.

As we indicated in the introduction to this textbook, the "John" identified by early church tradition as the author of the Gospel and Letters of John is the apostle **John, the son of Zebedee**. In the Synoptic Gospels, two sons of a fisherman named Zebedee, James and John, are called by Jesus to follow him (Mark 1:19–20; Matt 4:21–22; Luke 5:10–11). They leave their father and their nets and never look back. Indeed, they are often identified with Peter as the leaders of the inner circle of twelve. They are, however, never identified by name in the Gospel of John. There is one mention of the "sons of Zebedee" with several other disciples by the Sea of Galilee after the resurrection of Jesus at John 21:2, which places them in the inner circle, but they do not otherwise have a named role in the Gospel. The author of the Gospel and Letters of John, therefore, never identifies himself by name in the texts, nor does he give any indication what his name might be. This, as we have indicated, is not unusual. The evangelist does, however, indicate the authority behind his message through a different tactic.

The Gospel calls attention to an eyewitness at the cross, who is the disciple whom Jesus loved (19:26). This **Beloved Disciple** avows the truth of what he

---

The Emergence of the Beloved Disciple

The Beloved Disciple is first identified as such during Jesus's final meal with his disciples:

> One of his disciples—the one whom Jesus loved—was reclining next to him (13:23).

He is later identified as one among those at the cross of Jesus:

> When Jesus saw his mother and the disciple whom he loved standing beside her, he said to his mother, "Woman, here is your son." Then he said to the disciple, "Here is your mother." And from that hour the disciple took her into his own home (19:26–27).

That same disciple is then identified as the eyewitness testimony behind the Gospel:

> He who saw this has testified so that you also may believe. His testimony is true, and he knows that he tells the truth (19:35).

The final verses of the Gospel indicate he is the author:

> Peter turned and saw the disciple whom Jesus loved following them; he was the one who had reclined next to Jesus at the supper. . . . When Peter saw him, he said to Jesus, "Lord, what about him?"... This is the disciple who is testifying to these things and has written them, and we know that his testimony is true (21:20–24).

The Last Supper by
Vicente Macip

saw and the testimony he is sharing through this story (19:35). Once advised of this, audiences can reflect upon the story so far and realize that this same Beloved Disciple was first identified as he leaned against Jesus at the Last Supper (13:23). After the crucifixion, he is mentioned again along with Peter as the ones whom Mary Magdalene alerted to the empty tomb. In that instance he is identified as "the other disciple, the one whom Jesus loved" (20:2). Now audiences are reminded of the first two disciples who sought out Jesus at the urging of John the Baptist (1:35–42). One is identified as Andrew (1:40), but the other remained anonymous. This enigmatic, unnamed "other disciple" is present at all the crucial events of the narrative (see 13:23–25; 18:15–16; 19:26–27; 20:2–8; 21:7; 21:21–23) and is the first to *see* and *believe* when he found the clothes of death empty and folded in the tomb (20:3–10). John 21:24 claims this anonymous character, the disciple whom Jesus loved, to be the author of the Gospel.

As we also indicated in the introduction, the early church leader Irenaeus (ca. 180 CE) is the first to identify this disciple as John, the son of Zebedee, who lived at Ephesus until the time of the Emperor Trajan (ca. 98 CE). As a boy Irenaeus studied under Polycarp, Bishop of Smyrna, who is believed to have known and been a disciple under John, son of Zebedee. This identification, with the minor variation that he had assistants, subsequently received almost universal church acceptance. Was Ireneaus correct? It is impossible to be certain. Scholars generally recognize that later conjectures about figures and authorship from a century before were often simplified—and that *authority* behind a writing was the crux of such an identification. The fact that the author went to such pains to present his authority and yet remains anonymous is itself notable. The role of the Beloved Disciple in this narrative is to be a witness to Jesus and the source for the Fourth-Gospel tradition. We can, therefore, say that the narrative as we have it is the result of oral traditions directly stemming from the companions of Jesus. Several other possible authors have been suggested across the years, including Nathanael, Lazarus, Mary Magdalene, or some otherwise unidentifiable disciple. The massive support for identifying the Fourth Evangelist as John the son of Zebedee across the centuries lends weight to this identification that the evidence in the Gospel itself cannot support. We can, therefore, respect this long-standing tradition and continue to refer to the Gospel author as "John" and refer to him as a "he" even though we cannot be certain just who this disciple was.

Answering the Question of Genre

When we are establishing the world behind the text, asking the question "what," is really asking a question about what type of literature we have. This is a question of **genre**. We discussed genre in the last chapter when we introduced the methodology for studying the Gospels. The Gospel of John, like the other Gospels of the NT, is related to the ancient biography, or *bios* in Greek, and is therefore a narrative that has as its primary aim to share the good news of the Christ Event. All the narrative components of the text: plot, setting, characters, climax, resolution, etc., are geared toward that end. The hope is that upon

Saint John Theologos, icon in the monastery of Aptera, Crete

finishing the story, the audience will believe that Jesus is the Christ and that, through his life, death, and resurrection, God has put in place a new covenant that is available to everyone. As exegetes, our task is to take seriously the fact that the author in question chose, in this case, to compose a narrative; and we then ask our questions accordingly.

We indicated that in this chapter we will primarily act as historical critics. This is true, but we must also do a bit of textual criticism. In an introductory textbook, we will, for the most part, leave the textual criticism to the experts, and not only work from the final form of the text they have derived, but also read it in English. However, some textual issues are so significant or so difficult to determine that we must discuss them. We will begin this process below when we answer the question of purpose. At this point, it will serve us well to remember that to arrive at the contemporary English translations in our Bibles, translators use the work of textual critics who have examined hundreds and sometimes thousands of ancient manuscripts in the original Greek, as well as early translations into other ancient languages. This is, of course, also the case with the Gospel of John. With respect to the oldest manuscripts, Codex Vaticanus is usually considered to have the best original Greek text. Codex Sinaiticus and Codex Bezae are also important. These manuscripts written on parchment all date from the fourth and fifth centuries CE. Two more recently

Codex Vaticanus
© 2016 Biblioteca
Apostolica Vaticana

Early Papyrus of the Gospel: Papyrus 66 (P⁶⁶) of John 1:1–14

© Fondation Martin Bodmer, Cologny (Geneva)

discovered manuscripts are written on papyrus. Scholars call them P⁶⁶ and P⁷⁵, and they date from ca. 200 CE. These are the earliest texts we have, but quotations from the Gospel are found in writings of the early church leaders and in the Syriac translation, called the Peshitta, that can be dated earlier. Both where these manuscripts are identical and where they vary provide us valuable information about the world behind the text of the Gospel.

In this section, we must also include a brief discussion of the genre of the letter. The Greek word for "letter" is *epistolē*. This term comes into English as "epistle" and is usually reserved for formal letters with literary elegance, intended for groups of people for didactic, or teaching, purpose. The texts known as 1, 2, and 3 John are typically identified as epistles because of their formal literary character. In fact, although 2 and 3 John are good examples of Greco-Roman letters, 1 John is more of a theological tract. In addition to being studied alongside the Gospel of John, these texts also belong to a group of texts in the New Testament often referred to as the "Catholic Epistles." The term "catholic"

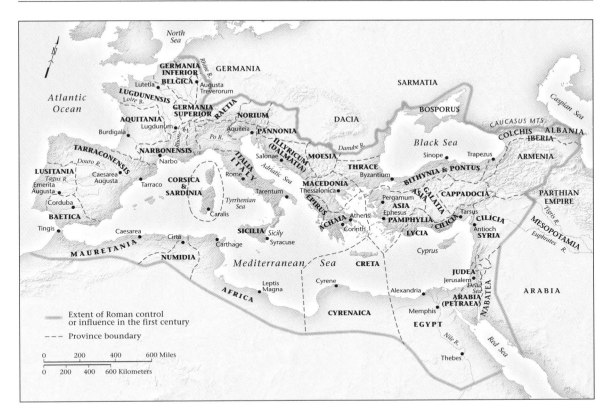

THE ROMAN EMPIRE, FIRST CENTURY CE

comes from the Greek language and means "universal" or "general." This identification reflects the notion that they are addressed metaphorically and intended for general circulation among a community of churches. For example, 1 John does not have an address as such, but provides a brief prologue before beginning its appeal for faithfulness, while 2 John is addressed to "the elect lady" (v. 1), a poetic reference to a sister church. We will discuss these letters and their role in the canon in much more detail in chapter sixteen. At this point, we simply want to acknowledge the distinctive genre in which they were written.

Answering the Question of the Location of the Writing Community

When we are establishing the world behind the text, to ask the question "where" is to ask about the origins of these texts. We are concerned with the **location** of the author and the writing community. If we know where the author and intended audience reside, we can couple information in the text with archaeological and other written evidence from that region to learn more about what was going on in that community, what images and symbols might be important to them, and how the community might be faring in their larger society and culture. As we clarified in the last chapter, the Gospel must have been written in and for a developing Christian community in the Roman Empire, but this is still a large area with a lot of diversity and both socio-economic and geographic disparity. So how might we narrow it down?

As we have already noted, scholars generally understand the Gospel and Letters of John as the literary expression of the community of the Beloved Disciple. More specifically, the epistles are theological reflections on the Gospel that reveal the development and challenges of this community over time. For centuries, this literature was often characterized as purely Hellenistic—a product of Greek philosophical thought and beliefs. As we will discuss in more detail in the next chapter, the evangelist's writing style includes the use of such abstract ideas as light and truth, the dualistic division of humanity into knowledge and ignorance, and a concept of the divine *logos* or "word" of God. This could lead scholars to conclude that the Gospel is a product of ethnically Gentile Christians living in the great metropolitan areas of the empire, interested in the philosophical ideas of Gnosticism.

Two major archaeological discoveries of the twentieth century, both in the 1940s, have challenged this conclusion and suggested John's historical rooting in first-century Judaism. The Dead Sea Scrolls are the more famous of the two important findings. These writings that were found in the caves of Qumran near the northern end of the Dead Sea make up the library of a first-century Jewish group. The scrolls include both Jewish Scriptures and contemporary writings of the community. This latter category of writings is full of the vocabulary and theological concepts found in John. For the first time in history, therefore, scholars had clear evidence that Jewish writers also used these more philosophical terms and concepts in the manner that John uses them. At about the

---

The Dead Sea Scrolls and the Nag Hammadi Library

The **Dead Sea Scrolls** typically refer to the religious writings found in eleven caves near Qumran by the Dead Sea. They reflect particular streams of Jewish thought in the first century CE. Although several intact scrolls were found, most of the collection consists of thousands of parchment and papyrus fragments. The writings are largely either manuscripts from the Jewish Scriptures or documents that describe the beliefs and practices of the community that composed them.

The **Nag Hammadi Library** is a collection of thirteen ancient codices containing over fifty texts discovered in Egypt in 1945. The collection includes a number of Gospels that date to the second century CE, including the Gospel of Thomas, the Gospel of Philip, and the Gospel of Mary.

Qumran
© Meg Stewart

same time, a library of Gnostic Christian manuscripts were found at a site called Nag Hammadi in Egypt. These writings show a profound difference from John, especially their ideas about God and the role and person of Jesus. This evidence leads scholars to believe that it is more likely that second-century Gnostics drew from the worldview of those at Qumran or the Johannine community, and not the other way around.

Within the pages of the Gospel, John reflects a familiarity with Judea and the surrounding regions of the Jewish homeland. He knows sites not mentioned in the other Gospels, and archaeological evidence often supports his accuracy. Some examples of references to specific locations include: the pool of Bethesda (5:2), the pool of Siloam (9:7), Solomon's portico in the temple (10:23), the village of Bethany (11:1, 18), and the Garden across the Kidron (18:1). He also knows the customs and practices of Judaism, including: the Jewish festivals (5:10; 6:4; 7:2; 10:22); purity rituals (2:6; 18:28); Passover practices and the preparation of the paschal lamb; and burial rituals (12:1–8; 19:36–42). That said, the evangelist explains some of these places, customs, and practices as if the audience might

The Gospel of Thomas and the Secret Book of John, Codex II of the Nag Hammadi manuscripts

The War Scroll from the Dead Sea Scrolls found at Qumran

not be familiar with them. Further, he translates the Hebrew words he uses into Greek (see 1:38, 41; 20:16) as if the audience might not know the sacred language of Judaism.

This evidence, both behind and in the text, leads most scholars to suggest that the writing community is made up of ethnically Jewish Christians living outside the Jewish homeland of Judea in the larger Greek-speaking empire. This would likely be a metropolitan area with a Hellenistic culture that also has a strong Jewish presence and influence. In addition, the community seems to have developed somewhat independently of other Christian groups and traditions, including those from which the Synoptic Gospels arose. **Ephesus**, a city located on the west coast of modern-day Turkey, is the location most often identified with the provenance, or origin, of this literature. This identification began in the earliest church tradition, and today tourists can visit both the site of this city and even the traditional tomb of the evangelist. Scholars, of course, are skeptical of this traditional attestation, and both the region of Syria and the city of Alexandria have also been suggested. Nonetheless, the city of Ephesus still occupies the majority position and remains the best candidate for the location of the writing community.

Ancient Ephesus, including the façade of the library of Celsus

Ancient Ephesus,
including the Roman
amphitheater

Answering the Question of Dating the Composition

In establishing the world behind the text, when we ask the question "when," we are trying to determine the **date of composition** for the literature. Sometimes this questioning is focused on when texts reached their final form, but some scholars also try to determine when earlier drafts were composed and how the text may have shifted before it was finalized. With the Johannine Literature, scholars have often gone this latter route and attempted to glean not only stages in the development of the texts, but also identify those "drafts" with stages in the development of the community of the Beloved Disciple. In this effort, they carefully analyze variations in the language of the text, including the manner in which Jesus and his opponents are characterized, how believers are called to respond, and what words and images are used to describe the situation at hand. Scholars then often establish a time frame in which the literature could have been composed and begin to narrow down the window from there.

When we study the language of the Gospel of John, we notice that Jesus is characterized as the Christ who is confident, clear on his mission, powerful, all-knowing, and in intimate relationship with God, whom he calls Father. Indeed, the first verses of the Gospel describe him as the divine Word of God who becomes human for a time in the form of God's only Son (1:1–18). This way of understanding Jesus is known as a **high Christology** and, as we indicated in the last chapter, is something that took time to develop in early Christianity. In addition, the Gospels are marked by conflicts between Jesus and opponents who are often characterized as "the Jews," as opposed to the more specific Jewish groups (the Pharisees, Sadducees, etc.) that we read about in the Synoptic Gospels and who would have been more influential before the First Jewish Revolt of 65–70 CE. Rather, John's terminology indicates the period of hostility between the emerging movement of Christianity and post-70 Judaism that eventually led to a full breakdown in relations between the two groups. Further, as a teacher, Jesus speaks not in parables but in long dialogues and speeches that focus not primarily on the "kingdom of God," as in the Synoptics, but rather on himself and the possibility of eternal life with God the Father for all those who believe in him. Much more will be said about these characteristics of the literary style of the evangelist and his writing in the next chapter, but at this point we can use these characteristics as evidence to draw the conclusion that the Gospel could not have been written before the First Jewish Revolt, or 70 CE.

To establish the other side of the time frame, we notice that John does indeed seem to reflect a later, more developed stage in the early history of Christianity, but his literature, particularly the Gospel and 1 John, is being quoted as authoritative by church leaders like Irenaeus by the mid to late second century CE. This alone means that they had to have been written by ca. 180 CE. Of course, for church leaders to be using these texts as credible sources for their own teaching, they had to have been in circulation for some time. As we introduced above, Irenaeus was teaching that these texts had been around for several generations and had their origins in the apostle John in the first century. This narrows our window a good deal. We can once again look to what the evangelist is teaching through his writing for more information.

On three occasions in the Gospel, mention is made of expulsion from the synagogue as the consequence for those who believe and publically profess that Jesus is the Messiah. The Greek term the evangelist uses is ***aposynagōgos***, literally, "**to put out of the synagogue**" (9:22; 12:42; 16:2). The first instance occurs when the man who was born blind was questioned by the authorities, after Jesus had given him sight. The narrator indicates that the punishment of expulsion for those who professed Jesus as Christ was already in place. The man stands firm against his interrogators and is eventually expelled (9:34). The second occurrence is found at the end of Jesus's public ministry, as the narrator is explaining the crisis caused by Jesus and the fear many had in coming forward with their belief (12:37–43). The third and final occurrence is found in the mouth of Jesus in his last discourse with his disciples, as he prepares them for leadership of the new community once his physical presence has left them. He warns them that this call to leadership is dangerous and they will likely give their lives for their beliefs (16:1–4).

The meaning of being "put out of the synagogue" and the actual action signified are not clear. Scholars draw different conclusions. As we suggested in chapter one, toward the end of the first century, the Jewish leaders gathered

John 9:22; 12:42; 16:2 and Expulsion from the Synagogue

When the parents of the man whom Jesus healed from blindness were called to speak for him, they redirect the questioning to him. The narrator specifies:

> His parents said this because they were afraid of the Jews; for the Jews had already agreed that anyone who confessed Jesus to be the Messiah would be put out of the synagogue. Therefore his parents said, "He is of age; ask him" (9:22–23).

At the end of Jesus's public ministry, the narrator sums up the response to him:

Nevertheless many, even of the authorities, believed in him. But because of the Pharisees they did not confess it, for fear that they would be put out of the synagogue; for they loved human glory more than the glory that comes from God (12:42–43).

Finally, Jesus prepares his disciples for the consequences of their discipleship:

> "I have said these things to you to keep you from stumbling. They will put you out of the synagogues. Indeed, an hour is coming when those who kill you will think that by doing so they are offering worship to God" (16:1–2).

at Jamnia to preserve Judaism after the devastation of the failed Jewish Revolt against Rome. In addition to reorienting worship away from the destroyed temple and establishing the Tanakh, these rabbis began to establish a more orthodox belief system. Differing beliefs about the messiah led to conflicts and eventually separated the Christians from the community of Judaism that was forming around the synagogues. This process was likely uneven and took a good deal of time to fully manifest. Nonetheless, it may have begun in the 90s CE and eventually led to the separation of the Christians from the mainstream Judaism that was developing.

What is clear, however, is that we have no evidence beyond the Gospel that professing Jesus as Messiah would have resulted in expulsion from the synagogue *during Jesus's lifetime* in the late 20s or 30s. Indeed, this sort of debate was a hallmark of life in the synagogues. The various Jewish groups had very different understandings of how God might intervene to rectify their current oppressive situation and what form the Christ might take. The lively arguments and theological reflection in and around both the synagogues and the temple area prior to 70 CE were part and parcel of the Jewish way of life. What we see in the Gospel, then, with this hostility, conflict, and fear about being expelled from the synagogue is actually a glimpse into the world behind the text of the Gospel. Although we cannot be sure that the evangelist and his community were being expelled from the synagogue in the 90s CE, it is clear they were undergoing some crisis as a consequence of their faith in Christ, which resulted in a strong sense of alienation from their original historical community. The evangelist is teaching about something happening in his own time through his narrative, set some sixty years earlier. He can then affirm for his audiences that what they are going through is to be expected, and even valued. Through the story of Jesus, he teaches them to stand strong and hold fast to their beliefs despite the challenges of the world around them.

This work we have done with the world behind and in the text allows us to date the Gospel in narrative form, very like we have it today, from ca. 90 to 100 CE, leaving room for minor redaction, or editing, later. The letters would have followed shortly thereafter, written near the turn of the first century CE. They reflect an ethnically Jewish Christian community in crisis over their faith and their future in an ever changing world.

Answering the Question of the Purpose for Writing

> **Jews and Christians**
>
> The well-known problem of John's negative use of the expression "the Jews" has been accurately and sensitively described by a significant Johannine scholar, John Ashton. On encountering this problem, he asks that one must "recognize in these hot-tempered exchanges the type of family row in which the participants face one another across the room of a house which all have shared and all call home" (*Understanding the Fourth Gospel*).

When establishing the world behind the text, asking the question "why" is to ask about the **purpose** for the writing. In earlier chapters we discussed the predominantly oral culture of the ancient world. Therefore, why did this author take on the arduous task of putting pen to paper (or quill to papyrus, as it were) in this context? All authors have agendas, reasons for writing. So what is the purpose behind the Fourth Evangelist's writing project in his Gospel and Letters? Answering this question while studying the Gospels is sometimes a difficult task for exegetes. Fortunately for us, the evangelist states his purpose in the conclusion of the body of the narrative (20:30–31). John says:

> Now Jesus did many other signs in the presence of his disciples, which are not written in this book. But these are written so that you may [come to] believe that Jesus is the Messiah, the Son of God, and that through believing you may have life in his name.

On first glance, this purpose is clear and simple enough. The evangelist wrote his Gospel so that audiences may believe that Jesus is the Christ. On closer analysis, however, we can glean more information, but also ask more questions. In the first verse (v. 30), for example, we find evidence for a claim that we made in the last chapter. The evangelist clarifies that he had much more information about Jesus and the things he did, but he chose from those traditions and shaped that material for his particular purpose in this telling. Like any author, this evangelist is not robotically restating data, but developing his source material to share his message, in this case the good news of the coming of the Christ. Further, in the second verse (v. 31), the evangelist shares his belief that Jesus is not only the promised Messiah, but also the Son of God. This falls in line with the "high" Christology that we discussed above. Jesus is the human Messiah who is also the divine Son of God. In addition, the evangelist also includes the consequence of believing his message for his audiences: that they "may have life in his name." Again, the evangelist teaches that this story has the power to change lives. The narrative up to this point has further taught us that this new life in the "name of" Christ is not bound by the reality of this world, and therefore is not bound by death. It is John's hope that all audiences can join in this eternal dwelling with God.

The issue that remains to be addressed is an important textual discrepancy in the early manuscripts of the Gospel. You will notice that the words "come to" in the quotation of 20:30–31 above are in square brackets. When a word or phrase is enclosed in square brackets in contemporary English translations of the Bible, this is an indication that there is a textual issue in the original Greek. The ancient manuscripts are so divided on which words or phrases are original that contemporary textual critics advocate leaving the terms in the English translations but using the square brackets to indicate the problem. Most study Bibles will also have a footnote explaining the issues at stake, thereby allowing readers to consider the options and make the final decisions for themselves.

In John 20:30–31, the issue surrounds the form of the verb "to believe." In Greek, the dictionary form of the verb "to believe" is *pisteuō*. Some ancient manuscripts of John 20:31 read *pisteusēte*, a form of the verb that grammarians call the aorist subjunctive. This word would be translated "you might come to believe." Other ancient manuscripts of John 20:31 read *pisteuēte*, a form of the verb that grammarians call the present subjunctive. This word would be translated "you might continue believing." What we are seeing is the difference of one Greek letter, sigma (pronounced like the English "s"), which changes not only the meaning of the verb but also the essence of the evangelist's purpose in writing the Gospel. Does he perceive his audience to be new to the good news and want them to come to believe? Or does he perceive his audience members to know the good news and consider them believers already, but members who need affirmation to continue in the faith?

This is a major exegetical question. It is certainly possible that John understood his task to be evangelical in the sense of sharing the good news with those who may not have heard it already. Given what we have established in the world behind the text thus far, however, it is also very likely that this evangelist wrote for a community who considered itself Christian, but was undergoing a severe crisis, including being alienated from the Judaism of their past. He wrote, therefore, to affirm their choices and further teach them about faith in this new world outside of traditional Judaism. A corollary to this primary purpose is connected to the location and cultural milieu of the community and their vision for the future. The Hellenistic world of the community and the Gospel it produced demanded a narrative that recast the Jewish story of Jesus in the language and style of the Greco-Roman world. The developing separation of Christianity from Judaism also necessitated a telling of the story that explained how the one who claimed to be the Jewish Messiah became known as Messiah to a wider group of Christians instead. Ultimately, as a foundational document, John's Gospel attempts both to adopt the traditions of Israel for the emerging faith and to reorient the movement away from the Jewish world of its past and toward the Hellenistic world of its future. This is why, as we will see in the coming chapters, the evangelist uses the language and metaphor of fulfillment throughout the text. In other words, the evangelist seems to understand his task to be to write about the continuation of God's work in creation through the new community founded on truth and belief in Jesus Christ, the Word of God.

Answering the Question of Sources

When establishing the world behind the text, when we ask the question "how," we are querying what **sources** the author used to compose his written works. In this case, how did John write his Gospel and Letters? From personal experience? Oral tradition? Written sources? Some combination of all these?

Scholars have argued about John's dependence upon the Synoptic Gospels throughout the history of Christianity. Some of the very early leaders of the church (especially St. Augustine) suggested that John provided his Gospel to "fill in" many of the details that Mark, Matthew, and Luke left out. This will not do. We can take for granted that as a gifted author and storyteller John molded and shaped the oral traditions that came to him, through his own experience and through the experience of his community, into a narrative whole. It is clear from a single reading of John that this Gospel is quite distinctive. Differences from the Synoptic Gospels include setting much of Jesus's public ministry in Jerusalem and Judea instead of Galilee, a significant absence of the "kingdom of God" motif, Jesus's teaching style in long discourses and dialogues instead of parables, and the presentation of Jesus's miraculous activity in seven distinctive signs, including three episodes unique to this Gospel. Yet there are also important similarities with the Synoptic Gospels especially at the beginning of Jesus's public ministry with John the Baptist, and in the concluding passion and empty tomb narratives.

Some argue for a direct source relationship with the Synoptics, particularly Luke, but no definitive reliance can be proven. Others argue for additional sources known only to John, most often a distinctive "signs source" that contains the seven or eight specific miracle stories found in the Gospel, and possibly an account of the passion and resurrection. Many contemporary scholars set this theory aside today, due to lack of clear evidence for an independent written tradition. At present, there is increasing agreement that John was certainly aware of the Synoptic Gospels, especially Mark and Luke. However, he does not use them as a source in the way that Matthew and Luke used Mark. John reflects creatively on traditions also found in the Synoptics, re-telling them in a way that reflects his own understanding of what God has done for humankind in and through Jesus Christ. In a French word that is easy to understand in English, scholars now talk of John's *réédition* (**reedition**) of passages from the Synoptic Gospels. Therefore, we can say that the independent traditions that came down through the Beloved Disciple had circulated long enough alongside the Synoptic traditions that the evangelist assumes basic knowledge of the events of Jesus's public ministry and life and arranges a few choice events for dramatic effect in the narrative to highlight the nature and mission of Jesus as Christ and Son of God.

Réédition in John 14 and 16

A careful reading of chapter 14 and chapter 16 shows that John 16 repeats, in different language, the same themes of John 14: the need for Jesus to depart, Jesus will not abandon the disciples, the gift of the Spirit-Paraclete will guide and teach them, the need for disciples to obey Jesus's commandments (love and believe), and the call not to fear but to pray and have courage. It is widely accepted that John 14 is the older form of Jesus's final discourse and that John 16 is a re-writing of it in more exalted language. This is a good example of what is meant by *réédition*.

What Have We Learned So Far? The World behind the Gospel and Letters of John

In this chapter, we have explored the immediate world behind the text of the Gospel and Letters of John. The historical context that we have established for this literature is built upon the larger history and theology of Judaism as well as the early Jesus movement of the first century CE that was developing into Christianity around the turn of that century. This means that our current topic, although crucial for exegesis and understanding the world in the texts, does not reveal a great deal of new information about the theology of the Johannine Literature. At the moment, therefore, we have nothing to add to our overall discussion of God, the world, or concepts of salvation. We can, however, say a bit more about Christology as well as the role of people and their church in this early Christian community.

Earlier in the chapter, we suggested that the Gospel's high Christology is an indication of its composition several decades into the Jesus movement and likely toward the end of the first century CE. We can say more about that here. As we discovered in the introduction, the study of Christology refers to how one understands the Christ (or Messiah, God's promised Anointed One). This includes the Christ's role in history as well as the nature of his being. In the last chapter, we discussed the basic Christian understanding of Jesus as the Christ, whose sacrificial death fulfilled God's promises of the covenants and put in place a new covenant. This is a reorientation of many Jewish messianic expectations away from a military ruler like King David. Although some Jewish messianic expectations did include the notion of a Prophet along the lines of Moses or Elijah, the Christian understanding was distinct from this belief as well. Early Christian theologians built on both of these concepts as well as their traditions about Jesus to build a Christology of Jesus as both fully human and fully divine. The titles that come to represent these two natures in the one person are Son of Man and Son of God.

In the Gospels, Jesus prefers to refer to himself and his mission in terms of being the Son of Man, while the evangelists and other characters in the stories sometimes identify him as the Son of God. More will be said about these titles in John in the coming chapters. For now, we can point out that, in discussing a particular biblical author's Christology (or that of any Christian, for that matter), when we see a focus on Christ's human nature, this can be identified as a "low Christology." And when we see a focus on Christ's divine nature, this can be identified as a "high Christology." In reality, most Christians fall somewhere in between these two ends of the spectrum, and indeed, we see various points on the continuum represented in the New Testament. Since a messiah who was both human and divine was unheard of in Jewish Scriptures, this belief took some time to develop in early Christianity. Therefore, scholars take the presence of a high Christology to be evidence that a text was composed later rather than earlier in the first century CE. Although John is careful to indicate that Jesus is fully human across his writings, and even in the opening verses of his Gospel (1:1–18), these same verses also establish a clear focus on the divine nature of Jesus as Christ and Son of God. This high Christology thereafter becomes a strong theme across the Gospel and Letters.

Other themes running through the literature (the world in the text) that seem to result from the world behind the text give us insight into John's anthropology and ecclesiology. John understands the human person in essentially the same manner presented in the Jewish Scriptures. Human beings stand in relation to God as unified wholes who cannot be separated into component parts and cannot be understood apart from their relationship with God. This has an important effect on the divisions and struggle that result from some believing in Jesus as the Messiah while others do not believe that he could be the Christ. We will see this more clearly as we explore the world in the text, but it does reflect a situation in which the community from which this Gospel developed and for which it was composed found itself separated from the Judaism of its past and struggling to reconcile this new reality while forging a way forward. This will have important implications for the ecclesiology, or understanding of church, that develops. We will see a focus on separateness from the rest of society, combined with a hope for equality, inclusion, and unity that is unique in the New Testament. It is to a broader study of the world in the text that we now turn.

Key Terms and Concepts

Aposynagōgos/"To Put Out of the
  Synagogue"
authorship
Beloved Disciple
date of composition
Dead Sea Scrolls
Ephesus
genre

high Christology
historical context
John the Son of Zebedee
location
Nag Hammadi Library
purpose
réédition
sources

Questions for Review

1. What do we mean by "historical context," and why is it important for responsible exegesis?

2. Who is the author of the Gospel of John? Why is this not a simple question? What does examining the answers provided by both the text and tradition add to our study?

3. How do questions of location, dating of the composition, and purpose overlap in the world behind the text? What are the best answers scholarship can provide to these questions with regard to the Johannine Literature?

4. What do scholars believe is the relationship between the Gospel of John and the Synoptic Gospels? Did the Fourth Evangelist use any of the other New Testament Gospels as a source? Are there other sources he might have used?

5. What does it mean to have a high or low Christology? Why is it best to speak of Christology on a continuum? What can we say so far in this regard about Johannine Christology?

Bibliography and Further Reading

Brown, Raymond E. *The Community of the Beloved Disciple: The Life, Loves, and Hates of an Individual Church in New Testament Times.* New York: Paulist, 1979.
———. *An Introduction to the Gospel of John.* Edited by Francis J. Moloney. Anchor Bible Reference Library. New York: Doubleday, 2003.
Martyn, J. Louis. *History and Theology in the Fourth Gospel.* 3rd ed. Louisville: Westminster John Knox, 2003.
Powell, Mark Allan. *Fortress Introduction to the Gospels.* 6th ed. Minneapolis: Fortress, 1998.

John as Storyteller and Evangelist

PURPOSE Chapter six introduces the world in the text in terms of the literary style of the evangelist and the storytelling techniques he uses to share his message of the good news through his particular voice. The chapter first explores the pervasive literary characteristics of the Gospel, then its recurring themes, and culminates in its plot and narrative structure.

ASSIGNMENT Read the Gospel of John, from beginning to end, in one sitting.

We have established the historical context of the Gospel and Letters of John in the world of first-century CE Judaism, but of course the roots of this literature can be traced back to the Jewish understanding of the very beginnings of God's creation of the world. These Jewish roots, together with Mediterranean culture and Greco-Roman civilization and rule, provide the historical and socio-political setting for Jesus and the Jewish movement in the first part of the century as well as John and his community in the latter part of the century. This broad world behind the text, however, also provides the language, symbolism, imagery, and geography for the world in the text. It is to this world that we now turn.

The World in the Text: The Literary Style of the Johannine Literature

Although we have been discussing the general worlds of all four texts of the Gospel and Letters of John, we must now turn our attention to the Gospel almost exclusively in order to prepare for the chapters that follow. We will return to the Letters in chapter sixteen. At that time, we will review the world behind those texts, including suggesting additional contextualization for them, then turn again to the world in those texts in terms of their outlines. This will allow for a deeper exploration of the world in front of 1, 2, and 3 John.

Like any writer, the Fourth Evangelist draws from the world he knows to make sense of his experience and share his message with others. Therefore, our task in this chapter is to uncover John's literary style and suggest what implications that style might have for exegesis. Although we will make some reference to history and the world behind the text, in this chapter we will primarily act as literary critics. Further, students will notice that the assignment above is to read the Gospel of John all the way through, from beginning to end. We suggest this task before reading further into the textbook because students now have the background necessary to begin to draw out some of the images and metaphors used by the author from his world and historical context. Students can then begin to put together a broad picture of the story and its intended meaning. We suggest an initial reading of the entire Gospel in an effort to respect the evangelist's decision to compose a narrative. Like any other story, this one has a plot, builds characters, and reaches toward a climax and resolution. When we read the Gospels in fragmented passages, as we tend to do if we attend church services where biblical texts are read, we cannot get the full sense of the story as it was composed and intended to be read. We must let John have his full voice and allow him to tell his story his way. This is the best way to grasp his overall literary style. We can reflect upon our experience and discuss the pervasive **literary characteristics** and overarching themes. We must also reflect upon the Gospel as a whole in terms of its overall flow and plotlines. This will allow us to sketch a broad outline of the Gospel's structure. Doing so will allow us to establish the literary context of each narrative unit as we proceed through a more detailed exegesis across the remainder of the textbook. To these tasks we now turn.

The Pervasive Literary Characteristics of the Gospel

In the following pages, we will draw out several of the most pervasive literary characteristics of the Johannine Literature. Although several of the motifs and techniques we discuss will be unique to the Fourth Gospel, a number of them will be apparent in the Letters as well. In addition, although we could focus broadly on characteristics found in the Gospels in general, that was the task of chapter four. Here we will draw out those features of the Fourth Evangelist's writing style that are particular to him. We are homing in on the evangelist's particular voice, which shares his perspective on Jesus Christ with audiences from the first through the twenty-first centuries. Exegeting the messages he composed through his distinctive style and characterization goes a long way toward hearing this ancient voice in our contemporary world. The following pages will discuss these literary characteristics in three categories: Symbolism and Other Storytelling Techniques, Jesus's Teaching Style, and Jesus's Opponents and Their Concerns. Each category will incorporate several characteristics.

Symbolism and Other Storytelling Techniques

Like any writer or teller of stories, John adopts images and figures of speech from the world around him and adapts them into his story world for particular effect. Symbolism and other storytelling techniques are crucial for affecting audiences and provoking desired responses in them. **Symbolism** is any use of symbolic language to represent larger ideas or qualities that are difficult to articulate in plain language. A symbol, of course, can be anything that represents or stands for something else. Material objects can be particularly useful symbols in storytelling in order to represent something abstract, like philosophical or theological ideas. Many people regard the use of the word "symbol" to mean that what is being represented by the symbol is not "real." The exact opposite can be the case! Authors (and we ourselves) regularly use symbols to express some of the most important things in our lives and in our experience. Language surrounding the human experience and expression of love is a very good example of this truth. By **storytelling techniques**, we are referring to any tools or practices storytellers utilize to engage, inspire, or otherwise connect with their audiences. In this category of literary characteristics, we will discuss the Beloved Disciple, examples from the variety of symbols the evangelist uses, as well as how he incorporates naïve misunderstanding and irony.

The Beloved Disciple

We begin with a discussion of **the Beloved Disciple** because this character is both unique to this Gospel and crucial to its plot and message. In the previous chapter, we discussed the Beloved Disciple in terms of the authorship of the Gospel and Letters of John. The narrative, although it is ultimately written anonymously, points to this figure in the Gospel as its author, whose eyewitness testimony serves as the story's foundation (see John 21:24–25). Nonetheless, this figure identified as "the disciple whom Jesus loved" can also be discussed as a mysterious and forceful storytelling technique that serves as a potent symbol for how Gospel audiences are called to respond to this narrative. Therefore, we can now review his role in the story in terms of a literary characteristic. In this vein the Beloved Disciple is both a symbol *and* a storytelling technique.

Before Jesus is arrested, during the last supper he shares with his disciples, as recounted in John 13, Jesus begins to teach them of his coming departure in order to prepare them for the new roles they will take once he is gone. This departure, Jesus shares, will be set in motion by a betrayal by one of his own disciples. In the wake of the confusion this revelation causes, Peter nods to the disciple closest to Jesus to find out what he means. This disciple, the narrator shares, is "the one whom Jesus loved" (13:23). This "beloved disciple" does as he is asked and begins to come to the forefront of the story as the disciple who is always closest to Jesus both physically and spiritually. In fact, readers can now

The Beloved Disciple

Peter turned and saw the disciple whom Jesus loved following them; he was the one who had reclined next to Jesus at the supper and had said, "Lord, who is it that is going to betray you?" When Peter saw him, he said to Jesus, "Lord, what about him?"

Jesus said to him, "If it is my will that he remain until I come, what is that to you? Follow me!" So the rumor spread in the community that this disciple would not die. Yet Jesus did not say to him that he would not die, but, "If it is my will that he remain until I come, what is that to you?" This is the disciple who is testifying to these things and has written them, and we know that his testimony is true. But there are also many other things that Jesus did; if every one of them were written down, I suppose that the world itself could not contain the books that would be written (21:20–25).

realize that one of the first two disciples who sought out Jesus at the urging of John the Baptist is identified as Andrew (1:40), but the other remained unnamed (1:35–42). This "other disciple" witnesses Jesus's arrest and is present in the courtyard of the high priest during Jesus's initial interrogation (18:15–16). Once Jesus is convicted of a capital crime and sentenced to crucifixion, "the disciple whom he loved" is there at the foot of the cross to witness his death and accept Jesus's mother into his home (19:25–27). This Beloved Disciple avows the truth of what he saw and the testimony he is sharing through this story (19:35). After the crucifixion, he is mentioned again along with Peter as the one whom Mary Magdalene alerted to the empty tomb. In that instance, he is identified as "the other disciple, the one whom Jesus loved" (20:2). Therefore, the "other disciple" and the "beloved disciple" are one and the same. Although he rarely speaks, this enigmatic, unnamed character is present at all the crucial events of the narrative and is the first to *see* and *believe* when he finds the clothes of death folded in the empty tomb (20:3–10). Further, he is the first to recognize Jesus at his final resurrection appearance, and his eventual fate receives special mention (21:1–23). The final verses of the Gospel claim the testimony of this anonymous character to be both the content of and the authority behind the Gospel (21:24–25).

This figure is so mysterious yet so powerful in the flow of the Gospel story that scholars have given him the title the Beloved Disciple (often BD, for short) in order to discuss his role and meaning. There are several reasons why an author might employ such a storytelling technique that carefully identifies and characterizes a key figure while just as carefully ensuring that he remains nameless. As a symbol, the Beloved Disciple is a human like anyone else who points to the ideal of living and walking in unity with Christ. He is the perfect disciple who believes through thick and thin and serves as a role model for all other

The Beloved Disciple.
Scenes from the Life
of St. John the Divine.

potential believers. His position near Jesus spiritually allows him to be loved by Jesus in some special manner. Readers can imagine that love for themselves as well. His often silent witness to Jesus is now recorded as Scripture for all to share. In the story, he often gives access to Jesus for other disciples, including Peter. Now as the eyewitness testimony behind the Gospels, he gives access to the good news to all.

As a storytelling technique, the evangelist can keep the spotlight on Jesus while affirming the veracity of the events through the eyewitness testimony of the Beloved Disciple. He can also keep his own identity disguised in the case of possible persecution. By keeping the Beloved Disciple nameless, the evangelist can also hope that audiences of the Gospel can identify with this ideal disciple more easily. There is a powerful indication of the author's desire for the readers to identify with the Beloved Disciple in John 20. Discovering the empty tomb, and Jesus's burial clothes, the Beloved Disciple "sees and believes" (see v. 8). But he does not see Jesus. Jesus's final words in the chapter are: "Blessed are those who do not see, yet believe" (v. 29). These words, directed to the audience, tell them that they are to be like the Beloved Disciple, who also did not see, yet believed. Any and all of these potential motives further allow for establishing the authority behind the Gospel's authorship.

Symbolism: Dualistic Imagery and Double Entendres

The next set of literary characteristics that we will discuss revolves around John's abundant use of symbolism in general. The evangelist uses many kinds of symbolism but is particularly notable for employing dualistic imagery and double entendres within individual words and larger metaphors.

Dualism refers to the conceptual division of something into two opposed or contrasting aspects. When we speak of **dualistic imagery**, then, we are referring to how an author uses opposite ideas or concepts to emphasize the contrasts inherent in the world or between this world and the divine. John makes the most extensive use of the effect rendered by opposing light and dark. Jesus is the light that shines in the darkness (1:1–18), and all who walk with him physically and spiritually walk in the light. This light gives the knowledge of salvation. By contrast, darkness pervades the world, and those who walk in the darkness remain in ignorance of the way of salvation. The evangelist also employs the dualistic imagery of life and death, above and below, as well as truth and lies. These opposite extremes appear across the narrative and powerfully evoke the images the evangelist is putting forth regarding the presence of both good and evil as well as the potential responses of right and wrong. In this way the evangelist

---

Dualistic Imagery

What has come into being in him was life, and the life was the light of all people. The light shines in the darkness, and the darkness did not overcome it (1:3b–5).

pushes audiences to make decisions about where they stand on the challenge and good news Jesus offers.

The term **double entendre** comes from an obsolete form of French and means "two meanings" in English. The expression refers to the phenomenon of using a word or phrase in such a way that it is open to two interpretations. Sometimes the speaker intends the word in one manner, while his or her dialogue partners take it in another. In this way an author can advance the plot or the conflict of the narrative. At other times the author might exploit the two potential meanings of a word or phrase such that both apply in different ways to the given situation. Although there are a number of these instances across the Gospel, here we give one example of each. In John 3:1–21, Jesus is approached by a Jewish man, a Pharisee named Nicodemus, at night who engages him in conversation. In this context, Jesus tells him of the necessity of "being born from *above*." The word translated here "above" is the Greek word *anōthen*, which can also mean "again." Nicodemus responds initially by asking how a grown man can be physically "born *again*." Jesus can then engage him further on the subject of spiritual renewal, being born from above.

Another example of a double entendre can be found in this same conversation. Here in 3:1–21, then again later in the Gospel, Jesus speaks of his coming crucifixion, but in a metaphorical manner that is confusing to those around him. To Nicodemus he says, "And just as Moses *lifted up* the serpent in the desert, so must the Son of Man *be lifted up*, so that everyone who believes in him may have eternal life" (3:14). The Greek word that is here translated "lifted up" is a form of the verb *hypsōthēnai*, which does indeed mean "to lift up" in the physical sense, as in lifting someone onto a cross, but it also means "to exalt" in the sense of honoring or glorifying someone. By using this particular term when Jesus talks enigmatically about his impending crucifixion, the evangelist can also symbolize the paradox that his death will also be his exaltation (see 8:28; 12:32). The evangelist can then teach that Jesus will glorify God and be glorified by God through his crucifixion, while also indicating why there is confusion around him among both his disciples and his opponents.

> **Double Entendres**
>
> Jesus answered him, "Very truly, I tell you, no one can see the kingdom of God without being born from above."
>
> Nicodemus said to him, "How can anyone be born after having grown old? Can one enter a second time into the mother's womb and be born?" (3:3–4).

*Storytelling Techniques: Literary Inclusions,
Naïve Misunderstanding, and Irony*

Finally, we will also highlight three of John's pervasive storytelling techniques that come together to make his literary style quite distinctive. These techniques can be identified as literary inclusions, naïve misunderstanding, and irony.

A **literary inclusion** is a storytelling device that is also often known by its Latin origin, the *inclusio*. Storytellers create inclusions by framing a particular section of the narrative with similar material, sometimes identical words or phrases and other times comparable episodes and events. By using these framing devices, storytellers can introduce and conclude a narrative unit and indicate that everything in between should be read with a particular theme in mind. In chapter two we spoke of the narrative and discourse levels of texts. Framing devices serve to bookend a section of the text such that everything on the narrative level of this section carries a primary discourse teaching. The repetition involved in literary inclusions is an effective way to mark off the narrative unit, summarize the discourse, and remind the audience of the messages being taught. John uses inclusions to great effect. We will discuss these in greater detail as we come upon them in the chapters to come, but we can introduce two instances here: John 2–4 and John 18–19.

John 2–4 is a clear example of an inclusion because John introduces and concludes this narrative unit by narrating Jesus performing signs in Cana, a town in Galilee: turning water into wine at the wedding feast (2:1–12) and healing the royal official's child (4:45–54). The narrator goes so far as to remind readers of the first episode twice in the latter episode in order to clearly mark the inclusion. Within these two signs, Jesus and his disciples journey from Galilee through Judea then back up through Samaria before returning to Galilee, while Jesus teaches all those he encounters about the true meaning of believing in him as the Messiah. We can identify the discourse teaching of this inclusion as an educational journey wherein authentic faith is belief in the word of Jesus.

John 18–19 narrates the passion narrative of the Gospel of John in that it tells the story of Jesus's arrest, Jewish interrogation, Roman trial, crucifixion, and burial. The evangelist narrates the passion narrative as a literary inclusion by clearly identifying the location of Jesus's arrest by his enemies as a garden where Jesus had often met with his disciples (18:1–2), and then identifying the place of Jesus's burial as garden with a new tomb into which his friends lay him (19:41–42). The opening and closing sentences of this crucial narrative unit thus mark the location as a garden. Garden imagery is very important in Judaism and echoes both God's activity of creation and the site where humankind dwelt in perfect relationship with God (Gen 1–3). The Gospel has indicated that faith allows believers to become children of God and Jesus's death will unite the

---

Literary Inclusions

On the third day there was a wedding in Cana of Galilee, and the mother of Jesus was there (2:1).

Jesus did this, the first of his signs, in Cana of Galilee, and revealed his glory; and his disciples believed in him (2:11).

Then he came again to Cana in Galilee where he had changed the water into wine. Now there was a royal official whose son lay ill in Capernaum (4:46).

Now this was the second sign that Jesus did after coming from Judea to Galilee (4:54).

dispersed children of God (1:12; 11:45–54), thereby establishing the possibility of a new relationship with God. Further, Jesus has taught that in his death he will glorify God and in turn be glorified by God (12:23–28; 13:31–33; 17:1–5). Therefore, we can identify the discourse teaching of this inclusion as: the death of Jesus, both tragic and sacrificial, reveals the glory of God and the creation of a new relationship in union with God.

John also uses **naïve misunderstanding** on the part of minor characters throughout the narrative in order to allow Jesus to teach about himself and the good news in more depth. As we will discuss in more detail in the following section, Jesus's teaching style is difficult for people to follow. He often speaks in metaphors and uses heavy philosophical language. This can be very confusing for both Jesus's opponents and his disciples. On a number of occasions in the Gospel, Jesus teaches in a very figurative manner, and his dialogue partner or partners take his words literally and ask how what he is suggesting can be. This storytelling technique offers a bit of comic relief in the story, but the person's naïve questioning also allows Jesus to teach the lesson at hand in more detail and possibly bring the person to a new, more spiritual, understanding of Christ.

A prime example of this technique is found in John 3:1–21, the dialogue between Jesus and Nicodemus that we discussed above with John's use of *double entendres*. In fact, John's use of *double entendre* is often associated with naïve misunderstanding. Whenever two or more meanings are possible, a character (or characters) choose the wrong, more literal, option. In the case of Nicodemus, whereas Jesus is using the word *anōthen* in the more figurative sense of "above," Nicodemus takes it in the more literal sense of "again," thus resulting in Nicodemus's question regarding the possibility of physically being born a second time. This allows Jesus to correct him and teach in more detail about God's love and being born of the Spirit, eventually culminating in one of Jesus's most famous teachings of the Gospel: John 3:16–17.

> ### Naïve Misunderstanding
>
> Jesus answered, "Very truly, I tell you, no one can enter the kingdom of God without being born of water and Spirit. What is born of the flesh is flesh, and what is born of the Spirit is spirit" (3:5–6).
>
> "For God so loved the world that he gave his only Son, so that everyone who believes in him may not perish but may have eternal life. Indeed, God did not send the Son into the world to condemn the world, but in order that the world might be saved through him" (3:16–17).

It takes Nicodemus the bulk of the dialogue to come around to Jesus's symbolic manner and the deeper meaning of who Jesus is, but his questioning of his Jewish counterparts' methods in 7:50–52 and his participation in Jesus's burial in 19:38–42 indicate that he ultimately believes. Some of Jesus's dialogue partners, however, do not recognize Jesus's symbolic manner of speaking and are never elevated to a more spiritual relationship with him. This, the evangelist seems to indicate, is what leads to Jesus's eventual arrest. The initial instance of this lack of understanding is found at John 2:13–22 when Jesus, dismayed at the commercialism he finds on the temple grounds, drives out the vendors and money changers. The shocked Jews there demand a justification for his actions. Jesus replies by telling them that if this temple is destroyed, he will raise it again in three days. Those questioning him take Jesus's statement as a reference to the literal temple, while the narrator explains that Jesus is referring to the temple of his body. The disciples eventually sort out this distinction, but the others present do not. We will note other examples of this clever storytelling technique, which draws in the audience even as it explains plot developments, as we exegete the Gospel in the coming chapters.

Irony is a common storytelling technique that uses words to convey a meaning far beyond, and sometimes in opposition to, their literal meaning by exploiting at least two potential ways of understanding these words or events. In literature, direct speech and narrative episodes can be reported factually and taken at their face value by other characters in the story; but readers and listeners are also made aware that the real meaning of these reported words and events is in some kind of opposition to what is said or done. Literary critics note various forms of irony, but the most common occurrences are verbal irony and dramatic irony.

In verbal irony, characters *say things* that at their face value have one meaning, but in reality convey a deeper truth that is the opposite to the meaning intended by the speakers. An example of verbal irony, which is so key to the Gospel of John that the narrator identifies it so that audiences do not miss it, occurs after Jesus raises Lazarus from death and the Sanhedrin convenes to decide what to do about him (11:45–54). The high priest Caiaphas indicates that it will be better for one person (Jesus) to die so that the whole nation may not perish. The narrator indicates that although he meant this on the literal level—if they get rid of Jesus, then the people will cease being riled up, and the Romans will not attack—his statement indicates a truth beyond Caiaphas's own understanding. Jesus's death will have far-reaching effects that will unite God's children and save many from the bonds of death.

Dramatic irony occurs when *certain events*—for example, Jesus's entry into Jerusalem (12:12–19)—appear to have an obvious meaning, but in reality they point the audience elsewhere. In that episode, the people may appear to be welcoming the Messiah, but Jesus's entry into Jerusalem was preceded by Mary of Bethany anointing Jesus's feet and Jesus's indication that they will

> ### Naïve Misunderstanding
>
> The Jews then said to him, "What sign can you show us for doing this?"
>
> Jesus answered them, "Destroy this temple, and in three days I will raise it up."
>
> The Jews then said, "This temple has been under construction for forty-six years, and will you raise it up in three days?" But he was speaking of the temple of his body. After he was raised from the dead, his disciples remembered that he had said this; and they believed the Scripture and the word that Jesus had spoken (2:18–22).

not always have him (12:1–8). Jesus's "triumphal" entry into Jerusalem also signifies the coming end of his own life. He will be the Messiah, but not in a way that matches the acclamation of Jesus as the long-awaited Son of David,

political king, and military leader. Rather, it is Jesus's death that will glorify God and mark his messiahship.

John further weaves both verbal and dramatic irony throughout his account of the passion and death of Jesus, making the tragic and cruel *words* and *events* that mark the end of the life of Jesus a *proclamation* of the fulfillment of God's design. On the one hand, Jesus is being violently executed, but for John he is bringing to perfection the task given to him by the Father, thus glorifying God and returning to the glory that was his before the foundation of the world (see 11:4; 17:4–5). Irony is thus a literary strategy used by the evangelist to guide readers and listeners into and around the world of the story of the life, passion, and death of Jesus, and thus into an awareness of its inner significance.

Irony

"If we let him go on like this, everyone will believe in him, and the Romans will come and destroy both our holy place and our nation."

But one of them, Caiaphas, who was high priest that year, said to them, "You know nothing at all! You do not understand that it is better for you to have one man die for the people than to have the whole nation destroyed." He did not say this on his own, but being high priest that year he prophesied that Jesus was about to die for the nation, and not for the nation only, but to gather into one the dispersed children of God (11:48–52).

Jesus's Teaching Style

The manner in which Jesus teaches in the Gospel of John is quite distinctive. Although many Christians and non-Christians alike know Jesus to be a miracle worker and the Synoptic Gospels are replete with Jesus's miraculous activity, the Gospel of John narrates only seven such actions and always refers to them as "signs." Likewise, whereas in the Synoptic Gospels Jesus teaches primarily by telling parables (brief stories that teach lessons relevant to the given context), in the Fourth Gospel Jesus engages in extended dialogues with other characters, often leading to passionate monologues. Although he makes use of metaphors (even extended ones), figures of speech, and other storytelling components, Jesus never uses a parable to teach in the Gospel of John. In addition, the content of Jesus's teaching focuses not on the kingdom of God as it does in Matthew, Mark, and Luke, but rather on himself as the Son who is at one with God the Father. In this effort, he uses important "I AM statements" to punctuate his identity and mission. As we will see, some of the "I AM statements" play a role in the Gospel of John that is similar to the role of the parables in the Synoptic Gospels. We will discuss these three aspects of Jesus's characteristic teaching style in the Gospel of John in more detail.

Signs

Again, in the Gospel, the evangelist always refers to Jesus's miracles as **signs**. Jesus and the people he encounters also use this term. In the Synoptic Gospels, Jesus performs many miracles and is particularly known for his power over the elements and miracle-working activity. However, this activity is typically described only in terms of its particular focus: a healing, an exorcism, a feeding, etc.; and not identified as a group. The Gospel of John is markedly different. Only seven of Jesus's miracles are narrated, and the story surrounding them—especially their consequences for Jesus and those involved—is often given in great detail. The choice of these signs seems to be careful and purposeful on the part of the evangelist. In biblical texts, the number seven is often symbolic of perfection. Seven, therefore, is the number of completion, the full count.

In addition, the signs John chooses to narrate seem to be carefully chosen to represent the full variety of Jesus's miraculous activity.

As we noted in our discussion of John 2–4 above, John also designates the first two miracles as "signs" and refers to Jesus's signs often across the Gospel (2:11; 4:54; 6:2, 14; 12:18, 37; 20:30). Jesus and those he encounters also often refer to his miraculous power in terms of "signs" (2:18; 3:2; 4:48; 6:26, 30; 9:16; 10:41; 11:47). Therefore, the evangelist is using this term for particular effect, and interpreters must ask why.

In general parlance, a "sign" is an object, event, or quality, the presence of which points to the existence or occurrence of something else. Signs are not ends in themselves, rather their purpose is to point to something else. Further, in the Old Testament, the phrase "signs and wonders" is often used to refer to the miraculous activity a person performs through the power of God. Moses, in particular, performed "signs and wonders" to *signify* the *wondrous* power of God throughout the Exodus and the covenant making activity in the Sinai wilderness. In the Gospel of John, therefore, the evangelist uses this particular term to teach that Jesus performs signs to point beyond himself to God as his Father as well as to draw people in so that he can teach more about himself as the Son. The signs are never the point of the narrative; it is the teaching that results from them that is always the goal. We will discuss this important feature of Jesus's teaching style in more detail in the coming chapters.

Seven Signs

1. 2:1–12   The wedding feast in Cana

2. 4:45–54   The healing of the royal official's child

3. 5:1–14   The healing of the crippled man

4. 6:1–15   The feeding of the multitude

5. 6:16–21   The walking on the water

6. 9:1–12   The healing of the man born blind

7. 11:1–44   The raising of Lazarus

The Feeding of the Five Thousand; Jesus Walking on the Water (1386)

Dialogues and "I AM" Statements

In John's Gospel, the content and style of Jesus's teaching are also unique. He regularly participates in extended dialogues with those he encounters, which often become ardent monologues and include the introductory formula "Amen, amen, I say to you" to mark key teachings (translated, "Very truly I say to you" in the NRSV). A **dialogue** is any verbal interaction between two or more people. Therefore, dialogues can be calm, amiable conversations between friends, tense, even hostile debates and arguments, or anywhere in between these two ends of the spectrum. Jesus's dialogical encounters with disciples, family, strangers, and opponents begin early in the narrative and span his entire ministry. They are as brief as a few lines or far more extensive. In these exchanges, Jesus is often the instigator and can even be very provocative. He pushes those he encounters out of their comfort zones and challenges them to be open to God working in their midst through him. Some people, like the Beloved Disciple or Jesus's mother in Cana, accept his role immediately; others, like his opponents among "the Jews," are closed to Jesus's challenge; while still others, like Nicodemus, take some time to rise to the challenge. Regardless, whether Jesus is approaching a Samaritan woman at a well (4:1–26), or facing the Roman governor Pontius Pilate on trial for his life (18:28–19:16a), he is always open to dialogue and intent on sharing the truth of who he is.

In these dialogues, Jesus uses a number of key **"I AM" statements** that are unique to the Fourth Gospel and become the hallmark of his teaching. Jesus uses these to identify himself with the name of God. As we introduced in chapter three on the Old Testament Story, in the book of Exodus, when God is calling Moses to his new role as prophet and leader of the Israelites, Moses needs to know, among other things, the name of God.

God, therefore, reveals his name as some form of the verb "to be." This particular form of the verb is difficult to translate into English and is often written simply as the equivalent of the Hebrew root: YHWH. The idea is that God is the essence of being, and so it is often rendered, "I AM." The Greek translation of "I am" is *egō eimi*. This is the phrase used in the LXX (based on Exodus 3) for the Hebrew name of God and also what we see in the Greek of John's Gospel when Jesus says, "I am." This phrase can also be translated, "I am he," or "It is I," depending on the context.

Across his ministry, Jesus uses two different types of "I AM" statements. In the first, Jesus claims "I AM" and follows with a metaphorical predicate. These statements, for which the Gospel of John is famous, allow Jesus to give himself a title that both is consonant with the current context of the dialogue and

---

Exodus 3:11–14

But Moses said to God, "Who am I, that I should go to Pharaoh and bring the Israelites out of Egypt?" And God said, "I will be with you. And this will be the sign to you that it is I who have sent you: When you have brought the people out of Egypt, you will worship God on this mountain."

Moses said to God, "Suppose I go to the Israelites and say to them, 'The God of your fathers has sent me to you,' and they ask me, 'What is his name?' Then what shall I tell them?" God said to Moses, "I AM WHO I AM. This is what you are to say to the Israelites: 'I AM has sent me to you.'"

Christ (St. Catherine's
Monastery, Mount Sinai,
Egypt)   © carulmare

allows him to point symbolically to his divinity and oneness with God. We can call these "predicated I AM statements." There are seven instances of these statements across the narrative.

Notice that these "I AM" sayings with a predicate always associate Jesus with something that the audience can experience: bread, light, gates, shepherds, life, way, vine. As the parables in the Synoptic tradition enable Jesus to tell of the presence of the kingdom of God by using the experience of the audience, so in John, Jesus reveals himself as the presence of the divine, also by using words that the audience understands. But Jesus takes their meaning to the edge of what audiences can accept. In the second type of statement, Jesus either just says "I AM" or uses the phrase as such in a larger sentence. We can call these "unpredicated I AM statements." There are also seven instances across the Gospel where Jesus speaks this way:

> ### I AM Statements
>
> 1. 6:35, 48, 51 I am the Bread of Life.
> 2. 8:12; 9:5 I am the Light of the World.
> 3. 10:7, 9 I am the Gate, you are the sheep.
> 4. 10:11, 14 I am the Good Shepherd.
> 5. 11:25 I am the Resurrection and the Life.
> 6. 14:6 I am the Way, the Truth, and the Life.
> 7. 15:1, 5 I am the Vine, you are the branches.

1. 4:25–26: The woman said, "I know that the Messiah is coming, the one called the Anointed; when he comes, he will tell us everything." Then Jesus declared, "**I am he**, the one who is speaking with you."

2. 6:19–20: When they had rowed three or four miles, they saw Jesus approaching the boat, walking on the water; and they began to be afraid. But he said to them, "**It is I**. Do not be afraid."

3. 8:24: "That is why I told you that you will die in your sins. For if you do not believe that **I AM**, you will die in your sins."

4. 8:28: So Jesus said to them, "When you lift up the Son of Man, then you will realize that **I AM**, and that I do nothing on my own, but I say only what the Father taught me."

5. 8:58–59: Jesus said to them, "Amen, amen, I say to you, before Abraham came to be, **I AM**." So they picked up stones to throw at him; but Jesus hid and went out of the temple area.

6. 13:19–20: "From now on I am telling you before it happens, so that when it happens you may believe that **I AM**. Amen, amen, I say to you, whoever receives the one I send receives me, and whoever receives me receives the one who sent me."

7. 18:4–8: Jesus, knowing everything that was going to happen to him, went out and said to them, "Whom are you seeking?" They answered him, "Jesus the Nazorean." He said to them, "**I AM**." Judas his betrayer was also with them. When he said to them, "**I AM**," they turned away and fell to

the ground. So he again asked them, "Whom are you seeking?" They said, "Jesus the Nazorean." Jesus answered, "I told you that **I am**. So if you are looking for me, let these men go."

Jesus uses this phrase repeatedly to identify himself with God and express the continuity of his teaching with that of God. Those who hear him speak this way are hearing him use the name of God for himself. In Judaism, the name of God is so sacred to the people that they do not speak it aloud out of reverence. Further, when humans identify themselves with God, this is considered blasphemy; and Jewish law dictates the punishment for blasphemy to be death by stoning. This is why, on several occasions, the crowds are moved to "pick up stones" against Jesus. Either one believes Jesus when he teaches that he is the divine Son of God the Father, or one believes he is committing blasphemy and should be condemned. Both the content and style of Jesus's teaching are so provocative that those he encounters are pushed, often beyond what they thought themselves capable, to make decisions about him that could render life or death.

Jesus's Opponents and Their Concerns

The final literary characteristic that we will explore in order to facilitate our exegesis of the Johannine Literature is the manner in which the opponents of Jesus and his mission emerge over the course of the narrative and how the evangelist characterizes them and their concerns. Although several characters or character groups are identified as wary of Jesus, opposing his ministry, or instrumental in his death, by and large John characterizes these antagonists as **"the Jews."** This has led to various misuses and abuses of the narrative throughout history. That said, Jesus and his disciples are also clearly characterized as ethnically and religiously Jewish. Further, many Jews support Jesus and his ministry, and Jesus articulates that "salvation is from the Jews" (4:22). Therefore, we cannot overstate how carefully we must proceed in our analysis of the identity and intention of this character group and their role as Jesus's sometime opponents in this narrative.

We tend to refer to the expression "the Jews" in quotation marks, as it does not refer to the Jewish people in general. As we indicated in chapter five, John and his community also seem to understand themselves as Jews. Rather, "the Jews"

Anti-Semitic Abuses of the Gospel of John

Because of its manner of identifying the opponents to Jesus's mission as "the Jews," the Gospel of John has long been a favorite tool of those Christians with anti-Semitic intentions. From Nazi passion plays to misguided homilies, the Gospel has been abused through the centuries. It is the modern exegete's duty to explain the complex and nuanced terminology of the evangelist, who was living and writing in a tense historical situation.

is a multifaceted term often used by the evangelist to encompass those who are opposed to Jesus and his disciples regarding the christological debate. The use of this term, instead of the more common "scribes and Pharisees" of the Synoptic Gospels, is likely a reflection of the further development of post-70 rabbinic Judaism, which itself was more communal and less sectarian and hierarchical. Historically, therefore, the opponents of the Johannine Christians were doubtless ethnic Jews fiercely committed to the religion of Israel and locked in bitter opposition to the emerging Christian community. By the end of the first century CE, mainstream Judaism is not accepting the new community's belief that the messiah has come in the person of Jesus of Nazareth. As Christian belief in the divinity of Jesus Christ (what we have called a high Christology) developed, this opposition developed into conflict and eventually became a factor in the split between Judaism and Christianity into separate religions. This struggle in the historical context of John and his community is reflected in the conflict that emerges between Jesus and "the Jews" in the Gospel.

In the story, initial hints that all is not well with "the Jews" in John 1–2 develop into public conflict in John 5, when a decision is made that Jesus must be killed. Thereafter "the Jews" are largely presented as hostile to both Jesus and his teaching about himself (see especially John 8) as well as those who profess him as the Christ (see John 9). Eventually they become the arbiters of his execution (11:45–57; 18:1–27). Even after his death, Jesus's disciples remain hidden for a time "for fear of the Jews" (20:19). That said, all "the Jews" do not turn against Jesus and his disciples. Over the course of the story, many of "the Jews" continue to come to believe that Jesus is the Christ right alongside his disciples (8:31; 10:19–21; 11:45; 12:11; 19:38–42). Therefore, Jewish people as such are not represented by the term "the Jews," and the Fourth Gospel must not be read as if they were. It bears repeating that, when reading the Gospel of John, we must recall that Jesus, his mother, his disciples, Nicodemus, John the Baptist, Lazarus, Martha, Mary, Mary Magdalene, Joseph of Arimathea, and most other characters are ethnically "Jews." The expression, although rooted in the breakdown between the synagogue and the Johannine believers, is not about a nation, but about belief and non-belief. It is important to note here that for John there is only one sin, encountering Jesus and his good news and not believing. The word "sin," the Greek term *hamartōlos*, is always

---

Papal Apology to the Jewish People for the Church's Role in the Holocaust

Pope John Paul II was born Karol Wojtyla on May 18, 1920, in Poland. Growing up he had Jewish friends and neighbors and witnessed the Holocaust first-hand. Once he became Pope in 1978, he devoted himself to condemning anti-Semitism and improving Jewish-Christian relations, calling for mutual understanding and respect. In 1994, he established full diplomatic ties between the Vatican and Israel and was instrumental in the 1998 document "We Remember: A Reflection on the Shoah," which expressed deep sorrow for the failures of the church. In 2000, he visited Israel and publicly apologized for the persecution of Jews by Catholics over the centuries. John Paul II died on April 2, 2005.

singular in this Gospel save for one anomaly. The majority of those called "the Jews," who become the antagonists of the narrative, fall under this sin, and it is this state of walking in darkness instead of light that determines their status as opponents—not their ethnicity.

The Recurring Themes of the Gospel

In addition to literary features that are characteristic of either John's storytelling style or the message he is sharing in these texts, there are a number of **literary themes** that are woven throughout the literature. A theme is an idea, message, or underlying meaning of a work that is sometimes stated directly, but is more often found indirectly in the expressions of the narrator or characters in the work. In the Johannine Literature, these themes are largely theological in orientation. We will discuss four of the most pervasive theological themes: the christological notions of Jesus as both fully God and fully human and Jesus as the true revelation of God, as well as the summons to the community to believe in the word of Jesus and love one another by abiding in Christ.

Jesus as Fully God and Fully Human

The opening verses of the Gospel state that the Word of God is of the same substance as God and became human for a time in the person of Jesus Christ to live among God's creation (1:1–18). This "both/and" understanding of the nature of Jesus permeates the entire story. There are moments in the story when Jesus's human nature comes to the fore, even though in many of these episodes the double entendre that we mentioned earlier is in evidence. For example, Jesus responds to his mother, and cares for the marriage couple who have run out of wine in 2:1–11. He turns to a Samaritan woman in the middle of a hot day, after walking all morning, and asks for water (4:7). He loves Lazarus, Mary, and Martha of Bethany and weeps over their loss. Above all, like all other human beings, he suffers death (19:30). But then there are remarkable claims that Jesus makes, showing his oneness with God. When he cares for the wedding couple, he miraculously changes water to wine. Jesus asking for water from the Samaritan woman culminates in his revelation as the Messiah and the villagers' proclamation that Jesus is the savior of the world. The loss of Lazarus culminates in the climactic sign of Jesus's public ministry. Further, in addition to the claim of the author that before all time the *logos* was one with God, and what God was, the Word also was (1:1–2), he tells "the Jews": "Before Abraham was, I AM" (8:58). Later he goes on to tell them: "I and the Father are one" (10:30), and "the Father is in me, and I am in the Father" (10:38). One of the challenges of this Gospel is its attempt to hold both the human and the divine together in this story of Jesus of Nazareth.

Jesus as the True Revelation of God

The opening verses of the Gospel also indicate that Jesus, in his human form, "makes God known" to the rest of humankind (1:17–18). This theme of revelation and Jesus as the true revelation of God continues to weave through the narrative until its conclusion. This theme is one of the major elements in John's message. As we have seen, his "signs" make God known, as they are more than just "miracles." They reveal the action of God. Given

Jesus, as Pantocrator (The Church of the Holy Savior)
© Guillaume Piolle

the fact that he is called the "*logos*" of God, which means the "Word" of God, he regularly speaks with authority about God, and what God plans for those who believe in him, and indeed, for the whole world. This is especially true of his long discourses, as they are found, for example, in John 6:25–51; 7:1–8:58; and 13:1–17:26. Jesus, the Word of God, makes God known through his word. In a special way in the Gospel of John, Jesus tells of a God who so loved the world that he gave his only son (see 3:16–17). This points to the fact that Jesus loves until death, and John's story of the crucifixion of Jesus is not only about the death of Jesus, but about the revelation of God's love for the world.

Jesus's Commandment to Believe in the Word

The opening verses of the Gospel further share that Jesus gives power to those who receive and believe in him to become children of God (1:11–13). Believing thus becomes the fundamental commandment by which Jesus calls people to live. Jesus then goes on to teach, however, that this believing must not be based on signs alone, but must be founded in the word of Jesus—both his being as the Word of God and the words of his teaching. Further, "belief" as a noun (*pistis*) does not occur in the Gospel, but forms of the verb "to believe" (*pisteuō/pisteuomai*) occur regularly and often (ninety-eight times). Thus, faith in the Gospel of John is always an action and is rightly described in terms of a process, or better, a journey. Jesus facilitates these journeys of believing in those he encounters across his ministry. Two important places in the story can be used as good examples of this theme. At the beginning of the Gospel, in a passage that we have seen is located between the "inclusion" of the two miracle stories at Cana (2:1–12 and 4:46–54), we see examples of a number of people responding to Jesus. Some believe in the word of Jesus (the mother of Jesus, John the Baptist, the Samaritans, the royal official), others want Jesus to respond to their expectations (Nicodemus, the Samaritan woman), while others will not listen to him ("the Jews," the Samaritan woman [initially]). At the end of the Gospel, in the story of Jesus's resurrection (John 20:1–29), the same journey of faith is made by Mary Magdalene, the Beloved Disciple, the Disciples as a group, and Thomas. That chapter ends as John tells his audience that this Gospel was written so that they may *go on believing* (vv. 30–31). This also becomes the summons to all who read the Gospel across the ages: to believe in the word of Jesus, Christ and Son of God, through John's story in the Gospel.

Jesus's Commandment to Love One Another and Abide in Christ

Jesus emphasizes love for one another as the great new commandment and the distinctive mark of his followers in symbolic terms of a covenantal relationship of truth. This becomes the second fundamental commandment by which Jesus calls people to live. There are many places across the Gospel where this theme is developed. It is especially important for Jesus's final evening with his disciples. It is at a meal with them that, after washing their feet as a servant, he asks them to follow his example (13:15). He then goes on to ask them to love one another as he has loved them (13:34–35). At the center of the account of this final evening, he urges the disciples to "abide" in him, so that he might "abide" in them. In this way they will bear much fruit (15:1–11). He again commands them to love one another, as he has loved them (15:12, 17), and reminds them that he has chosen them; they did not choose him. A God who loves (3:16) sends a Son who makes that love known, so that disciples will love one another, following the example that he has given them. As we will see, John often uses the verb "to remain/to abide" (Greek: *menein*) to speak of the mutuality of loving and being loved. This expression is especially important across Jesus's last discourse with his disciples, before his passion.

The Narrative Flow of the Gospel of John

In our study of the world in the text of the Gospel of John, we have developed the general literary characteristics and themes of the narrative. Our task now is to conclude our overview of the world in the text of the Gospel and thereby set the stage for more detailed exegesis of this world even as we begin to explore the world in front of the text. The pervasive characteristics of the evangelist's literary style coupled with the underlying themes he weaves through his writing provide the substance from which he shapes his narrative to tell the story he believes his audiences need to hear. This shaping results in an overarching outline and narrative flow to his plot and message. Closer examination of the Gospel of John, therefore, entails an initial exploration of its basic structure.

The term **structure** refers to a composition and its parts and the organization of something. In literature, the structure of a text is the organization of its parts composed as a whole. Interpreters study the final composition of a biblical author and try to glean what the original outline would have been if the author had written one. Because we do this after the fact and we cannot ask the author about his structuring techniques, we can never be certain about this process. Nonetheless, this is done in order to get a big picture of the author's flow of thought in writing, which in turn aids in exegeting, or drawing out, his intention in writing. As we introduced in chapter two, where we discussed the process of exegeting biblical texts, by establishing a broad outline of the narrative, we are respecting the fact that the author chose to write a story as opposed to a letter, a sermon, or any other genre of literature. Stories unfold in certain manners, and knowing where we are in the story helps us exegete any particular passage. Thereafter, we will explore and exegete the text along this structure. In this way we can make sense of what happens when. This is called establishing **literary context**. This does mean, however, that responsible biblical scholars can devise different structures to given passages that do not agree with each other. These varying structures can sometimes affect interpretations, but exegetes must simply do the best they can and work in dialogue with one another and the larger tradition.

It may be helpful, therefore, to discuss structures in terms of guides or roadmaps for entering the narrative world of the Fourth Gospel. In order to arrive at this roadmap that will guide us through our exegesis, we look for textual markers that serve as signposts along the way. The prologue (1:1–18) provides the clear words of an insider—the narrator who communicates to the audience everything he believes they need to know to begin the Gospel. John 1:19 starts the story itself, yet at John 13 something different happens. The audience is provided with what can be regarded as almost a new prologue at 13:1. It opens the period of private ministry and departure that flows through to 20:29, with the final verses (20:30–31) serving as a conclusion to the body of the Gospel—a first ending. Then we read John 21, an epilogue to this story that looks to the future of the community formed by the narrative. In John 1:1–20:31, therefore, the evangelist writes a powerful and cohesive narrative to show audiences that Jesus is the Messiah and Son of God and how a community of believers can find life in his name. In John 21 the evangelist provides a continuation of the community and an indication for how it is to go on in an ever-changing and challenging world. The epilogue provides a basis for leadership and the church that is not addressed in chapters 1–20. Consequently, a common approach to structuring the Gospel according to John is to note four fundamental components: a prologue (1:1–18) is followed by the body of the Gospel, which is presented in two sections: the public ministry of Jesus, commonly referred to as the Book of Signs (1:19–12:50), and the departure of Jesus, which includes a last discourse, the passion narrative, and post-resurrection appearances, commonly referred to as the Book of Glory (13:1–20:31). The conclusion to the body of the Gospel is then followed by an epilogue (21:1–25). Each of these larger narrative units can then be further detailed along the same lines.

The structure of the Gospel of John that will provide the roadmap for exploring its narrative world and exegeting its meaning for this textbook can be diagrammed as follows:

1:1–18 **The Prologue**
— Introduction to the Nature and Mission of the Word

1:19–12:50 **The Book of Signs**
— The Word Reveals Himself to the World and His Own through a Public Ministry

    1:19–51   The Opening Days of the Revelation of Jesus
— The Calling of the First Disciples

    2:1–4:54   From Cana to Cana—Jesus's Instruction on Faith
— The Educational Journey of Belief in the Word

    5:1–10:42   Jesus and the Jewish Festivals
— The Perfection of the Old Testament Traditions of Worship

    11:1–12:50   Jesus Moves toward the Hour of Death and Glory
— The Arrival of the Hour of Jesus

13:1–20:31 **The Book of Glory**
— The Word Makes God Known and Is Glorified in Death and Resurrection

    13:1–17:26 Jesus's Last Discourse
— The Foot Washing, Betrayal, and Jesus's Final Teaching to His Disciples

    18:1–19:42 Jesus's Passion
— The Arrest, Trial, Crucifixion, Death and Burial of Jesus

    20:1–31   Jesus's Resurrection
— The Empty Tomb and Jesus's Appearances to His Disciples

21:1–25 **The Epilogue**
— Conclusion of the Mission of the Word That Leads the Community into the Future

From this point forward, we will explore and exegete the Gospel text along this structure. Beginning with the next chapter, we will exegete a narrative unit established in this overall flow. Once we develop and discuss the literary context of the given narrative unit, we will then structure it in further detail and explore what occurs in it (the narrative level and the world in the text). This will lead us to suggest what it reveals about the world behind the text and what the author may intend audiences to do as a result (the discourse level and the world in front of the text). In the conclusion of each chapter we can draw all this together to answer what we will call the "so what" question. So what have we learned, and what does it all mean? This, of course, is the goal of exegesis.

What Have We Learned So Far?
The World in the Gospel and Letters of John

Our work in this chapter as literary critics, studying a broad reading of the Gospel of John, has allowed us to gain a general picture of the world in this text. Although we can draw some conclusions from these underlying literary characteristics and themes, we must be careful not to overreach at this early stage before we do more detailed exegesis. That said, general discussions of the worlds behind and in the text do allow us to begin to get a sense of why the evangelist composed his Gospel in the manner he did. Our discussion in the previous chapter, showing the developing Christology of early Christianity, was reinforced in this chapter when we saw how the Beloved Disciple understood Jesus and how Jesus, in turn, taught about himself. Jesus performed "signs," which grounds him in the story of Judaism, especially in God's work through Moses during and after the Exodus; however, Jesus taught primarily through dialogues, in which he identified himself as the Son of God the Father. The literary themes that the evangelist wove through his story further establish both this newly developing Christology as well as the theological and ethical responses to which humankind is summoned. In his Gospel, therefore, the evangelist is grounding his story in the world of Judaism while he is telling the story of God working in a new way through Jesus.

In the early chapters of this textbook, we saw that the story of Judaism as preserved in the Old Testament is grounded in the concept of a covenant relationship between God and humankind. The Sinai covenant mediated through Moses provides the Ten Commandments and the full Torah to guide humankind's relationship with God as well as the ethical interaction between people. The Gospel of John is steeped in this history and theology. In keeping with this covenantal history, therefore, the evangelist presents Jesus providing two commandments as the fundamental guide through this new way. Although we will see this in more detail in the chapters to come, we can already suggest that the evangelist is presenting Jesus as the true revelation of God who fulfills the former and puts in place a new covenant. In this new covenant available to all humankind, Jesus commands that all who seek this relationship *believe* in him as the Word of God and *love* one another as God has loved them. These two commandments are foundational to the new community. Receiving Jesus Christ and believing in God the Father through Jesus the Son is the theological summons, and accepting one another through mutual abiding love is the ethical summons this story of the good news makes to all who encounter it. We will begin to explore more deeply how the evangelist presents these commandments of the new covenant in the next chapter as we exegete the prologue to the Gospel.

Key Terms and Concepts

dialogues

double entendres

dualistic imagery

"I AM" statements

irony

literary characteristics

literary context

literary inclusions

literary themes

naïve misunderstanding

signs

storytelling techniques

structure

symbolism

teaching style

the Beloved Disciple

"the Jews"

Questions for Review

1. Why is it important to be aware of the literary style of a biblical author in order to properly exegete the text?

2. Identify and discuss several key literary characteristics of the Johannine Literature.

3. What is the identity and role of the character group known as "the Jews"? Why is it important to be careful and nuanced in such a discussion?

4. Identify and discuss the key literary themes of the Johannine Literature.

5. What is meant by the structure of a piece of literature? Why is establishing the flow of a text important for exegesis? How does the literary context of a passage or larger narrative unit aid in its interpretation?

6. What is the broad narrative flow and structure of the Gospel of John?

Bibliography and Further Reading

Brown, Raymond E. *The Gospel according to John.* 2 vols. AB 29–29a. New York: Doubleday, 1966–1970.

Brown, Sherri. *Gift upon Gift: Covenant through Word in the Gospel of John.* Princeton Theological Monograph Series. Eugene, OR: Pickwick, 2010.

Culpepper, R. Alan. *The Anatomy of the Fourth Gospel: A Study in Literary Design.* Foundations and Facets. Philadelphia: Fortress, 1983.

Moloney, Francis J. *The Gospel of John.* Sacra Pagina 4. 2nd ed. Collegeville, MN: Liturgical, 2005.

Powell, Mark Allan. *Fortress Introduction to the Gospels.* 6th ed. Minneapolis: Fortress, 1998.

The Beginnings of the Word in John 1:1–18

PURPOSE Chapter seven establishes the prologue (1:1–18) as the gateway into understanding and interpreting the Gospel of John.

ASSIGNMENT Reread John 1:1–18 before proceeding with this chapter.

In this chapter we will focus on the beginning of the Gospel of John as the gateway into both the narrative itself and the good news the evangelist is teaching through this story. The spotlight will rest upon the prologue (1:1–18). In doing so, we will set the stage for crossing from the narrator's introductory remarks in the prologue into the first half of the body of the gospel narrative, the Book of Signs. Indeed, we will present the prologue as the key for understanding the entire gospel narrative. The characters in the story who cross the prologue into the body of the Gospel are John the Baptist and Jesus. Therefore, we will pay particular attention to their roles. We will open by discussing the concept and function of a prologue as the beginning of a story or drama, then turn our attention to the structure of John's prologue before we spend some time interpreting its meaning and function in the larger gospel narrative.

Beginnings: The Prologue to the Body of the Gospel (1:1–18)

The term **prologue** comes to us from the Greek word *logos*, which literally means "word" but has larger connotations of "speech" or "study," and the prefix *pro*, meaning "before." The term *logos* becomes an important concept in the content of the prologue, but initially it also helps us understand that the first eighteen verses of the Gospel of John serve as a speech or message before the body of the narrative that serves as a key to appreciating the full force of the story to come. Just as we sometimes see in contemporary novels, the prologue serves as an introduction, giving a good deal of background that sets up the action and helps audiences make sense of the story to come. Likewise, prologues have a particular purpose in ancient Greek drama, which is much closer to John's original context. In Greek tragedy, the prologue was the first component of the play that set forth the subject and protagonists of the drama when the chorus entered the stage. The prologue would typically give the mythological background necessary for understanding the events of the play. By "mythological," we refer to the interaction of the divine with the earthly, and in the case of the Gospel of John, to how God interacts with God's creation. The prologue, therefore, introduces the setting, previews the main characters, and establishes the primary themes and message of the work. All of this becomes information that audiences have and that most characters in the story *do not* have. Thus it puts us in a privileged position as we participate in the action of the story, identifying with characters and waiting, even hoping, for them to catch on, as it were, and begin to grasp the fullness of what is at stake. Although biblical scholars typically agree on very little, the vast majority of those who work on the Gospel of John understand John 1:1–18 to be a carefully composed prologue that is essential to understanding the rest of the narrative.

As a first page, the prologue is therefore fundamental to the narrative structure of the Gospel. Scholars have argued over its placement, with some claiming it to be the last part of the Gospel to take definitive shape after a long history of development within the community. This was the majority position for some time in the history of scholarship. Nonetheless, its positioning must be understood as part of the author's strategy, even the key to understanding the narrative to come. This position has come to the fore in contemporary scholarship as commentators have come to realize that, however it was initially composed, the prologue in its final form of eighteen verses at the beginning of this story introduces every theme in the narrative to come and does indeed give audiences a great deal of information that the characters in the Gospel would likely wish they had. Although audiences may not fully understand the enigmatic philosophical ideas and motifs of the prologue, these are precisely what create the tension that raises the question of the *how* of God's action in the world. The subsequent narrative *shows* what the prologue *tells*.

The Narrative Flow and Structure of John 1:1–18

Now that we have discussed the role and purpose of a prologue in general and John's prologue in particular, the next step in exegeting what the evangelist is teaching in this "first page" of the Gospel is to try to determine how he has structured it. With regard to its literary form, these verses are largely a poetic hymn with a strong use of parallelism. Biblical scholar Robert Alter argues that highly structured epic poetry was the accepted oral and literary expression of polytheistic religions (think of the Greek poet Homer and his epic poems, the *Iliad* and the *Odyssey*, that tell of the history and religion of the Greek Empire).

Therefore, the fact that so many biblical authors from Judaism and developing Christianity chose to use prose narrative to tell their stories is a conscious break from that custom, in an effort to say something different. As distinct from their Greco-Roman religious counterparts, the Jewish and Christian traditions teach the covenant faithfulness of the one creator God alongside the freedom of humankind to choose to live in right relationship with that God. The Fourth Evangelist is writing firmly within this tradition. However, by writing a Gospel, he is also sharing good news and teaching that God has broken into history with a new act of covenant. God is faithful and, yet, has done something distinctive through Jesus. Therefore, John's use of the poetic prologue as a foundation for his Gospel that suddenly and definitively breaks into prose narrative can be understood as a reflection of his theological perspective. The **incarnation** of the Word of God suddenly and definitively turns the custom and "truth" of the world on its ear. The epic qualities of these poetic verses establish an ordered system of relationships between God, creation, and history. The narrative then unsettles that order, as events do not occur as the prologue audiences expect, for this is the story of God's self-revelation in history in human form.

Now we can discuss the structure of this poetic hymn in more detail. Remember from chapter six that, as interpreters, or to use the technical term, as exegetes, we study the final composition and try to glean what the author's original outline would have been if he had written one. This helps us get a big picture of the author's flow of thought in writing, which in turn aids us in exegeting, or drawing out, his intention in writing. Some compositions are very clear and straightforwardly structured, while others are more complex and intricately constructed. Because we are doing this after the fact and we cannot ask the author himself about his structuring techniques, we can never be certain about this process. Thus, responsible scholars can derive very different structures for the same passage, segment of a text, or even an entire book. The structure of these eighteen verses of the prologue to the Gospel of John is elusive, and biblical scholars have made numerous attempts over the years to capture the flow of this poetic prelude, coming up with sometimes widely varying structures. Discussing these in detail is beyond the purpose of our task and would not be helpful in introducing the

---

Ecumenical Councils and Christian Doctrine

Christianity and its Scriptures burst onto the religious scene of the Mediterranean world, making extraordinary claims about God, God's presence and revelation in and through Jesus, and the gift of the Spirit. It took the Christian Church centuries to debate and clarify what this all meant. The great Christian doctrines were the result of meetings of Bishops and Christian leaders, generally at the request of the Emperor, called Ecumenical Councils. The most important were Nicaea (325 CE: the Trinity), Constantinople I (351 CE: Christology), Ephesus (451 CE: the role of Mary as mother of God), Chalcedon (451 CE: Christology), and Constantinople II (553 CE: Christology).

The Christian doctrine of the Incarnation was formally defined at the Council of Chalcedon in 451. The official teaching of Christianity is that Jesus Christ is at once both fully God and fully human. Jesus is the eternal Son of God in human form.

Gospel of John. Therefore, we have chosen the structure that we believe gives us the best roadmap for understanding the evangelist's intention both for the prologue as well as for his larger teaching across the gospel narrative. For our purposes in this textbook, therefore, the work of R. Alan Culpepper on the prologue proves most helpful.

Recognizing the complexity of these eighteen verses, Culpepper acknowledges that more than one structuring technique may well be in play in the prologue. Thus, any diagram of it should be open to the fluidity of the evangelist's style, since various literary techniques are often not mutually exclusive. Nonetheless, Culpepper suggests that the underlying framework of the Johannine prologue is the **chiasm**. As a structuring technique, a chiasm is a placing crosswise of words, phrases, or concepts that may comprise whole passages as well as single sentences. This structure is called a *chiasm* because, when the passage is diagrammed, the resulting graphic looks like the left side of the Greek letter *chi*, which resembles the English letter X. These words and phrases that are placed in corresponding positions could be synonyms, or they could share themes. Often there are inversions of similar ideas rather than identical terms. Authors might use a chiasm in a story, letter, or speech in order to introduce the main point generally, and then give more and more information as they move toward their climax. Instead of concluding at that point, however, these authors will revisit the initial information in reverse order to show how it has been affected by that climax. This means that the structure and content of a passage move from general to more and more specific claims that typically turn on a central assertion. In addition to chiastic structures in which there is no middle term (which could be structured as, e.g., ABB′A′), there are chiasms at whose center is a single, central segment (which could be structured as, e.g., ABCB′A′). In this second type of chiasm, this central segment becomes the pivot of the passage ("C" in our example). This pivot is the climax of the passage's thematic presentation.

Culpepper builds upon the work of his predecessors, who have also understood the prologue to be structured as a chiasm, and isolates both its flow and its pivot. He investigates these eighteen verses by analyzing them in three ways: (1) language—primarily the occurrence/repetition of catchwords; (2) parallel concepts across the passage; and (3) statement and restatement of content—in terms of the theme or themes of each segment. He concludes that the evangelist presents the prologue in an extended chiasm with seven corresponding elements, with the chiasm turning on the pivot of v. 12b: Jesus gives to those who receive him "power to become children of God." This suggests that the crux of the prologue is to teach that the mission of the Word that has become human is to give the gift of truth that empowers those who receive and believe in him to become children of God. This central thesis further indicates how the prologue is also the key to understanding the entire Gospel.

Notice that we identified the pivot of the prologue as "v. 12b." When a verse is made up of several clauses in the same sentence, or even several sentences, and we want to focus on just part of the verse, the convention is to mark each phrase with a letter of the alphabet, beginning with the letter "a." This division of phrases usually, but not always, follows punctuation marks such as commas, semi-colons, and periods. In this case, John 1:12 can be divided into three phrases, vv. 12a, 12b, and 12c. In the original Greek text of the Gospel, a direct translation of the full verse would be, "But to those who did receive him, he gave power to become children of God, to those who believe in his name." Verse 12b is the central phrase of the verse and the central concept of the prologue. In their attempt to make the flow of the sentence more understandable, not all English translations preserve this original word order. This is an acceptable practice; therefore, we must highlight the evangelist's syntax in order to make sense of Culpepper's overall structure.

A diagram follows:

The Prologue   1:1–18

A   vv. 1–2   The Word in the Beginning with God
  B   v. 3   What Came to Be through the Word
    C   vv. 4–5   Life and Light in the Darkness
      D   vv. 6–8   John, Sent from God for Testimony
        E   vv. 9–10   The Light in the World
          F   v. 11   His Own Did Not Receive Him
            G   v. 12a   Receiving Him
              H   v. 12b   Becoming Children of God
            G′   v. 12c   Believing Him
          F′   v. 13 His Own Born of God
        E′   v. 14   The Word became Flesh in the World
      D′   v. 15   John's Testimony
    C′   v. 16   Gift upon Gift
  B′   v. 17   The Gift of Truth in Jesus Christ
A′   v. 18   The Son Reveals the Father

This is the narrative flow and structure of the prologue that we will use as our guide for exegesis.

Interpreting John 1:1–18

"Both in life and in literature beginnings are consequential, but risky undertakings." Given our discussion of the prologue to the Gospel of John thus far, this declaration of biblical scholar Werner Kelber holds particular weight. Likewise, beginnings are the manners by which our evangelists present the key to understanding all that follows. This view of the function of the prologue coupled with

Culpepper's roadmap will serve as the guide through which we can examine the key that the Fourth Evangelist provides to open the passageway into his Gospel.

1:1–11 In the Beginning Was the Word

The first part of the prologue's chiasm introduces themes, concepts, and characters and leads audiences to the climax of its presentation.

1:1–2 The Word in the Beginning with God

The first words of the prologue, and thus of the entire Gospel, are identical to the opening words of Genesis in the OT: "in the beginning." They serve to bring John's first audiences to "the beginning," not only of this narrative but to the beginnings of their sacred narrative of history, when God literally spoke creation into existence (Gen 1). By echoing this shared story of God's action in history, the evangelist firmly grounds his following story in the world of Scripture, particularly the Scripture of Israel. This literary intention is furthered with the fullness of the initial phrase: "In the beginning was the Word." The Greek term for "word" is *logos*, and the use of this terminology here has been discussed a great deal by biblical scholars. The evangelist's concept of "the **Word** of God" is rooted in both the Jewish Torah and Wisdom traditions as well as the Greek philosophical tradition. John's choice of it here allows for rich and varied symbolism, evoking God's revelation in Torah as well as the broader voice of the sages through the Greco-Roman cultural milieu. On the narrative level, it also allows for a fundamental identification of the *logos* with the creative activity of God. The "word" that is introduced here corresponds with God's own word of creation in the beginning.

The parallelism that proceeds in v. 1 picks up the introduction of the *logos* and affirms that the "Word was with God." The eternal nature of the Word is indicated here with the form of the verb "to be" ("was"), which is differentiated from all that is created or "becomes" in vv. 3, 6, and 10. What is most notable in this second step of the first verse, however, is the use of the preposition that links the existence of the Word with God. Although typically translated as "with," the power of this preposition, *pros* in Greek, is found in its literal translation as "to" or "toward." What this means is that, in its eternal state of being, the Word is turned toward God. This wording conjures an image of inherent relationship between the *logos* and God. The two beings are turned toward each other in a face-to-face relationship. This image is reinforced in the final step of this first verse: "and the Word was God." Since the first two clauses of this sentence already indicate that the Word is in relationship with God, we know that this phrase is not claiming that the two are the same being. Rather, the syntax of the original Greek suggests that we might understand this phrase to claim that "what God was, the Word also was." In this poetic fashion, John teaches that as an independent being of the same divine essence as God, the Word is fundamentally oriented toward union with God. The expansiveness of this first verse prepares audiences for God's revelatory action in the story to come. The deeds and words of Jesus in the following pages are the deeds and words of God. In this same light, the second verse reflects a second layer of parallelism as it succinctly reiterates and affirms the claims of the first verse: "This one was in the beginning toward God" (v. 2).

1:3 What Came to Be through the Word

Verse 3 pushes the chiasm of the prologue forward by further presenting the nature and role of the *logos* as the vehicle for creation. Verse 3 emphasizes (as does its counterpart, v. 17) what "came to be" through the as-yet-unnamed *logos*, who himself always existed. We can reflect once again on Gen 1, where God says, "Let there be . . .," to facilitate creation and appreciate the symbolism of the action of the Word as God spoke creation into existence. Indeed, nothing came to be without it. The Word's role in all creation is, therefore, foundational for understanding him as the giver of "life" and "light."

1:4–5 Life and Light in the Darkness

This new segment further characterizes the Word as the giver of life (v. 4) who stands fast in the darkness, lighting the way for humankind (vv. 4–5). John introduces these themes of **life**, **light**, and its corresponding **darkness**, which will play out across the rest of the narrative, but he also continues an exposition of Genesis 1 that echoes the eternal creative force of God. Throughout his ministry, Jesus will teach about life in his name, and here the evangelist identifies that with God's gift of creation. Likewise, Jesus will be portrayed as the light, a beacon to all who are searching for God, and the evangelist will make ample use of this symbolism. The final words of v. 5 further hint at the conflict to come between the Word as giver of light (Gen 1:3–5) and the darkness that exists among the people who are the caretakers of God's creation (Gen 1:26–30). Audiences are told that regarding the shining light, the darkness "did not overcome it." This verb can carry the sense of "overtake" in the physical sense as well as "apprehend" in the sense of "comprehend." Thus, a physical threat is implicated as well as the notion of the Word already in the world, in the form of Torah, which has not been fully understood. This statement leads directly to the introduction of John, the one who comes to give testimony and who also becomes part of the driving force toward the crux of the entire prologue.

1:6–8 John, Sent from God for Testimony

The next segment of the prologue's chiasm is formed by verses that introduce the first human being (*anthrōpos*) into the story, a man named John (vv. 6–8). We should clarify here that, although the evangelist never calls him "the Baptist," this John is the same person that the other Gospels call "John the Baptist." This John is *not* the same person as the evangelist, who is traditionally identified as John the son of Zebedee. In the prologue, this human being is characterized as having "come to be," in distinction from the eternally existing Word. In the same breath, however, the evangelist describes this man as "sent from God," the only fully human character in the narrative to be identified as such. John, then, is special: he is sent into the world from God with a mission. Audiences are, therefore, alerted right away that this man can be trusted. His mission is to testify (vv. 7–8). John is to bear witness to the light of the eternal Word identified in v. 4. As the witness sent from God, everything that John says about Jesus can be trusted as true. Through the introduction of John and his role, the evangelist also introduces the concept of **believing** in the Word. As we noted in chapter six, scholars often notice that "belief" as a noun (*pistis*) does not occur in the Fourth Gospel, but forms of the verb "to believe" (*pisteuō/pisteuomai*) occur regularly and often (ninety-eight times). Thus, faith in the Gospel of John is always an action and is rightly described in terms of a process, or better, a journey. Verse 8 carefully clarifies the distinction between John, the human witness, and the light, but his role is crucial to point to the light and thus facilitate the process of faith.

John the Baptist

The figure of John the Baptist appears in all four Gospels as one whose ministry precedes and points to that of Jesus. That said, the evangelists characterize the role of the Baptist and his relationship somewhat differently. Interestingly, in John's Gospel we may have preserved some of the oldest traditions about the relationship between Jesus and John the Baptist, even though John is never called the Baptist. Here he speaks of Jesus as "the one who comes after me" (1:15, 27, 30), indicating that Jesus may have once been a follower of John the Baptist. In 3:22–26 we may have traces of a very old tradition that indicates John and Jesus carried on parallel baptismal ministries for a time, before the imprisonment and execution of John. Nonetheless, John the Baptist's primary role in the Gospel of John is to be a witness to Jesus.

1:9–10 The Light in the World

The next segment of the prologue flows out of the final words of vv. 6–8 and returns focus to the light, now further characterized by way of **truth** (vv. 9–10). The true light, whose enlightening reign reaches everyone, is coming into the world. The incarnation foreshadowed here comes to pass in the counterpart to these verses, v. 14. The imminent conflict of the Gospel story is also reaffirmed, this time in terms of **knowledge** (v. 10). The very **world** that the light was instrumental in creating "did not know him." The evangelist will characterize the world as consumed by darkness, and, though claiming a great deal of knowledge, lost in ignorance. The verb "was" indicates that the *logos* (characterized as light) was already in the world. This could be a further identification of the *logos* with Torah, making these verses a reference to the giving of Torah to Israel and a failure to understand its fullness. Describing this conflict with the concepts of truth and knowledge also brings the language and symbolism of the Prophets into the prologue's presentation of the person and mission of the Word.

1:11 His Own Did Not Receive Him

Verse 11, although a distinctive segment in the prologue's chiasm in its own right, provides powerful parallelism to this disconnect between the light and the world through the intimate language of "his own." The Word, instrumental giver of life and light in intimate relationship with God, comes into what is his own and is not received by his own people. This is a reference to the Jewish people who are in covenant relationship with God, the people through whom and to whom the Word is coming in the world. In this way, audiences are given more information about the impending conflict of the story to come. Giving, receiving, and rejecting in relationship thus become the operative interactivity of the Word in the world with his own people as well as with anyone he encounters.

1:12 The Children of God: The Pivot of the Prologue

At verse 12, the audience arrives at the pivot of the prologue (v. 12b, marked H) and the hinges upon which the pivot turns (vv. 12a and 12c, marked G and G′). Put another way, the force of the entire prologue is poised on the axis of the mission of the Word: "he gave power to become children of God." As we mentioned above, the balance of the three phrases of v. 12 can be lost in some English translations, including the RSV/NRSV. In effect, however, the evangelist's Greek syntax allows the central assertion of the Word's giving action (v. 12b: "he gave them power to become children of God") to be framed by the introduction (v. 12a: "but to all who received him") and the description of the potential recipients of the gift (v. 12c: "who believed in his name"). In v. 12a the subject builds upon those to whom the Word came ("his own," v. 11), while v. 12b delineates the indirect object of the power the word gives ("them"), and v. 12c characterizes "them" as "those who believe in his name." Verses 12a and 12c are thus corresponding phrases that hinge upon the core assertion of v. 12b. Therefore, this verse can be discussed as:

> Receiving Him (v. 12a)
> > Becoming Children of God (v. 12b)
> Believing Him (v. 12c)

This central assertion, the giving of power to become **children of God** to those who receive the Word, is understood to be the crux of the prologue's message to its audiences. Therefore, this core must also profoundly affect the corresponding elements that provide the balance of the prologue's message. This language of family will often be used in the Gospel to describe relationship with God. Becoming God's children through the Son of God is the culmination of all God's dealings with the world, the goal of the creator and creation. Thus v. 12 can be regarded as the pivot that facilitates the entirety of what is achieved by the incarnation of the Word. This expressed aim will affect every statement that follows. This effect is already apparent in v. 12. The claim is that those who receive the Word will be given the power to become children of God, but how does one go about receiving him in order to achieve this status? By believing in his name. The remainder of the prologue can be studied in this way, which will also shed light on what it means to become "children of God" and how this could be the goal of the whole Gospel.

1:13–18 The Word Became Flesh and Dwelt among Us

The latter parts of the prologue's chiasm lead audiences to its conclusion by revisiting all the thematic claims of the first half, in light of the central claim of its core, v. 12.

1:13 His Own Born of God

Those who believed received the Word and thereby received a gift in return, the power to become children of God. Verse 13 stands in apposition to v. 12 and also corresponds antithetically to v. 11, which shared that the Word's own people did not receive him. Verse 13 continues the "how" of the central claim of v. 12. If v. 12c describes the role of the "receivers" in this relationship, then v. 13 describes the role of God and the "how" of becoming God's children. Three standard (human) ways of how this could happen are listed negatively by way of dismissal, followed by the positive assertion that children of God are indeed born spiritually of God. Natural descent, ordinary human sexual desire, and the husband's will are no longer operative, for spiritual birth comes from above, from heaven. This notion is more fully articulated in John 3 but is introduced here in terms of the mission of the Word. Because of the coming of the Word into the world and the rejection by "his own," heritage and ethnicity are rendered irrelevant to birth from God, and the privilege of becoming the covenant people of God also changes forever. Anyone who believes in the Word can now become a child of God.

1:14 The Word Became Flesh in the World

Concluding this initial characterization of the children of God, the evangelist returns to what God did to make this possible. Verses 9–10 revealed that the Word, characterized as "the true light," was "coming into the world." Corresponding to this proclamation, v. 14 majestically announces how this happened, who the Word becomes, and what he gives in the process.

> And the Word became flesh and made his dwelling among us, and we beheld his glory, the glory as of a father's only son, full of the gift that is truth.

Scholars who oppose a chiastic structure to the prologue typically point to this verse, describing the glory of the incarnation of the eternal Word as the climax of the hymn. These words are powerful indeed, and their impact should not be minimized. With regard to the flow of the prologue, they announce an event long coming, made possible by the plan of God to re-envision the covenant people as children of spiritual, not human, birth. Just as God's action in the Sinai covenant and the giving of the Torah changed the nature of God's relationship with creation, the incarnation of the Word, while very much in accord with that history, once again decisively alters the manner by which creation can relate to God.

The evangelist leaves no doubt about the full humanity of the incarnate Word, with the use of "flesh" to describe this in-breaking of God's action. Further, the Exodus event and the covenant-making time in the wilderness at Sinai are brought to mind with the action of dwelling "among us." The verb *skēnoō* means literally to "pitch a tent," and the form here is generally translated as "lived" or "made his dwelling." The evangelist's verb choice, however, resonates with Exodus 33–40, where God renews the covenant with Israel mediated by Moses, and the people are told to make a tent (the Tabernacle, or *skēnē*,) so that God can dwell among them. After a lengthy description of the Tabernacle and its construction, Exodus 40 recounts the erection of the Tabernacle and the placement of the tablets of the Ten Commandments in the Ark of the Covenant and its setting in the Holy of Holies. Depicting the incarnation of the Word in terms of the *shekinah*, or dwelling presence of God, thus also preserves the Word's divinity as a new presence of God and God's covenantal activity in creation. This echo would not have been lost on the evangelist's first audiences.

The incarnate Word made his dwelling "among us." The narration shifts to the first person plural as the narrator speaks inclusively from the perspective of the children of God. This inclusive narration also serves to draw audiences into the potentiality of becoming part of this group. "We have seen his glory." The visible and powerful manifestation of God likewise harks back to the revelation of the **glory** of God to Moses on Mount Sinai (Exod 33:18–22). Verse

14 also describes the glory of the incarnate Word in the context of a father's only son. This phrase introduces the evangelist's characteristic christological formulation: **Jesus as the Son** of God. The verse also offers a very human image of the incomparably privileged status of Jesus as "the only son" of **God the Father**, ensuring that Jesus's status in relation to God is understood to be unique.

Verse 14 then concludes this powerful statement by further describing the incarnate Word and at the same time continuing the articulation of *how* he gives believers power to become children of God. The incarnate Word is full of "grace" and "truth." Most scholars simply understand this phrase as descriptive and take the juxtaposition of "grace" and "truth" as expressing the OT covenant love of God, reflecting the common OT pairing of covenant love and truth (Exodus 34:6). This reading has much to commend it, but we must note the evangelist's use of the Greek word *charis* instead of the word for "love." Thus, without dismissing a reflection of pure covenant love, a more complete interpretation includes translating the Greek word *charis* with its more widely held denotation, "an expression of good will, a gift, an unexpected favor," and reading the "and" as explanatory, thus allowing the second term, "truth," to clarify the first term. The phrase is rendered more clearly as "full of a gift that is truth." The Word, giver of light and life, now human, is filled with a new gift, truth. The giving and receiving of this gift of truth is intimately connected to the power to become children of God and, thus, to the crux of the mission of the incarnate Word. The remainder of the prologue returns to where it began by continuing to elucidate this gift, integrating it into the life and being of the Word now made human.

1:15 John's Testimony

This incarnate Word is then firmly grounded in history as the narrator returns to John, the human witness sent by God and whose testimony audiences can trust (v. 15). In this role, John provides the first direct speech about the Word and the first direct speech of the Gospel. To assert both the correspondence of this verse to vv. 6–8 as well as the trustworthy nature of John's message, the evangelist places in the mouth of John the narrator's major verbs about him and has him repeat them, thereby confirming in direct speech what the narrator claimed for him. John testifies that the Word is "the one who comes" after him temporally, but ranks before him. John explains that this is so "because he was before me." With this historical grounding and temporal designation in place, as well as the corresponding element to John's initial witness (vv. 6–8), the prologue surges forward with the mission of the Word.

1:16 Gift upon Gift

In v. 16, the narrator picks up from v. 14 by way of explanation, determined both by the return to the first person plural ("we have all received") and the reference to the "fullness" of the gift of the incarnate Word. The narrator continues to speak in the collective voice of the children of God as he details the process of God's action in creation in terms of their reception of God's gifts. Retaining the earlier understanding of *charis* as "gift," what God has done through the incarnate Word is to give the gift (of truth) upon a gift.

1:17 The Gift of Truth in Jesus Christ

The nature of the new gift has been introduced in v. 14, and the nature of the first gift has been behind the very characterization of the Word in vv. 1–5, but both are illuminated in v. 17: "The law indeed was given through Moses; the gift of truth came to be through Jesus Christ." The law was a gift from God, and the reference to Moses ensures that the covenantal gift of Torah echoes through this proclamation. The gift of truth was given through the incarnation of the Word, who is finally identified in history as Jesus Christ. This gift of truth is likewise a gift of God that acts in history in covenant with creation. One cannot "replace" the other. One perfects the never-ending graciousness of God: the gift of the law is perfected in the gift of truth in the incarnation of the Christ. The giving of the gift of the Torah was God's covenantal activity at Sinai. The incarnation of the Word that is full of the gift of truth is God's activity in Jesus.

1:18 The Son Reveals the Father

The final verse of the prologue, v. 18, returns to the beginning (v. 1–2) while illuminating the relationship of Jesus as "only son" to the Father who is turned toward that Father, now in history. It is that one who makes God known, and in this way he gives humankind the ability to become children of God. Jesus, the Word of God made human, will make God known through his life and ministry. The concept of **revelation** is now introduced into the narrative. Jesus will reveal God by revealing himself and his relationship as Son to God the Father across his ministry and through his passion and death. The remainder of the Gospel will narrate the "how" of the claims that the prologue introduces. In essence, the new covenant gives the power to become children of God through receiving the gift of truth as revealed by the incarnate Word, Jesus Christ the only son who is in perfect relationship with God the Father.

What Have We Learned So Far?
Beginnings

The prologue to the Gospel of John is one of the most famous texts of the New Testament. It is poetic and beautiful, even while it is enigmatic and provocative. We cannot give such detailed attention to every passage in the Gospel, as we have in this chapter on John 1:1–18. We participate in such careful exegesis of the prologue, however, because of how crucial it is to understanding both the narrative and discourse levels of the rest of the Gospel. As a prologue, it sets the stage for all that is to come, introducing key characters (God, Jesus the Christ and Word of God, John the Baptist who is witness to Jesus, the world, and Jesus's own people, the Jews) and key themes (word, life, light, darkness, truth, knowledge, family, glory, and the revelation of God) of the Gospel. As such it is indispensable information for audiences as we launch into the body of the narrative. The chiastic structure of the prologue further points us toward the mission of the Word made human in this world and the hope of the new activity of God in truth: that everyone who encounters the Word may receive and believe in him, thus becoming the new children of God in the family formed by Jesus, the Christ and Son of God. Therefore, it is available to anyone and everyone, regardless of race or ethnicity. All humankind has to do is receive him and believe in his word.

The prologue also gives audiences a great deal of insight into the theology of the Gospel. The evangelist presents the creative, sovereign power of God in divine union with his Word. The goodness of humankind is reinforced in the gift of the Word to history in human form through the incarnation. This gift of life, light, and truth cannot be overcome by the darkness that was reigning in the world. Through his life, ministry, and passion Jesus the Son reveals God the Father to the world and thereby creates a new family of God in which all humankind can become children. This, then, is also the soteriology of the Gospel. Humankind can experience salvation now through a life that is not bounded by death. Armed with these insights, we can now turn our attention to the process of the revelation of the glory of God through Jesus's life and ministry.

Key Terms and Concepts

believing	knowledge
chiasm	life
children of god	light
darkness	prologue
glory	revelation
God the Father	truth
incarnation	Word/*logos*
Jesus the Son	world

Questions for Review

1. Why is so much attention given to the prologue to the Gospel of John?
2. How is the prologue structured? How does this structure help in understanding it? What is its purpose in the flow of the gospel narrative?
3. What key terms and concepts are introduced in the prologue?
4. What characters are introduced in the prologue?
5. How might reading or hearing the prologue first affect how we come to the rest of the story? On the other hand, if the Gospel did not have the prologue, how might this affect how we understand the rest of the story?

Bibliography and Further Reading

Alter, Robert. *The Art of Biblical Narrative*. New York: Basic Books, 1981.

Barrett, C. K. *The Prologue of St John's Gospel*. London: Athlone, 1971.

Culpepper, R. Alan. "The Pivot of John's Prologue." *New Testament Studies* 27 (1980): 1–31.

Hooker, Morna. *Beginnings: Keys That Open the Gospels*. Harrisburg: Trinity, 1997.

Kelber, Werner H. "The Birth of a Beginning: John 1:1–18." *Semeia* 52 (1990): 121–44.

Moloney, Francis J. *Belief in the Word: Reading John 1–4*. Minneapolis: Fortress, 1993.

The Opening Days of Jesus's Public Ministry in John 1:19–51

PURPOSE Chapter eight introduces the first part of the body of the gospel narrative, known as the Book of Signs. We can then explore the opening days of Jesus's public ministry (1:19–51), which make up the first narrative unit.

ASSIGNMENT Reread John 1:19–51 before proceeding with this chapter.

In this chapter, the spotlight will rest upon the opening days of Jesus's public ministry (1:19–51). We will cross from the narrator's introductory remarks in the prologue into the first half of the body of the gospel narrative, the Book of Signs. The characters in the story who journey from the prologue into the body of the Gospel are John the Baptist and Jesus. Once we establish the structure of the Book of Signs, we can turn our attention to the first narrative unit, which tells of the foundation of Jesus's public ministry: the opening days of his revelation.

Introduction to the Book of Signs

After the prologue, there is a continuous narrative, from John 1:19 to 12:50, through which Jesus emerges and conducts his public ministry. The end of chapter 12 and the beginning of chapter 13 mark a break in the Gospel. The final two paragraphs of John 12 offer a summary description and analysis of Jesus's public ministry and its effect (vv. 37–43), followed by the last words of Jesus in public, directed to the people in general (vv. 44–50). John 13:1–3 marks a shift in emphasis, and all Jesus's teachings in John 13–17 are directed to "his own"—the new children of God—described in the prologue, whom Jesus has gathered across his public ministry. The spirit of these divisions was introduced in vv. 11–12 of the prologue. Jesus came into his own people, who did not receive him, but for all those who do, during his earthly ministry and beyond, Jesus continues to teach and give the gift of truth as members of the new family of God.

John 1:19–12:50 is often designated **the Book of Signs** because these chapters largely concern Jesus's miracles, what this evangelist always refers to as **signs**, and the discourses that interpret those signs. It is important to remember that although this title for these chapters is so common that many interpreters of the Gospel use it without further explanation, it is not a title given to this section by the evangelist himself. It is a designation used by scholars and audiences to help us determine a structure for the evangelist's narrative. For his part, the evangelist wrote a continuous story without sub-headings or a designated outline. That said, we continue to attempt to uncover an outline, or structure, for the story as a whole as well as its constituent parts in order to give ourselves a roadmap of sorts to guide us through both the narrative and discourse levels of his story.

What we can say is that these signs of the first half of the body of the Gospel anticipate the glory of the second half (John 13–20). In turn, the action of the second half accomplishes in reality what was anticipated in the first half. Further analyzing the structure of the Book of Signs is a bit more difficult. The Gospel gives some indication of the passing of time, particularly by way of marking Passovers in 2:13; 6:4; and 11:55. Indeed, it is this marking of the annual festival of Passover that gives evidence of a historical ministry of two to three years for Jesus. The other Gospels in the NT refer to only one Passover festival, at the time of Jesus's arrest, and thus do not give this duration to Jesus's ministry. Nonetheless, in the Gospel of John, these markers of time seem merely to do just that: mark the passing of time and the setting of a given portion of the narrative. They do not provide a direction for the overall flow of the narrative.

It is not impossible that the signs themselves may indicate a key to the book's structure. We mentioned in chapter five that some scholars have even argued that the evangelist used a written text that recounted Jesus's signs as a primary source for his work. But looking to the signs as a structuring technique also proves inadequate, as only the first two are marked (2:11; 4:54), and passing references to signs not described are made in 2:23; 4:45; 7:4; 12:37; and 20:30. As we indicated in chapter six, this evangelist seems to choose seven representative signs of the many Jesus performed in order to signify the wondrous power of God through Jesus, much like that of God through Moses during the period in the Sinai wilderness recounted in the book of Exodus. By way of reminder, here again is a list of those signs:

1. 2:1–12   The wedding feast in Cana
2. 4:45–54   The healing of the royal official's child
3. 5:1–14   The healing of the crippled man
4. 6:1–15   The feeding of the multitude
5. 6:16–21   The walking on the water
6. 9:1–12   The healing of the man born blind
7. 11:1–44   The raising of Lazarus

The placement of these signs, however, does not really help us structure the overall flow of the narrative of the Book of Signs. In fact, we will see that if the people Jesus encounters understand the signs as ends or goals in themselves, Jesus will push them further to believe in his word as the revelation of the new covenant in God. The signs are not enough for a sustainable faith. Jesus calls people into a deeper and more challenging relationship. This seems to be true for the evangelist's storytelling structure as well. Thus, some sort of bigger picture is necessary. In this light, the Book of Signs seems to flow in four parts from the early days of the revelation (1:19–51), through a journey that teaches about faith (2:1–4:54), into the heart of the ministry and the feasts of Judaism (5:1–10:42), and onto a final movement toward glory (11:1–12:50). The following structure attempts to capture the narrative flow of this portion of the Gospel and also provides a roadmap for a more detailed exploration of the Book of Signs.

The Structure of the "Book of Signs" in the Gospel of John—1:19–12:50

Part One: The Opening Days of the Revelation of Jesus   1:19–51

1:19–34	The Testimony of John the Baptist	
	1:19–28	Day 1: Concerning Who He Is Not
	1:29–34	Day 2: Concerning Jesus
1:35–51	John the Baptist Points Disciples to Jesus	
	1:35–42	Day 3: Two Disciples—Jesus as Rabbi
		Simon Peter—Jesus as Messiah
	1:43–51	Day 4: Philip—Jesus as Fulfillment of the Law and Prophets
		Nathanael—Jesus as Son of God and King of Israel
		Jesus—A Saying about the Son of Man

Part Two: From Cana to Cana—Jesus's Instruction on Faith   2:1–4:54

2:1–12	The Encounter with Jesus's Mother and the First Sign at Cana	
2:13–25	The Encounter with "the Jews" in the Temple Area in Jerusalem	
3:1–21	The Encounter with Nicodemus in Jerusalem	
3:22–36	The Encounter with John the Baptist and His Final Witness in Judea	
	4:1–3	Transition—Jesus Leaves Judea and Moves into Non-Jewish Territory
4:4–15	The Encounter with the Samaritan Woman at Jacob's Well (part 1)	
4:16–30	The Encounter with the Samaritan Woman at Jacob's Well (part 2)	
4:31–44	The Encounter with the Samaritan Villagers	
4:45–54	The Encounter with the Royal Official and the Second Sign at Cana	

Part Three: Jesus and the Jewish Festivals   5:1–10:42

5:1–47	Sabbath—Jesus Performs Works Limited to God on the Sabbath
	5:1–15 Gift of Life [Healing] to the Man at Bethesda Pool
	5:16–47 Discourse on the Giving of Life and Sabbath Work
6:1–71	Passover—Jesus Gives Bread Perfecting the Manna of the Exodus
	6:1–21 Miraculous Feeding of the Crowd; Walking on Water
	6:22–59 Jesus's Discourse on the Bread of Life
	6:60–71 Disciples' Responses to the Discourse
7:1–10:21	Tabernacles—Jesus Perfects the Water and Light Ceremonies
	7:1–8:59 The Tabernacles Dialogues

7:1–13   Introduction: Will Jesus Go Up to the Feast?

7:14–36   Scene 1: Dialogues on the Middle Day of the Festal Week

7:37–52   Scene 2: Dialogues on the Last Day of the Festal Week

[7:53–8:11   The Woman Caught in Adultery]

8:12–59   Scene 3: Dialogues Conclude: Jesus, Light of the World

9:1–10:21   Continuation of Tabernacles

9:1–38   The Healing of the Man Born Blind

9:39–10:21 Jesus as the Sheep-Gate and Shepherd

10:22–42	Dedication—Jesus Perfects the Temple as the Dwelling Presence of God
	10:22–31 Jesus as the Messiah
	10:32–42 Jesus as the Son of God

Part Four: Jesus Moves toward the Hour of Death and Glory   11:1–12:50

11:1–12:8	Jesus Gives Humankind Life; Humankind Condemns Jesus to Death
	11:1–44 Jesus Gives Life to Lazarus—Jesus as the Life
	11:45–57 The Sanhedrin Condemns Jesus to Die as Passover Draws Near
	12:1–8 Jesus is Anointed for Death at Bethany
12:9–36	Preparation for Passover and Death
	12:9–19 The Crowds Acclaim Jesus as He Enters Jerusalem
	12:20–36 Arrival of the Greeks Marks the Arrival of the Hour
12:37–50	Conclusion of Jesus's Public Ministry
	12:37–43 Evaluation of Jesus's Ministry to His Own People
	12:44–50 Jesus's Summary Proclamation

With this bigger picture of the flow of the narrative, we can proceed with a more detailed interpretation of the first part of the Book of Signs.

Part One: The Opening Days of the Revelation of Jesus, 1:19–51

The prologue of the Gospel of John presents Jesus Christ as the incarnate Word who fulfills the Torah of the Sinai covenant and gives a new covenant, the gift of truth, to those who would be children of God (1:1–18). The bridge from the prologue to the action of the body of the Gospel is manifested in the human witness, sent from God, named John. He becomes the embodiment of the prologue as he continues to give valuable information about the person of Jesus as well as about the story to come, now in the form of dialogues with other human characters. The prologue tells the reader the *who* and the *what* of the events at hand, but it leaves open the *how*. The story itself is necessary to understand how it all happens. **John the Baptist**, introduced so strongly in the prologue as the human **witness** sent from God, opens the narrative as the first character in the story with dialogical force. In other words, he is the first human character to speak, and in his first dialogue he takes control and begins to teach the *how* of the good news.

We have discussed the importance of literary context for the interpretation of a passage or larger narrative unit. In the case of 1:19–51, we are finding ourselves at the beginning of the body of the gospel narrative. Therefore, we can expect to be introduced to key characters and get a glimpse into both the relationships and the conflicts that will play important roles across the development of the plot. Although this narrative unit is brief, it serves a major purpose in setting the tone for the exegesis of the larger story.

The Narrative Flow and Structure of John 1:19–51

John 1:19–51 occurs over the course of four consecutive days. During the first two days and the beginning of the third day, John gives his testimony. The detail of his witness over this three-day progression directly parallels the pattern set forth in vv. 6–8. On day one John declares he is not the light (vv. 19–28), on day two he witnesses positively to the light (vv. 29–34), and on day three people begin to believe through him (vv. 35–36). As day three progresses, the two disciples whom John points to Jesus are welcomed by Jesus and bring Simon Peter on board (vv. 35–42). They begin to address Jesus with a variety of titles. As day four commences, the focus remains upon Jesus and his gathering disciples, as Philip and Nathanael also join the group (vv. 43–51). The disciples continue to heap praise upon Jesus by using titles of honor, and yet they all remain within well-known Jewish categories of authority: Rabbi, the Messiah, he of whom Moses in the Law and also the Prophets wrote, Rabbi, Son of God, King of Israel. These opening days culminate as Jesus responds to Nathanael with his first major teaching of the Gospel, through which he identifies the title that will be his preferred self-designation for his ministry: the Son of Man (v. 51). Therefore, this first narrative unit can be structured as follows:

Part One: The Opening Days of the Revelation of Jesus   1:19–51

1:19–34	The Testimony of John the Baptist	
	1:19–28	Day 1: Concerning Who He Is Not
	1:29–34	Day 2: Concerning Jesus
1:35–51	John the Baptist Points Disciples to Jesus	
	1:35–42	Day 3: Two Disciples—Jesus as Rabbi
		Simon Peter—Jesus as Messiah
	1:43–51	Day 4: Philip—Jesus as Fulfillment of the Law and Prophets
		Nathanael—Jesus as Son of God and King of Israel
		Jesus—A Saying about the Son of Man

We can proceed with an exegesis along this structure.

Interpreting John 1:19–51:
Part One—The Opening Days of the Revelation of Jesus

As we indicated above, this first part of the Book of Signs serves to introduce audiences to key characters and the general setting and tone of the plot. John the Baptist brings audiences from the timeless omniscience of the prologue into the discrete history of Jesus's earthly life and ministry. As John proceeds to fulfill his mission to testify to Jesus as the Word of God incarnate on earth, the spotlight of attention shifts from John to Jesus, where it will remain for the rest of the Gospel. John's testimony is a key precursor to Jesus's own ministry of revelation of the glory of God. It begins when he is approached by a delegation from Jerusalem.

The "Days" of the First Week

The evangelist carefully marks the passing of time over the first week of Jesus's public ministry by noting "the next day," *tē epaurion* in the Greek language, three times: vv. 29, 35, 43. The marking of these early days culminate in 2:1 when Jesus and his new disciples arrive in Cana for a wedding "on the third day," *tē hēmera tē tritē* in Greek. The evangelist employs these temporal markers to build toward the revelation of the glory of Jesus in 2:11, which symbolically reflects the revelation of the glory of God in the Sinai wilderness after the Exodus. See the discussion at the end of this chapter.

1:19–34 *The Testimony of John the Baptist*

As audiences often notice, John is not referred to as "the Baptist" in this Gospel, as his role in this narrative is as a witness who testifies to God's action in and through Jesus. We will, however, often refer to him by his accepted title, John the Baptist or, simply, the Baptist, in order to continue to distinguish him from the Gospel's traditional author, John the evangelist. Since the narrator placed the audience's trust in this man named John, this character, upon entering the story (and even launching the story), thus becomes an embodiment of the prologue. He is the one character who witnesses accurately to the Word made flesh, just as he was sent to do. He may not know everything about Jesus's mission and ministry, but what he does testify is true. His first dialogue at 1:19–28, followed by the monologue of 1:29–34 and coupled with his final initial witness in 1:35–36, provides readers the grounds from which to form decisions about the characters in the narrative, and about their own belief in the Word.

1:19–28 Day 1: Concerning Who He Is Not

On the first day John is approached by a delegation and finds himself in dialogue over his identity. His task at this point is primarily to counter their misconceptions about who he is and what he is doing, and thus his initial testimony is largely negative. John focuses on explaining who he is not by rejecting the titles suggested for him. Nonetheless, even while John rejects any messianic titles or claims for himself, he points to a coming one who will indeed fulfill God's promises.

The opening of this scene further connects the action of the day at hand with information provided in the prologue: "This is the testimony given by John" (v. 19). Both the demonstrative pronoun "this" and the subject noun "John" are carefully chosen words that point back to John's mission as stated in the prologue and focus audience attention on the beginning of the action proper. John is first interrogated by a delegation "sent from Jerusalem." The one who is sent from God (v. 6) is confronted by "the Jews" sent from Jerusalem (v. 19). They approach him with the question that will mark these first days, and indeed, the first part of the gospel story, "Who are you?" They focus their attention on John and the identity in question. The beginning of John's testimony is a response that actually characterizes what he is *not*. "I am not the Christ" (v. 20). The narrator's introductory formula of this first direct speech ("He confessed and did not deny it, but confessed") correlates the content of the testimony with

---

Baptism

The rite of initiation into the Christian community is known as **baptism**. The term comes from a Greek verb that means "to immerse;" thus, the ritual always involves water and is performed in the name of the Father, Son, and Holy Spirit.

the act of confessing. Notice that in response to their general question, "Who are you?" John chooses to turn the dialogue to the question of Christology. Historically, questions of the Baptist's messianic claims likely circulated around the region and thus specifically spurred this delegation to come to him; however, the force of John turning the dialogue to the question of Christology affirms his role as the witness sent from God. John points negatively to himself in a manner that will correspond to the positive claim that Jesus will make about himself time and again over the course of the Gospel: "I AM."

The delegation continues with its quest for identification, "What then?" (v. 21). The Baptist's succeeding denials progress more concisely, cutting short any designs his interlocutors may have for information or even the upper hand in the conversation: "He said, 'I am not'. . . . He answered, 'No.'" We can then almost feel the frustration of the interrogators as they find themselves where they began, "Who are you?" They must have an answer "for those who sent us," but they concede all identification of power, and thus the lead in the dialogue, to John: "What do you say about yourself?" Only then does John testify positively about who he is by accepting the role of the voice in the wilderness, proclaimed by the prophet Isaiah in the OT (v. 23; see Isa 40:3). The NT Gospels agree in giving John the Baptist this voice of Isaiah (Mark 1:3; Matt 3:3; Luke 3:4), but only the Fourth Evangelist allows John, the witnessing agency, to give voice to his own self-identification. The Baptist "says" that he is the "voice crying out in the wilderness" in order to prepare the people to "make straight the way of the Lord." He allies his own voice with that in the book of the prophet Isaiah and, finally, positively asserts his role as the witness. As the human link between the prologue and the narrative of the Gospel, John prepares a way for the new children of Israel to receive the revelation of the Word.

This dialogue is followed by an interlude in which the narrator states that "they had been sent from the Pharisees" (v. 24). In this way, the narrator lays out what will be the full range of the opposition to the good news on this first day. The delegation initiates a further exchange. Repeating the Baptist's three-part denial of vv. 20–21, they ask him why, then, he is baptizing. This first reference to baptism indicates indirectly what prompted the delegation in the first place. John's practice of baptizing must have brought him to the attention of the Jerusalem authorities and has now given him the opportunity to fulfill his particular testimonial role in this gospel narrative. When the interrogators inquire why John is baptizing if he is not the messiah, Elijah, or the prophet, they are referring to various roles connected to the beginning of the messianic era. If John does not claim any recognizable identity of the messianic era, why is he performing an act of purification like baptism? The question thus serves to keep the christological issue before audiences. John affirms his baptizing role, even as he continues to reject a messianic claim for himself and to witness to the one coming after him. The strength of this image is magnified by his claim

Elijah and the Prophet as Messianic Figures

John the Baptist's interrogators ask whether he is Elijah or the prophet, once he rejects any notion that he is the messiah. The story of the prophet Elijah is found in 1 Kings 17:1–2 Kings 2:18. In those early verses of 2 Kings 2, Elijah is taken up into heaven in a chariot of fire. As God's true prophet who does not die, but is taken directly to God, many expectations of Elijah's return developed over time. The later prophet Malachi refers to Elijah as a messianic precursor who will prepare the way for the Day of the Lord (4:5). By the first century CE, great hopes were in place for Elijah's return. The "Prophet" is a reference to a prophet like Moses. In Deuteronomy 18:18, God tells Moses, "I will raise up for them a prophet like you from among their own people; I will put my words in the mouth of the prophet, who shall speak to them everything that I command." Since the death of Moses, the people had been hoping for a "prophet like Moses" as part of their messianic expectations. Later in the Gospel, the people will even wonder whether Jesus has taken this role (6:14; 7:40).

that the one who is coming is already standing among them, and they do not know him. John's revealing allusion to the hidden one to come emphasizes what the interrogators "do not know," and the messiah they will be hard-pressed to recognize and receive in the narrative to come.

1:29–34 Day 2: Concerning Jesus

On the very next day, vv. 29–34, John's witness continues in terms of fulfillment as he, seeing Jesus come toward him, points verbally to the "coming one" he promised on day one. The first day's dialogue becomes a monologue on this second day of promise fulfillment. John's interlocutors have left the scene, and John bears witness to any and all who would hear. He begins his testimony with an interjection that points to Jesus: "here!" Audiences can imagine him extending a hand toward Jesus as he speaks. He then gives Jesus the title, **Lamb of God**, and mission, "who takes away the sin of the world," that link the human being Jesus, who has finally come onto the scene of the gospel drama, with the divine *logos* of the prologue. Jesus is the "Lamb of God" who has come into "the world" (see vv. 1–2, 9–10). John now also indicates a correlation between Jesus the Lamb's role in "taking away sin" and Jesus the incarnate Word's mission of giving the gift of truth that empowers receivers to become children of God (see vv. 12, 14, 17). John's pointing to Jesus as the Lamb of God becomes particularly poignant, as both the characters in the story and audiences of the story later experience the passion narrative. Jesus is condemned at the moment the paschal lambs are being sacrificed (19:14) and is led to the slaughter like the suffering servant discussed in the book of the prophet Isaiah (see 53:7). We will discuss that in more detail later. For now, we can note that much of the story to come is revealed in this first sight of Jesus by the Baptist and the witness that encounter evokes.

John grounds this testimony by referring to and repeating his witness from the prologue ("This is he of whom I said . . .," v. 30; see v. 15). Again, John is the one entirely human character who bridges the omniscient narration of the prologue into the discrete narrative of the body of the Gospel. The demonstrative pronoun that points to Jesus ("this is he") and the personal pronoun that points back to himself ("I") both strengthen these verbal connections. The one sent by God to witness continues to give information that transcends the space, time, and culture of the story world and keeps audiences apprised of God's action in history.

John's testimony on this second day continues through v. 34. The issue of human knowledge that he first mentioned on day one (v. 26) comes up again as he now affirms the limits of his own powers of perception. He acknowledges that his entire ministry of baptism is so that, through the movement of the Spirit (in the form of a dove, v. 32), he might hear the word of the one who sent him and recognize Jesus as the coming one who will baptize with the Holy Spirit. The other Gospels in the NT recount John baptizing Jesus in this scene, something that is not narrated in this account. By not reporting the actual baptism, this evangelist maintains focus on the Baptist's role as witness and Jesus's burgeoning role as the one who reveals God through the Spirit. John is then able to initiate God's revelation in Jesus. With these statements affirming his own role and alluding to the role of Jesus in God's plan, John can also conclude this second day's witness with the declaration that he is fulfilling the mission God sent him to complete: "And I myself have seen and have testified that this is the Son of God" (v. 34). Jesus is the Son of God who has broken into the world and who will transcend all human expectations for his mission. Therefore, this second day of preparation for the gift of truth and the glory of God further informs audiences of the story, but not the other characters in the story, of *who* Jesus is and *what* he does. The question of how all this will play out becomes more pressing.

1:35–51 *John the Baptist Points Disciples to Jesus*

On days three and four, Jesus and his gathering disciples are introduced during the Baptist's teaching (1:35–42) and can then take over the dialogue for the final verses of the chapter (1:43–51). Jesus has already been introduced to the story, but now he begins to speak to and even challenge those he encounters. Audiences get their first insights into Jesus's character as well as the nature of his mission and the ministry to come.

1:35–42 Day 3: Two Disciples—Jesus as Rabbi; Simon Peter—Jesus as Messiah

On day three, the focus turns to disciples and discipleship. Jesus's disciples begin to gather, and his first interaction with them sets the tone for their relationship and future role. This third day of the Gospel begins with John again, this time standing in partnership with two of his disciples. His introductory testimony declared and fulfilled, John now bridges the narrative into the ministry of Jesus as he verbally points his disciples to Jesus, who is passing by ("he says, 'look!'"). He links this day's testimony to his previous witness by once again using his title of choice for Jesus and his mission: "the Lamb of God." This designation from their first teacher becomes a direction for these two disciples as they in turn follow Jesus. John the Baptist, his mission complete for the moment, now fades from the scene as audiences turn with the disciples along the path of John's pointing, now following on the journey of these disciples as they begin to participate in the mission of Jesus.

For his part, Jesus takes up the mantle of control in the dialogue, which he will guide and maintain for the rest of the Gospel, and initiates conversation with his new followers. His first direct speech of the narrative will mark his questioning discourse to all who would encounter him for the rest of his ministry and beyond: "What are you seeking?" The disciples respond positively, yet firmly within their Jewish religious and cultural categories, "Rabbi (which translated means 'Teacher'), where are you staying?" The narrator's translational aside further clarifies the limits of their initial perception. They see Jesus only as a new teacher. Their question about where he is staying is also typical of potential disciples to a new rabbi. The idea is that they would stay with and look after him in return for the teaching he might share. And yet their deeper question of abiding will indeed be answered as Jesus will have much to teach them about where he and they are ultimately to abide (see John 13–17). For now, Jesus responds with an ambiguous openness that paves the way for the theological pushing that will characterize following him as well as the new sights and insights that will be revealed to his followers. He says, "Come and see" (v. 39).

Although one of these disciples remains unnamed, the other one is identified as Andrew. The unidentified disciple seems to be the unnamed disciple

Titles in John

John uses few titles and he uses them very carefully. Jesus himself never claims to be "the Christ." Rather, John proclaims that he is the Christ (see 1:17; 20:31). Jesus does, however, accept the messianic title of "the Good Shepherd" (10:11–21). John associates the title Son of Man (3:14; 8:28; 12:32–34) with Jesus's revelation of God in being "lifted up" on the cross. Jesus is also, however, "the Son of God." Because he is "Son of God," the one who has come from God (1:1–18), all the other titles are possible, especially the exalted words of Jesus himself when he claims, using words used for God in the OT: "I AM" (e.g., 6:20; 8:28; 13:19).

who appears across the gospel story and is eventually characterized as Jesus's "beloved disciple." For his part, Andrew continues this ingathering by finding and bringing in his brother. Upon hearing Andrew's claim of finding the Messiah, Simon joins them and Jesus renames him **Cephas** (vv. 41–42). This is the Aramaic version of the Greek name for which this disciple eventually becomes famous: **Peter**. Day three comes to a close with the mission of the Word underway.

1:43–51 Day 4: Philip—Jesus as Fulfillment of the Law and Prophets; Nathanael—Jesus as Son of God and King of Israel; Jesus—A Saying about the Son of Man

On this last of the opening days, Jesus begins to teach his new followers what it means to be disciples as well as who he is. Day four commences with a trip to Galilee, and the gathering of eager disciples continues as they heap titles upon Jesus. For the most part, the disciples find each other in this telling of the Gospel, but on this fourth day, Jesus picks out Philip and commands him to "follow me." For his part, Philip finds Nathanael and urges him to "come and see" the fulfillment of the Law and the Prophets. Philip's description of Jesus as "Jesus of Nazareth, the son of Joseph" indicates to the audience that he is full of good will, but that he has not yet understood the person of Jesus. After experiencing the prologue, the audience knows that Jesus is not "of Nazareth" or "of Joseph." He is "from above" and "of God." Nathanael, however, is not convinced that God's Anointed One could come from somewhere as inauspicious as Nazareth. This allows Jesus to "wow" him with his insight and even add a little humor with a play on the "duplicity" of the first Israel, Jacob, when he calls Nathanael a "true Israelite" and refers to his sitting "under the fig tree," a symbol for Israel.

This series of "findings" culminates in v. 49 when Nathanael replies, "Rabbi, you are the Son of God! You are the King of Israel!" In Jewish usage of the time, "son of God" was employed in a sense that does not refer to Jesus as "Son of God" in the way intended by the prologue, but as a designation of a Davidic messianic figure who will behave like a loyal son. This comes from Jewish reflection on the promises of 2 Samuel 7 and Psalm 2. Nathanael, as a good Jew, recognizes Jesus as a son of God messiah. But audiences know from the prologue that he is more than that. Jesus then stops and begins to reorient their vision to the mission at hand. These titles are accurate, but they do not capture the full picture of who he is. Furthermore, discipleship cannot be based upon being "wowed" since that will not sustain them in life. They must be open to "greater things." Jesus concludes by offering his first major teaching of the Gospel introduced by the double-amen formula, "Amen, amen, I say to you, you will see heaven opened and the angels of God ascending and descending upon the Son of Man" (v. 51).

Across the Gospel of John, Jesus employs the designation "the Son of Man" to highlight that he is the earthly one who comes from God. In referring to himself as the Son of Man, then, Jesus underscores that he, in all of his humanity, is the point of communication between heaven and earth (v. 51; see Daniel 7:13–14). In all their titles of respect for Jesus, the disciples have not yet come to identify Jesus as the one turned toward God in intimate relationship both from the beginning and now in history. With the acclamation of Nathanael as the Israelite without duplicity, Jesus turns the image of Jacob, who would become Israel, onto himself and claims that he, Jesus, will be the new Jacob's ladder (see Gen 28:12–17). The Son of Man is the new ladder and gateway to heaven, and he will be the new revelation of God in and to the world. Jesus stops Nathanael and the rest of his neophyte disciples with this strong word so that they can begin to open themselves to the new action of God in history through Jesus.

The first chapter of the Gospel thus comes to a close. John has witnessed to Jesus as the Lamb of God (vv. 29, 36). Discipleship in the Fourth Gospel has been illustrated as being and abiding with Jesus (v. 38). The nature of Jesus's promise in response to Nathanael's confession in vv. 49–50 is significant. Jesus indicates that greater faith than that manifested by Nathanael will be required. If only the disciples are able to reach another depth of faith, they will see greater things. This vision of "greater things" points to the future. The vision of the open heavens, and God communicating with humankind through his Son, Jesus, the Son of Man, lies before the disciples and the audience. Both the disciples and audiences are now ready for the revelation of God in Jesus, the Son of Man (vv. 50–51).

Concluding Thoughts on the Opening Days of the Revelation of Jesus

The movement of the beginning of the body of John's Gospel (1:19–51) is most clearly delineated by the temporal markers that push the story forward through a flurry of activity across the span of a first week (vv. 29, 35, 43; then 2:1). Thus, 1:19–28 narrates day one, 1:29–34 narrates day two, 1:35–42 narrates day three, 1:43–51 narrates day four, followed by a distinctive three-day gap before the narration picks up again (2:1). This temporal structuring is often seen as the week of a new creation, and this could very well be part of the evangelist's plan, especially with the imagery from the book of Genesis we have seen across both the prologue and these first days. We should, however, also note that a primary motif of these early verses that remains in play throughout this Gospel is *revelation*. If a cue is taken from Exod 19:15–16 ("on the third day . . ."), then the first four days plus the three-day narrative gap does not only point to creation but is also a direct reference to the revelation of God on Mt. Sinai that results in God's covenant with Israel. The *Mekilta on Exodus* is a work from later Jewish rabbis that presents explicit instructions on how the people are to spend four days preparing prior to the three days of preparation for the ancient celebration of

Pentecost, the commemoration of the gift of the law on Sinai. The first three days show John the Baptist living out everything claimed about him in the prologue; he thus accurately portrays his own role (on day one) and points to Jesus as the Lamb of God (on day two). In days three and four, the gathering disciples begin to heap titles onto Jesus, but none of these titles go far enough—they all remain in the religious and political categories within which the disciples are comfortable. Jesus constantly shatters comfortable categories and the titles that go with them. Thus, at the end of day four Jesus rebuffs Nathanael and prepares them all for the revelatory process to come in terms of his own role as the Son of Man (v. 51) who reveals God's glory. The tension sparked by the word of Jesus creates dramatic interactions, through dialogue, that actively move his story forward toward its fulfillment on the cross, which glorifies both God and the Son and produces a new community of God's children who have received the Word. Just as the festival of Pentecost celebrates the revelation of God in the Sinai covenant, now Jesus Christ as the Son of Man reveals God to all he encounters.

What Have We Learned So Far?
Jesus as the Son of God and the Son of Man

We can now conclude the study of part one of the Book of Signs by reflecting on new aspects of the components of theology that have come to light. John 1 teaches its audiences much about God and how God is working in the world. The prologue affirms that God is creator, and the activity recounted in the Gospel to come is grounded in God's creative activity of Genesis 1. Further, this story has to be understood in terms of God's covenantal activity at Sinai, as recounted in Exodus. That covenant was a gift of God through Moses; this new covenant is a further gift given by God, a gift of truth, made possible by the incarnation of God's Son, Jesus Christ. The role of this Word of God in human form is to communicate, to reveal and make God known to all who will listen. The authority given the Word made flesh is to make all who receive him into children of God. This hints at soteriology. Somehow salvation is connected to becoming part of this new family of God. Union with God is the goal, and the achievement of this goal is characterized in terms of childhood. The remainder of the story will be necessary for the details of this relationship, but much is suggested in these early verses.

The bulk of the first days of the ministry of Jesus also points to Christology; and these important passages provide the foundational christological beliefs of Christianity. Jesus the Christ pre-existed creation and was in union with God. As the Word of God, creation came to be through his communication of life and light. Further, being a child of God is possible for believers who receive Jesus Christ as the incarnation of God, the Word become flesh. He shares in the divinity of God, yet he has taken on the human condition completely: Jesus is the uniquely begotten Son of God who fulfills God's earlier gift of the law to Moses through the new gift of himself in truth. He is the Lamb of God who heals the broken, sinful relationship between God and humankind, and the Son of Man who reveals God in the human story by challenging disciples and audiences to "come and see."

Key Terms and Concepts

baptism	Lamb of God
Book of Signs	sign
Cephas/Peter	Son of Man
John the Baptist	witness

Questions for Review

1. Why is John 1:19–12:50 often called the Book of Signs? What is a sign, and what does it have to do with believing in the good news of Jesus as the Messiah?

2. In John 1:19–51, the evangelist describes the first days of Jesus. What might be the effect of narrating the opening of Jesus's public ministry in terms of "days"?

3. Why might the evangelist not narrate the baptism of Jesus by John? What is the role of John the Baptist in this Gospel?

4. In John 1:19–51, what are the titles given to Jesus by his disciples? What is the meaning of Jesus's interaction with Nathanael? How might this foreshadow coming encounters in the Gospel?

Bibliography and Further Reading

Brown, Raymond E. *The Gospel according to John*. 2 vols. Anchor Bible 29–29a. New York: Doubleday, 1966–1970.

Brown, Sherri. "John the Baptist: Witness and Embodiment of the Prologue in the Gospel of John." Pages 145–62 in *Characters and Characterization in the Gospel of John*. Edited by Christopher W. Skinner. Library of New Testament Studies. London: T&T Clark, 2013.

Hooker, M. "John the Baptist and the Johannine Prologue." *New Testament Studies* 16 (1970): 354–58.

Moloney, Francis J. *The Gospel of John*. Sacra Pagina 4. Collegeville, MN: Liturgical, 1998.

Neirynck, Frans. "The Anonymous Disciple in John 1." *Ephemerides Theologicae Lovanienses* 66 (1990): 5–37.

Neyrey, Jerome. "The Jacob Allusions in John 1:51." *Catholic Biblical Quarterly* 44 (1982): 586–605.

The Beginnings of Jesus's Ministry: Journeys of Faith in John 2–4

PURPOSE Chapter nine examines the next narrative unit of the Gospel, a journey that teaches about believing in the word of Jesus as he and his disciples travel "from Cana to Cana" (John 2–4).

ASSIGNMENT Reread John 2–4 before proceeding with this chapter.

As an audience to John 2–4, we participate in Jesus's travel from Cana in **Galilee**, south into Jerusalem and the environs of **Judea**, north through **Samaria**, and finally back into Galilee and Cana, but we also have the discipleship-oriented episodes of 1:19–51 at the forefront of our consciousness. At the close of those first days, we cannot help but feel that the disciples are coming to authentic faith and understanding of Jesus and that we are grasping the Christology of the Gospel. But then we encounter Jesus's semi-reprimand of Nathanael. This is part of the teaching strategy of the Gospel: whenever people (characters in the Gospel and audiences of the Gospel) seem to come to a solid articulation of faith, Jesus engages them in dialogue and challenges them to go further. But if the disciples need to go further, where must they go? The evangelist answers this question across the narrative journey **from Cana to Cana**, providing an early Christian catechesis, or "education," on authentic faith.

The Narrative Flow and Structure of John 2–4

In John 2–4, the second narrative unit of the Book of Signs, we begin to see a number of strategies that are characteristic of John's storytelling style. As we noted in chapter six, the discourse level of this portion of the narration of Jesus's public ministry—the narrative from Cana to Cana—provides the Johannine instruction on the nature of authentic faith. The two signs at Cana in Galilee that form the beginning and ending of this teaching are the literary frames of the journey of faith. The physical movement between these two events mirrors

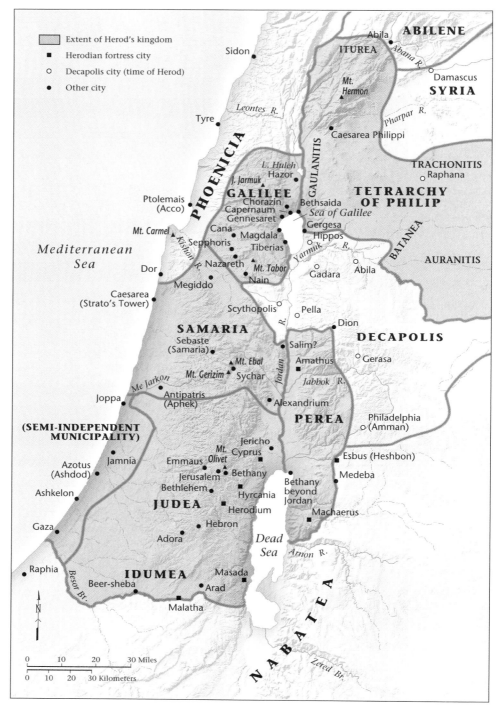

GALILEE, SAMARIA, AND JUDEA

the theological journey through which Jesus brings himself and his message, as the Word of God, to people across the world, first in a Jewish setting then in a non-Jewish setting. We will also begin to see both how John portrays faith as an action and how he identifies Jesus's miracles as "signs." Faith, according to John, is dynamic and communicative, and often when those Jesus encounters think they "have" it and have "arrived," Jesus verbally challenges them to go further. To do this, Jesus often draws people into dialogue by performing signs. These signs "wow" audiences, but they are not ends in themselves; rather their intention is always to "point to" the power of God. The revelation of God in Jesus must always be anchored in the message he teaches, not in the fleeting "wow" of a miraculous experience. Therefore, we will see a constant tension in the acceptance of "signs faith" over against the more challenging belief in the word of Jesus.

This portion of the Gospel thus offers the universal possibility of a journey of faith. In John 2–4, Jesus encounters different people or groups of people and challenges them to move out of their comfort zones and religious preconceptions and into a new relationship with God the Father through himself, the Son. This narrative unit can thus be structured as follows:

Part Two: From Cana to Cana – Jesus's Instruction on Faith   2:1–4:54

2:1–12	Encounter with Jesus's Mother and the First Sign at Cana in Galilee
2:13–25	Encounter with the Jewish Leaders in the Temple Area in Jerusalem
3:1–21	Encounter with Nicodemus in Jerusalem
3:22–36	Encounter with John the Baptist's Disciples and His Final Witness in Judea
	4:1–3 Transition—Jesus Leaves Judea and Moves into non-Jewish Territory
4:4–15	Encounter with the Samaritan Woman at Jacob's Well (part 1)
4:16–30	Encounter with the Samaritan Woman at Jacob's Well (part 2)
4:31–44	Encounter with the Samaritan Villagers
4:45–54	Encounter with the Royal Official and the Second Sign at Cana in Galilee

In this structure, we see examples of different types of responses to Jesus's challenge, both from within Judaism and from the broader non-Jewish, or **Gentile**, world. Each encounter provides a model for a faith response, some positive, some negative, and some, like Nicodemus, who try to ride the fence between both reactions. Although this may be acceptable for the meantime, Jesus in this Gospel will ultimately push all those he encounters to make a firm decision of faith. Each of these encounters will also move the plot of the story forward as Jesus reveals more about himself, and audiences move toward his inevitable arrest, passion, and glorification. We can also diagram the flow of this narrative in this way:

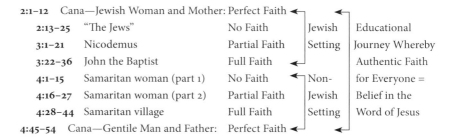

2:1–12	Cana—Jewish Woman and Mother: Perfect Faith			
2:13–25	"The Jews"	No Faith	Jewish	Educational
3:1–21	Nicodemus	Partial Faith	Setting	Journey Whereby
3:22–36	John the Baptist	Full Faith		Authentic Faith
4:1–15	Samaritan woman (part 1)	No Faith	Non-	for Everyone =
4:16–27	Samaritan woman (part 2)	Partial Faith	Jewish	Belief in the
4:28–44	Samaritan village	Full Faith	Setting	Word of Jesus
4:45–54	Cana—Gentile Man and Father: Perfect Faith			

This structure and diagram will guide us through the exegesis of John 2–4.

Gentiles

The term **Gentile** or **Gentiles** comes from the Latin *gentilis*, which means "of a family or nation; of the same clan." This term was first used in the Latin translation of the Bible, called the Vulgate, to translate the Greek word *ethnē*, or *ethnoi* in the plural, meaning "nation" or "nations." The term is used in the NT to refer to anyone who is not Jewish. It is not an ethnic designation in and of itself but can be used generally of any non-Jew.

Interpreting John 2:1–4:54: Part Two—From Cana to Cana, Jesus's Instruction on Faith

The first days of Jesus's public life were focused on the testimony of John the Baptist and the gathering of the first disciples (1:19–51). The ministry of John the Baptist pointed to Jesus as the Word, set forth in the prologue (1:1–18). The gathering disciples, however, seem trapped in the categories of their religious and cultural milieu. All the titles they give to Jesus are restricted to this worldview. With the powerful image of angels of God ascending and descending upon him, Jesus articulates the title that will fit his earthly mission: the Son of Man (1:51). This creates a palpable tension whereby both the disciples and audiences are ripe for the promised revelation. With this tension in the air, Jesus and his disciples arrive in Cana.

2:1–12 The Encounter with Jesus's Mother and the First Sign at Cana in Galilee

The public ministry of Jesus is fully inaugurated at a wedding feast at Cana in Galilee (2:1). This first sign looks back to the preparatory days of Jesus's public appearances, while it also begins to reveal the fullness of his ministry and passion. From its opening words, the symbolism of the scene points inevitably to the revelation with which it ends. On the discourse level, the content of that revelation is the perfection of God's activity at the Jewish festival of **Pentecost**. The verses that narrate the beginning of the signs that Jesus performs throughout his public ministry open with the temporal designation "on the third day" (2:1). This explicit designation of time resonates the experience of God's revelation at Sinai, as narrated in Exodus. In that event, "On the third new moon after the Israelites had gone out of the land of Egypt, on that very day, they came into the wilderness of Sinai" (19:1). When presented with the opportunity to become God's "treasured possession out of all peoples" if they make a covenant with God, the people respond without qualification, "Everything that the LORD has spoken we will do" (19:5–8). In response, God says to Moses, "Go to the people and consecrate them today and tomorrow. Have them wash their clothes, and prepare for the third day, because on the third day the LORD will come down upon Mount Sinai in the sight of all the people" (19:10–11). This is followed by the promised revelation of the glory of God, including the covenant beginning with the Ten Commandments, which takes place "on the third day" (19:16). Therefore, marking the narrative of the wedding feast at Cana "on the third day" brings the revelatory event of the Sinai covenant to the forefront.

Following on this temporal marker, the first two verses set the stage for the action at hand and bring all the relevant characters onto the scene. What happens on this third day is a wedding feast in Cana, Galilee. The wedding celebration itself would have lasted seven days, but the festivities began with a procession in which the groom's friends brought the bride to the groom's house where the entire party gathered for a wedding supper. There, in the midst of this celebration, was **the mother of Jesus**. Although she is never named, the mother of Jesus is given primacy of place as the first character introduced in this passage, indicative of her role in the events to come. In fact, her designation as "mother" by the narrator (four times) is set in relief against how Jesus eventually addresses her as "woman" (v. 4). Her son Jesus, along with his disciples, was also invited to the wedding. Thus, the major characters are assembled, and the stage is set through symbols of a messianic banquet and the revelation of the glory of God.

The action begins as Jesus encounters his mother in this environment. Their dialogue alternates with the verses both instigated and concluded by Jesus's mother. The narrator quickly puts forth the problem and provides the motivation for the dialogue between Jesus and his mother. The wine for the wedding feast gave out, putting the groom in a potentially shameful position. Although the narrator has explained the situation, which is to be understood as a social

---

Redundant Narration

Redundant Narration is a storytelling technique whereby the narrator uses language that characterizes people, objects, times or places, which is then also used by a character in dialogue, usually repeated verbatim. This technique serves to confirm the veracity or integrity of those characters. An example from early in the Gospel of John is when, in the omniscient prologue, the narrator characterizes John the Baptist as saying of Jesus, "He who comes after me ranks ahead of me because he was before me" (1:15). John then utters these exact words in 1:30. He is one whom readers should trust. We see this same technique here in John 2:1–12.

crisis, Jesus's mother's words focus the scene and bring her to center stage. She says to Jesus, "They have no wine." Jesus's mother's brief statement, however, only magnifies the tension. Is she requesting something from him? A miracle? Or just a run to the market? Moreover, she virtually repeats what the narrator has just stated. Although it may seem to be repetitive in the context of the narrative, she becomes the character who perceives the problem and makes it known to Jesus. This technique of "redundant narration" confirms for audiences the integrity of the mother of Jesus. She can be trusted and sought for guidance in responding to Jesus. This makes Jesus's response all the more challenging, "Woman, what concern is that to you and to me? My hour has not yet come."

The question Jesus puts to his mother has been described as one of the most difficult phrases of this Gospel. The full reply, the only thing Jesus says to her in this passage, presents a twofold response, each side of which is challenging. His first words are ambivalent and followed by an apparent non sequitur about his "hour." That he then proceeds to do something about her statement only intensifies the ambiguity. The verbless clause in Greek can be translated literally in English, "What (is) to me and to you?" The expression is terse even in the original. The question then becomes, what *is* between the two of them, if anything? If the presumption of negativity is set aside, we can note that, on the more personal level, the "what" of this expression seems to invoke the idea of relationship. Given the established symbolic context of revelation and the Sinai covenant celebrated at the feast of Pentecost, this idea of relationship language begins to make sense of the interaction between Jesus and his mother at the wedding feast. She makes known to him the lack of wine; he responds with a sharp question of challenge. But what is the nature of this relationship? The second part of Jesus's response seems to indicate what it is not: "my hour has not yet come." With this statement, the theme of **the hour** is introduced to the Gospel. Jesus's cryptic references to his hour will drive his entire public ministry (4:21, 23; 5:25, 28; 7:30; 8:20), and its arrival (12:23, 27) will mark the turning point of the Gospel (13:1), the content of his passion (17:1), and the future of his church (19:27). With this statement in response to his mother's declaration of the lack of wine, Jesus signifies that the hour of his full glorification has not yet arrived and that part of his covenant will have to wait for its full expression.

The mother of Jesus accepts this without qualification. Her next words confirm her acceptance and indicate the role that she will take. Resonating with the words of the Israelites at Sinai, and again at the ritual that seals the covenant, "Everything that the Lord said, we will do" (Exod 19:8; 24:3, 7), she turns to the servants and says, "Do whatever he tells you" (v. 5). She accepts his challenge just as the Israelites accepted the covenant at Sinai, and her imperative sets in motion the revelation. Her role fulfilled for the moment, she fades from the scene. The remaining verses are marked by command and response as the servants respond to his mother's command by further obedience to the commanding word of Jesus (vv. 7–8). As silent "doers" of the word, they implicitly partake of the relationship established by the interaction between Jesus and his mother. The rest of this episode is a continual acting out of this "doing" the word of Jesus. He commands them to "fill the jars with water," and they "filled them up to the brim." This is another example of redundant narration, this time direct speech followed by narration to confirm the right response of the servants. Jesus then commands them again, "Now draw some out, and take it to the chief steward," and "so they took it." The word of Jesus and the responsive action of the servants resolve the problem at the wedding feast.

The chief steward then enters the scene and steps into the spotlight (vv. 9–10). His role in this narrative is to verify the sign. Jesus also fades from the scene for the moment. The characters who bridge the narrative this time are the servants who bring what they have drawn from the jars. The chief steward tasted the water become wine and immediately called the groom to confirm the abundance of wine, the miraculous nature of which he has no knowledge. It is the servants who have full knowledge of the event. They are still silent but nonetheless witnesses to the sign. They can attest that what the chief steward says to the groom is profoundly true, regardless of his own superficial understanding. The chief steward notes the goodness of the wine in what he understands to be the exceptional act of the groom. By mistakenly crediting the groom with this extraordinary act, the chief steward evokes images of a wedding banquet through which the groom inaugurates the messianic age with an abundance of wine. The dramatic irony is that the true "groom" is only just beginning to reveal himself.

The narrator returns to summarize the event and affirm its effects on several characters. The evangelist is not simply emphasizing the power of Jesus but his sovereignty as well. Jesus is the one whose word has the power to initiate covenant, made apparent through signs. Jesus "revealed his glory; and his disciples began to believe in him" (v. 11). The evangelist then makes clear the nature of the time before the arrival of "the hour." It is manifested through "signs" and its purpose is to begin the revelation of his glory. The full manifestation of the glory of God cannot be known until "the hour" arrives and God becomes the agent of the revelation. Here Jesus begins his participation in that glory so that his disciples may begin to believe in him. The disciples, who were present with Jesus at his arrival in Cana, are mentioned again for the first time since the action began. They have apparently been standing by all along and, like the servants, have become silent witnesses to the sign. Unlike the servants, however, they are merely observers at this stage. They have yet to become doers of the word. At this point, they are just becoming believers. And, unlike the mother of Jesus, they are farther still from perceiving the fullness of authentic faith. This process of becoming is a journey for the disciples that will span the rest of the Gospel. At Cana, it has only just begun.

The final verse of this passage brings the major characters back together and introduces the brothers of Jesus to the Gospel. Their unbelief, over against the developing belief of the disciples, will come into play at a later stage (7:1–10). These last verses taken together form a frame with vv. 1–2 and bridge the narrative to the next events in Jesus's ministry. The narrative of the wedding feast at Cana thus captures in twelve verses the essence of the beginnings of the ministry of Jesus, as depicted in the Gospel of John with the mother of Jesus emerging as a model disciple with perfect faith.

2:13–25 *The Encounter with "the Jews" in the Temple Area in Jerusalem*

Once the wedding feast in Cana ended, Jesus and his entourage went down to Capernaum and remained there a few days (2:12). When the feast of the Passover drew near, he goes up to Jerusalem where his demonstration against commerce in the temple area brings him into his first confrontational dialogue with **"the Jews"** there (2:13–22). This is the first mention of the Passover in the narrative. Its annual recurrence becomes a major temporal marker in the Gospel (6:4; 11:55; 12:1). The passing of more than two years' time in this narrative allows for more growth and development of Jesus's ministry than seems to be indicated in the Synoptic Gospels, which mention only one Passover festival situated at the end of his life. At this point in our narrative, the drawing near of the springtime Passover celebration serves to motivate Jesus's travel to Jerusalem with thousands of other pilgrims during an intense period of celebration and remembrance of the presence and action of God in the life and history of Israel. The repeated mention of Jewish festal celebrations also allows for Jesus's frequent travel to, from, in, and around Jerusalem—something also not apparent in the other Gospels, which orient their narratives toward a single climactic journey to Jerusalem. More will be said about Passover and the Jewish festivals in the following chapter, but this intensity in the air sets the stage for this initial encounter between Jesus and his fellow countrymen in the temple area.

What Jesus finds on his first arrival in Jerusalem and the temple grounds is a "market-place," something he cannot condone in his "Father's house" (v. 16). He sees the selling of animals for sacrificial offerings as well as currency-exchange businesses, providing for the financial offerings that pilgrims will give during their time at the festival. Savvy entrepreneurs saw the need for these small businesses in the temple area since pilgrims traveling in convoys for days and weeks at a time from the surrounding regions could not be expected to bring their own livestock across such arduous journeys. In addition, coinage with engraved images was not allowed in the temple proper, and since most Roman money carried just such portraits of famous personages, pilgrims once again found themselves in need, this time of money changers for the temple fees. Therefore, not unlike gift shops and other souvenir options that pop up around contemporary shrines and sacred spaces, a niche market in the ancient world had been identified and served by these local businesspeople. Such commerce was not illegal. For Jesus, however, it is an intolerable commercialization of the house of God. He fashions a whip and overturns the tables, causing a scene and driving the sellers out of the area. With a reference to the OT prophet Zechariah (14:21), Jesus demands that they all get out of his Father's house. His disciples connect Jesus's activity and declaration with a psalm and being consumed by zeal for his Father's house (v. 17; Psalm 69:9). "The Jews," however, were not impressed.

By disrupting the preparations, Jesus challenges what had become standard religious practices. We must here remember our discussion of the role of "the Jews" in the Gospel of John from chapter six. Here, "the Jews" serve as the voice of reaction to Jesus's prophetic action and challenge to the temple proceedings. They ask for a sign to justify his challenge, questioning the source of his authority and giving the first indication that "signs" might not really be the focus of Jesus's ministry. The dialogue between Jesus and "the Jews" serves as a sharp contrast to the abundance and commitment of the Cana narrative and pres-

---

The Temple Area

The period of Jesus's life is generally identified as the time of the Second Temple (e.g., Second Temple Judaism). The very large space occupied by the Jerusalem Temple in Jerusalem was made up of three discrete regions, surrounded by a large area where Gentiles were permitted, called the court of the Gentiles. Furthest from the Sanctuary (the Holy of Holies) was the court of the women. Closer to the Sanctuary was the court of the Israelites, strictly reserved for suitably prepared Jewish men. The final court was for the Priests. It contained the altar of sacrifice and the Holy of Holies. It was regarded as the dwelling place of God. After its destruction in 70 CE the rabbis looked back on the memory of the temple as the dwelling place on earth of the "glory of God."

---

ents the initial indication of a sharp misunderstanding of Jesus's often enigmatic and metaphorical words, which will eventually lead to the opposition and rejection introduced in the prologue. Jesus speaks metaphorically of the impending destruction of the temple of his body, and "the Jews" take him literally, referring to the current renovations of the temple begun under Herod the Great ca. 19 BCE. This tremendous rebuilding effort was not completed until ca. 63 CE. The reference to 46 years would place this encounter at ca. 28 CE. The conversation ends here, for they have reached an impasse at the moment. It is once again the disciples who continue to be silent observers of the words and actions of Jesus, such that after his earthly ministry has completed, they can understand the fulfillment of his word as Scripture (v. 22). Audiences of the Gospel, however, are provided the interpretation of Jesus's metaphor now by the narrator in v. 21. The evangelist continues his practice of inviting audiences into the deeper symbolic world of Jesus's teaching. If the temple is the locus of the dwelling presence of God in Jewish belief and practice, Jesus is teaching that as the incarnate Word of God, he is now and will fully become the dwelling presence of God at the consummation of his death and resurrection.

This episode, often called the "cleansing of the temple," is indeed found in all four Gospels of the New Testament, but in the other three it is placed toward the conclusion of Jesus's public ministry during his one and only visit to Jerusalem. In those narratives, it serves as a "last straw" that puts Jesus in the crosshairs of his enemies and brings his passion rushing to the foreground. In the Gospel of John, however, we find this same well-known account at the onset of Jesus's public life in what will be the first of many activities in and around Jerusalem and the temple grounds. The two traditions cannot be reconciled. By placing it here, the evangelist presents Jesus in the stead of the OT prophets who constantly challenged the veracity of the religious authorities and their commitment to covenantal relationship with the God whose word they professed. More importantly, the presentation of Jesus as the new revelation of the glory of God develops, and the acceptance of his word as the mark of the new relationship with God continues, this time with the result of tragic misunderstanding and rejection.

The final verses of John 2 bring to the forefront this tension of knowledge and understanding, a tension between believing in the word of Jesus and seeing the signs he performs. Audiences begin to suspect more clearly that, although the signs and activity of Jesus will draw people to him, true faith in relationship with him is far more of a challenge (vv. 23–25). The narrator's tactical repetition of what Jesus "knows" of "people" also prepares audiences for Jesus's next encounter, this time with a "man" from the Pharisees who believes he "knows" what to expect from God.

The Temple Scene in the Synoptic Gospels

John narrates his understanding of Jesus's stand in the Temple Area as an inaugurating event of his ministry in Jerusalem (2:13–25). The Synoptic Gospels, however, narrate a strikingly similar scene as the capstone event of Jesus's public ministry (Matt 21:12–16//Mark 11:15–19//Luke 19:45–48). The timing of both scenes places Jesus in the crosshairs of the Jewish authorities; but while it sets an ominous tone to the rest of Jesus's ministry in John, it catapults the plot directly to the passion narrative in the Synoptics. All of the evangelists understand Jesus to be in conflict with the status quo of the temple area; how they narrate this seems to be a function of their larger storytelling strategies.

3:1–21 *The Encounter with Nicodemus in Jerusalem*

The narrator's comment about the knowledge and faith of Jesus leads into an extended dialogue instigated by **Nicodemus**, a leader of the Jews (3:1–21). Just as the negative encounter with "the Jews" in the temple area served as contrast to the positive encounter with his mother at the wedding feast in Cana, Jesus's encounter with Nicodemus shows that all is not lost even with the officialdom of Judaism. The somewhat naïve and literal questioning by Nicodemus provides Jesus the opportunity to teach about heavenly things, including God's love and plan for the world and the role of the Son of Man in that plan. Nicodemus, another new character in the narrative, comes to Jesus in Jerusalem. There has been no change of location from the previous encounter; therefore, Nicodemus has undoubtedly been attracted to Jesus's activity and comes to him. Nevertheless, he comes by night, a potential echo of the theme of darkness from the prologue. That he is coming to the light indicates his desire to believe in Jesus and his message. However, Nicodemus proves his journey will be a long one, as his understanding remains quite literal, and he will take some time to fully receive the metaphorical word of Jesus and let go of his preconceived religious categories.

We have already introduced Nicodemus in chapter six in terms of John's literary style. In this chapter, we will note how his initial encounter with Jesus can be interpreted. The dialogue proceeds in two stages, and these few verses contain both an enduring concept (v. 3) and one of the most famous lines of Christianity (v. 16). Nicodemus approaches Jesus with what he "knows" about Jesus as a rabbi from God, focusing on Jesus's signs. Jesus accepts this, but he immediately begins to push Nicodemus's knowledge further with an important teaching that begins with his characteristic double-amen statement. He speaks about the necessity of "being born from above" in order to "see the kingdom of God" (v. 3). As we outlined in chapter six, this term "above" comes from the Greek word *anōthen*, which has several connotations and has been variously translated as "anew" and "again." Jesus plays on this double meaning to challenge Nicodemus to a deeper understanding of God's work in the world. Nicodemus would have been familiar with the notion of God as king, but this challenge to be born from above/again in order to "see" this kingdom pushes him to expand his notions of God and kingship and "see" Jesus as something beyond a God-sent teacher and miracle-worker. Nicodemus, however, shows that he has not grasped the spiritual intention of Jesus's use of "above" when he asks about the biological possibility of being born "again." This kind of naïve misunderstanding will happen time and again across Jesus's ministry, but it allows Jesus the opportunity to speak more about the nature of the Spirit and the need to be born of the Spirit to truly be a part of his kingdom. John had testified that he baptizes with water, but the one coming would baptize with the Holy Spirit (1:29–34). This promise is now fulfilled in the Spirit brought by Jesus. Unfortunately this does not bring Nicodemus, who is just beginning his journey, any closer to understanding, and he says as much. Jesus responds in such a way that he concludes this initial dialogue and shifts the image of the heavenly things and the role of the Son of Man, not unlike what he did with Nathanael in the early days of his ministry (1:50–51).

John's Unique Understanding of the Cross

Already this early in the narrative (John 2–4), John indicates that he has a special idea of the cross: yes, a physically painful "lifting up," but *also* an exaltation that manifests the glory of God and sets in motion the glorification of the Son. This understanding is developed further as the story progresses. See, for example:

> So Jesus said, "When you have lifted up the Son of Man, then you will realize that I am he, and that I do nothing on my own, but I speak these things as the Father instructed me" (8:28).

> "And I, when I am lifted up from the earth, will draw all people to myself." He said this to indicate the kind of death he was to die (12:32–33).

Jesus teaches that the Son of Man has descended from heaven and will teach all who will hear about both earthly and heavenly things, and he will give all who receive this teaching eternal life in the kingdom of God (vv. 11–13). Just as Moses pointed to the signs and wonders of God for the children of Israel in the desert after the Exodus by "lifting up" the serpent, so must the Son of Man be lifted up to bring this promise to fulfillment. Here again Jesus makes use of the fullness of a potential double meaning of the lifting up in the physical sense: Moses lifting the rod over his head, as well as the potential meaning of "lifting up" in terms of exaltation and the wonder of God. In this way, Jesus is able to point metaphorically to his coming crucifixion and lifting up on the cross as a new sign of the wondrous power of God to forge relationship (vv. 14–15). The cross will be *both* a physical "lifting up" *and* an "exaltation." Jesus can then utter the line that has become the encapsulation of the entire gospel story: "For God so loved the world that he gave his only Son, so that everyone who believes in him may not perish but may have eternal life" (v. 16).

Another theme of the Gospel emerges here as the immensity of God's love is proven integral to the mystery of salvation. The gift of the Son is the essence of the saving power of the new covenant, and this salvation is and will be available to any and all who receive and believe in him. Indeed, the entirety of this mission is not for condemnation, in the sense of sentencing people to punishment, but rather to bring light into the world and make possible salvation from its darkness (vv. 17–18). However, an openness to this light and the action of God and the Son of God is necessary. In a reference back to the verses that closed the previous chapter and transitioned into this encounter, Jesus refers to the darkness that lives in the hearts of some and that leads them not to come to the light (vv. 19–20). Jesus closes, however, with a renewed reference to truth and life and the grounding of their lives in the presence of God (v. 21).

As Jesus's dialogue with Nicodemus slips into a monologue, he brings into words and thus the story world of the narrative the promises the narrator has made about him. In this way, the evangelist continues the narrative's task of *showing* what the prologue *told*. Jesus is forming new children of God through the gift of salvation for all who are open to his word. This encounter with Jesus concludes without resolution for Nicodemus. In coming to Jesus, he showed the openness necessary for full relationship, but he came expecting to have what he already "knew" confirmed, and thus his restricted religious categories stifled his progress. Jesus, as we have seen, destroys these categories and challenges those he encounters to full relationship with him. There is hope for Nicodemus, and audiences often identify with him, even if they sense they shouldn't!

The Temporal Marker "After This"

The evangelist uses the Greek phrase *meta tauta* to mark the passing of time across the Gospel (2:12; 3:22; 5:1; 6:1; 7:1; 11:7; 19:38; 21:1). Although it literally means "after these things," it is often translated simply as "after this." The use of this temporal marker seems to indicate the passing of a good deal of time, relative to the situation.

His openness is a sign that his believing process has begun, but his faith is partial. For the rest of his story, audiences must press on (see 7:45–52; 19:38–42). The scene ends with Jesus's final words hanging in the air: "But those who do what is true come to the light, so that it may be clearly seen that their deeds have been done in God" (3:21). It is time to encounter once again someone sent from God who witnesses to the truth of the light.

3:22–36 *The Encounter with John the Baptist and His Final Witness in Judea*

The narrator indicates that, after these things, Jesus and his disciples move from Jerusalem to the Judean countryside where they spend some time baptizing (3:22). We are coming to understand that this phrase "after these things" or "after this" serves as a temporal marker for the evangelist. It marks the passing of some time, possibly a good deal of time, and it moves the plot forward to the next event the evangelist believes is necessary to share in order to deliver his good news.

As in the first verses of the wedding scene in Cana, key characters are gathered early on into a scenario that provides the basis and motivation for the dialogue that follows. Jesus and his disciples are participating in a baptizing ministry. John was likewise continuing his own baptizing ministry. The narrator then informs audiences that "John, of course, had not yet been thrown into prison" (v. 24). Through this last comment, the narrator points beyond the story at hand, indeed beyond what he will ever narrate. Yet with this one aside, he provides a reason for this current encounter and alludes to the entirety of John the Baptist's story. By assuming that audiences are already familiar with the end of John the Baptist's life, the narrator exchanges a knowing nod with them and punctuates this final scene of the model witness introduced in the prologue.

A debate arises between the disciples of John the Baptist and "a Jew" regarding purification (v. 25). Although no details of this controversy are provided, it spurs John the Baptist's disciples to come to him with concern over the increasingly successful baptizing ministry of Jesus. John the Baptist's disciples address him as "Rabbi" and inform him that "the one who was with you across the Jordan, to whom you testified, here he is baptizing, and all are going to him" (v. 26). This rather pointed way of speaking emphasizes the contrasting subjects of John and Jesus, while illustrating the disciples' anxiety over the situation. The exaggerated "all" confirms that John the Baptist's ministry is declining noticeably. In the shame and honor culture of the ancient world, we should expect this information to be very concerning. For his part, however, John continues his persistent defiance of human expectations by responding counter-culturally and offering his final witness to Jesus.

The heart of this passage is John the Baptist's response, which is solemn and definitive. He begins by speaking not of Jesus directly but of the sovereignty of

---

Shame and Honor in the Culture of the Ancient World

Students of the New Testament and the ancient Mediterranean world in general must bear in mind the important place of honor and shame in these societies. Honor was universally regarded as the highest asset for human beings, while shame was the ultimate burden. Much of public life, therefore, revolved around ensuring one's family received honor and avoided shame. This means that, with such a high value placed on honor, humility was rarely considered virtuous. Unlike modern society, activity such as boasting and other efforts at self-congratulation and promotion were esteemed, but deference and self-effacement were shameful. This makes John the Baptist's attitude toward Jesus and his mission in John 1 and here again in John 3 both counter-cultural and an exceedingly important witness for those around him.

God. A human being is able to receive only what is given from heaven (v. 27). Just as he was presented in the prologue, John the Baptist continues to highlight the gift-giving prerogative of God and the receiving power of humankind. Then, echoing his first witness to the Jewish delegation, John the Baptist calls his own disciples to be his witnesses and repeats, "I am not the Messiah" (v. 28; see 1:20). The one proclaimed in the prologue as sent to witness to the light continues to fulfill this role. Here John the Baptist points to Jesus verbally, just as he did those first days (1:29, 35–36), thereby clearly linking the expected messiah with Jesus, whose ministry is now in question.

John the Baptist then turns to the messianic imagery of marriage and applies the role of the friend of the bridegroom, what we might call the "best man," as a metaphor for his role in the events at hand. As the friend, he rejoices at the success of the groom. John is the voice of one crying in the wilderness (v. 28; see 1:23) who witnesses to Jesus, whom he now characterizes with the messianic image of the bridegroom. He is not the voice of the groom. Therefore, as the friend "who stands and hears him," rather than being envious or in any way upset, he "rejoices greatly" on account of that voice. John the Baptist can then proclaim that his "joy has been fulfilled," indicating with emphasis the finality of his current witness. He now refers directly to Jesus: "He must increase, but I must decrease." Contrary to ancient societal expectations of one whose ministry has achieved what John's has until now, he willingly yields to Jesus's expanding ministry. John the Baptist explodes convention precisely because his role lies outside human bounds, so that his very decline in the face of Jesus's increase means that his duty is complete and his role fulfilled.

The final words of this scene, and the final verses of this journey through Jewish territory, expand upon the role and experience of the one who comes from above (3:31–36; the geographical shift in 4:1–4 is discussed below). Scholars have debated from whose lips these words are uttered, John the Baptist's or the narrator's? It seems, however, that this passage is a final discourse by the narrator to summarize and conclude this first leg of the journey from Cana to Cana. These verses affirm why Jesus must increase, and they also reject the concern of John the Baptist's disciples, who can be included among those who belong to "the earth" and speak about "earthly things." At the same time, these condemning words also apply to "the Jews" who rejected Jesus at the temple in Jerusalem (2:18–22) as well as to Nicodemus who has not yet let go of earthly categories and concerns (3:1–21). The narrator then repeats key positive actions introduced in the prologue and manifested in the narrative thus far: witnessing, giving, and receiving. The trustworthiness of John the Baptist, the one sent from God, is affirmed, and whoever receives his witness confirms that God is true.

This section then closes by introducing the love of God for Jesus as the relationship of the Father to the Son. Because of this familial relationship, the Father has given all things to the Son. The words and actions of Jesus in the story thus far, and in the fullness of the Gospel to come, flow from this relationship. This gift of God, however, puts a choice before the world. Believing in the Son is the decision that confers eternal life, while the alternative to believing is characterized not as disbelief but as disobedience. The one who disobeys chooses not life but to abide in God's wrath (v. 36). This may seem to be a difficult, even surprising, way to end this encounter. When we explore the OT, however, we find that the phrase "wrath of God" is used in Exod 32:10–12 to describe God's reaction to Israel's disobedience as the people turn to the golden calf. This phrase is also found in the prophets to describe God's judgment upon Israel's turning from its relationship with God (e.g., Isa 9:19; Jer 30:24; Ezek 38:19; Hos 13:11; Zech 7:12). Just as Israel's covenant obligations to God were based on obedience, the evangelist uses the concept of disobedience to narrate the action of all who do not believe the Word of God. John has already taught that this Word gives life, and this is the activity of Jesus that is increasing, even as John the Baptist's witness completes and, his role fulfilled, he must decrease.

4:1–3 Transition—Jesus Leaves Judea and Moves to Non-Jewish Territory

Jesus's journey with his disciples continues, now through a conscious decision to leave Judea and return to Galilee by way of Samaria. This route is remarkable in and of itself. Many Jews would have taken a longer and ostensibly safer route across the Jordan River through the Gentile region of the Decapolis to avoid the region of Samaria with whose residents they have a long tradition of discord and animosity extending from the time of the divided monarchy ca. 920 BCE. That Jesus "had to go through Samaria" is probably both a political expedience and a theological necessity (v. 4). He had made some enemies in Judea, and good judgment may dictate that he move on as quickly as possible. However, theologically speaking, it may also be time for Jesus to make his way out of Jewish territory and take on the wider world. This is part of God's plan for Jesus's saving presence. With whom would it be better to initiate this foray than those who share so much history and faith with the Jewish people, yet with whom they are so divided? So Jesus and his disciples move into Samaria and make their way to the village of Sychar. Thus, the remainder of the journey from Cana to Cana moves through territory outside the world of Judaism. After an extended discussion with a Samaritan woman at a well, which is presented in two segments (4:4–15 and 4:16–30), Jesus has a brief interlude with his disciples alone (4:31–38). This account of Jesus's time in Samaria then concludes with him spending several days in the Samaritan woman's village teaching all the people there to believe in his word (4:39–44).

4:4–15 *The Encounter with the Samaritan Woman at Jacob's Well (part 1)*

This is a challenging encounter for scholars to interpret, and much has been written on it across the centuries. Audiences familiar with the other Gospels may notice that, like all the encounters in this section of the narrative, this passage is unique. Like the wedding feast at Cana, no other Gospel contains an encounter in this setting, with a woman from a Samaritan village at a well. Audiences will also notice that, like the mother of Jesus with whom this section begins and the royal official with whom this section ends, this woman with whom Jesus has an even lengthier dialogue is never identified by name. In addition, like Nicodemus, this character does not appear in the other Gospels. Even the cleansing of the temple scene, the final encounter with John the Baptist, and the upcoming encounter with the royal official are all unique and "out of place" with the rest of the gospel tradition. Therefore, John's distinctive traditions about Jesus continue to be recounted in particular ways to teach his community about Jesus and about believing in his word. But what are we to learn in 4:4–44? We have already suggested that this segment of the journey from Cana to Cana will teach us about the impact of Jesus and the availability of the relationship of faith with him outside of Judaism; but what of *this* woman and her *Samaritan* ethnicity?

Historically, the traditional interpretation has focused on the gender of the woman and, more specifically, her sexuality; the implication being that this is simply a(nother) case of Jesus reforming a sexually promiscuous, outcast woman and bringing her back into a community of faith. More recent interpretations have focused on her ethnicity, as we have done, and understood her to be a representative figure for all Samaritans and this encounter to be an incorporation of the Samaritan people into the new community. At the same time, recent feminist interpretations have attempted to reclaim her gender in order to understand her role as becoming a disciple of Jesus and apostle to the rest of her community, thus establishing a leadership role for women in the new community. The rather brief discussion that follows continues to build upon these recent explorations of the encounter between Jesus and **the Samaritan woman** to draw out both her womanhood and her "Samaritan-hood" as integral to understanding what the evangelist is teaching his community in this passage.

The encounter begins as Jesus, tired from his journey, comes to rest in Sychar by Jacob's well at about midday (vv. 5–6). By setting the scene in this way, John associates this encounter with the OT patriarchs in general and Jacob who becomes Israel in particular. The city of Sychar has been associated by some scholars with the OT city of Shechem, where the twelve tribes of Israel came together in a union of covenant renewal (Joshua 24). Since the time of the divided monarchy after the death of King Solomon, when Samaria became the capital of the northern kingdom that seceded from Judah, the Jewish people had considered their northern counterparts apostates from the true faith in God. In the first century CE, Samaritans held to a Torah-centered faith that focused on the patriarchs, centralized worship on Mount Gerizim, and looked for a messiah who would be a prophet like Moses, while the Jewish people held to a broader scriptural tradition that included the prophets, centralized worship in Jerusalem, and looked for a messiah-king in the line of David. Although sharing the same founding history, the two ethnic groups currently shared nothing else in common, including food, drink, and utensils. In this environment, Jesus takes a break alone as the disciples go for food and meets a Samaritan woman who comes to the well for her daily chore of drawing water (vv. 7–8). The scene is thus set for an encounter through which Jesus once again explodes social convention and incorporates a woman who is also a Samaritan into his ministry. At the same time, on the discourse level of the Gospel, the evangelist can teach that Jesus also fulfills the expectations of the Samaritans and reconciles this long-standing division.

> **Samaritans**
>
> The Samaritans occupied the central section of the land formally occupied by the nation of Israel. After the destruction of the northern kingdom of Israel in 722 BCE (see 2 Kgs 17), the conquering Assyrians introduced various other ethnic groups into the region and deported many Jewish people elsewhere. The Samaritans developed their Law (Torah) and had their own temple on Mount Gerizim. The Jewish people of Galilee (north) and especially Judea and its capital in Jerusalem (south) regarded them as no longer of Jewish ethnicity and tradition.

Jesus initiates a dialogue with the woman, a surprising move in itself, by asking for a drink in the command form, "Give me a drink" (v. 7). With the imperative he takes an authoritative tone, even as he puts himself in the role of a supplicant requesting hospitality for a basic need from a person with whom his people deny kinship. Therefore, he implies that he is rejecting the religious and familial division between these ethnic groups from the outset. For her part, the woman takes a strong tone herself and implicitly denies his request by questioning his actions based on these long-standing divisions (v. 9). Jesus responds in his now typically metaphorical way with a reference to the gift of God and living water. By using the Greek term *pēgē* to identify this well in v. 6, the narrator has indicated that it is a spring-fed well, fed by running, or living, water. The language of the prologue has already introduced the "gift" of God as covenant (1:14–18). Therefore, in putting forth the condition of knowing "who it is" speaking with her in terms of knowing the gift of God, Jesus is once again challenging his dialogue partner, this time a woman from outside of Judaism, to new relationship available through him (v. 10). Further, he hints at the coming revelation of himself as the "I am" of God in v. 26.

The Samaritan woman's response is twofold and could simply indicate naïve misunderstanding on par with Nicodemus, but then seems to go further and break into the symbolic level. She first points out his lack of a bucket and the deepness of the well, then making what could simply be a mocking reference to the "living water." But then she asks how he compares to Jacob, "our ancestor" and giver of the well. On a more symbolic level, her question could be quite serious. Who *is* Jesus in relation to their shared history? Jesus responds, as is becoming his practice, not by answering her question directly but by challenging her to think further, on the theological level, about the living water he gives, as it will become "a spring of water gushing up to eternal life" (vv. 13–14). Now it is the Samaritan woman's turn to demand water. She says, "Sir, give me this water . . ." Is she accepting his challenge for herself, representing all Samaritans? Her answer is twofold again, and this time the second part indicates that she is not quite there yet, as she refocuses on the daily chore of drawing water (v. 15).

4:16–30 The Encounter with the Samaritan Woman at Jacob's Well (part 2)

Jesus, therefore, redirects the dialogue with a new command, "Go, call your husband, and come back" (v. 16). So we have a new start, this time with a focus on the woman's married life and Jesus's status as a prophet. But on a symbolic level, the language remains that of relationship. Jesus and the woman continue to explore covenant and the potentiality of relationship. The woman admits that she has no husband, and Jesus affirms her truth but not until he articulates a lengthy marriage history that is no doubt an unhappy one (vv. 17–18). Audiences might remember that Hosea, the prophet to the northern kingdom, primarily used the language of marriage, and broken marriage, to speak of the northern kingdom's covenant relationship with God and what he considered its breach of that covenant. Thus, Jesus is also articulating the current broken state of the Samaritans' relationship. The woman gleans this and begins to see Jesus is a prophet. This, for her as a Samaritan, opens the discussion to the possibility of Christology. Any mockery is gone as she opens herself to what Jesus may have to give. She pursues this by asking about worship and the divisions between them (v. 19–20). Her openness now also begins to look like that of Nicodemus

Christ and the Woman of Samaria by Benedetto Luti

and allows Jesus to teach her about the coming reconciliation of all worship in and through spirit and truth from the Jews by way of knowledge of the Father. In response to this, she speaks specifically of the role of the messiah, and Jesus responds with his first explicit acceptance of this title and self-identification with God, the Father of both Jews and Samaritans. The "I AM" of v. 26 is the "I AM" of the sacred name of God revealed to Moses at the burning bush (Exodus 3:14) and unfolds the promise of v. 10. In accepting her hope for the Messiah, relating this encounter with that between God and the prophet Moses, and identifying himself with the sacred name of God, Jesus presents himself to the

Samaritan woman as the fulfillment of covenant, worship, and messianic expectations of both Jews and Samaritans. Although the woman makes no verbal acceptance of Jesus's revelation and challenge, she does, like many disciples before her (e.g., Mark 1:6–20), leave her belongings and earthly responsibilities where they lay and run to share her message. Seeking confirmation for her encounter, she also becomes an apostle sent to the village to share the news of the one coming to them (vv. 28–30).

4:31–44 *The Encounter with the Samaritan Villagers*

Before this encounter is complete (i.e., Jesus's encounter with the world outside of Judaism, with his closest ethnic siblings, the Samaritans), Jesus has an interlude with his disciples. They pass the woman on her way and seem concerned about Jesus's interaction with her and what she may be seeking from him, but they say nothing (v. 27). On the discourse level, some scholars take this as the voice of concern about the role of either the Samaritans, women, or both, in the Johannine community. Up to this point, the disciples have been largely silent observers and go-betweens in Jesus's ministry. Here Jesus addresses their earthly concerns about his food as well as their more religious concerns about his mission plans. In response to their inquiries, he gives them their first clear teaching about his mission and their ministry, which will ultimately result from it (vv. 31–38). His food is to do the will of the one who sent him, and in this case, it is to incorporate the Samaritans into relationship through the discipleship of this woman. Their labor will come later as they embark upon their own ministries in his stead.

Jesus's time in Samaria closes in 4:39–44 with many of the Samaritan villagers believing in Jesus, first because of the witness of the woman and then because of Jesus's own word. Her mission is finally perfected in the full faith of the entire village, resulting from their own encounter with Jesus and his saving word. In this journey that gives instruction on who Jesus is and the progression of individual witness and group faith, the evangelist's purposes are made clear particularly in the final declaration of the Samaritan villagers, as they reflect upon their experience of the word of Jesus: "we know that this is truly the Savior of the world" (v. 42). The word of Jesus is now proclaimed to be meaningful and effective, not only for Judaism, but for the entire world. With this pronouncement in the air, Jesus returns to Galilee (vv. 43–44).

4:45–54 *The Encounter with the Royal Official and the Second Sign at Cana*

As he has in the previous encounters, the narrator sets the closing scene in this educational journey of faith temporally and geographically, reflecting with audiences upon where they have been while at the same time providing the motivation for the event at hand. As the narrative moves back out of Samaria and into Galilee, we also recall the events at the Passover festival in Jerusalem as John mentions the notoriety Jesus has achieved as word of him and his actions spread through the countryside with the returning Galileans. In the midst of this setting, the narrator inserts a traditional saying attributed to Jesus himself regarding a prophet's lack of honor in his own country. It may seem difficult to situate this saying within the context of Jesus traveling, after two successful days in Samaria, into Galilee where he is also welcomed. By relating this bit of information here, however, the narrator achieves two things. First, he punctuates the reality that with John the Baptist's witness complete, it is now Jesus who must give voice to testimony (v. 44; see 5:31, 36; 7:7; 8:14, 18; 10:25; 13:21; 18:37). Second, John signals once again that this sort of welcome based on signs and bold acts may not be the authentic faith that the prophetic figure of Jesus truly desires. Audiences are alerted to the notion that in the events to come, this sort of faith understanding may continue to be corrected. The scene itself is then introduced and heightens this alert by locating Jesus in Cana and harking back to the authentic faith that brought about the beginnings of his ministry (v. 46; see 2:1–12). Finally, the last new character in this scene is introduced: a certain **royal official**; and the motivation for the scene is set: his son lay ill in Capernaum.

The heart of the encounter between Jesus and the royal official is narrated in vv. 47–50. Although this title could identify either a Jew or a Gentile, the context of this dialogue—because it concludes Jesus's journey through the world outside of Judaism and because the evangelist tends to explicitly identify Jewish characters—suggests that audiences are to understand this official as a Gentile, and potentially a Roman centurion. Upon hearing that Jesus had returned from Judea to Galilee, the official went out and asked Jesus to go down (to Capernaum) and heal his son, for he was about to die. The next three verses recount the dialogue between Jesus and the official. The similarity between this encounter and that of Jesus's first visit to Cana is notable (2:1–12). In this passage, the primary dialogue falls again into three parts, beginning and ending with the word of Jesus and his conversation partner providing the central assertion. In the first Cana event, the primary dialogue was instigated and carried forward by his mother, with Jesus's covenantal challenge holding her statement and response together. What we see here is a progression in the discourse based upon the fullness of the journey that has occurred from Cana to Cana.

Jesus responds to the official's entreaty with another provocative challenge: "Unless you see signs and wonders, you will not believe" (v. 48). The narrator has recounted the official's act of requesting, and since Jesus has not been characterized as a physician of any sort, audiences must understand this entreaty, as does Jesus, in terms of "signs and wonders." This again is a progression from the first Cana story, for now it is Jesus's renown that has led this official from the larger world to him. For his part, Jesus seems to be challenging the official to communicate what it is he really wants, and what he truly believes. He challenges the official beyond signs and wonders. But Jesus directs his verbal challenging not just to the official. He accuses "you people" of not believing without seeing signs and wonders. His statement in the plural extends beyond the official, who faces him, to the Galileans, who stand behind this dialogue as festive hangers-on (v. 45).

The royal official responds to Jesus's harsh words in the face of his dire need by, instead of retreating, taking a verbal step closer to Jesus. He says, "Sir, come down before my little boy dies" (v. 49). He refers to the child as "my little boy," while the narrator described him as "his son." This more intimate way of referring to his sick child would begin to humanize this government official even to the most skeptical audience member. Jesus acknowledges the official's verbal approach in response to his challenge in command form. Jesus tells him to "go, your son is living" (v. 50). The official, now further humanized as "the man," began to believe, not in signs and wonders, but "in the word of Jesus," and went. The redundant narration of Jesus's command ("go. . . . and he went") affirms the right response of the man to Jesus's challenge and direction.

The final verses of John 4 narrate the consequences of the man's belief in the word of Jesus (vv. 51–54). Even as he is going down to Capernaum, he is met by his slaves who tell him that his child would live. Upon his inquiry about "the hour" of his child's improvement, the men respond precisely, which allows the official, here characterized solely in the familial role of a "father," to come to know that this healing correlates directly with the word of Jesus, "Your son will live" (v. 53). The restatement of the father's process of believing now includes his entire household's process of coming to belief. This seems to be the key to understanding the evangelist's intention here. Even authentic belief is not static, but it is a dynamic journey of coming to knowledge that deepens hand in hand with the missionary aspect of witnessing. It is in sharing his belief in Jesus, however authentic in foundation, that the royal official, who is also fully human and a father, can realize its full consequence for living. The final verse brings this encounter to a close in a manner that once again parallels the first sign at Cana in Galilee between Jesus and a Jewish woman and mother (v. 54; see 2:11–12). This now is the second sign that Jesus did here. The journey from Cana to Cana is complete, concluding in many ways the way it began, with a response of authentic faith, this time from a Gentile man and father.

What Have We Learned So Far?
Teaching People to Believe

The journey from Cana to Cana in John 2–4 is an educational one, through which the evangelist teaches the nature of authentic faith. As we arrive at 4:54, the ministry of Jesus has come a long way. All those he has encountered have been affected by his word and deed, some changed forever (John the

Baptist, the Samaritan villagers), others resolutely unchanged ("the Jews"), and still others slowly making the first steps along their own journeys of faith (Nicodemus, the Samaritan woman). Jesus, too, has been affected by these encounters. His interactions with people along the way are marked by his human experience of them and with them. As his renown spreads he is brought into contact with more and more people. Yet, in these ensuing encounters, he pushes harder for those he meets to believe in his word, despite that renown. His disciples, too, are journeying, watching, and remembering. This is a dynamic process of ever-challenging and deepening belief in the word, based in relationship. Audiences, likewise, are making this journey along with them.

The theological focus of this narrative unit, therefore, is on belief and its role in uniting people with God in relationship through Jesus. This new commandment of believing has emerged strongly over the course of these early chapters. Jesus is open to everyone he encounters, but he is also provocative and challenging. By approaching Jew and Gentile, man and woman, Samaritan and royal official alike, Jesus welcomes all, even as he makes strong christological claims about his relationship to God his Father. At the same time, Jesus also pushes people to a new openness both to God and to each other. In this way, believing also becomes part of the ethic of the Gospel. In the introduction to this textbook we noted that ethics refers to good or "right" action. The Gospel of John teaches that right action involves believing in the word of Jesus, which reveals God and God's welcome to everyone. This, in turn, leads those who receive and believe in Jesus to be open to and welcoming of all others, regardless of race, ethnicity, gender, or socio-economic class. We might refer to this call to believe as a vertical commandment between believers and God—one that is theological, christological, and ethical and that also leads to a horizontal summons to accept all others as fellow children of God. The evangelist will have much more to say about these commandments in the coming chapters, but John 2–4 fully establishes believing in the word of Jesus as foundational to the new relationship offered by God through Christ.

Key Terms and Concepts

Cana	Nicodemus
Galilee	Pentecost
Gentile	redundant narration
hour	royal official
"Jews"	Samaria
Judea	Samaritan woman
Mother of Jesus	

Questions for Review

1. In what ways does John 2–4 form the primary instructional section of the Gospel of John? What is the evangelist trying to teach his audience?

2. How are belief, sin, and authentic faith characterized in this journey of encounters? In other words, how does belief in the "Word" of the prologue play out in these chapters?

3. How and why might the mother of Jesus be understood to inaugurate the public ministry of Jesus and take the role of the model disciple during that ministry in John 2?

4. What is distinctive about John's story of Jesus cleansing the temple, and how does it introduce audiences to the key role of "the Jews"?

5. How does John the Baptist complete his role as witness in John 3? What does he mean by saying Jesus "must increase" while he "must decrease"?

6. Why is Jesus's traveling into Samaria something he "had" to do as part of his mission? With this in mind, identify and describe three ways the Samaritan woman at the well is symbolic of the character of the new covenant people Jesus is gathering; then conclude how Jesus can be proclaimed the "savior of the world" by the Samaritan villagers.

7. What does it mean to talk about a "journey of faith"? How might it make sense to understand the disciples as being on a journey of faith with Jesus from Cana to Cana?

Bibliography and Further Reading

Collins, Raymond. "The Representative Figures in the Fourth Gospel." *Downside Review* 94 (1976): 16–46.

Lee, Dorothy A. *Flesh and Glory: Symbolism, Gender and Theology in the Gospel of John*. New York: Crossroad, 2002.

Moloney, Francis J. *Belief in the Word: Reading John 1–4*. Minneapolis: Fortress, 1993.

Newsom, Carol A., Sharon H. Ringe, and Jacqueline E. Lapsley. *Women's Bible Commentary*. 3rd ed. Louisville: Westminister John Knox Press, 2012.

Schneiders, Sandra M. *Written That You May Believe: Encountering Jesus in the Fourth Gospel*. Revised and expanded ed. New York: Crossroad, 2003.

The Heart of Jesus's Public Ministry: People and Festivals in John 5–10

PURPOSE Chapter ten presents the next narrative unit of the public ministry of the Gospel (John 5–10) as the heart of Jesus's teaching. Focus will rest upon the Jewish festivals and Jesus's dialogues in Jerusalem, spoken in the context of these feasts as he challenges the people to faith.

ASSIGNMENT Reread John 5–10 before proceeding with this chapter.

In this chapter we will focus our attention on the third narrative unit of the Book of Signs, John 5–10. Jesus's public ministry is now in full swing, and as we work through these chapters we experience his actions and interactions during several **Jewish festivals**, or religious holiday celebrations. John 4 concludes with the narrator affirming the second sign Jesus performed in Cana in Galilee (v. 54), thereby providing the closing frame to the second narrative unit "from Cana to Cana." In John 2–4, the evangelist introduced the audience to the advent of Jesus's public ministry and the nature of authentic faith as believing in the word of Jesus. This new section opens with a temporal marker indicating that some time has passed, followed by the announcement of a Jewish festival (5:1). John 5–10 will take the audience through a year in the life of Jewish worship, teaching that the gift of Jesus has fulfilled the purpose of the Jewish feasts for those who believe in his word. The presence of God can now be experienced through faith in Christ. The evangelist's primary discourse, or teaching, of this narrative unit, therefore, focuses on bringing to completion in Jesus Christ God's original gift through Moses (as introduced in the prologue, 1:17).

The Narrative Flow and Structure of John 5–10

The signs, dialogues, and discourses of John 5–10 are contextualized by the central feasts of the Jewish ritual calendar. A year's time in the narrative passes, marked temporally by the general phrase, "after these things" (5:1; 6:1; 7:1), until the culminating designation "it happened then" (10:22). The feast of Pentecost was presented symbolically at the inauguration of Jesus's public ministry in Cana (across 1:19–2:12). Following his return to Cana (4:46–54), Jesus goes up to Jerusalem to an unnamed "feast of the Jews" (5:1) where he eventually engages in dialogue about the weekly feast of Sabbath (5:10). John 6 focuses on the spring festival of Passover (6:4). John 7 introduces an extended narrative section that runs through 10:21 and contains both a sign and several discourses and dialogues, all contextualized by the autumn feast of Tabernacles (7:2). In the midst of the Tabernacle festival, the final form of the gospel narrative has Jesus encountering a woman caught in adultery (7:53–8:11); while the aftermath of that same festival allows Jesus to heal a man born blind, the act of which has consequences of its own. The final feast that "was taking place" in these chapters is the winter festival of Dedication (10:22). Through perfection of the liturgical celebration of God's presence, belief in the word of Jesus pervades the evangelist's teaching across each festival narrative and discourse.

Therefore, the narrative unit constructed through John 5–10 can be diagrammed as follows:

Part Three: Jesus and the Jewish Festivals   5:1–10:42

5:1–47	Sabbath—Jesus Performs Works Limited to God on the Sabbath	
	5:1–15	Gift of Life [Healing] to the Man at Bethesda Pool
	5:16–47	Discourse on the Giving of Life and Sabbath Work
6:1–71	Passover—Jesus Gives Bread Perfecting the Manna of the Exodus	
	6:1–21	Miraculous Feeding of the Crowd; Walking on Water
	6:22–59	Jesus's Discourse on the Bread of Life
	6:60–71	Disciples' Responses to the Discourse
7:1–10:21	Tabernacles—Jesus Perfects the Water and Light Ceremonies	
	7:1–8:59	The Tabernacles Dialogues
		7:1–13 Introduction: Will Jesus Go Up to the Feast?
		7:14–36 Scene 1: Dialogues on the Middle Day of the Festal Week
		7:37–52 Scene 2: Dialogues on the Last Day of the Festal Week
		[7:53–8:11 The Woman Caught in Adultery]
		8:12–59 Scene 3: Dialogues Conclude: Jesus, Light of the World
	9:1–10:21	The Continuation of Tabernacles
		9:1–38 The Healing of the Man Born Blind
		9:39–10:21 Jesus as the Sheep-Gate and Shepherd
10:22–42	Dedication—Jesus Perfects the Temple as the Dwelling Presence of God	
	10:22–31	Jesus as the Messiah
	10:32–42	Jesus as the Son of God

Using this structure as our guide for exploring Jesus and his interactions through the festival and ritual life of Judaism, we will exegete John 5–10.

Interpreting John 5:1–10:42: Part Three—Jesus and the Jewish Festivals

In the Jewish Scriptures, the **feasts** of Israel are presented as **cultic** (i.e., group ritual) **celebrations** that recall God's saving action in the past and render that action present in the current community. Leviticus 23:1–44 narrates God's appointment of the feasts through Moses. The celebration of a Jewish feast is a *zikkārôn*, a "memorial," of God's past active presence in the lives of his chosen people (Lev 23:24). Although the term "feast" is a good translation of the original Hebrew and Greek words, it might be more descriptive to use the term "festival" since, for many contemporary audiences, "feast" conjures images of huge meals. By contrast, these celebrations were often multi-day affairs with several rituals as their focus. For the Jewish people, celebrating the liturgy of the feast manifests God's presence in previous times and events among the people in the current age.

As we discussed in chapter five, if the Johannine Christians had been expelled or felt alienated from the synagogues, they were not simply being excluded from these celebrations (a social experience), they may have felt that they were losing contact with the God of creation and God's saving action in history (a religious experience). As believers in the saving action of the Christ Event, they had been taught that relationship with God is engendered through the word of Jesus. But this presents other problems. What about the festivals and the experience of God's presence they facilitate? Not only does the Fourth Evangelist have to care for the community members pastorally because they

---

The Depth of the Hebrew Verb *zkr*

For modern languages, and especially English, "to remember" normally means to recall an event of the past in one's mind, or to remember important facts in order to establish what happened *in the past*. The biblical notion of "memory" and "to remember" (the noun *zikkārôn*, and the verb *zkr*) is richer. As the Israelites looked back upon their past and "remembered" God's creative actions (Sabbath), the Exodus (Passover), God's care for wandering Israel (Tabernacles), and God's dwelling in the Temple (Dedication), they did not just recall the past, as something that happened a long time ago. "Memory" and "to remember" meant to recall an action of God in the past in a way that *renders present* the Sabbath, Passover, Tabernacle, Dedication, and the God who dwells among them. This sense of memory is important in Christianity, as in the Eucharist it obeys Jesus's command: "Do this *in memory* of me." Christians celebrating Eucharist "remember" Jesus's death and resurrection and *render it present*.

are no longer in that world, he also has to show God's fidelity to them and God's continuing presence in their lives as members of a new community. This problem of having to rethink the celebrations of God's presence was not exclusive to the Johannine Christians at the end of the first century CE. Following the First Jewish War, Judaism was shifting from temple to synagogue-centered worship. The liturgy of the temple and the piety of the people were in a state of transition, since by this stage (end of the century) neither the temple nor its priesthood class (the Sadducees) existed. The temple had been destroyed by the Romans, and the Sadducees gradually joined mainstream Judaism. Reshaping the experience of God in the life of the community is, therefore, the background for this "**feasts section**" in John 5–10.

The evangelist renders "christological" the feasts of Judaism. What we mean by this is that he is teaching that it is Jesus the Christ who is the perfection of Jewish liturgy and theology. It is Jesus the Christ who brings God present in the ongoing lives of the community. This process began in John 2–4 in the presentation of the festival of Pentecost as the theological canvas behind the portrait of the wedding feast at Cana and the ensuing catechetical journey of faith from Cana to Cana. In John 5–10, the evangelist turns to the remaining major feasts of Judaism, Passover and Tabernacles, as well as the weekly feast of Sabbath and the minor festival of Dedication. The climactic close of John 10 is the revelation that Jesus and God are one.

This revelatory claim of Jesus as Christ and Son of God, coupled with the reality of being forced to worship outside the synagogue, is the crux of the emerging conflict between the Johannine Christians and mainstream Judaism as it is developing in the 90s CE. We see this reflected in the narrative as the spark of conflict between Jesus and "the Jews" catches fire across these chapters. Therefore, it bears repeating that "the Jews" in the Gospel typically form a group character that serves as the voice of opposition to this claim. The debate gets heated and the rhetoric becomes venomous as these opposing forces advance. We must take care to read it in its own context for the evangelist's specific literary and theological purpose, and not extend it generally into our own time and situation. On arrival at John 10, the audience has encountered a growing tension in the narrative between Jesus and his opponents. This tension leads to conflict (especially in John 7–8) and also involves his disciples (John 9). The conflict that will lead to a decision that Jesus must die (John 11–12) is now out in the open. With these historical and literary contexts in mind, we can turn our attention to a closer analysis of John 5–10.

Jewish Celebration of Sabbath

Sabbath is the fundamental feast of the Israelite religion. Looking back to God's resting on the seventh day (see Gen 2:1–4), each Sabbath celebrated the lordship of the God of Israel, creator and judge, the beginning and end of creation. John's message of Jesus the judge and giver of life in 5:1–47 reflects this Jewish understanding of the God of the Sabbath, placing Jesus likewise in that role.

5:1–47 Sabbath—Jesus Performs Works Limited to God

The next major movement in Jesus's public ministry, therefore, begins in John 5 at an unnamed "feast of the Jews" (5:1). The narrator's designation of this setting introduces themes of the next six chapters: how Jesus relates to the presence of God celebrated in the Jewish feasts and how the Johannine community is to begin to reshape its liturgical life. Audiences learn that the weekly feast of **Sabbath** is the focus of this first narrative and discourse, as Jesus sees a man lying near the pool by the Sheep Gate in Jerusalem and heals him on the Sabbath (vv. 2–9). As part of the healing command, however, Jesus instructs the man to carry his pallet. The man complies, thereby breaking Sabbath law. The controversy (vv. 10–15) and dialogue (vv. 16–47) that results is based upon the question of Jesus's authority to make such demands.

Although there may be another unnamed feast occurring during this episode, the audience is told explicitly that these events also occur on the weekly feast of Sabbath, or **shabbat** in Hebrew. The term is related to the verb "to rest," and the heart of festal celebration is setting this day apart each week by resting from the toils of daily life. Although the practice of keeping the Sabbath is detailed in both accounts of the Ten Commandments provided in the Old Testament (Exod 20:8–11; Deut 5:12–15), its origins necessarily reach back to the narrative of creation when God "rested" upon gazing at the "very good" expanse of his work (Gen 2:1–4). In the Ten Commandments, the faithful are instructed to "remember" and "observe" the Sabbath to keep it holy, or set apart. The rabbis developed many instructions about how to do this in the worship of God. One of the prohibitions pertinent to John 5 is "taking out anything from one domain to another." God, however, continued to work on the Sabbath to give life and sustain the moral governance of the universe. Behind Sabbath observance, therefore, is a belief in the creator-redeemer God who gives creation a holy day of rest in order to encounter God in worship.

Understanding this background helps us appreciate just how provocative it was for Jesus to perform this healing on the Sabbath, and then to take the extra step of commanding the man to take up his pallet and walk. In the ensuing discourse, he further shocks his audience by claiming the authority of God to do so, "My father is working still, and I am working" (5:17). This provokes the double accusation of breaking the Sabbath and blasphemy (5:18). In the discourse, Jesus can then take on the role of God on the Sabbath for himself in order to teach "the Jews" just who he is.

5:1–15 Gift of Life [Healing] to the Man at Bethesda Pool

Across John 5:1–47, therefore, Jesus performs works limited to God on the Sabbath, first by performing a sign, then by discoursing on his ability to do such work as allowed to God his Father. Jesus approaches one among the sick and infirm at the pool of Bethesda and offers him the gift of life through healing his crippled legs (vv. 1–15). Unlike the two previous signs, this man does not ask for help or even seem interested in the miracle that follows. Following the miraculous healing itself (vv. 1–9a), the narrator informs the audience that it is a Sabbath (v. 9b). This surprising detail makes sense of the coming verses and why "the Jews" question the man's movement with his pallet (vv. 10–13). Jesus then reveals himself to the man, who then, in a show of complete lack of gratitude, reports this to the authorities, thus bringing Jesus into their crosshairs "for making himself equal to God" (vv. 14–15).

5:16–47 Discourse on the Giving of Life and Sabbath Work

The bulk of the chapter is taken up with the resulting discourse, during which Jesus defends his authority to give life and to work on the Sabbath (vv. 16–47). Jesus is the only speaker in this extended scene, revealing to the audience the impetus for the healing on the Sabbath: to give him the opportunity to teach about himself and to give both his audience in the story and the audience of the story the opportunity to believe in his word. The focus of John 5, therefore, is not the sign but the discourse that follows from it. Indeed, the evangelist takes twice as many verses to narrate the latter as he does the former.

Jesus does not deny the charges that result from healing on the Sabbath, but he says that as the Son he can and must mirror the work of his Father, including giving life and judging. As the divine emissary of God, Jesus stands on behalf of God (vv. 16–21). Acceptance or rejection of Jesus is, therefore, acceptance or rejection of God. Belief in Jesus, however, brings the gift of eternal life (vv. 22–24). A double-amen statement prepares the audience for a significant teaching on Jesus as the judge who does the will of the Father who sent him (vv. 25–30). This allows Jesus to make the Gospel's final statement about John the Baptist as his witness sent from God. This language continues to give the scene the air of a trial. The focus is to give evidence of Jesus as likewise a giver of life (vv. 31–40). He shows an authority as life-giver and judge and suggests that he has been granted functions traditionally restricted to God. He can then close with a provocative challenge, justifying his work on the basis of covenant and Moses as God's prophet (vv. 41–47).

John's Use of Signs to Focus Discourses

It is imperative by this point in the narrative that audiences of the Gospel of John recognize that the signs that Jesus performs are not ends in themselves; that is they do not prove that Jesus is the Messiah. Signs simply draw people in and "wow" them. Although this sort of signs faith is a good start, it is not the faith that sustains through life's challenges. John narrates Jesus performing signs to provoke dialogue, even confrontation, so that he can teach the people to believe in his word—that he is the Word of God in human form. Pay special attention to the way the evangelist presents the signs and discourses across John 5, 6, 9, and 11.

What Jesus claims in these verses about his relationship to God and Sabbath is essential for further understanding who he is and the revelation of God that he brings. Jesus, as the Son of God the Father, transcends human bonds chronologically, historically, and legally (vv. 17, 19–47). "The Jews" reject this claim of transcendence and understand his words and actions to be blasphemous. Thus, they begin to seek "all the more to kill him" (v. 18). The healed man begins with full faith in his response (v. 9), becomes fragile as he shifts responsibility (v. 11), then falls away as he turns to stand with "the Jews" and accepts their authority and their categories as well as the application of both of these to his life (vv. 15–16). For his part, Jesus remains constant and in control ("My Father is working still, and I work," v. 17). The Sabbath was established for rest because God rested, but the sun keeps rising, and babies continue to be born. Therefore, God rests save for two primary functions: giving life and judging. Through this discourse Jesus places himself in the roles of life-giver and judge as well. He claims that he transcends Sabbath law by fulfilling the roles the Father has given him without destroying or replacing it. Jesus teaches that he is the new Moses in his humanity—the one who mediates God's covenant. But he is also more: he is the Son of the Father. In this way, he can give life through healing and is the embodiment of the Sabbath. He is rest. He is the presence of God. He is re-creative. The audience either believes in his word or takes up stones against him for blasphemy.

John 5 is the first episode in the body of the Gospel to clearly delineate Jesus's divinity as introduced in the Prologue (1:1–18). Jesus has been given titles by others among his gathering disciples (1:19–51) and taught those he encountered to believe in his word as Messiah (2:1–4:54), but now he makes the next, very challenging step of beginning to teach his divinity alongside his humanness. As the Son of the Father, he works alongside the Father and has such authority. The evangelist is teaching his audience that they no longer need to practice Sabbath in the traditional way in the synagogue from which they may have been expelled. Now they can experience the Sabbath in their new community through the presence of Christ among them. As the rabbis teach, God continues his creative and sustaining work even on the Sabbath. John uses his thoroughly Jewish understanding of the Sabbath to teach that Jesus is the new covenant of the creator-redeemer God. Indeed, he understands Jesus to perfect the Sabbath feast. The faith of the community in Jesus fulfills what they have lost and provides for an even deeper relationship with God and with each other.

6:1–71 Passover—Jesus Gives Bread Perfecting the Manna of the Exodus

John 6 opens with a new scene set and the active characters gathered at the outset. The expression "after these things" (6:1) once again marks a new time that allows for a new geographical setting as well. As the feast of Passover drew near, Jesus and his disciples, followed by a large crowd, went to the other side of the Sea of Galilee (vv. 1–4). This annual spring festival will contextualize the events and discourse at hand. The narrator also clarifies the reason for the presence of the crowds: "because they saw the signs he did on those who were sick" (v. 2). All this takes place as Jesus positions himself "on a mountain" (v. 3). These introductory remarks bring to mind images of Moses and his prophetic leadership in the Sinai wilderness after the Exodus and lead into the miraculous feeding of five thousand people with a boy's provision of five barley loaves and two fish (vv. 5–15). The crowds clamor to make Jesus king by force, leading him to withdraw (v. 15). He later comes to his disciples by night across the sea during the storm (vv. 16–21). The crowd is then regathered for the so-called Bread of Life discourse (vv. 22–59), which marks a new shift in the narrative of Jesus's public ministry as both the crowd and the disciples respond (vv. 60–71).

Some scholars suggest that the symbolism of Passover contributes more to the Gospel of John than any other festival. Three occurrences of the annual pilgrimage feast are noted: at 2:13, which provides the context for the rest of John 2; at 6:4, which contextualizes all of John 6; and at 11:55, which contextualizes all of John 12–20. To understand John 6 better, we will discuss the background, symbolism, and celebration of Passover in more detail. Alongside the festivals of Pentecost and Tabernacles, in the Second Temple period of Judaism (ca. 515 BCE–70 CE), **Passover** was a major pilgrimage festival that brought to bear both God's presence in the historic event of the Exodus and the messianic hopes of the nation. The celebration of the passage from winter to spring and the rebirth of creation also symbolized God's liberation of the people from all forms of slavery. The population of Jerusalem would swell as Jewish pilgrims from the diaspora would travel sometimes great distances to share in the celebration first described in Exod 12–14, in such a way that the memorial continually makes present God's saving action of freedom.

> **Jewish Celebration of Passover**
>
> The Jewish practice of Passover combined the memory of the slaying of the lamb and an ancient feast of unleavened bread that marked the Exodus. At the time of Jesus the celebration focused upon the liberation of Israel from slavery in Egypt, and the journey of God's people through the desert, nourished by God with the manna—bread from heaven. That "bread" ceased to fall once Israel entered the Promised Land, and Jewish teachers then taught that the Law (Torah) was now to be their "bread from heaven." These aspects of the feast are applied to Jesus in 6:1–71.

The book of Exodus narrates three distinct ceremonies in the Passover festival: the Passover sacrifice, the feast of Unleavened Bread, and the consecration of the firstborn. What were originally separate pre-Israelite rituals were adopted by the Israelites and reinterpreted in light of their experience of the Exodus and called *Pesach*. The two feasts acquired characteristics of the flight from Egypt and journey to freedom, while the blood of the lamb marked the new people of God. The communal aspect of the entire festival heightened this understanding of their relationship with God. In the Second Temple period, the feast of Passover came to be observed on the fourteenth of the month of Nisan. The feast of Unleavened Bread began on the fifteenth of Nisan and lasted seven days. In the afternoon of the fourteenth of Nisan, the lambs were ritually slaughtered and offered to God in the temple. The Passover meal included the *haggadah*, which is the telling of the story of the Exodus and its meaning for the current participants, and songs of praise from the Psalms in addition to the meal itself.

In John 6, the evangelist employs the rich imagery and meaning of Passover to cast Jesus in the light of Moses and God's gift of freedom both then and at the current moment. The evangelist recalls the gift of manna in the miraculous feeding and the authority of God over the sea when Jesus walks on water. The abundance and power evoke images of the messianic banquet and the liberation of the messianic age. Jesus can then communicate how all this power and presence of God is embodied in his person and mission, both inviting and challenging those around him to this new experience.

6:1–21 Miraculous Feeding of the Crowd; Walking on Water

The first of the two signs that Jesus performs during the Passover season of John 6 begins as Jesus, from the vantage point of the mountain, sees a mass of people drawing near to see what he might do and hear what he might say. The narrator reminds audiences of Jesus's knowledge and plan as he tests Philip's understanding of his mission with the question of how they might acquire bread to feed the people. Although Philip fails the test, Andrew presents a boy with a meager offering of barley loaves and fish, through which Jesus provides food for all. The language of thanksgiving, or *eucharist*, comes into play as Jesus blesses and distributes the meal (v. 11). Scholars often note that the Christian practice of the **Eucharist**, also called the "Lord's Supper" or the "Communion Meal," is reflected in this act as well as the discourse that follows. The evangelist's first audiences were likely very familiar with this early ritual and welcomed this imagery as well as the teaching Jesus provides about it.

As the meal concludes in vv. 12–15, the narrator notes that the people are all "satisfied," before sharing that Jesus ensured that all the leftovers were gathered so that nothing would be lost. Indeed, twelve baskets are filled. This reflects the abundance that Jesus provides, over against the limited resources of the manna in the wilderness after the Exodus. Jesus is the prophet like Moses, but he also is the perfection of what God did through Mo-

---

The Feeding Miracles in the Gospel Tradition

All four Gospels present Jesus miraculously feeding a crowd of thousands with a few loaves of bread, though the details vary a bit. Indeed, both Matthew and Mark narrate two such events (Matt 14:14–21; 15:29–39; Mark 6:31–44; 8:1–9), while Luke and John recount only one (Luke 9:10–17; John 6:1–15). These are clearly ancient traditions about Jesus that formed early in the Christian tradition.

ses. The people affirm their basic understanding of this idea based on the sign, but Jesus realizes the limits to their understandings of how he is to be messiah and king, and he withdraws to the mountain by himself.

Jesus and the Title of King in John

In John 6:15, we learn of the people's initial attempt to take Jesus by force and make him king. They are acting upon their expectations of what the Messiah's mission would be. Jesus, however, is unwilling to accept the title of King in the Gospel of John until the passion narrative (see John 18:28–19:16a). It seems that he wants to use his public ministry to challenge the people to believe in his word and redefine their messianic expectations.

The second sign performed during this Passover is contained in the relatively brief narrative of Jesus walking on water in John 6:16–21. Setting the scene after the miraculous feeding in the wilderness allows the evangelist to continue the echo of God providing manna for the Israelites after the Exodus. This miraculous water event then furthers the resonance of God's presence. Although it immediately follows the feeding, there is no direct connection to that activity, thereby allowing the event to be a "sign" of the wondrous power of God through Jesus in its own right. Further, as distinct from the Gospels of Mark and Matthew, the episode is narrated completely from the perspective of the disciples, and Jesus's intentions are not indicated. As evening approaches, the disciples go down to the lake and embark, destined for Capernaum on the western shore. Through the night, the waters become rough, due to the winds. The evangelist takes care to indicate that they are three or four miles into their journey before they see Jesus "coming near." The disciples are terrified. Here, however, Jesus counters their fear more directly by simply stating, "It is I; do not be afraid." In this way, the evangelist continues to present this self-revelation of God in Jesus as a primary theme of Jesus's mission and ministry. He began his story this way (1:1–18), incorporates it into the dialogue with the Samaritan woman, and will continue to narrate Jesus as the true "I AM" across the Gospel.

The story concludes with the disciples "wanting to take him into the boat" and their immediate arrival at their destination. John 1:12 indicates receiving and believing in Jesus to be the mark of authentic faith. This same verb of receiving is behind the disciples' desire to take Jesus into the boat. Jesus has already begun to reveal his glory, and the disciples have begun to believe in him at the wedding in Cana (2:11). This encounter further strengthens the disciples' faith in Jesus's true nature as the presence and revelation of God in human form.

These two signs and the discourse that interprets them portray a revelatory moment in the Gospel of John. The feeding miracle that precedes the walking on water shows Jesus's power and the crowd's burgeoning acclaim. Indeed, John reports that "Jesus realized that they were about to come and take him by force to make him king" and this is why "he withdrew again to the mountain by himself" (6:15). The disciples too may be caught up in this enthusiasm. Jesus must divert his disciples and teach them that he is not the political sort of king, nor is he merely a prophet like Moses. Rather, Jesus is God incarnate who has the power to control nature as only God can. However, he is also the God who comes to those who need him, be their hearts hardened, their faith little, or their willingness to receive him in faith whole-hearted. He is the Messiah who is Son of God and whose power and presence on earth and in the lives of people are palpable. We can now turn to the discourse through which Jesus begins to teach these things.

6:22–59 Jesus's Discourse on the Bread of Life

The narrator regathers the characters and details of the scene once again to prepare for the so-called Bread of Life discourse. There are clear textual markers that enable us to trace the "flow" of the discourse. It opens with Jesus challenging the superficiality of the crowds and insisting that they work for food that endures for eternal life—a nourishment that the Son of Man will give them (vv. 25–29). There are two hints here: the high point for the gift of this food is in the future, and the food is not just "bread." They will be nourished if they believe in the one whom God has sent. The discourse will face the question of true faith in the one sent by God. The next step in the discourse opens with a question from the crowd, asking Jesus for a sign (vv. 30–31). They are happy with the sign of the bread from heaven, provided in the wilderness by Moses. Here we find an indication, often present in John, that "the Jews" are locked into a closed religious system. They are happy with what God has done for them through Moses and have no inclination to look elsewhere. But Jesus tells them they must transcend that understanding of bread and seek the "true bread" given from heaven by God. The crowd again intervenes: "Sir, give us this bread always" (v. 34). This leads Jesus to identify himself as the true bread of life, from heaven. He is the sent one of God who comes to do the will of God, to draw all who believe in him into eternal life, both here on earth and hereafter, in heaven (vv. 35–40).

> **True/*Alēthinos***
>
> Our contemporary Western thought generally understands the words "true" and "truth" to indicate that what is said, thought, or done, corresponds with facts, or what should be done. For the ancient mindset, the notion was less concrete, and for John it becomes a key expression. For John, "the truth" refers to the authentic revelation of God, in and through Jesus. The adjective "true," so often used in John 6, means that what is described is exactly what it is claimed to be: the real thing. There are many "breads," but only one of them is the "true bread," the authentic revelation of God that is provided by Jesus.

The discourse proceeds as "the Jews" begin to complain: how is it possible that he can claim to be the true bread from heaven? They know his origins, his mother and father. This question leads to Jesus's self-revelation as the only one who can make God known. Who Jesus is and what he does to bring others to life are possible only because of his relationship with God, whom he calls "the Father who sent me." Because of Jesus's *origins* in God, he alone can make God known and give life both here and hereafter. However, this can happen only as the result of belief in Jesus as the bread of life. Those who ate the bread given by Moses are dead. This will not be the case with those who believe in Jesus, the true bread from heaven (vv. 41–49). Even though the miracle of vv. 1–15 recalled the Eucharist celebrated by the Johannine community, nothing has been said of Eucharist in vv. 25–49. For Israel, the manna stopped when the people of God took possession of their land, but a new "bread from heaven" continued: the law of Moses. Jesus has insisted throughout the discourse that he is the "true" bread from heaven. He does not annul God's former gift but brings it to completion. In these verses, therefore, Jesus establishes himself as the true bread from heaven that will give life so that those who eat of it will neither hunger nor thirst. He is the perfection of the gift of God to Israel in the Sinai wilderness, giving life to all who partake of his offer of himself.

The Gospel's audience, a group of people who believe without seeing Jesus, are faced with a problem. Where do they encounter the Son of Man who will give them the bread of life? When "the Jews" grumble about his origin and ability to speak in this way, Jesus responds with further claims of his heavenly origin: "I am the bread of life" (v. 48). He begins to speak about "eating" the bread for the first time. This leads into a Eucharistic application of all that has been said thus far. He speaks of his flesh as the living bread, the perfection of God's wilderness gift of manna at Sinai. Using the ceremonial imagery of eating and drinking the eucharistic meal—and offering himself as that meal—Jesus challenges the characters in the story, both the crowds and those who claim to be his disciples, to open themselves to the ongoing revelation of God in himself and into eternal relationship with him. But any talk of "eating" the bread that is the flesh of Jesus generates a horrified question from "the Jews": "How can this man give us his flesh to eat?" (v. 52). The questioning of "the Jews" only prompts Jesus to press further, establishing the Son of Man, sent from the Father, whose flesh and blood sustains life, as the one in whom they can abide forever. The final section of the discourse (vv. 52–58) points the audience to their celebration of the Eucharist as the place where they will encounter the broken body and the spilt blood of Jesus, the Son of Man. It is there that they will be called to the belief that in him the Father is revealed. That belief will lead to eternal life. The discourse closes as the evangelist indicates that this all took place in the syna-

The Eucharist

The term **Eucharist** comes from the Greek verb that means "to give thanks." Associating giving thanks with a meal of bread and wine is based in Jesus's actions as recorded in the NT. Different Christian denominations have varying understandings of what happens during this ritual, which is also known as the Communion meal or the Lord's Supper. Some take part in it as a sacrament that conveys the real presence of the body and blood of Christ, while others reflect a memorial that symbolically commemorates Christ's gift of his body and blood. All Christians believe that by participating in this meal, they are giving thanks to God for feeding and nourishing the soul.

gogue at Capernaum. The narrative has come full circle, from a bread miracle that pointed to the celebration of the Eucharist (vv. 1–15), to Jesus's teaching that a decision of faith in Jesus as the one who makes God known should be made at the Eucharist (vv. 52–58).

6:60–71 Disciples' Responses to the Discourse

With these provocative words, Jesus verbally challenges the crowds further than he has thus far in his public ministry, to the very limits of their religious worldview. The enormity of the progression of Jesus's public challenge in these verses is borne out by the varying responses to it narrated in vv. 60–71. Curiously, only responses of the disciples are recounted here. The audience recalls that the disciples experienced Jesus's self-revelation as "I AM" on the stormy sea, but they are the ones who now falter. "The Jews" mentioned in v. 41 and v. 52 as those facilitating Jesus's discourse by murmuring and disputes do not yet respond, as in John 5. As for the disciples, many find Jesus's teaching hard to bear: "This is a hard saying; who can listen to it?" (v. 60). Their response is to reject Jesus by no longer following him. For in their worldview, Moses, manna, and Torah exhaust all possibilities for God's action and presence in their lives. Jesus understands this, and in this context challenges the Twelve directly: "Do you also wish to go away" (v. 67)? This is the first time in the story that Jesus's inner circle of the Twelve is identified, and their number is mentioned three times in this passage (vv. 67, 70, 71), both in the context of acceptance and the ultimate rejection by Judas (v. 71). The only other time in the Gospel that Jesus's inner circle is identified as the Twelve is at the first resurrection appearance to the disciples (20:24). Simon Peter, for the first time in the story, takes a leadership position and responds on behalf of the disciples by making a public confession of their growing belief in Jesus as well as their determination to follow him. He professes, "You have the words of eternal life; we have come to believe and we have come to know that you are the Holy One of God" (vv. 68–69). Peter recognizes that Jesus is "of God," which is so essential to authentic understanding and faith. These sincere words of acceptance, however, are marked with the foreboding of trial and betrayal, as in the final words of this episode Jesus reveals that intrinsic to this choice is the path to the hour of his suffering and glory (v. 71).

The signs, discourse, and dialogue of John 6 lead to a turning point in the narrative, as audiences participate not only in the mass exodus of the crowds and some of Jesus's disciples from uncritical following of and belief in Jesus, but also in the foreshadowing revelation of the beginning of the end of the Son of Man's earthly mission. If there is a betrayer, then there will be a betrayal. The shadow of a violent death, which has been across much of this celebration of the Passover (see vv. 15, 27, 51, 53–54), emerges as the account of Jesus's activity on the occasion of the feast comes to a close (vv. 70–71). The author is working at several levels, indicating to the audience that although much has been accomplished in Jesus's ministry, much is still at stake. Further, even correct confessions of faith are not the end of the journey; there is also a message of a future betrayal and death that will test the disciples who have been the recipients of all Jesus's actions and words across the celebration of the Passover, including his self-revelation as "I am he" in the boat (v. 20).

7:1–10:21 Tabernacles—Jesus Perfects the Water and Light Ceremonies

The narrative tempo and tone shift once again with the marker "after these things" and the information that "Jesus went about in Galilee," for in Judea "the Jews were seeking to kill him" (7:1). The entirety of John 7:1–10:21 takes place in the context of the Jewish festival of **Tabernacles** (v. 2). This lengthy section falls in two major sections once Jesus goes up to Jerusalem (vv. 3–13). The first section is primarily dialogue as Jesus uses the backdrop of the feast of Tabernacles as the canvas for his teaching of himself as the living water and light of the world that brings about the integration and fulfillment of their scriptural history (7:14–8:59). The second section takes place in the aftermath of these Tabernacles dialogues (9:1–10:21) and focuses on Jesus's healing of a man born blind and its consequences (9:1–38). Here the evangelist gives audiences a model for how to respond in faith to this conflict, even in the face of expulsion from the synagogue. This sign further provides for an extended discussion of Jesus's identity by others as well as Jesus's own self-identification as the Good Shepherd who will lay down his life for his own (9:39–10:21).

Again, the backdrop of all of these events is the festival of Tabernacles. Tabernacles was regarded as the most popular of the three pilgrimage feasts, known in the OT as the "feast of God" (Lev 23:39; Num 29:12; Judg 21:19) or simply "the feast" (1 Kgs 8:2; Ezek 45:25; Neh 8:14). The Jewish historian Josephus (ca. 37–100 CE) describes Tabernacles as "especially sacred and important to the Hebrews" (*Antiquities of the Jews* 8 §101). This feast, designated the Feast of Ingathering in the earliest liturgical calendars (Exod 23:16; 34:22) and the Feast of Booths or Tabernacles (*sukkot*) in the later calendars (Deut 16:13, 16; Lev 23:34), was originally an autumn celebration of the grape and olive harvest that was later associated with the Sinai covenant and God's care and guidance during the wilderness experience. By the later prophetic age and into NT times, the celebration included explicit hopes for the coming of the messiah and messianic age (see Zechariah 14).

Ancient sources for ritual practice and celebration of the feasts of Israel are found in rabbinic literature, dated well after NT times and the existence of the temple. Depicting how it would have been celebrated in Jesus's time is, therefore, necessarily speculative. Nonetheless, the sources describe the feast beginning on the fifteenth day of the seventh month, Tishri (September–October).

The hallmark is the building of tabernacles, or shelters, representing the tent experience of the Israelites in the wilderness, who were cared for by the God with whom they were now in covenant. For seven days, the men celebrating the festival ritual sleep and eat in their shelters. After the initial seven days there is an additional eighth day that specifically recalls God's protection in the wilderness.

Three major elements form the festival ritual. The festival begins with the Water Libation Ceremony. At the dawn of each day, a procession accompanied by blasts of the shofar moves down to the pool of Siloam to gather water in a golden container, before returning through the Water Gate. According to the rabbis, this gate marked the source from which the waters of life, issuing from the temple, would flow in the messianic age. Singing psalms, the procession arrives at the altar, where the water is mixed with wine and allowed to flow out onto the altar (repeated seven times on the seventh day of the feast). This ritual was linked with the giving of rain in the wilderness but also with current messianic expectations. The rabbis looked to a time of the final giving of the water. This expectation linked the messiah with a Moses-like teacher and the definitive gift of water from the well of Torah, the ultimate perfection of the Law. The second component of the ritual is the ceremony of light. Four menorahs are placed at the center of the court of the women. To the sounds of psalms, celebrations under these lights last most of the night each of the seven days of the feast. The temple then also becomes the beacon that looks back at God's guidance in the wilderness through the pillar of fire and forward to the pillar's expected return in the age of the messiah. The daily celebration culminates with the Rite of Facing the Temple. This ritual, greeting the light of the new day, affirmed that God is the one true God to whom all honor, glory, and obedience are due.

Therefore, we can suggest that what marked a first-century Tabernacles celebration was increased messianic expectation coupled with profound symbolism of God's covenantal action in Israel, manifested in daily water libation rituals and the lighting of great candelabra. This tenor in the air provides the sensory backdrop of Jesus's encounters in the temple area during and following the feast of Tabernacles recounted in John 7:1–10:21.

7:1–8:59 The Tabernacles Dialogues

John 7–8 is one of the most difficult movements in all of the gospel narratives. After an introduction focused on the question of whether Jesus will go up to the feast (7:1–13), the flow proceeds through a series of dialogues on the middle and last days of the week (7:14–36; 7:37–52; 8:12–59), interrupted by an encounter between Jesus and a woman caught in adultery (7:53–8:11). When the dialogue between Jesus and the Jewish leaders and the crowds in the temple area during the Feast of Tabernacles reaches its climax, it is a passionate, and even vitriolic, conflict. Both sides of this encounter are very heated: "the Jews" accuse Jesus of having a demon (i.e., "possessed" or "crazy;" v. 48), and Jesus calls them children of the devil, the father of lies (i.e., "liars": vv. 42–47).

The entire encounter brings the people in the story (and audiences of the story) to a crisis, to a point where they are forced once again to begin to make decisions about where they stand in the mounting christological conflict between Jesus and the Jewish authorities. Is Jesus the Christ, or is he just crazy? The conflict is now public and will become terminally violent.

Jewish Celebration of Tabernacles

The Jewish celebration of Tabernacles lasted 8 days. It recalls the celebration of the end of the harvest season and God's care of Israel during the Exodus. In Jerusalem in the Second Temple Period, its main features were water libations, the lighting of a large menorah in the Temple area, expectation of the coming messiah, and a confession of the true God of Israel. These aspects of the feast are applied to Jesus in 7:1–10:21.

7:1–13 Introduction: Will Jesus Go Up to the Feast?

The narrator opens John 7 with a word about the threat rising in Judea against Jesus as the Jewish festival of Tabernacles drew near (vv. 1–2). After a conflict between Jesus and his brothers about how he should manifest himself "to the world" (vv. 3–9), Jesus goes up in secret to Jerusalem. He seems to want to go and teach on his own terms, not those of the "world." The narrator's additional remark that even his brothers did not believe him (v. 5) continues the theme of Jesus having to reconstitute "his own" family based on belief. His absence to this point caused division among "the crowds," though fear of "the Jews" had kept such speculation private (vv. 10–13). The dialogical encounters that ensue between Jesus and "the Jews" and "the crowds" unfold in two major sections: the dialogue that occurs "about the middle of the festival" (7:14–36); and the dialogue that is engaged "on the last day of the festival" (7:37–8:59).

7:14–36 Scene 1: Dialogues on the Middle Day of the Festal Week

The initial encounter that takes place when Jesus arrives at about the middle of the festival (7:14–36) is marked by two exchanges (vv. 14–24; vv. 32–36) centered around the division among the people that Jesus's teaching in the temple area causes (vv. 25–31). Imagery of Moses dominates as Jesus brings the historical backdrop of the festival to bear on his teaching about himself. When they are astonished at the content and boldness of his teaching, Jesus claims that it comes from "the one who sent" him. He refers back to his healing on the Sabbath in chapter 5 and urges them to use "right judgment" about such things. This leads to messianic questions regarding his origin and destiny, creating conflict for the people. Even those who are positive focus on his signs, however, and struggle with his claims to be like Moses and more, the Son of God the Father.

Concerns culminate in a thwarted attempt to arrest Jesus for such disturbances. Violence threatens.

7:37–52 Scene 2: Dialogues on the Last Day of the Feast

The encounters at Tabernacles begin to reach their climax on the last day of the feast when Jesus reveals that he personifies the water rite of the feast (vv. 37–39). He beseeches all those who are thirsty to come to him and have their thirst sated spiritually. This claim, to be the embodiment of the living waters in fulfillment of Torah, creates a crisis of judgment and a schism among the people, particularly about whether Jesus is the expected messiah (vv. 40–44). Jesus's origins are the focus here, and the primary question comes into clearer focus: could Jesus's claims about himself be true regardless of their traditional expectations?

When the arresting party from the previous scene must account for their failure to the chief priests and Pharisees, they exclaim their awe at Jesus's teaching. For their part, the Pharisees defer to authority to condemn Jesus without further hearing, indicating that the crowds are simply easily swayed by such talk. Nicodemus, who came to Jesus by night in chapter 3 and is now standing with these fellow Pharisees, now takes a step forward into the light and refers to this same authority in defense of Jesus. He reminds his colleagues that the Law requires more of an investigation before such verdicts are cast. The accused must be heard, and what he does must be seen. Regardless, he is shut down quickly as they dismiss the possibility of a prophet coming from Galilee (vv. 45–52). The encounter comes to a halt for the moment.

[7:53–8:11 The Woman Caught in Adultery]

We have placed the heading for the next scene in square brackets to indicate that there is a text-critical issue here. Most study Bibles do the same. The narrative of this encounter between Jesus, a woman caught in adultery, and those who want to test Jesus to her harm is as popular today as it was in the earliest church. That said, a survey of the ancient manuscripts shows that this little vignette was not originally part of the Gospel of John. Although it was an early written tradition about Jesus, our evangelist did not compose it nor did he include it in his initial narrative. Study Bibles will also often have a footnote indicating briefly the textual history of this passage. Most ancient manuscripts of the Gospel of John lack 7:53–8:11. Some include the scene, but between 7:36 and 7:37, or at the end of the Gospel. Other ancient manuscripts include the passage after Luke 21:36, and many scholars suggest the tone and language is more typical of Luke than John. What is remarkable is that this little story was so powerful and so well loved that even though none of our evangelists included it in their original drafts, it nonetheless found a home in the canon here at 7:53–8:11 in John. Now audiences of all time can experience this profound vignette of wisdom and compassion.

The Woman Taken in Adultery by Lorenzo Lotto

That the passage was somewhat hastily inserted here is revealed in the narrative transition. In the midst of the intense interaction in the temple area, suddenly everyone goes home and Jesus retreats to the Mount of Olives (7:53). Although he returns the following morning, the dialogues of John 8 still seem to take place on the last day of the festival. Regardless, vv. 2–11 recount that while Jesus was teaching the people, the scribes and Pharisees bring a woman to stand before him as if to stand trial. They claim to have caught her "in the very act of adultery," a crime punishable by stoning according to Torah (see Lev 20:10 and Deut 22:22–24). They ask Jesus to render judgment, but the narrator confirms that he too is on trial. That the woman is of no real concern to them is evidenced by the lack of interest in her partner in crime as well as their sole apparent interest in what Jesus might say.

Jesus, in fact, initially says nothing; rather he bends down and begins to write with his finger in the sand. The one whose words have flowed so freely across these chapters now refuses to speak. Perhaps this is an indication that they are asking the wrong questions. Upon their insistence, he responds with his famous encouragement to the one among them without sin to throw the first stone at her before returning to his writing. Audiences are always most curious about the content of Jesus's writing in the sand. We simply cannot know what he wrote, but the narrator affirms that this action coupled with his provocative suggestion leads the eldest to give up the test first. One by one they depart until even the young have moved away, leaving the woman standing on her own before Jesus. Although the popular gloss of this passage is that he forgives her, he does not. Rather, he asserts her autonomy as one who will make her own decisions and have her own relationship with God. He calls her "Woman," and when she affirms that no one is left to condemn her, he agrees and sends her off with the commandment to change her ways. The passage concludes and this unnamed woman goes on to make her own way and decisions accordingly.

8:12–59 Scene 3: Dialogues Conclude: Jesus Light of the World

As the dialogue proper resumes, the scenes at Tabernacles flow to their climax. In 8:12–30, Jesus reveals himself as the giver of the light of life. He continues the teaching he began at 7:37–39 and claims to be the fulfillment of the remaining symbolism and purpose of this Jewish feast: "I am the light of the world" (8:12). Verses 12–20 mark the first stage of this dialogue, presenting the fundamental divide between Jesus and his opponents. In vv. 21–30, the characters openly debate the issue simmering under the surface in the first section: Jesus's origins and destiny. Jesus and his opponents come closest to a meeting of hearts here (v. 30). Then, however, Jesus characteristically begins to challenge those who profess belief in him further, beyond their earthly categories. Thus the narrator recounts: "Then Jesus said to the Jews who believed in him . . ." (v. 31). This leads to a conflict concerning the identity of the true children of God based on the progeny of Abraham that takes up the rest of the passage (8:31–58). By v. 47, the tension has increased such that Jesus pronounces that they "are not from God." "The Jews" begin to respond in v. 48 and it becomes apparent just how wide the gulf is between them. As Jesus challenges his opponents beyond their expectations and rigid worldview to understand his being as the incarnate Son of the one Father, they retreat to their former position and no longer venture even a partial belief. Father and child imagery pervades this portion of the dialogue, and Jesus eventually resorts to characterizing his opponents as children of the devil (v. 44). Jesus, by contrast, is the Son who is the "I AM" (*egō eimi*): the incarnation of God and fulfillment of messianic expectation (8:58).

The gulf separating Jesus and "the Jews" that he encounters at the feast of Tabernacles is a profound *closedness*. Audiences of John 7–8 have the prologue resonating in their ears as they listen to Jesus's teaching in this most heated segment of his public ministry. They have been given information about Jesus and the glory of God's action in and for the sake of the world through the gift of truth manifest in Jesus. Thus, when audiences experience Jesus verbalizing what God is doing through him in the tenor of his own voice, there is room for *openness* to his word. The evangelist teaches that "the Jews," who stand outside the world of the prologue, are ultimately not open to hearing and seeing God the Father in the voice and person of Jesus the Son. Although many can come to a partial faith in the messianic mission of Jesus when it rings familiar to their long-standing religious system, they cannot take root and abide in his word when he reveals the full implications of the life-giving truth of his messiahship. They can neither appreciate nor participate in the openness of the very figures of their religious history to which they appeal. Thus, even as authentic progeny, they choose to remain outside the realm of the children of God, for children hear the word of their Father and do as their Father does, as manifest in the Son the Father gives to them. The challenge given by Jesus to "the Jews" in the setting of the feast of Tabernacles is initially taken up in part by "many of the Jews" (v. 30). However, when the full messianic implication of abiding in the word of Jesus is revealed, they ultimately reject the gift to become children of God.

For his part, Jesus stands in the temple area in the midst of the feast of Tabernacles, which celebrates the experience of God's care for the children of Israel in the wilderness at Sinai, and he presents himself as the fulfillment of the experience of God's life-giving care now and forever. As the participants in the Tabernacles celebration relive their ancestors' experience of God through rituals of water and light, Jesus shows himself to be the living water and true light that reveals God to all who would open themselves to him and take root in his word, thus empowering them to become the covenantal children of God. In the dialogue of Tabernacles, Jesus reveals that all that is accomplished in that annual feast is perfected in him through the covenantal love between the true Son and the living Father, now and forever.

The formal debate that manifests through these dialogues is forensic in nature, manifesting the tone of a trial scene in the tradition of the covenantal lawsuit of the prophets. Jesus acts as both witness and prosecutor in the name of God the Father. He extends the challenge to abide in his word, claiming himself to be the incarnation of God's covenant love for the world and putting "the Jews" on trial, including those who have made the partial move of belief. He pronounces them guilty, depicting them as children not of the covenant of God but of the lies of the devil. In turn, "the Jews" attempt to put Jesus on trial, but his dialogical prowess eventually renders them speechless. They attempt to condemn him of blasphemy in their spontaneous physical response of taking up stones against him. But the true verdict of God in this "lawsuit" is presented in Jesus's successful evasion of their action. The hour of the glory of the Son of God will come on God's time, when Jesus's mission to the world can be perfected.

9:1–10:21 Continuation of Tabernacles

The second major segment of the Tabernacles events commences in the aftermath of these dialogues and includes the sign of the healing of the man born blind (9:1–38) and Jesus's Good Shepherd discourse (9:39–10:21). During the sign, Jesus continues to teach that he is the light of the World (9:5), and he relates this metaphor to the challenge of blindness and sight. In the discourse, he turns his attention to the new community he is forming through his mission and ministry by teaching of himself as both the Gate (i.e., the way in; 10:7, 9) and the Good Shepherd (i.e., the one who cares for the new community; 10:11). A more detailed structure of this masterpiece of Johannine storytelling focuses on the encounters between the key characters in each scene: Jesus and the disciples (9:1–5), Jesus and the man born blind (9:6–7), the Man and his neighbors (9:8–12), the Man and the Pharisees (9:13–17), the Pharisees and the man's parents (9:18–23), the Pharisees and the man (9:24–34), Jesus and the man (9:35–38), and Jesus and the Pharisees (9:39–10:21). All the while a schism continues to form among the crowd about Jesus. Could he be the messiah? His background does not fit the expectations of many, and they voice the negative. His signs and teachings, however, have many others leaning toward the positive. Jesus continues to push everyone he encounters beyond their easy answers and closed categories to a new openness to how God is acting through him in the present.

9:1–38 *The Healing of the Man Born Blind*

As Jesus and his disciples walk along away from the temple area, they encounter a man who is blind from birth. The insistence that he is not sightless simply from some passing illness or injury but from some sort of "permanent" defect from birth persists across this passage. The point is that Jesus is doing something beyond even the typical healers of the time. The disciples voice an ancient understanding of God and sin found in the book of Deuteronomy among others that illness and misfortune of any sort is the result of sin—some sort of breach of the covenant with God. The teaching would be that if one keeps the covenant one will be blessed, but if one breaks the covenant one will be cursed in some way. That said, history had shown that many who do not live good lives nonetheless succeed, and many who do live in right relationship with God struggle and suffer. Initially, it was taught that misfortune can therefore transcend generations; that is, a child could suffer from the parents' sin, hence the question in v. 2. Even by the centuries prior to the life of Jesus, however, the sages were teaching that this sort of theology did not hold weight. Both God and human life are more complex than this scheme allows. Jesus gives voice to this later understanding when he indicates in vv. 3–5 that they have asked the wrong question. The purpose of this encounter, rather, is to further reveal that Jesus is the light of the world and life-giving water. As the passage proceeds, we see that its telling also reveals how humans should respond to this light.

Much in the same fashion as he did with the crippled man in chapter 5, Jesus approaches this man who does not request a healing and sets to work. By contrast, however, this becomes an intimate encounter that changes this man's life. Jesus forms mud with dirt and his own saliva as a salve of sorts, but he then sends the man off to wash and complete the healing. This man likewise does as he is told, but unlike the earlier healed man, this newly sighted man stands firm in testimony about Jesus. The crowd is amazed and begins to question him, eventually bringing him before some Pharisees. Only at v. 14 does the narrator reveal that all this occurred on a Sabbath. Audiences of the Gospel may be thinking, "here we go again!" as these leaders begin to grumble and wonder just who this man and his healer think they are.

> **Journey of the Man Who is Blind to True Sight**
>
> As elsewhere in the Gospel (Cana to Cana, 2:1–4:54, and the resurrection, 20:1–29), the blind man makes a journey of faith. He begins blind (9:1), refers to Jesus as "the man," then calls him "a prophet" (v. 17), suggests that he might be "from God" (v. 33), and finally, fully sighted, worships Jesus, believing that he is the Son of Man (v. 38).

What follows is a trial of sorts as "the Jews" formally question first the man, then his parents, then the man again about his background and what he has experienced. The narrator mentions once again that the people and the leaders are divided over Jesus (v. 16). This is becoming a major scene in the second part of the public ministry. For his part, the newly sighted man responds to the questioning with the truth as he knows it so far: "he is a prophet" (v. 17). Not only is this not sufficient for his interrogators, they begin to question the honesty of his claims. They call in his parents who confirm both his identity as well as the veracity of his birth defect, but they wish to stay out of the current situation. At this point the narrator provides the first indication of the world behind the story that we discussed in chapter five: that those who confess Jesus to be the Messiah would be expelled from the synagogue. Therefore, it is the man who must make his stand alone. He does and is duly expelled (v. 34).

The episode does not conclude, however, without Jesus once again coming to the man and affirming his decision and stand (vv. 35–38). Jesus affirms his identity as the Son of Man, the one whom the man can see and hear, and the newly sighted man likewise affirms his belief. In this way, Jesus resolves the man's experience of the trial and alienation by confirming that he had made the right choice and that true worship was now found in him. This is what it means to truly see. By narrating this entire series of encounters in this way, the evangelist is simultaneously teaching audiences of the Gospel how to "stand trial" for their faith, the realities of "blindness" and "sight," as well as the ongoing presence of Jesus in their lives.

9:39–10:21 Jesus as the Sheep-Gate and Shepherd

John 9 concludes with Jesus continuing to challenge the "closedness" of religious systems that lead to claims of knowledge and clarity instead of openness to God's action. In this way he transitions into the final scene, what is sometimes called the "Good Shepherd Discourse" in the context of the festival of Tabernacles. Jesus's "Amen, amen, . . ." introductory formula for his next statement indicates the significance of the teaching to come as well as how it links to what has just occurred, especially his summons to what we "see" and "hear." Jesus shares a metaphor about the behavior of good and bad shepherds. But the Pharisees do not understand. He then describes himself as the gate that is the way to nourishment, life, and security, in contrast to thieves and bandits who have no care for the sheep. Jesus then uses the image of the Good Shepherd, finally identifying himself with an expected messianic figure in Israel's hope. But he describes the activity of the "hired hands" who are bad shepherds. His extended use of the shepherd imagery to describe himself resonates with God's self-characterization in the words of the prophet Ezekiel. There God calls himself the "shepherd" who will seek out and care for his sheep so that "they will know that I am God" (Ezek 34:15–31). By employing the shepherd imagery here at the conclusion of the events in the context of the feast of Tabernacles, Jesus reverberates the declarations of God in Ezekiel. He identifies himself first as the gate (v. 9) through which anyone can enter the fold of the sheep of God, then as the Good Shepherd (vv. 11, 14) who is known by his own and God the Father.

In the final section, therefore, Jesus makes no further reference to the bad sheep, but describes how and why he is the Good Shepherd. As always with Jesus, who he is and what he does depend upon his oneness of love with his Father. Because of this he will give his life for his sheep, and he will take up his life again, a clear indication of the oncoming death and resurrection of Jesus. For the first time, the theme of "gathering" appears. Jesus will lay down his life not only for his own flock, but also for "other sheep that do not belong to this fold" (v. 16). As so often in this Gospel, Jesus's self-revelation as the light of the world, the living water, and now the Good Shepherd who gathers together all God's "flocks" creates division among the people. Some regard him as out of his mind (v. 20: "he has a demon"), while others recognize that he is bringing goodness into the world (v. 21). The schism continues to develop as Jesus pushes all those he encounters out of their comfort and toward a new realm of belief and relationship with the Father and Son as one.

10:22–42 Dedication—Jesus Perfects the Temple as the Dwelling Presence of God

The final temporal and festival marker of this "feasts section" is found at John 10:22, when the narrator indicates that "at that time the festival of Dedication occurred in Jerusalem." This relatively brief scene (21 verses) closes this narrative unit by focusing on Jesus's teaching, framed by minimal narrative. In this final teaching Jesus focuses first on his role as the Messiah (vv. 22–31), then climaxes in his self-revelation as the Son of God (vv. 32–42). Jesus's exit and the speculation it produces close the episode. These few verses, however, are nonetheless important for understanding the conclusion to this larger section that moves through the annual feasts of Judaism.

The narrator designates that it is now winter and Jesus is walking in the portico of Solomon during the festival of **Dedication** (*Hannukah*, which occurs during the month of Kislev: November–December). The celebration of this festival relives the experience of rededicating the temple after the Hellenizing "desolating sacrilege" of Antiochus IV Epiphanes was destroyed and the altar was cleansed, following the successful Maccabean revolt of 167–164 BCE (see 1 Maccabees 1–4 and our discussion in chapter three). The festival was held for eight days and was a joyous celebration including music, singing, and parades with waving palm branches. The ritual was modeled on Tabernacles and commemorated the victory of the Jewish people over both their oppressors as well as those from within their own community who were content to let go of their faith. The very identity of the Jewish people as the distinctive, chosen people of God was embedded in this celebration. Likewise the centrality of the temple as the dwelling place of God among the people is affirmed. It is in this context that Jesus responds to their demands for clarity and certainty that he is their Messiah and Son of God, though not conforming to their expectations. Rather, he is sanctified (v. 36), in his oneness with God (vv. 30 and 38).

10:22–31 Jesus as the Messiah

The evangelist sets this new scene by announcing the arrival of the festival of Dedication in winter and placing Jesus once again in the temple area (vv. 22–23). Solomon's portico, the oldest colonnade on the eastern face of the temple, is a fitting backdrop for this final confrontation that occurs during the festival commemorating Judaism's resistance to blasphemy, idolatry, and apostasy. Speculation about the messiahship of Jesus has been in the air for some time and "the Jews" seek to put an end to it: "If you are the Messiah, tell us plainly" (v. 24). In response, Jesus intensifies the imagery and teaching of his relationship with God as the Son to the Father. He takes up the shepherding imagery of his previous discourse to place himself once again in the role of a shepherd who draws his sheep to him. In doing so, he presses far beyond his interrogators' messianic expectations as well as their comfort by presenting his oneness with God: "I and the Father are one" (v. 30).

10:32–42 Jesus as the Son of God

Even as "the Jews" take up stones against him for his perceived blasphemy (v. 31), Jesus responds verbally to their unspoken accusation by appealing to Torah specifically, Scripture generally, and his own divine works (vv. 32–38). But his final declaration, "that you may know and understand that the Father is in me and I am in the Father," falls on uncomprehending ears as "the Jews" attempt to arrest him. His hour, however closer, has not yet come, and Jesus once again escapes from their hands (v. 39). This narrative section comes to a close with Jesus returning across the Jordan where "many began to believe in him" (vv. 41–42). This lengthy portion of Jesus's public ministry that explores and perfects Israel's remembrance and celebration of the presence of God in and through Jesus as Christ and Son of God draws to a close in belief rather than condemnation. As "the Jews" celebrate the temple as the dwelling place of God, Jesus teaches that he is the consecrated one (v. 36), one with God (vv. 30, 38), and the dwelling place of God. In many ways, all that Jesus has claimed in John 5–10 is true precisely because "the Father and I are one" (v. 30).

What Have We Learned So Far?
Jesus as the Presence of God in Human Lives

Across John 5–10, the signs and symbolic language of Jesus's dialogues challenge those he encounters to embark upon a journey of faith into relationship with him. The action his speech evokes in his dialogue partners is a movement toward him or a turning away from him in acceptance or rejection of his challenge to life in the family of God. Throughout, he verbally points to himself as the revelation of the Word of God who gives this gift of truth to those who would become children of God. The narrative imagery of the feasts of Israel, all of which are intimately connected to the experience of God's action in and with creation, forms the backdrop of all that Jesus says and does in this major segment of his public life. The identity of Jesus is revealed in his relationship to the God who is celebrated through these festivals. He embodies a unique Father-Son relationship, a relationship of family. Further, the Father has sent the Son for the purpose of summoning all the children of God to himself. These children know the voice of the Son and respond as sheep to a shepherd, gathering and abiding in the light of life that he gives. As Jesus moves through the feasts of Israel, he voices a continual clarion call, heard by the disciples, the crowds, "the Jews," and the audience. The ever-increasing intensity of both his rhetoric and the potential consequences imposed on those who reject his self-revelatory challenge mark the progress of the Gospel story.

In John 5, within the literary context of the feast of Sabbath, Jesus heals a man who is crippled and instructs him to carry his pallet, thereby having them both break Sabbath law (5:1–18). In the conflict with "the Jews" that follows, Jesus claims that his oneness with the Father transcends Torah, allowing him to continue God's good works. The healed man, who initially responds with obedience to the word of Jesus (v. 9), ends by pointing Jesus out to "the Jews" who "were seeking all the more to kill him" (v. 18). The scene comes to an end with no resolution. Jesus's accusers make no response to his challenge. The healed man does not seem to have understood a challenge was even at stake.

The entire chapter serves to introduce this series of christological perfections of the Jewish feasts.

In the extended narrative and dialogue of John 6, Jesus stands in the countryside of Galilee during the time of Passover and teaches that he is the true bread from heaven. He is the perfection of the gift of God to Israel in the Sinai wilderness that gives life to all who partake of his offer of himself. Using the ceremonial imagery of eating and drinking—and offering himself as that meal—Jesus challenges the characters in the story, both the crowds and those who claim to be his disciples, to open themselves to the ongoing revelation of God in himself and to eternal relationship with him. "The Jews" mentioned do not yet respond, as in John 5. As for the disciples, many find Jesus's teaching hard to bear, and their response is to reject Jesus and no longer follow him. Simon Peter responds on behalf of the inner circle by making a public confession of their growing belief in Jesus as well as their determination to follow him. These sincere words of acceptance, however, are marked with the foreboding of trial and betrayal.

In the dialogues of the feast of Tabernacles (John 7:1–8:59) Jesus stands in the temple area and asserts his messianic origins and destiny in the context of the light of God's gift of Torah to the faithful. These extended scenes of dialogue and narrative that escalate to violent controversy are the point in this feasts section where "the Jews" begin to come to decision about Jesus. The evangelist narrates their ultimate response of rejection to his challenge of abiding in his word as they attempt to stone him for blasphemy. The controversy continues as Jesus heals a man born blind, and the evangelist gives a glimpse into the conflict of his own time as the threat of expulsion from the synagogue to those who follow Jesus is articulated (9:1–41). Jesus affirms that acceptance and belief have their own rewards, for he is the Good Shepherd who lays down his life for his sheep (10:1–21).

In the brief encounter during the feast of Dedication that closes the feasts section (10:22–42), Jesus challenges all those in doubt and discussion about him to accept his word and works in the name of the Father who sent him. He concludes: "I and the Father are one" (v. 30). The general schism seems to have come to an end as "the Jews" once again take up stones against Jesus for blasphemy. Jesus denounces their accusation and acknowledges that their rejection of him is rejection of God the Father. He escapes their renewed attempt to arrest him and continues unhindered to find acceptance in new believers.

This review of the "Feasts Section" of the Gospel of John allows us to draw some conclusions about the evangelist's Christology as well as his soteriology and eschatology. In fact, the discourse level of this narrative unit is primarily aimed at Christology as the evangelist teaches his audience about how Jesus is the Christ through his narration. To an extent, Jesus fulfills the messianic expectations of those who are looking for authority through signs and wonders. However, once he gains the attention of those who seek such power, he pushes them spiritually to open themselves to the God from whom they claim to be descendants. He takes a new christological step by claiming to be the Son of that Father who cares for his true children as a shepherd cares for his sheep. This leads Jesus to challenge them to accept the power and presence of God in him just as they celebrate it in the annual festivals of Judaism. This is hard. Many, even those who want to do so, cannot make that next step. But the evangelist teaches that it is just this level of faith that is necessary both to understand and participate in what God is doing in and through Jesus as the Christ, God's Anointed One, in order to redeem his children.

This leads us to soteriology. Salvation and the glory of God often have a decidedly present-tense orientation in this Gospel. What we mean by this is that the evangelist is careful to show through his narration of Jesus's teaching that one can experience salvation *right now* when one believes in the word of Jesus that he is Christ and Son of God sent to gather into one family all the children of God. Biblical scholars identify this manner of teaching as "**Realized Eschatology**." Remember that we taught in the introduction that eschatology refers to the study of the last things or end times. These ideas are often associated with beliefs concerning life after death, judgment, and the end of the world as we know it. We said then that John has a distinctive idea of when and how "end time" is understood. In John 5–10, the evangelist is beginning to illustrate this vision. One does not have to wait until some vague "end time" to participate in life in the presence of God through Jesus. It is available the moment one makes the leap of faith to believe that Jesus is who he claims to be. In the coming chapters of the story, this teaching will come to a head as Jesus's public ministry reaches its climax.

Key Terms and Concepts

cultic celebrations

Dedication/*Hannukah*

Eucharist

Feasts

Jewish feast/festival

Passover/*Pesach*

realized eschatology

Sabbath/*Shabbat*

Tabernacles/*Sukkot*

zikkārôn

Questions for Review

1. Given what we have discussed as the potential world behind the text of the Gospel of John, why might the evangelist include a narrative unit that presents Jesus and his disciples moving through a year in the worship life of Judaism in the world in the text?

2. How does learning about the Jewish festivals celebrated in John 5–10 help in exegeting Jesus's actions and dialogues in their midst?

3. How do Jesus's relationships with the disciples, the crowds, and his opponents "the Jews" develop and change over the course of this year in his public ministry?

4. What suggestions can you make about the overall discourse level and the evangelist's purpose in John 5–10?

Bibliography and Further Reading

Asiedu-Peprah, Martin. *Johannine Sabbath Conflicts as Juridical Controversy*. Wissenschaftliche Untersuchungen zum Neuen Testament 2.132. Tübingen: Mohr Siebeck, 2001.

Martyn, J. Louis. *History and Theology in the Fourth Gospel*. 3rd ed. Louisville: Westminster John Knox, 2003.

Moloney, Francis J. "Narrative and Discourse in the Feast of Tabernacles." Pages 155–72 in *Word, Theology, and Community in John*. Edited by John Painter, R. Alan Culpepper, and Fernando Segovia. St. Louis: Chalice, 2002.

———. *Signs and Shadows: Reading John 5–12*. Minneapolis: Fortress, 1996.

Yee, Gale A. *Jewish Feasts and the Gospel of John*. Eugene, OR: Wipf & Stock, 2007.

Jesus and the Arrival of the Hour: Moving toward Glory in John 11–12

....

PURPOSE Chapter eleven provides a close reading of the last narrative unit of the public ministry as the hour of Jesus arrives and he begins to move toward his glorification (John 11–12).

ASSIGNMENT Reread John 11–12 before proceeding with this chapter.

....

The narrative unit that explores how Jesus fulfills and completes the festivals of Judaism in a christological fashion comes to a close at 10:40–42. Jesus moves back across the Jordan and abides there for a time. A final reference to the truthful witness of John allows the narrator to provide a moment of reflection for the audience. The words of the prologue resonate as the testimony of Jesus and about Jesus reconstitutes "his own," not just as the ethnic Judaism of the past but as all those who "receive him"—the many who believe in him (10:42; see 1:11–12). With these suggestions in mind, we begin John 11–12, the last narrative unit of the Book of Signs. Upon learning of the illness of his friend Lazarus, Jesus eventually travels to Bethany, a village close to the city of Jerusalem. He enters the city for the final time. There he concludes his public ministry and takes a step closer to his glorification: "The hour has come for the Son of Man to be glorified" (12:23).

The Narrative Flow and Structure of John 11–12

Chapters 11–12 of the Fourth Gospel are crucial to the theological flow of this good news because they move the narrative out of the ministry and toward the cross. In the words and actions of Jesus, the evangelist culminates the themes of life and light that have permeated his Gospel from their introduction in the prologue (1:3–5). Unlike the Gospels of Mark, Matthew, and Luke, Jesus never speaks openly of his death up to this point in the story of the Gospel of John. He has, however, spoken of an "hour" that had not yet come (see 2:4; 7:6, 30; 8:20).

On two occasions he has also used a double-meaning word to speak of his being **"lifted up"** (Greek: *hypsōthēnai*; 3:14; 8:28). He is clearly speaking of his death, but words associated with death and dying never appear. John has a very special understanding of the cross. It is not only a death, but it is also a crucial turning point in his life, mission, and his relationship with his Father—a moment when he will be both physically "lifted up" on a cross and "exalted" by his Father. Across John 11–12 the words "death" and "dying" appear for the first time, and regularly (see 11:4, 14, 16, 21, 25–26, 32, 37, 39, 44, 50, 51, 53; 12:1, 7, 10, 17, 24–25, 33).

Simply reading these verses will show how the death and resuscitation of Lazarus prepare the way for the death and resurrection of Jesus. But there is a crucial difference between the death and resuscitation of Lazarus, and the death and resurrection of Jesus! In John 11–12 Jesus turns toward the cross, but it will be a life-giving death and resurrection. In this way, they both look back to the person and teaching of Jesus in the story up to this point, yet they also point the audience beyond the events being reported into a future that has been hinted at (with terms like glory, hour, lifting up, death, resurrection, and life), without, as yet, providing all the answers. In literary terms, these final events in Jesus's ministry generate a **literary tension**. We have some answers, but we need to go further into the story to see all of them resolved.

The entrance into a new segment in the story is indicated by the introduction of a different setting (Bethany, 11:1), and fresh characters (the siblings Mary, Martha, and Lazarus, whom Jesus loves [vv. 1–3]). The story begins strangely. The narrator offers a flash forward (what literary critics call a **prolepsis**) that Mary is the one who anointed Jesus (v. 2), as if that bit of information is something we know. But it has not yet happened. These words raise a note of tension about the events that are to come. When Mary does eventually anoint Jesus, his impending death has already been established (12:1–8). Although it is Lazarus whose physical life is at stake, the intricately constructed narrative that unfolds across 11:1–12:8 emphasizes the faith journeys of Jesus's friends, Mary and Martha, as he challenges them to see in him not the culmination of a historical religious system, but the perfection of life in the spirit through believing in God. In the midst of this story of friendship and faith, the arrival of the final Jewish festival of this story is announced at 11:55. The final Passover is at hand, and the many who have arrived in Jerusalem are abuzz with what might occur. The tension is high and the crisis is at hand. This is confirmed as John 12 begins with the narrative that reports Mary's anointing of Jesus with perfumed oil. What was announced in 11:2 comes to pass in 12:1–8. Defending her actions, Jesus

---

Prolepsis

The storytelling technique known as **prolepsis** comes from the Greek noun of the same pronunciation that means "anticipation." It is used to represent an event as happening or a thing as existing before it actually does so. It serves to alert readers of the impending occurrence by raising questions about plot sequence and the storyteller's integrity. It can also have the effect, as in John 11:1–12:8, of framing a narrative unit so that its contents can be interpreted accordingly.

confirms its purpose: "so that she might keep it for the day of my burial . . . . You will not always have me" (12:7–8).

The narrator's description of the impact of the raising of Lazarus on the Jewish people and the chief priests transitions the unit into the preparations for Passover and the impending death of Jesus (12:9–36). The crowds acclaim Jesus as he enters Jerusalem in fulfillment of the prophet Zechariah's messianic expectations (vv. 9–19; see Zech 9:9). In the wake of the Pharisees' dismay that the "whole world is going after him," Jesus's disciples are indeed approached by some Greeks who have come to meet him. The entire world is seeking him out. For Jesus, the arrival of these Greeks marks the arrival of the hour of his death and glorification (vv. 20–36). The "hour" has come (v. 23). Even as those closest to him do not understand the magnitude of this moment, a turning point in human history, Jesus will next spend time with them, showing them with symbolic gestures, speaking to them, and praying for them (John 13–17). His love for them knows no bounds, and they will be challenged to follow his example (13:15), loving as he has loved (13:34–35; 15:12, 17).

But before those moments of intimacy begin, Part Four of the Book of Signs comes to a close with the conclusion of Jesus's public ministry narrated in two summary statements (12:37–50). They add nothing to the *action* of the story, but they use words to *tell* of the significance of all that has happened up to this point. In the first statement, the narrator evaluates Jesus's ministry to his own people, made up of his own ethnic kin and all those who hear his voice (vv. 37–43). In the second, Jesus cries out his final words in the public sphere, giving a climactic voice to the themes of mission and light first introduced in the prologue (vv. 44–50; see 1:1–18). With these words, he summarizes the way his public ministry has made God known and how acceptance or refusal of that revelation leads to light or darkness. The stage is set for his passion and glorification.

The structure of this narrative unit can be diagrammed in the following manner:

Part Four: Jesus Moves toward the Hour of Death and Glory   11:1–12:50

11:1–12:8	Jesus Gives Humankind Life; Humankind Condemns Jesus to Death	
	11:1–44	Jesus Gives Life to Lazarus—Jesus as the Life
	11:45–57	The Sanhedrin Condemns Jesus to Die as Passover Draws Near
	12:1–8	Jesus is Anointed for Death at Bethany
12:9–36	Preparation for Passover and Death	
	12:9–19	The Crowds Acclaim Jesus as He Enters Jerusalem
	12:20–36	Arrival of the Greeks Marks the Arrival of the Hour
12:37–50	Conclusion of Jesus's Public Ministry	
	12:37–43	Evaluation of Jesus's Ministry to His Own People
	12:44–50	Jesus's Summary Proclamation

This structure will serve as the roadmap for our journey through this final movement in the Book of Signs. As we make our way, we must be aware that this is a richly layered story. Very often events are reported that may represent facts, but John is using his story of those "facts" to give "meaning" to what God has done for humankind by means of them.

Interpreting John 11:1–12:50: Part Four—Jesus Moves toward the Hour of Death and Glory

We can now move into a more detailed exegesis of this final moment in Jesus's public ministry. In terms of literary context, these scenes bring us to the midpoint of the Gospel and one of its watershed moments. As we have just mentioned, we will be meeting reported "facts" (narrative) that have "meaning" (discourse). On the narrative level, the characters in the text find themselves in **crises of faith**. Do they believe in the word of Jesus? Is he the one in whom they should place their hopes, the messiah they have been promised? On the discourse level, the evangelist is bringing his audience to this same point. Audiences have read the prologue and know much more about Jesus than the characters in the text, but are they prepared to stand up and stand fast for what they believe? This is a crucial moment for John's original audience, but audiences across time are likewise pulled into the fray. Is it enough to believe that Jesus is the expected Jewish messiah? Is there, perhaps, more at stake? The worlds behind, in, and in front of the text collide as we move with Jesus toward the hour of his death and glory.

11:1–12:8 Jesus Gives Humankind Life; Humankind Condemns Jesus to Death

This long and dramatic passage narrates transitions of faith as the story is led gradually away from Jesus's public ministry into the hour of his glorification. It is framed by the first mention of Jesus's anointing, the description of friends **Mary**, **Martha**, and **Lazarus**, and Mary's eventual anointing of Jesus's feet (11:1–10; 12:1–8). Within this "frame" a great deal happens, especially the spectacular raising of Lazarus. Across the narration of these "events" many are called to decision: the disciples (see 11:15–16), Martha (see vv. 25–27), Mary (see vv. 32–34), "the Jews" (see vv. 45–46), and the Jewish leadership (see vv. 47–50). As we follow this amazing story, we are also drawn into it, called to decision by the person who claims to be resurrection and life (see vv. 25–26). The question that Jesus directs to Martha is also directed to the audience: "Do you believe this?" (v. 26).

11:1–44 Jesus Gives Life to Lazarus—Jesus as the Resurrection and the Life

Several tensions emerge as this chapter begins. We have already seen that the narrator tells us about the future role of Mary (v. 2). But in another strange encounter, although Jesus loves Lazarus and his sisters Mary and Martha, when he hears that Lazarus is ill, he stays where he is for two more days (v. 6). Is this what we do when he hear that our loved ones are ill? The explanation for this delay is found in v. 4: "This illness does not lead to death; rather it is for God's glory, so that the Son of God may be glorified through it." This is the underlying discourse of John 11–12. So much is said about "death" in these chapters, but the death of Lazarus is not about death, as we would normally understand that reality. Jesus will raise Lazarus from the dead and thus show forth God's glory (see v. 40), and this event will lead to the plot to crucify Jesus. Jesus's crucifixion is, however, **the "hour"** of his **"exaltation."** Through the cross he will reveal the love of God and return to the glory with the Father, which was his before the world was made.

But the characters in the story do not see this. Invited to come to Jerusalem with Jesus so that the experience of Jesus's encounter with the death of Lazarus might produce true faith (vv. 7–15), Thomas speaks in their name and accepts that they should go to Jerusalem to die with him (v. 16). But Jesus has not asked them to be martyrs with him; he wants them to believe in what God is doing in and through him (v. 15). They are good people, but they do not understand. Martha regrets that Jesus was not there to heal Lazarus when he was sick. She accepts that Jesus is a messianic miracle worker. But when Jesus tells her that her brother will rise, she instructs Jesus on her knowledge about resurrection at the end of time (vv. 20–24). In unforgettable words, Jesus reveals his role as the resurrection and the life (vv. 25–26), asking her to transcend her messianic hopes. She will not make that step and reaffirms her belief that he is the Christ, the son of God (a Jewish messianic title), the one who is to come into the world (v. 27).

Mary has the same difficulty. Initially she falls at Jesus's feet, ready to accept what he has to offer, but then she joins "the Jews" in their weeping and their hopes that he might work miracles. Jesus is deeply frustrated by his inability to bring anyone to true faith in him as the sent one of God, the resurrection and the life (vv. 32–37). At the tomb Martha again shows her lack of faith in Jesus as the resurrection and the life, as she suggests that the odor from the tomb after four days would be unacceptable; and Jesus warns her about her lack of faith (vv. 39–40).

In a prayer to his Father, Jesus again states his purpose in raising Lazarus from the grave: "I have said this that they may believe that you sent me" (v. 42). Through raising Lazarus from the dead, Jesus wanted to bring the disciples, Martha, Mary, and "the Jews" who had come to the tomb to faith in him as the sent one of God. He has not been successful. They mourn, weep, and expect him

The Resurrection of Lazarus by Giovanni di Paolo

to behave as a messianic miracle worker. Little wonder that he is deeply upset by this failure. On two occasions Jesus is "greatly disturbed" (11:33, 38). The Greek verb **embrimasthai** actually means **to be angry**, to express frustration. Its original meaning is associated with the snort of a horse. Jesus is not joining everyone in sorrow; he is expressing deep emotional disappointment, because no one comes to true faith.

Lazarus comes forth and must be freed from the clothes of death (vv. 43–44), something that will not be necessary when Peter and the Beloved Disciple find the empty tomb of Jesus (see 20:4–8).

11:45–57 The Sanhedrin Condemns Jesus to Die as Passover Draws Near

Some believe, but others report these events to the Jewish leadership (vv. 45–46). The council of leadership, called **the Sanhedrin**, under the direction of **Caiaphas, High Priest** that year, make their decision: it is better that Jesus "die for the people than have the whole nation destroyed" (vv. 47–50). But as the early audiences read and listen to these words, late in the first Christian century, they know that the nation has been destroyed by the Romans and that Jesus has been raised and is alive! The deeper meaning of Jesus's death is clarified as

the narrator steps in to explain that Caiaphas had uttered a prophetic word. Jesus was about to die, "not for the nation only, but to gather into one the dispersed children of God" (v. 52). We mentioned this passage in chapter six when we discussed the evangelist's use of irony as a storytelling technique. At this crucial moment in the story, the narrator is careful to ensure that his audiences understand his deeper discourse. In the face of death Jesus gives the gift of life in relationship as a child of God to all who call on his name. Indeed, the irony is that Jesus's death will affect the restoration and union of the covenant people of God, a reconstituted Israel, as the true children of God. This **gathering** also continues a theme that began in Jesus's Good Shepherd discourse. There he said: "I have other sheep that do not belong to this fold.

> **The Sanhedrin**
>
> A high court in the period of the Second Temple is sometimes identified in the NT as simply "the council" but is often identified by what is taken to be a proper name, "the Sanhedrin" (e.g., Mark 14:55; 15:1; Matt 5:2; 26:59; Luke 22:56; John 11:47; see Acts 4–6; 22–24). The historical role and composition of the council of Jewish leadership is disputed. Some suggest it was more political; others claim it was composed of religious leaders (e.g., including priests, Pharisees, and scribes) knowledgeable in the Torah.

I must bring them also, and they will listen to my voice. So there will be one flock, one shepherd" (10:16). This theme will gather momentum in John 12.

12:1–8 Jesus Is Anointed at Bethany in Preparation for Death

All four Gospels in the NT share a story about a woman who anoints Jesus's feet in an intimate act of devotion just before he enters Jerusalem for his final Passover celebration. In the Synoptic Gospels, this woman remains unnamed. In the Gospel of John, however, she is Mary of Bethany, friend of Jesus and sister to Martha and Lazarus (see 11:2). In this case, her move toward Jesus is set within the context of the unbelieving Judas, and her faith is symbolized by the odor that fills the house. As her sister Martha showed her lack of faith when she objected to the odor from the tomb of a dead man, Mary fills the whole house with the odor that symbolizes her faith-filled preparation of Jesus's body for a death that will reveal the love of God and will be the "hour" of Jesus's "lifting up." As we have already seen, this passage brings to closure many episodes where the characters in the story (disciples, Martha, Mary, "the Jews," the Jewish leaders) show their inability to accept what God is doing in and through Jesus, his sent one. What began in 11:1–6 concludes in 12:1–8.

12:9–36 *Preparation for Passover and Death*

Jesus's final public moments with "the Jews" and their leaders are reported in this section of the story. It features some significant actions: Jesus's entry into Jerusalem for the last time (vv. 12–16), "framed" by discussions among the Jewish leaders about Jesus's increasing popularity (vv. 9–11, 17–19). The arrival of **the Greeks** and the advent of "the whole world" (see v. 19) leads to a discourse from Jesus in which he announces the arrival of the "hour" of his "lifting up," met by the usual rejection and misunderstanding (vv. 20–34). Before leaving "the Jews" and hiding from them, Jesus pleads with them, one last time, to believe in him so that they might walk in the light (vv. 35–36).

12:9–19 Jesus Enters Jerusalem, and the "Gathering" Continues

Jesus enters Jerusalem, greeted by the waving of palm fronds, a sign that they are welcoming a military hero, and is acclaimed as the King of Israel (vv. 12–16). This is the event celebrated by Christians as a "triumphal entry" on Palm Sunday, the Sunday before Easter, every year. Jesus's entry in this way fulfills the promise for the messiah given by the prophet Zechariah. In this sense, Jesus is indeed the long-awaited messiah, and he enters the city one last time victoriously. Attentive audiences, however, also know that he is not a military hero; this is not the kind of messiah he is destined to be. Jesus has been calling those he encounters to a deeper understanding of how God is acting in the world through him. In this second sense, therefore, the lack of authentic faith that we saw in 11:1–12:8 continues. Only after Jesus's death and resurrection will the disciples fully come to understand what was happening to Jesus. Even here, however, the entry is surrounded by concerns from the Jewish leadership (vv. 9–11 and vv. 17–19) that *ironically* develop the theme of "gathering." Initially they are concerned that, because of the resurrection of Lazarus, "many of the Jews were deserting and were believing in Jesus" (v. 11) and—even worse—that "the world has gone after him" (v. 19).

12:20–36 Arrival of the Greeks Marks the Arrival of the Hour

In fulfillment of the complaints of the Jewish leadership that "the world has gone after him" (v. 19), Greeks who seek to see Jesus arrive and two disciples with Greek names, Andrew and Philip, repeat this "request" from "the whole world" to see Jesus (vv. 20–22). After indications throughout his ministry that his hour had "not yet" come (see 2:4; 7:6, 30; 8:20), Jesus now announces: "The hour has come for the Son of Man to be glorified" (v. 23). What this "hour" means for Jesus, and also for the disciples, is spelled out in vv. 24–26, and the theme of "gathering" returns. Only by falling and dying can the grain of wheat bear fruit. Such is the destiny of Jesus, and also the destiny of anyone who would claim to be his servant: "Where I am, there will my servant be also." But as Jesus's loving self-gift makes the Father known, so will the loving self-gift of the disciple: "Whoever serves me, the Father will honor" (v. 26).

The hour of his glorification is also an hour of distress for Jesus, who, despite his foreknowledge, is no less affected by his mission as the Son of Man in the world. To be crucified necessarily means to suffer, but Jesus has come for this hour and will not swerve from the will of the one who sent him (v. 27). He is assured by the voice from heaven that God has already glorified his Son throughout the ministry and will shortly glorify it again, in and through his death (v. 28). The discussion among the people that results from this voice again indicates their inability to recognize the relationship between Jesus and God (v. 29). This is not thunder but a voice from above! Jesus reaffirms his role as the Son of Man who must be "lifted up" and in this way "draw all people" to himself: "He said this to indicate the kind of death he was to die (vv. 32–33). The theme of "gathering" at the cross continues.

In a final appeal to "the Jews" Jesus urges his misunderstanding audience, "While you have the light, believe in the light, so that you may become children of the light." Tragically, they will not listen. Jesus departs "and hid from them" (v. 36). "The Jews" can no longer "see Jesus." The next time Jesus will appear before them will be in his trial and his passion, fulfilling the prophecy of Jesus from 8:28: "When you have lifted up the Son of Man, then you will know that I am he." For the moment, they have chosen to walk in the darkness.

12:37–50 *Conclusion of Jesus's Public Ministry*

The final passage of this larger narrative unit is made up of two summary statements, the former by the narrator and the latter by Jesus. In terms of literary context, we are coming to the midpoint of the story. The central conflict is established, and characters are responding in kind. For the moment, the story of Jesus, "the Jews," his disciples, and other characters is over. The dialogue is now between the storyteller and the audience (vv. 37–43), and then between Jesus and the audience (vv. 44–50). No other characters play a role: just words spoken—and heard.

12:37–43 Evaluation of Jesus's Ministry to His Own People

These few words from the narrator are initially puzzling. In fulfillment of the word of the prophet Isaiah who saw his glory, the narrator explains that "the Jews" failed to accept Jesus because their eyes were closed and their hearts hardened (vv. 37–41). The puzzle comes from the fact that throughout the Gospel there has never been any indication that God wanted them to fail. Indeed, they are challenged to believe that Jesus is the sent one who has come to make God known to them at every turn. It is to that issue that the narrator turns in vv. 42–43. Many did believe, even from among their leaders, but they were afraid of losing their human esteem and in this way missed out on the revelation of the glory of God. The narrator again plays upon a single word that has two meanings. The Greek word *doxa* means "**esteem**, honor," but it also means "**glory**." "The Jews" did not want to be excluded from the synagogue and the world they knew. The "esteem" (*doxa*) in which they are held might be at risk. They reject Jesus's challenge and lose sight of the presence of the divine among them. Those who do believe in Jesus accept that, in him, the glory (*doxa*) of God has been made visible. They accept Jesus's challenge and are thus empowered to become children of God.

12:44–50 Jesus's Summary Proclamation

The final words of the Book of Signs come from Jesus, who "cries out" (v. 44). This is a dramatic and climactic voice that looks back across the Gospel story to this point. The themes of mission and light first introduced in the prologue (1:1–18) reappear steadily as Jesus exercises his public ministry from 1:19 to 12:36. Jesus thus summarizes the challenge of God's revelation in and through Jesus, which has been at the heart of all that he has said and done. He has been sent by God, he announces the word of God, and he thus brings people out of the darkness into the light (vv. 44–46). Also paralleling the many events across the public ministry, Jesus announces that his presence within the human story brings **decision** and judgment (see 3:11–21, 31–36; 11:1–55). Those who accept him, whom he has empowered to be the true children of God, speak out the words the Father has commanded, regardless of the earthly consequences. Those who reject him do not; God will be their judge. Jesus defers all motivation and honor for his life and mission to the Father who sent him. His word is the word of the Father, and his mission is to give eternal life (vv. 47–50).

These verses resonate with the covenantal themes of Deuteronomy. The words of God are now uttered by the prophet like Moses, incarnate in Jesus the Son of God (see Deut 18:15, 18–19), and these commandments set the pattern of daily life for the people and breathe the life of Israel (see Deut 32:45–47).

The word of God in the new covenant spoken through Jesus now encapsulates the obligations of believers. Through the intimacy of the relationship between God the Father and Jesus the Son, as well as their shared desire to extend this relationship of family to all who would become children of God, we move to the glory of the hour of Jesus.

What Have We Learned So Far?
Jesus as the Resurrection and the Life

The narratives and dialogues that close Jesus's public ministry bring the themes of life and light to their peak, as Jesus places himself in the midst of the Jewish people and reveals himself to be the resurrection and the life on the eve of the hour of his glorification (11:25–26). In the drama surrounding the illness, death, and raising of Lazarus, the people who are called to decision and fail include: the disciples, Martha, Mary, "the Jews," and the Jewish leaders. The Jewish authorities are prompted to make their final decision: Jesus must die. Death is now decisively "in the air." The evangelist continues to distinguish between superficial belief and abiding in the word of Jesus, which reflects the authentic faith of true children of God. Mary, Martha, and the disciples continue on their journeys of faith, and Mary breaks through to show her acceptance of the saving revelation of God's love in Jesus's death as she prepares his body with her anointing (12:1–8). But the persistent unbelief of the crowds is finally confirmed (12:35). Many among the authorities believe but are afraid to confess Jesus as the Messiah, lest they be expelled from the synagogue. The narrator condemns their fear as a failing of human will (12:42–43).

Audiences find themselves in the midst of these journeys of faith. They, too, are being brought to a crisis and must determine with whom to identify as they decide the direction their own journeys will take. The Book of Signs closes as Jesus sums up his discourse that has made God known: Jesus has been sent to save the world, and those who receive him receive the commandment of God, which is eternal life (12:47–50). Jesus now turns toward his own and the hour of his glorification (see 13:1). There and then the mission of his gift to the world will be fulfilled.

This fairly brief narrative unit that closes the Book of Glory, therefore, has much to say about Christology—how Jesus is the Christ and how humankind is to respond to him—as well as ethics—how humankind is then to act in community. In John 11 we learn that Jesus is the "sent one" of God who is also the resurrection and the life. This is how he is the Messiah, as the Son of Man who by overcoming death will give life to those who accept the challenge to believe. In John 12, however, we also see how Jesus fulfills more traditional messianic expectations through his triumphant entry into Jerusalem. Although he will not be the military hero and king like David, audiences are prepared for a royal end to his story. He will be king, just not of this world. And the kingdom of God is built for those who can transcend even the most profound human sorrow: death. The ethics of the children of God include the hope of Martha and Mary, however imperfect it may be, the Greeks' desire to see Jesus, and even Thomas's and the disciples' desire to die with Jesus. The promise that Jesus gives is life in his name, and this life is lived in a community of hope and support that sustains through the deepest sorrow.

Key Terms and Concepts

angry/*embrimasthai*	hour
Caiaphas the High Priest	Lazarus
crisis of faith	lifting up/*hypsōthēnai*
decision	literary tension
exaltation	Martha
gathering	Mary
glory/esteem/*doxa*	prolepsis
Greeks	Sanhedrin

Questions for Review

1. In chapter six, we discussed the evangelist's use of literary frames as a story-telling strategy. What might be the interpretive force in framing the raising of Lazarus, first with the mention and second with the action of Mary anointing Jesus beforehand for burial?

2. How do the journeys of faith proceed in the telling of the raising of Lazarus? In other words, who is this story really about, the disciples, Martha, Mary, "the Jews," or Lazarus?

3. When the Sanhedrin gathers after the raising of Lazarus, they condemn Jesus to death. With this in mind, explain the irony on the part of the high priest Caiaphas and how it serves to share a message with audiences.

4. What is the significance of the theme of "gathering" that began in John 10:16 and that increases in importance in 11:51–52; 12:20–24, 32–33? Does this theme play a role in generating a "narrative tension" in the story?

5. Why does the arrival of Greeks, who want to see Jesus, mark the arrival of the hour of his passion and glorification? How is this a part of Jesus's larger mission as the Son of Man who is Messiah and Son of God?

6. The Book of Signs closes with Jesus making a final evaluation of his ministry and retreating from public life. The people are divided. What is the nature of their crisis of faith as it is characterized by the narrator? How does this prepare audiences for the Book of Glory?

Bibliography and Further Reading

Lincoln, Andrew T. "The Lazarus Story: A Literary Perspective." Pages 211–32 in *The Gospel of John and Christian Theology*. Edited by Richard Bauckham and Carl Mosser. Grand Rapids: Eerdmans, 2008.

Moloney, Francis J. "Can Everyone Be Wrong? A Reading of John 11.1–12.8." *New Testament Studies* 49 (2003): 505–27.

————. *Signs and Shadows. Reading John 5–12*. Minneapolis: Fortress, 1996.

Thompson, Maryanne M. "The Raising of Lazarus in John 11: A Theological Reading." Pages 233–44 in *The Gospel of John and Christian Theology*. Edited by Richard Bauckham and Carl Mosser. Grand Rapids: Eerdmans, 2008.

Jesus and His Own:
Glory, Love, and Discipleship in John 13–17

PURPOSE Chapter twelve introduces the Book of Glory and focuses on Jesus's last discourse with and preparation of his disciples for life and leadership in the glory of God and through love for one another (John 13–17).

ASSIGNMENT Reread John 13–17 before proceeding with this chapter.

We now turn our attention to the second half of the body of the narrative of John's Gospel, known to many as **the Book of Glory**. After introducing this major component of the narrative and its overall structure, the spotlight will focus on the first narrative unit of the Book of Glory, Jesus's last meal and discourse with his disciples found in John 13:1–17:26. This is a lengthy and complex unit that transitions the story from the public ministry of Jesus narrated in the Book of Signs (John 1–12) to his ultimate glorification through his passion and death (John 18–19). Therefore, we must take care in unpacking the evangelist's nuanced storytelling on both the narrative and discourse levels.

Introduction to the Book of Glory

The Book of Signs (John 1:19–12:50) depicts the public ministry of Jesus. His words and deeds address a wide audience and provoke a crisis of faith wherein some believe and some refuse to believe. The Book of Glory (John 13:1–20:31) can be characterized as the result of that crisis. It is addressed to the restricted audience of those who believe. If the Book of Signs anticipated what Jesus would do for humankind once glorified, the Book of Glory describes that glorification. This, finally, is "the hour" of his passion, crucifixion, and resurrection. The unique feature of the Gospel of John is that the "glory" of Jesus takes place by means of the cross. Through his death and resurrection he will return to the glory that was his before all time. John is also unique in presenting Jesus's self-gift in love on the cross as the revelation of the love of God. Thus, John claims, the cross itself makes God's glory visible. For that reason, as he ends his passion narrative, he reports: "They will look on the one whom they have pierced" (19:37).

It is obvious that we are entering another part of the story in the very first verse of what we call the Book of Glory: "Now before the festival of the Passover, Jesus knew that his hour had come to depart from this world and go to the Father. Having loved his own who were in the world, he loved them to the end" (13:1). The Book of Glory reverses the narrative action of the Book of Signs. In that first part of the body of the Gospel, Jesus's dialogues and discourses followed and served to interpret the signs. In this second part, the last supper and discourse (13:1–17:26) precede the action of glorification and serve to foretell and interpret that action before it takes place (18:1–19:42). What follows 13:1 spells out in word and action Jesus's instructions to his disciples on his imminent departure (14:1–16:33), his unfailing love for them—despite their frailty (13:1–38; 17:1–26), the revelation of the glory of God (18:1–19:42), and the glorification of the Son as he returns to his Father through his resurrection and ascension, and commissions his disciples (20:1–31).

In terms of the "action" of the narrative, everything slows down, as Jesus pauses, along with his disciples, as John 13–17 anticipates the meaning of what follows in John 18–21. Indeed, John 1–12 covered events that took place over more than two years; whereas John 13–21 reports the climactic moments of just three days. Although we will discuss each narrative unit in more detail in its respective sections, the Book of Glory—the second half of the body of the Gospel of John—can therefore be structured as follows:

The Structure of the "Book of Glory" in the Gospel of John 13:1–20:31

Part One: The Last Discourse   13:1–17:26
- **A**   13:1–38   Making God Known: The Foot-Washing and the Morsel
  - **B**   14:1–31   Departure: The Promise of God's Abiding Presence and Guidance
    - **C**   15:1–16:3 The Call to Abide, to Love, and to Be Hated
  - **B′**   16:4–33   Departure: The Consequences of Discipleship
- **A′**   17:1–26   Making God Known: Jesus's Final Prayer Consecrating the Community

Part Two: The Passion   18:1–19:42
- **A**   18:1–11   Jesus Is Arrested by His Enemies in a Garden
  - **B**   18:12–27 Jesus Is Interrogated by "the Jews"—Condemnation
    - **C**   18:28–19:16a Jesus Stands before Pilate—The Challenge of Truth
  - **B′**   19:16b–37   Jesus Is Crucified before "the Jews"—Completion
- **A′**   19:38–42 Jesus Is Buried by His Friends in a Garden

Part Three: The Resurrection   20:1–29

Part Four: The First Conclusion to the Gospel   20:30–31

With this bigger picture of the flow of the narrative in mind, we can proceed with a more detailed interpretation of the first part of the Book of Glory, Jesus's last meal and discourse with his disciples (13:1–17:26).

Part One: The Last Discourse, 13:1–17:26

The form and content of the **last discourse** has lent itself to considerable scholarly discussion regarding its structure and integrity. Repetitions and discrepancies in sequence and content in these chapters have resulted in various approaches to interpreting the extended scenes narrated within them. The final text is most likely the result of many years of story-telling and remembering. It is made up of a narrative (13:1–38), two very similar discourses (14:1–31 and 16:4–33), a further quite different discourse (15:1–16:3), and a final prayer (17:1–26). These elements were very common in other Jewish and Greco-Roman literature and are classified as **farewell discourses**. Most of them contain narrative and instructions for the next generation, and they close with a prayer. Against this history and background, John 13–17 must be interpreted as a coherent narrative unit. There are twenty-one chapters in our present Gospel of John. Five of those chapters are found in the last discourse. The evangelist has deliberately constructed 13:1–17:26 and used it to form one quarter of his story. It is our task to see why he did that and what he wants to say in his use of the farewell discourse literary form.

The Narrative Flow and Structure of John 13–17

We have already seen that the literary "background" to John 13–17 is a traditional form of a "farewell discourse." Closer attention to the structure and message of the passage uncovers a deliberate literary strategy. In the first place, this section opens with a narrative that insists upon Jesus's revelation of the remarkable love of God, and he calls his disciples to follow his example and to love as he has loved (13:1–38). Although couched in different language and form, the closing **prayer** makes the same point: Jesus makes known God's remarkable love, and he calls his disciples to love one another so that the world might know that he is the sent one of the Father, that they might be swept into the love that unites the Father and the Son (17:1–26).

The **discourse** proper (14:1–16:33) insists twice on the need for Jesus to depart, the gift of the Paraclete, and the love and belief that must mark the lives of his disciples while they live the time between his departure and his return (14:1–31; 16:4–33). At the center of the discourse—surrounded by Jesus's command that the disciples must abide in him and the indication that they will be hated as he has been hated—Jesus's command to love reappears, calling disciples to love as he has loved them, because he has chosen them to be his friends (15:1–16:3). Taking this into account, we suggest the following literary structure for the narrative unit known as the last discourse (13:1–17:26), located between Jesus's ministry (1:19–12:50) and his death and resurrection (18:1–20:31).

Part One: The Last Discourse   13:1–17:26

    A   13:1–38   Making God Known: The Foot-Washing and the Morsel

        B   14:1–31   Departure: The Promise of God's Abiding Presence and Guidance

           C   15:1–16:3 The Call to Abide, to Love, and to Be Hated

        B′ 16:4–33 Departure: The Consequences of Discipleship

    A′ 17:1–26 Making God Known: Jesus's Final Prayer Consecrating the Community

Notice that we have diagrammed this structure in the same manner that we diagrammed the prologue (John 1:1–18) in chapter seven. We call the initial narrative segment **A**, the first part of the discourse segment **B**, and the center of this narrative unit segment **C**. As we proceed through the final part of the discourse and the final narrative episode, we call those segments **B′** and **C′** respectively. We are therefore suggesting once again that the evangelist has plotted this narrative unit as a **chiasm**. He has carefully centered the last discourse around Jesus's call to his disciples to abide in his love, even as they will be hated by much of the world. This is the climax of the narrative unit, and the prior segments build to this call while the latter segments proceed from it. We can now move forward with a detailed discussion of John 13–17 along this structure.

Farewell Discourses

A farewell address or discourse is a literary form found in both the OT and the NT. The typical pattern presents a leader at the end of life or who is about to leave due to external forces. This leader takes the opportunity to remind the audience of their shared traditions and instruct followers on how to carry on the work in his or her absence. The book of Deuteronomy is often interpreted as the farewell address of Moses. John 13–17 presents the farewell address of Jesus and is thus generally identified as "the last discourse."

Interpreting John 13–17: Part One—The Last Discourse

On arrival at 13:1 the audience is the product of the experience of John 1:1–12:50. The first page of the narrative (1:1–18) leaves no doubt about the author's point of view concerning *who Jesus is* and *what he does*. However, the remarkable nature of these claims, even for one well-versed in the Christian story, leaves the audience wondering. They demand a narrative that spells out *how* all this could possibly take place in the life-story of Jesus of Nazareth. Questions about authentic faith, which emerged from the Opening Days (1:19–51), were resolved in the journey from Cana to Cana (2:1–4:54). The problem of Israel's traditional way to God through their feasts and liturgy was addressed amidst increasing bitterness and threats of violence in 5:1–10:41. A decisive turn toward that violent end, known to the audience as Jesus's death on the cross, was taken in 11:1–12:50. But this is to plot the story in terms of its external features. From the beginning of the story the author has insinuated a theology of the cross that created more problems than it solved. Jesus's ministry was marked by "the hour" that was "not yet," an inevitable movement toward a time to be determined by God (see 2:4; 7:6–8, 30; 8:20). Only when people from beyond the boundaries of Israel seek to see Jesus does he announce that "the hour" has come (12:23). From that point on, the audience is caught up in "the hour" as it moves toward consummation. The Son of Man was to be the unique revelation of God, yet lifted up on a stake, as Moses lifted up the serpent in the wilderness (3:13–14). Three times Jesus refers unmistakably to the cross as his necessary "lifting up" (3:14; 8:28; 12:32), and the narrator adds a comment for the audience after the final use of the expression, so that there may be no doubts about what is meant by Jesus's being "lifted up": "He said this to show by what death he was to die" (12:33). But that is not all. We know from the prologue to the Gospel that his story tells the story of a God whom no one has ever seen (1:18). Jesus makes God known as he speaks the word of God.

Moreover, there are other themes from the earlier part of the narrative that point to Jesus as the revelation of God. There have been several uses of the expression **"glory"** (Greek: ***doxa***) throughout the ministry, which suggest to the audience that the revelation of the glory of God associated with the gift of the law at Sinai has been perfected in the gift of Jesus Christ. This is already present in the wedding feast at Cana in John 2, where the disciples see the "glory" as the culmination of a series of "days" that match the days of the Jewish celebration of Pentecost. It becomes explicit in the final reflections of the narrator, at the close of the public ministry, in an explanation of why "the Jews" failed to accept the revelation of God in and through Jesus. Earlier in the story, there was a play on the secular and religious meaning of the expression "glory" (*doxa*). This is repeated in 12:43 as the narrator comments: "They loved human glory (the *doxa* of human beings) more than the glory that comes from God (the *doxa* of God)." An inability to abandon the established, recognized ways in which they found their self-identity and self-esteem led them to reject the revelation of God in Jesus.

Toward the end of the story of the public ministry, a link emerges between Jesus's death and glorification as he informs his disciples that the events to take place at Bethany will be "for God's glory, so that the Son of God might be glorified through it" (11:4). The glory of God shines through in the miracle, but it is because of the miracle that a decision is taken that Jesus must die. The link between "the hour" and the glorification of Jesus, the Son of Man who must be lifted up is made explicit for the audience in 12:23: "The hour has come for the Son of Man to be glorified." The purpose of "the hour" of Jesus is to glorify the name of the Father, and a voice from heaven informs Jesus—and the listening audience—that the ministry of Jesus has already rendered glory to God and that the oncoming death of Jesus will render further glory. A final confirmation comes in 12:32: "And I, when I am lifted up from the earth, will draw all people to myself." This is a further reference to another theme that has criss-crossed the final chapters of the ministry: the gathering. It has been present since Jesus first spoke of the Good Shepherd's gathering sheep from other folds into one and further developed by the narrator's comment on Caiphas's decision that Jesus was to die for the nation: "and not for the nation only, but to gather into one the dispersed children of God" (11:52). In John 12 this movement toward oneness begins. The narrator comments that "many of the Jews were deserting and were believing in Jesus" (12:11), while the Pharisees complain, "Look, the world has gone after him" (v. 19). As if in fulfilment of these words, some Greeks come to Jesus, and this leads to his words indicating that the gathering will take place when he is lifted up from the earth, drawing everyone to himself.

As the Book of Glory opens in 13:1 crucial questions remain unanswered: how is it possible that "lifting up" on a cross can be glorification, gathering, and the revelation of God? John opens the final encounter between Jesus and his disciples with words that begin to answer those questions: on the eve of Passover, Jesus, knowing that the hour had come to depart from this world to the Father, loved his own to the very end. But further explanation is necessary. The linking of Jesus's consummate love for "his own" with the hour of his departure from this world to the Father has no prior precedent in the story. The result makes John 13:1–20:31 ("the Book of Glory") a symbolical acting out in the footwashing and the gift of the morsel in 13:1–38, explained in Jesus's discourse in 14:1–16:33, and closed with Jesus's prayer for himself, his disciples, and all who will come to believe in Jesus through them in 17:1–26.

A 13:1–38 *Making God Known: The Foot-Washing and the Morsel*

The narrator begins by informing the audience, which is already reasonably informed on these matters, that Jesus knows the hour has come for his return to the Father. Jesus has brought to perfection the work his Father gave him to do, having loved his own on earth. Now he announces "the hour" of his return to the Father. Without further ado, however, something dramatically new is introduced. The audience is told that the moment of "perfection" has arrived in a love that is both the final act in a human story (Jesus's crucifixion) and a gesture of love that cannot be surpassed (**consummate love**). This is the double meaning involved in the expression "he loved them **to the end**" (Greek: *eis telos*). The mounting violence of John 5–10, Jesus's indications of the significance of the events that will surround the raising of Lazarus, the

decisions taken by the Sanhedrin thereafter, and the comment made by the narrator upon Jesus's words on his being lifted up to draw everyone to himself lead the audience's awareness that Jesus's departure from this world to the Father, in a consummate act of love for **"his own,"** will be *via* the cross. Toward the end of this first part of Jesus's final moments with his disciples, this awareness is further clarified in terms that are familiar. As the Greeks arrived, the hour of the glorification of the Son of Man was announced and explained as a "lifting up." Now, as the narrator continues to set the scene with talk of the devil's intention for betrayal (v. 2) and Judas eventually leaves the room to go into the darkness of the night, this theme returns. The Son of Man is now glorified, and God is glorified in him (13:31–32).

In many ways, 13:1–38 spells out the meaning and consequences of glorification. In what is often referred to as **the foot-washing**, Jesus engages in an intimate act of service by washing the feet of his disciples to reveal God and signify his coming self-gift in love. But the disciples are swept up into this love, despite their failure, ignorance, and even **denial** and **betrayal**. The theme of the future betrayal of **Judas** echoes across the narrative even as the character and relationship of **Peter** and **the Beloved Disciple** emerge more clearly. For his part, Peter wants his own way with the foot-washing, with following Jesus wherever he might go, but Jesus counters that he does not fully grasp his own promises and will deny him three times. Not one of the disciples, not even the Beloved Disciple (mentioned by that name in v. 23 for the first time in the story) understands what is happening, and Judas will betray Jesus. Nonetheless, they have part with Jesus, symbolized in his washing of their feet

---

The Eucharistic Undertones of the Last Discourse Meal

Even though there is no account of the institution of the Eucharist with words over the bread and wine, as in Mark, Matthew, and Luke, John takes the celebration of the Eucharist for granted as he reports the gift of the morsel to Judas. In 13:18, when he speaks of the one who eats his bread but will raise his heel against him (citing Psalm 41), he changes the Greek verb from a word normally used for human eating (*esthiō/phagomai*) to a word that indicates physical crunching with the teeth (*trōgō*). The only other place where this verb is found is in the clearly Eucharistic passage of 6:51–58. The audience would see the link. Similarly, although early scribes eliminated it, 13:26 has the words: "he took and he gave it to Judas." The use of the words "he took and he gave" are found side-by-side in all New Testament reports of the institution of the Eucharistic meal.

and the sharing of this final meal. With **Eucharistic symbolism**, Jesus even shares the **gift of the morsel** of bread with Judas, the darkest character in the story (vv. 26–27).

Whatever one might make of these failures, Jesus challenges the disciples to do as he has done and to act as he has acted. Jesus gives an example, that they might do to one another as he has done to them, and a new commandment, that they be known as his disciples because they love one another as he has loved them. In this is Jesus glorified, and in him God is glorified. The love that is to be revealed in Jesus's self-gift will be continued in the lives of "his own," whom he leaves in the world. Jesus tells these things to failing disciples, whom he has chosen and whom he will send out, so that when this moment of glorification takes place, they might believe that Jesus is the revelation of God (v. 19: "you may believe that I am he").

In this initial segment of the last discourse, the Beloved Disciple emerges as the model who is particularly close to Jesus. Even as Peter likewise emerges as the leader and primary spokesperson for the disciples, it is the Beloved Disciple who gives him access to Jesus. Even as the audience begins to identify with them, however, that they have much to learn is also clear. The spotlight remains on Jesus. The audience exits from 13:1–38 informed that Jesus makes God known in the perfect love that he shows for his fragile disciples. In and through his loving, Jesus is glorified, and God is glorified in him. The disciples are to be recognized as the sent ones of Jesus by the unity created through the love that they have for one another.

Washing the Feet of the Disciples by Tintoretto

B 14:1–31 Departure: The Promise of God's Abiding Presence and Guidance

John 13:1–38 makes it clear that Jesus's self-gift in death will be a consummate act of love. Following hard on the heels of this information, the second segment of this narrative unit, 14:1–31, is dedicated to a further, obvious, clarification: the death of Jesus marks his **departure**. On the one hand, the audience meets an affirmation of unconditional love, but on the other, a statement that Jesus is about to leave "his own" whom he has loved "to the end." But the departure of Jesus is unlike any other departure. He instructs his disciples that it is not a moment for consternation or fear. Jesus departs to return to the Father, to initiate an in-between time, filled by the presence of another **Paraclete** who will be with the disciples "forever" (vv. 16–17, 26). During that time they are to follow Jesus's commandments: to believe in him and to love God.

Until this point in the story, Jesus has been the unique revelation of the Father. Now another character enters the story, continuing the revealing task of the earthly Jesus. Jesus is about to depart and leave the disciples. His promise to come to them will be fulfilled in the ongoing revealing mission of the Paraclete. The earthly Jesus has opened the way to the Father. Once Jesus has begun his teaching on the gift of the Paraclete, his promise casts a light across the final discourse. There are now two characters sent by the Father: Jesus, who is with the disciples now but is about to depart; and the Paraclete, who will remain with them forever. This term that we are using, "the Paraclete," is not often found in English translations of the Bible. Rather this is an English form of the Greek word *paraklētos*, which is typically translated as "the Advocate," though sometimes also "the Counselor" or "Comforter." This term for the "spirit of truth" (v. 17) or Holy Spirit is unique to John's Gospel and reflects the judicial sense of a defense attorney—one who will always advocate for them in the world.

The promise is not to be limited to those few words explicitly dedicated to it in vv. 16–17 and v. 26. Before the promise of the Paraclete and surrounding Philip's request that Jesus show the disciples the Father (see v. 8), Jesus restates one of the fundamental messages of the Gospel: Jesus's oneness with the Father makes his words and his works the unique revelation of God (14:7–11). His going away from the disciples does not end this revelation. The gift of the Paraclete will continue this revelation forever, ensur-

The Paraclete and the Holy Spirit

John uses the expression "the Paraclete" to refer to the Holy Spirit (see 14:26, where the two expressions appear together). The notion of the Spirit of God as the divine presence hovering over creation is part of Jewish tradition. In the Christian church, the Holy Spirit is seen as the gift of God, made possible by the death and resurrection of Jesus and his return to the Father. This is especially important for Luke-Acts. John continues this tradition but by adding the term "the Paraclete" he enriches the theme. It has its origins in the world of the law courts. In John, the expression carries with it the ideas of protecting, speaking up for, continuing the teaching of Jesus, reminding the community of the teaching of Jesus, and acting as a witness against evil.

ing that the oneness that exists between the Father and the Son will be revealed in disciples who love Jesus and keep his commandments, now swept into that same oneness (vv. 18–21). This promise of an in-between time undermines all expected responses to a departure by death. In place of consternation and fear, the Spirit-filled disciples will experience love, further belief and joy (vv. 22–28). The gift of the departing Jesus to the disciples is his peace, a peace that cannot be matched by anything that the world can provide.

Has the departure of Jesus initiated a utopia where life is made up of the abiding presence of the Spirit? Does the disciple, swept up into the oneness that unites Jesus and the Father, experience only love, belief, joy, and peace? The disciples, the members of the Johannine community who first received this Gospel and all subsequent Christians, recognize that the hostility of the world to Jesus has not disappeared, despite Jesus's claim that the ruler of this world has no power over him. There is a tension in the closing sentences of this first part of Jesus's discourse. He announces that he will no longer talk much, but that the ruler of this world is coming (vv. 29–30). This tension exists between the revelation of God in the word of Jesus, now no longer spoken but available through the gift of the Paraclete, and the ongoing presence of this world. This is the tension that lies behind Jesus's summons to rise and face this world (v. 31) and the need for further words from Jesus that will guide his disciples through the conflicts and hatred of the in-between time (see 15:1–16:3).

The discourse, therefore, begins in 14:1–31 as Jesus instructs his failing disciples on his departure and the conditions and challenges that will face them. Guided by the Paraclete in his physical absence, love, faith, joy and peace should be theirs, swept up into the love that unites the Father and Jesus, the sent one.

C 15:1–16:3 *The Call to Abide, to Love, and to Be Hated*

The focus of Jesus's argument changes in 15:1–11. The use of the symbol of the vine, part of which is Jesus's claim to be **the *true* vine**, is linked to traditional Israel's claim to be a vine or a vineyard (see many references in the prophets such as Hos 10:1–2; Isa 5:1–7; Jer 2:21; Ezek 15:1–5; 17:1–21; 19:10–14; as well as in Psalm 80). Although 15:1–11 focuses upon Jesus's words to his disciples, an atmosphere of polemical contrast between Jesus's exclusive claim to be the true vine and Israel's claim to be a vine is present from v. 1. Fascination over the image of the vine, however, must not overlook the central theme of vv. 1–11: the command to abide and Jesus's explanation of what this abiding will mean for them. Some form of the verb **"to abide"** or **"to remain"** (Greek: ***menein***) appears ten times in vv. 1–11 (vv. 4 [three times], 5, 6, 7 [twice], 9, 10 [twice]). The audience's attention is drawn to the repeated insistence on the need to abide, which is more than a command to go on believing. Given the strategic place of this discourse, Jesus's command asks that disciples take on a new and deeper reciprocity with

Icon of Christ the Vine
(fifteenth century)
© Tilemahos Efthimiadis

one who is about to come to his glory through a cross. The metaphor, based on the everyday experience of a vine and the vinedresser, is the springboard for the theologically significant call to abide, maintaining and deepening the uniqueness that the disciples have been granted: they are already made clean by the word of Jesus (v. 3; see 13:10). Continuing to use the images provided by the metaphor of the vine and the branches, but gradually moving away from it into more explicitly theological statements, Jesus speaks of the creative and fruitful unity that flows between the reciprocity of love in Jesus and the Father and the disciples being swept up into that love by their abiding in Jesus. The subordination of Jesus to the Father demands that the disciples' oneness with Jesus lead them into the oneness that exists between the Father and the Son. The joy of Jesus's oneness with the Father will also fill the lives of the disciples.

The exhortations, admonitions, consolation, and polemics found in vv. 1–11 are united by the theme of the oneness and joy created by abiding in Jesus, the true vine, and being swept up into his abiding oneness of love with the Father. Another theme is struck as, in vv. 12–17, the new commandment of love, already unequivocally stated in 13:34, returns: "This is my commandment, that you love one another as I have loved you." The addition "as I have loved you" is crucial. It looks back to John's comment on the love of Jesus for his own in 13:1, with its link to the cross, and thus asks for a remarkable quality of love from the disciples. The cross also lies behind Jesus's statement of the principle that the greatest act of love is the gift of one's life for one's friends. **The new commandment** is not something that the disciples do of their own ability. They are now in a new situation, where old slaveries have disappeared because Jesus has made the Father known to them. This has been made possible because of the initiative of Jesus, summed up with words that look back to the image of the Good Shepherd: "No one has greater love than this, to lay down one's life for one's friends" (v. 13), and others which remind the reader of the use of the metaphor of the vine: "You did not choose me but I chose you. And I appointed you to go and bear fruit" (v. 16). But the audience also recalls Jesus's earlier words to his chosen, appointed, and missioned friends who will deny and betray him. It is in their being chosen and sent that Jesus's unique revelation of God's love ("that I am he") takes place (13:18–20). The love of Jesus for his own surpasses all paradigms of love for one's friends. John 15:12–17 forms the centerpiece of 15:1–16:3, highlighted by Jesus's command that the disciples love as he has loved, as a consequence of all that he has done for them.

The tone changes in 15:18–16:3, as the world's hatred, rejection, and expulsion become the subject of Jesus's discourse. As Jesus has been hated, so also will the disciples **be hated**, rejected, and even murdered because they are the chosen ones of Jesus, no longer part of this world's system. The rejection of the word of Jesus continues in the rejection of the word of his disciples. As with the abiding, so also with the hatred, the issue is fundamentally theological. The problem arises because those who have hated Jesus will also hate, reject, and kill the disciples: "because they do not know him who sent me" (v. 21); "they have seen and hated both me and my father" (v. 24): "they will do this because they have not known the Father or me" (16:3). Thus, they stand condemned, rejecting the revelation of God brought by Jesus and fulfilling the Scriptures by hating without reason. But, as the pain created by the separation that flows from Jesus's departure is to be enriched and guided by the Paraclete, so also the pain of rejection will be comforted by the witness of the Spirit of truth, who is sent from the Father. The truth of the Father and Jesus will be made clear by the witness of the Spirit, and even in the midst of conflict the disciples will have the responsibility to continue this witness to later generations.

Is there any indication of who these enemies are? Who is **"the world"** that will have no part with the Father, the Son, and the disciples? Balancing Jesus's insistence that he is the *true* vine, the disciples are told that they will be cast out of the synagogues and even killed (16:2) by people who do not accept the word of Jesus and who refuse to believe that Jesus is the sent one of the Father (16:2–3). The audience recognizes non-believers from the story of 1:19–12:50 as the *false* vine. Therefore, teaching on the love and joy that will flow from abiding in Jesus the true vine (15:1–11) is reversed as Jesus instructs the disciples on the way they will be treated by the false vine (15:18–16:3). The fruits of abiding in Jesus and the Father are matched by the hatred, rejection, expulsion, and slaying of the disciples, which will result from the actions of non-believers, the false vine that has rejected Jesus and the Father. This call to abide and to love and the consequences of hatred are the crux of Jesus's final teaching to his disciples.

B' 16:4–33 Departure: The Consequences of Discipleship

In 16:4–33 the form and themes from 14:1–31 return, as the theme of Jesus's imminent departure returns. The earlier discourse, interspersed with remarks and objections from the disciples, was driven by the theme of Jesus's departure and the new situation in which the disciples would find themselves because of that departure. The disciples have remained silent throughout the central segment of 15:1–16:3. They return as interlocutors in 16:4–33 as the theme of departure and the form of a discourse interspersed with words from the disciples reappear. But in 16:4–33 the tone of the discourse is more exalted, confident, and richer in Johannine profundity. Many have suggested that 16:1–33 is a later, more pondered Johannine "rewrite" of 14:1–31. That may be so, but 16:1–33 has its own role to play in the Johannine account of Jesus's final discourse.

Jesus returns to the theme of his departure to the Father and of his coming back to the disciples. As in 13:1–38 and 14:1–31, the disciples fail to understand. The disciples played no active role in 15:1–16:3, and thus their failure did not appear. Despite the failure and misunderstanding, Jesus promises the presence of the Paraclete to expose the failures of the world and to guide and instruct the disciples in the time of his physical absence. This aggressive presence of the Paraclete over against "the world" is different from the teaching and remembering role described earlier and developed further here, but these roles—one internal and the other external—are two aspects of the same reality. A further deepening is added to Jesus's instructions to the disciples. The theme of prayer to the Father in the name of Jesus, present in the earlier discourse, now also returns as a central motif in 16:21–24. The allegory of the woman in labor is based on a pattern of "before and after." *Before* the hour of birth, she has tribulation; but by passing through the hour, *after* the birth, she has great joy, as a child has been given to the world. The disciples are now sorrowful over the departure of Jesus, but they will finally arrive at a time when they will be seen by Jesus in joy that no one can take from them, and they will no longer have need to ask for anything. But they must live through the **in-between time** in the fullness of joy, given in the name of Jesus when they turn to the Father in prayer. Jesus has added a further element of instruction to the disciples, given *before* the hour, on the way they must live in the period *after* his departure through the hour of the cross. The disciples are assured that their prayer will be answered.

The Father will give them anything asked in his name as they live through the in-between time, after which they will no longer need to ask anything of Jesus. This instruction prepares the audience for the final segment in 17:1–26, where Jesus prays to the Father, supremely confident that the prayer will be answered.

As the disciples have believed that Jesus comes from the Father, the Father loves them. Jesus's return to the place of oneness with the Father leads the disciples to a final glimmer of understanding. They see that Jesus's origins assure the uniqueness and authority of his revelation. But they make no mention of his departure. Their confession is limited by their present circumstances (a subtle change exists between the Greek for the "now" (*nun*) of the disciples in v. 29 and the "now" in Jesus's rhetorical response in v. 31). Between the "now" of the upper room and the "then" of perfect faith among the disciples there are to be moments of suffering and loneliness. Jesus too is about to experience suffering, but his oneness with the Father overcomes all loneliness. Jesus has overcome the world, and the disciples' awareness of this victory should bring them joy in the midst of tribulation (v. 33).

We can therefore observe that the themes of 14:1–31, however much developed, return in 16:4–33. Jesus instructs his failing disciples on his departure, and the conditions and challenges that will face them. Guided by the Paraclete in his physical absence, joy and confidence should be theirs, loved by the Father who sent Jesus.

> **Two Commandments: Believe and Love**
>
> In John's Gospel there are only two explicit commandments for all potential disciples, and both are found in chs. 13–17: "to believe" and "to love." Two of the most significant characters in the Gospel embody these commands: the mother of Jesus believes (2:1–5), and one of the disciples is the disciple whom Jesus loved (see 13:25; 19:25–27; 20:2; 21:20–23).

A' 17:1–26 Making God Known: Jesus's Final Prayer Consecrating the Community

At the opening of John 17, John's comment that Jesus adopts a traditional position of prayer and Jesus's words of prayer directed to the Father initiate a change in literary form. Jesus moves from discourse (14:1–16:33) to prayer (17:1–26). The audience soon becomes aware that words and themes central to the narrative of the foot-washing and the gift of the morsel have returned. It is not that the message of 13:1–38 is repeated; there is a linear development of the argument, as well as a return to earlier themes. The narrative does not go back to the beginning, but—as with the deepening and broadening of 14:1–31 in the discourse of 16:4–17:26 deepens and broadens 13:1–38, as the report of the words and events of Jesus's final evening with his disciples comes to a close. One must not be too concerned by the prayer form. It may be a prayer, but Jesus continues to teach. John 17:1–26 is at once a prayer and a profession and a revelation. Jesus's prayer moves in three stages. In the first place he prays for himself (v. 1–8). He then prays for "his own" (vv. 9–19). For the audience, they continue to be the foundational disciples, present with him around the table, which they have not left since 13:2 (despite 14:31). Finally he prays for the generations of believers who will believe through the word of the disciples (vv. 20–26).

Themes that were central to 13:1–38 return: "the hour" (v. 1; see 13:1), the glorification of the Son and the Father (vv. 1, 4–5; see 13:31–32), Jesus's self-gift having brought to perfection the task given him by the Father (vv. 3–4; see 13:1), and his ongoing love for his fragile disciples (vv. 9–19; see 13:4–17; 21–31a). The disciples continue to be presented as the fragile sent ones of Jesus who will nevertheless reveal the one who sent Jesus by the unity that their love for one another creates (vv. 11b, 21–23; see 13:18–20, 34–34). He has revealed God in his life (and death) in a unique and authoritative way. Jesus now seeks a return to glory with the Father. The disciples have believed in Jesus's revelation of the Father and in the basis for the truthfulness of that revelation: Jesus comes from the Father. They are now presented to the Father as the worthy successors of Jesus, because Jesus has done what was asked of him.

As Jesus turns to pray explicitly for these disciples, their fragility is recalled. Jesus asks his Father to care for them and to sanctify them. He first asks his Father, who is **holy**, to be Father to them, to care for them and keep them safe in the hostile world. They are not of the world, as Jesus is not of the world. The audience, encountering this Gospel after the death and resurrection of Jesus, is aware that disciples have succumbed to the attractions of the world on more than one occasion. Indeed, Judas has already gone out into the darkness. Jesus next asks the Father to make them holy so that they may perform the same sanctifying mission as Jesus. The audience is aware that the disciples are in need of greater holiness, as a gift from God, if they are to parallel the saving action of Jesus's self-gift. This is what he wants from them: to be one as Jesus and the Father are one, and to be filled with the perfection of the joy of Jesus.

The covenant theology of the OT associates knowing God's name with the eschatological realization of God's covenant relationship with Israel in the age to come (Isa 52:6). The prologue of the Gospel of John associated the "children of God" with those who receive Jesus, who is full of the gift of truth, and believe in his name (1:12). Here in this final prayer on behalf of his disciples, Jesus acknowledges that they have received his gift of truth and consecrates them in the name of the Father. They are the first fruits of the community of the children of God. The seriousness of their mission and the mission of future generations of followers makes this even clearer. The oneness of love that marks the unity between the Father and the Son is to be repeated within the community of believers, so that the world

---

Glory

John reveals his unique interpretation of Jesus's being "lifted up" on a cross in his version of the passion. As Jesus said of the consequences of the resurrection of Lazarus: it was "for God's glory, so that the Son of God may be glorified through it" (11:4).

may believe that Jesus is the sent one of God and that God loves the disciples just as he has loved the Son. The prayer closes with a request that the disciples of all generations be swept up into the oneness of love that exists between the Father and the Son.

As the theme of love opened 13:1–38, it closes 17:1–26. In and through this love God has been glorified, and the Son is glorified. The unity of love granted to the disciples, aware of the truth about God in a way unknown to the world, will enable them to contemplate that glory. The last discourse, therefore, closes with a prayer, as do other farewell discourses. But the Johannine final prayer returns to themes that opened the discourse. Jesus makes God known in the perfect love that he shows for his fragile disciples. In and through his loving, Jesus is glorified, and God is glorified in him. The disciples are to be recognized as the sent ones of Jesus by the unity created by the love that they have for one another.

What Have We Learned So Far?
Jesus, Glory, Love, and Discipleship

Two fundamental issues determine the discourse of John 13:1–17:26: the immediate future of Jesus and the more distant future of the disciples and subsequent generations of believers. But within the narrative strategy of the Fourth Gospel the narrative of 13:1–38, the discourse of 14:1–16:33, and the prayer of 17:1–26 have a rhetorical function that is not entirely determined by its literary forms. There are crucial theological and elements in John 13–17 that are determined by the story so far, in John 1–12. These same themes look forward in a way that is normal for a farewell discourse.

Without claiming to exhaust everything that is said across this section of the Gospel, we have observed that John communicates fundamental truths about *Jesus*, revealing more of his Christology. Jesus will be glorified through the revelation of perfect love, both for his Father and for "his own." The disciples have now been told that, when the events that Jesus has foretold happen, they will recognize the immensity of his love for those he has chosen and sent out, but who have not understood, who have denied and betrayed him; and they will come to believe that Jesus is the revelation of God. These events, which will take place in the near future, will lead to the glorification of God and the return of Jesus to the glory that was his before the world was made. The "glory" that will be revealed in and through the love of Jesus for his own is rooted in the love that he has for the Father and that the Father has for him. The "perfection" of the "love" is intimately linked with the "glory" of both Jesus and God and "the hour" of Jesus's passing from this world to the Father, by means of the cross. The audience senses that, as the passion story approaches, the promises of the prologue are about to be fulfilled within the narrative: And the Word became flesh and dwelt among us, the fullness of a gift that is truth. We have gazed upon his glory, the glory of the only Son from the Father. No one has ever seen God; the only Son, who is turned toward the Father, has made him known. What is surprising is that the sight of the "glory," the final word in Jesus's telling of God's story, is intimately associated with the cross.

John's message on *the disciples* is equally challenging, revealing more of his anthropology and ethics. Jesus has loved them in a consummate fashion until his final breath. They have failed and will continue to struggle in a hostile world that will not accept Jesus as the sent one of God. Within this hostile world they will not remain orphans. Awaiting his return, they are to abide in Jesus, marked by a unity of love, which will be the revelation both of their being the disciples of Jesus and of the fundamental truth that, behind the mystery of both Jesus and his disciples, Jesus is the sent one of God. They must follow the commandments of Jesus, but there are only two commandments: to love and to believe. After his departure, another Paraclete will replace Jesus in their midst, guiding, strengthening, supporting and instructing them, and judging the world, as they become the sent ones of the sent one.

There is a sense, however, that all this lies beyond the borders of a narrative of the life, death, and resurrection of Jesus. It will belong to the story of the on-going audience of the Gospel of John, living the in-between time. That such is the case is made obvious by the lack of promises within 15:1–16:3, which could be realizable within the story of Jesus. The disciples are told to abide and to love; they are told that they will be hated, expelled, and slain. This impression is enhanced by the clear indications in 16:2–3. The concrete experience of the original audiences of the Gospel is present: put out of the synagogues and slain by people who believe that they are offering service to God, because, in not recognizing Jesus, they have not come to know the Father. The revelation of the glory of God, the glorification of Jesus (13:1–38; 17:1–26), and the departure of Jesus (14:1–31; 16:4–33) belong to the story of Jesus, but the abiding, believing, loving, and being hated belong to the story of his followers (15:1–16:3) and in the lives of all who experience this story of Jesus.

Whatever its sources and its literary history, John 13:1–17:26 is part of the rhetorical strategy of the Johannine narrative. It depends upon the preceding narrative for its meaning and encourages the audience to look further into the story for the resolution of the many questions that flow from this insistence *that Jesus's loving is the revelation of God*. In short, we must read on to find out *how this happens in the life (and death) of Jesus*. But the narratives, discourses, and prayer of John 13–17 do more than that. They address both the *disciples in the narrative* and the *disciples who form an audience for the narrative*. They make a statement and raise a question, which point the audience beyond the boundaries of the Jesus-story as it is told in the Gospel of John. The disciples *in the narrative* are instructed that Jesus has made God known in a consummate act of love. But only the audience *of the narrative* can answer the question posed at the structural heart of the story of Jesus's last encounter with his disciples

(15:1–16:3). Is God still being made known by fruitful disciples of the Johannine Jesus? Are they abiding in him, believing and loving in the midst of a hostile world? Does their love for one another proclaim that they are no longer servants? This should be the case, as they have been chosen by Jesus and have heard all that the Father made known to him.

Key Terms and Concepts

abide/*menein*	hated
Beloved Disciple	"his own"
betrayal	Holy
Book of Glory	in-between time
chiasm	Judas
consummate love	last discourse
denial	new commandment
departure	paraclete
discourse	Peter
eucharistic symbolism	prayer
farewell discourses	"to the end"/*eis telos*
foot-washing	true vine
gift of the morsel	world
glory/*doxa*	

Questions for Review

1. Describe the change of audience and atmosphere that begins in John 13:1. Despite these changes, do certain themes from the Book of Signs continue into the Book of Glory? Does one prepare for the other? If so, how?

2. What is the importance of 13:18–20 and Jesus's use of the words "I am he" in v. 19?

3. On reading 14:1–31 and 16:4–33 carefully, do you find similar themes? What is different between the two chapters, and what is new in John 16 that cannot be found in John 14?

4. What is the central theme of John 14 and 16? Describe the role of the Paraclete.

5. What is more important in 15:1–11: the image of the vine or the command to abide? Why?

6. Can you detect a relationship between the abiding of 15:1–11 and Jesus's indications of the hatred the disciples will encounter in the future of 15:18–16:3? Can you imagine a real-life situation in the early church where this relationship was important, especially in the light of 16:1–3?

7. Some scholars regard 15:12–17 as the very center, the heart, of John 13–17.

Now that you are familiar with the whole passage, what do you think? How might this be so?

Bibliography and Further Reading

Brown, Raymond E. *The Gospel according to John*. 2 vols. Anchor Bible 29–29a. New York: Doubleday, 1966–1970.

Brown, Sherri. *God's Promise: Covenant Relationship in John*. New York: Paulist, 2014.

Chennattu, Rekha M. *Johannine Discipleship as a Covenant Relationship*. Peabody, MA: Hendrickson, 2006.

Kurz, William S. *Farewell Addresses in the New Testament*. Zaccheus Studies: New Testament. Collegeville, MN: Liturgical, 1990.

Moloney, Francis J. "The Function of John 13–17 within the Johannine Narrative." Pages 43–66 in *"What Is John?" Volume II. Literary and Social Readings of the Fourth Gospel*. Edited by Fernando F. Segovia. Symposium Series 7. Atlanta: Scholars Press, 1998.

The Passion of Jesus:
Crucifixion, Kingship, and Truth in John 18–19

PURPOSE Chapter thirteen presents the passion narrative as the culmination of the good news of the Gospel of John, with a focus on Jesus and his glorificaton through crucifixion (John 18–19).

ASSIGNMENT Reread John 18–19 before proceeding with this chapter.

Jesus's last discourse in John 13–17 provides teaching for his disciples to prepare them for his coming arrest and death and the reality of his future physical absence. As he closes his final prayer, Jesus is ready to face the last task of his earthly mission and depart. Christian tradition has long identified Jesus's willing acceptance of these events to come as his **passion**. Although in contemporary English we use this word in many ways, from hunger for success or accomplishment to sexual desire, the term comes into English from the Latin word for "suffering." Christians understand Jesus's willing suffering, even to the sacrifice of his life, to be foundational for understanding him as the Christ. And yet, in the Jewish tradition from which the Gospel arose, Messiahs do not get crucified. Thus, the earliest Christians had to struggle with this historical fact both to make sense of their experience of Jesus as well as to form their own identity as a church. Therefore, preservation and telling of the passion story must have had its beginnings in the earliest development of the church. These accounts are called **passion narratives**. Each evangelist gives his own perspective to illustrate his particular theology, but they all tell the same essential story along the same plotlines: the arrest, a Jewish trial process, a Roman trial process, the crucifixion, burial, and an empty tomb (see Matt 26–27; Mark 14–15; Luke 22–23). The Fourth Evangelist narrates his unique understanding in John 18–19, and this is the focus of our current chapter.

The Narrative Flow and Structure of John 18–19

Biblical scholars have long observed the characteristics of ancient Greco-Roman drama in the Gospel of John. The evangelist seems to use a number of techniques of playwriting as he composes his narrative. He likely does this for several reasons, including the reality that he knew his good news would most often be shared in formal and informal gatherings of oral story-telling. Employing the techniques of drama allows the evangelist to set the stage and visualize the scene for the storytellers who can in turn act out these verbal cues for audiences. Across John 18–19 the telling of Jesus's passion moves through five distinct geographical locations: the garden across the Kidron valley (18:1–11); the house of Annas, the father-in-law of the high priest (18:12–27); the Roman praetorium (18:28–19:16a); Golgotha, the Place of the Skull (19:16b–37); and the new garden of Jesus's burial (19:38–42). As Jesus moves to each new location, the narrator describes the place as well as the characters and activity that will be involved there. This action on the part of the evangelist has become his typical pattern of distinguishing new acts in the story. Therefore, the Johannine passion narrative can be divided in five acts through these changes in location.

John, therefore, presents his understanding of Jesus's passion as a five-act play. In addition, the narrative acts begin and end in a garden, first as Jesus is confronted by his enemies and finally as he is buried by his friends. Similarly, the interrogation process of Jesus before his enemies in the second act is countered by the further formation of his own community in the fourth act. All of this action turns on the central encounter at the Roman praetorium between Jesus and Pilate, which concludes with Pilate handing Jesus over to be crucified. The passion narrative, like the prologue and the last discourse is thus presented in a chiastic pattern, unfolding along the following structure:

Part Two: The Passion   18:1–19:42
- **A**   18:1–11   Jesus Is Arrested by His Enemies in a Garden
  - **B**   18:12–27 Jesus Is Interrogated by "the Jews"—Condemnation
    - **C**   18:28–19:16a Jesus Stands before Pilate—The Challenge of Truth
  - **B′**   19:16b–37   Jesus Is Crucified before "the Jews"—Completion
- **A′**   19:38–42 Jesus Is Buried by His Friends in a Garden

This chiasm will provide the guide for exploring the content and discourse of the passion narrative and for establishing the crucial dialogue between Jesus and Pilate on the nature of kingship and truth through Jesus as its crux. In this way we can interpret the evangelist's teaching, or discourse, in telling the story in this way.

Interpreting John 18:1–19:42: Part Two—The Passion

In John's Gospel, the cross is presented as Jesus's most significant human experience (contrary to typical Christian understanding). God exalts Jesus in this "lifting up" on the cross. This same phenomenon of circumventing human understanding and expectation appears in the evangelist's use of the term "glory" across the Gospel. The glory of God and the means by which Jesus is glorified (through his crucifixion) flow from the evangelist's understanding of revelation. Remember, John teaches that God so loved the world that he handed over his only Son (3:16). This handing over is an incredible act of love. Further articulation of this self-gift in love was presented in the last discourse as the revelation of God that Jesus brings. Jesus the Son, given to the world, loved his own to the end (13:1). The glory of God and God's glorification of Jesus lie in this gift of the Son that begins with the incarnation (1:1–18) but is not complete until he is lifted up on the cross (see Jesus's promises in 3:14; 8:28; 12:32; as well as his final word on the cross, "It is finished," 19:30). The passion narrative is the climax of the story of this mission on earth.

A *18:1–11 Jesus Is Arrested by His Enemies in a Garden*

Act One begins with Jesus departing with his disciples upon the conclusion of his prayer, connecting the events to come with the teaching and preparation of Jesus's last discourse. They make their way across the Kidron valley, a river bed just outside the Jerusalem city walls, to a **garden** that is a common meeting place for the group. As is his custom, the evangelist quickly gathers all the major characters in this new setting. Jesus, his disciples, Judas, and an arresting party come together in this garden that had likely been a place of solace and learning. Jesus is surrounded quickly by enemies who appear in the dark—an odd collusion between Rome and "the Jews" that continues through this process. Judas, who has always been identified as the betrayer since his introduction to the story at the conclusion of Jesus's Bread of Life discourse (6:71), fulfills his own mission, launched at the meal of the previous evening (13:21–30), by leading the arresting party that is equipped with lanterns, torches, and weapons. Upon Judas's departure from Jesus, the evangelist indicated the onset of night (13:30). Now we see the fullness of the irony in this scene, since Judas has chosen darkness rather than the light that has come into the world, and now he needs artificial light of the enemies.Jesus, knowing everything, assumes the lead in the interrogation. In terms that resonate his first words to his disciples ("What are you seeking?" 1:38), Jesus asks the arresting party, "Whom are you seeking?" What results from their response of "Jesus the Nazorean" is the "I AM"—the self-revelation of Jesus in the face of the collusion of his enemies in the world (vv. 4–8). Here we see another theme that comes to the forefront of

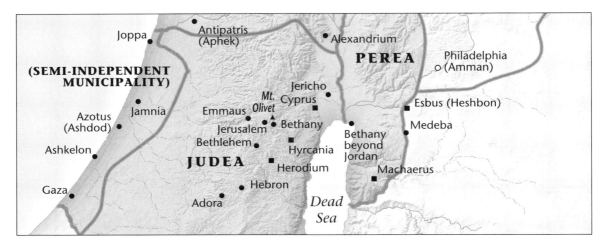

JERUSALEM AND ENVIRONS

this passion narrative: **fulfillment**. The action of Jesus's passion fulfills either the Jewish Scriptures, Jesus's own promises during his ministry, or both. In this introductory Act, Jesus reveals himself to be the revelation of God in creation, whose concern is for his disciples. He commands the arresting party to "let these go"—a reference to his disciples who, as a consequence of the prayer of Jesus in John 17:18–20, are to go forth.

Jesus's mission on earth is coming to an end. For his part, however, Peter merely begins his journey through the passion of Jesus as he tries to fulfill his own promise to Jesus during the last discourse by stepping forward with a sword against the arresting party in an effort to lay down his life for Jesus physically (v. 10; see 13:36–38). His limited efforts are thwarted by Jesus himself, who speaks to him once again in terms of his destiny: "Shall I not drink the cup that the Father has given me?" (v. 11). Although Peter's response to Jesus's question is not recorded, his behavior in the acts to come shows that his self-understanding has been thrown such that he must continue on his own journey of faith through Jesus's passion and resurrection before he can fully regain his composure and sense of mission in the community of disciples.

B 18:12–27 Jesus Is Interrogated by "the Jews": Condemnation

Act Two commences following introductory verses that describe the change of place and introduce new characters. The collusion between Roman and Jewish law enforcement takes the bound Jesus to Annas, the father-in-law of Caiaphas, the high priest, for interrogation. The roles of Annas and Caiaphas in this narrative are complex. Annas was high priest from 6 to 15 CE. Caiaphas was high priest during the historical period of the passion narrative, 18–36 CE. To use our contemporary language, Annas was "retired," or, to use the language of a university, he was an "emeritus." As such, he could still act with authority. Although this evangelist narrates only an interrogation before Annas, he is careful to note the prophecy of Caiaphas that is being fulfilled in the current narrative action by reminding audiences of his earlier role in determining what must be done with Jesus. Caiaphas is now completing his own role in God's plan by facilitating this process and sending Jesus to the Romans so that "one man should die for the people" (vv. 13–14; see 11:45–54).

The narrative of this Jewish hearing process is framed by the continuation of the journey of Peter who, on the discourse level, models the struggle of the early Christians in finding and asserting identity in Jesus (vv. 15–18, vv. 25–27). Within the frame of Peter's denial, Jesus is claiming that he has spoken openly but that his teaching to "the Jews" is over. Yet there are those who know, claims Jesus, and the high priest should therefore ask them (vv. 19–24). These scenes exemplify the frailty of the early church and its propensity to fail even as it struggles to find its way and identity in a hostile world. On the narrative level, the action that this scene narrates has the "other disciple" give Peter access to the court of the high priest. Other than his implicit desire to remain with Jesus, the Beloved Disciple has no other active role in this act. His presence, however, allows him to witness the events. For his part, Peter, apparently disturbed by the gatekeeper's query about whether he is a disciple of the accused, responds, "I am not," and warms himself by the charcoal fire with Jesus's enemies. Peter's encounter thus sets the scene for the interrogation of Jesus about "his disciples and his teaching" (v. 19). Jesus speaks boldly in defense of his teaching and is beaten and bound as a result. The focus returns to Peter as the narrator indicates that at the same time Jesus is condemned for his open integrity, Peter, the disciple who has claimed so much from Jesus's teaching, is preserving himself with three distancing denials.

The act closes with the cockcrow. Peter has actively moved from the true light of Jesus to the human-made light of the charcoal fire and is literally standing with Jesus's enemies embodied in the arresting party. In contrast to Jesus's self-revealing "I AM" of the first act, Peter repeats "I am not" in the face of the variety of challenges to his identity. He tries to warm himself in that coldness, but the cockcrow punctuates his choices. The word of Jesus continues to be fulfilled as the narrative of his passion hurtles toward its inevitable climax.

Jesus's Approach to Death

The Gospel of John tells the story of Jesus's passion, but interprets it very differently. This is obvious in the very first passage in the account. Comparing John 18:1–11 with Mark 14:35–36, the audience finds that Jesus is in command at all times. He surprises those who come to arrest him with the words "I am he," and he insists that his disciples be allowed to go and that the passion begin. There is no agonizing prayer, asking that the cup of suffering be avoided, as in Mark 14:35–36, but Jesus goes willingly into the passion, saying: "Shall I not drink the cup the Father has given me?"

Peter's Denial of Jesus
by Rembrandt

C 18:28–19:16a Jesus Stands before Pilate: The Challenge of Truth

There is a gap in the narrative of Jesus's trial process from the time he was bound and sent to Caiaphas (18:24) until he is led from the house of Caiaphas to the praetorium to stand trial before **Pontius Pilate**, the Roman governor, now that morning has broken. This **narrative gap** breeds a tension as audiences wonder what has happened and in what state Jesus arrives before the Roman government. Act Three, which presents Jesus's Roman trial, unfolds as Pilate moves outside and inside the praetorium to speak with "the Jews," who refuse to come inside for fear of defilement, and to speak with Jesus, who has been handed over to him for crimes against the state. This act further provides for a distinctive dialogue that focuses on kingship and truth. As Pilate investigates the crime set before him and travels between the accusers and accused, he is stopped momentarily by his own question on the nature of truth. The truth of Jesus as King is diminished neither by Pilate's questioning and flogging nor by "the Jews'" accusing and mocking. Jesus's passion ultimately flows from Pilate's inexorable decision to hand him over to them to be crucified—and only in the Johannine narrative does Jesus go to the cross dressed as a king. Since we are suggesting that this act is the crux of the chiasm formed by the Johannine five-act drama of Jesus's passion, we will explore it in a bit more depth.

The Roman trial is structured, after an introduction (18:28), in seven scenes as Pilate moves outside and inside the **praetorium**, the official residence of a Roman officer, in order to speak with both "the Jews" and Jesus. The final verse concludes this act as Pilate makes his decision (19:16a). The narrative is marked by verbs of motion to show that Pilate or Jesus comes out of or goes into the praetorium. These verbs, coupled with the change of place and dialogue partners they produce, facilitate the distinction among the seven scenes. After Jesus was brought into the praetorium, Pilate went outside to speak with "the Jews" twice (18:29, 38b). In addition, Jesus went outside with Pilate to be presented to his accusers (19:5). Pilate also entered the praetorium to speak with Jesus on two occasions (18:33; 19:9) before he brought Jesus outside to face his accusers one last time (19:13). In the

> **Narrative Gap**
>
> The storytelling device known as "ellipsis" is also sometimes called the "narrative gap." Authors can leave a gap between what the narration indicates is happening and what they allow audiences to learn first-hand. Omitting a portion of the sequence of events serves to involve the audience more deeply in the plot as they question what may have been missed and "fill in the gap" for themselves.

concluding moment of the trial Pilate handed Jesus over to be crucified (19:16a). Of these seven core scenes and their narrative frame, only one scene, 19:1–3, contains no verb of motion and no dialogue. In that scene, which takes place inside the praetorium, Jesus is crowned, dressed as a king, and ironically hailed "the King of the Jews" (v. 3). This narration and ironic proclamation of the kingship of Jesus, which stands at the center of the passage, becomes the scene around which the entire Roman trial narrative turns. The truth of the kingship of Jesus and how this affects and is affected by Pilate, "the Jews," and Jesus's own life and mission are all at stake.

The passage is thus structured as follows:

18:28   Introduction: Gathering at the Praetorium for the Roman Trial
      18:29–32   Scene 1: Pilate and the Jews, Outside
      18:33–38a   Scene 2: Pilate and Jesus, Inside
      18:38b–40   Scene 3: Pilate and the Jews, Outside
      19:1–3   Scene 4: Pilate and Jesus, Inside
      19:4–8   Scene 5: Pilate, Jesus, and the Jews, Outside
      19:9–11   Scene 6: Pilate and Jesus, Inside
      19:12–15   Scene 7: Pilate, Jesus, and the Jews, Outside
19:16a   Conclusion: Handing over for Crucifixion

The effect of the refusal of "the Jews" to enter the praetorium at the onset of the trial is to send Pilate shuttling back and forth between Jesus and his accusers, acting on two stages as it were, a front stage and a rear stage. Pilate's physical movement inside to Jesus and outside to "the Jews" illustrates his own ambivalence about Jesus as he tries to discern who Jesus is and what threat he might pose to Pilate himself and to the larger social structure. Further, "the Jews" do not hear Jesus's self-disclosing claims before Pilate, while Pilate becomes the only figure who appears in every scene. Through oral performance of the passion narrative in particular, the audience experiences Pilate's encounter with Jesus and his intellectual ambivalence toward the challenge Jesus presents through his physical wafting between the pulls of the earthly and heavenly realms. Questions that the audience wants answered include: will Pilate recognize the truth when he faces it? And what will that recognition or lack thereof lead him to *do* about Jesus? Nonetheless, it is Jesus himself and the nature of his kingdom as Messiah that occupy the spotlight.

The introductory verse sets the stage for the subsequent action and establishes the irony of the proceeding. Those who have brought Jesus refuse to enter the Roman structure lest they be defiled and thus prevented from eating the Passover. Jesus, the Lamb of God (1:29), is handed over for trial by those who desire to maintain ritual purity in order to partake of the Passover lamb that very evening. The irony and staging of the act are set and the opposing forces are initially separated so that audiences are called to judge for one or the other.

Pilate is introduced in Scene 1 without qualification. A known personage who needs no further introduction, he goes outside to those who have delivered Jesus to him and asks for the charge brought against "this man." His question formally opens the proceedings. The accusers respond in a manner that does not so much answer the question as it offers a defense of their own action. They affirm that "this man" in custody, Jesus, is indeed worthy of the arrest, due to his wrong actions, and refer to their own action as "handing him over." Although prior to this point only Judas has been cast in the role of "the betrayer," or "one who hands over," now Jesus's accusers place themselves in this same role. Doing wrong is not a formal charge, so this lack of cooperation is oppositional. Pilate responds in kind and reassigns responsibility to them and their own law. Jesus's accusers, now identified as "the Jews," are forced to acknowledge the limits of their jurisdiction. They also reveal their objective in bringing Jesus to Pilate: capital punishment. The scene concludes when the narrator confirms God's plan and Jesus's prescience: Jesus was brought before the Roman governor so that he might be convicted and put to death by the Roman method of execution, **crucifixion**. This sends Pilate back inside to Jesus.

Scene 2 begins as Pilate enters the praetorium again and begins to interrogate Jesus on the charge that is at stake for the Roman state: the claim of **kingship**, which would indicate sedition or rebellion. The "inside" interaction between Jesus and Pilate forms the heart of the Roman trial. The fundamental questions at stake are what it means to be king and what it means to be "of the truth." Pilate questions Jesus, "Are you the King of the Jews?" Kingship in the political sense is his only concern. Jesus's initial reply is to answer the question with a question of his own: on whose behalf is Pilate speaking? This parry asserts Jesus's control and provides for the extended interaction on the nature of

Crucifixion

Death by crucifixion was the most horrible process used by the Romans, reserved for the worst criminals and those who rebelled against Roman authority. These criminals were hung on a cross of wood on the main road leading into the city to indicate that the rule of law governed the area. The uprights of the cross were often left in place to act as deterrents to all who entered the city. Victims would typically be left on the cross for days to succumb to the elements. Death would often come by suffocation, as the crucified could no longer hold themselves up to inhale and their lungs would collapse.

The horror of Jesus's death must not be forgotten. However, John rereads this horror as a moment of "lifting up," the revelation of the "glory of God," and the means by which he will return to the glory that was his before the world was made. There is suffering in John's story, and a "lifting up" as Moses raised up the serpent in the wilderness (3:14) certainly indicates Jesus's crucifixion on a cross, raised from the ground in agony. But this historical fact has been played down, and even overcome by the theological and christological interpretation of John's point of view. The crucifixion of Jesus is the consummate achievement of God's manifestation of his love for the world (see 3:16; 15:13).

kingship. On the defensive now, Pilate attempts to distance himself from any personal stake in Jewish matters of nationalism. He confirms that Jesus's own people and religious leaders have handed him over and puts the onus for the proceedings back onto Jesus, "What did you do?" The verbal sparring bristles as Jesus speaks not of himself but of his kingdom. His kingship is not part of the political system about which Pilate is concerned. It is not "of the world." Nonetheless, it can be witnessed in the world. Therefore, Pilate pursues the question, "So you are a king?" This base understanding of kingship allows Jesus to assert his identity positively, "You say that I am a king." The rejoinder is not a simple affirmative, nor is it a negative, and indeed Pilate will "say" that Jesus is "king" four times in the coming scenes (18:39; 19:14, 15, 19). Jesus clarifies who he is and what he offers, laying bare the real issue at stake in this trial: "Everyone who is of the **truth** hears my voice." Those outside are not of the truth, and their accusations all come down to this. Jesus, however, continues to fulfill his mission. He bears witness to the truth even on trial. Implicit in this final statement is also a challenge to Pilate, but Pilate abruptly cuts off the dialogue with the question, "What is truth?" With this timeless question coupled with his immediate exit, Pilate refuses Jesus's offer by shutting himself off from its voice and moving back outside.

For the evangelist, the irony lies in Pilate's dismissal of even the possibility of knowledge of the truth while standing face to face with its embodiment. The criterion for authentic belief in Jesus is openness to his word as the revelation of God. Like many in the story before him, particularly those who now stand outside as Jesus's formal accusers, Pilate is closed to that revelation and dismisses the word of Jesus. This is Jesus's final challenge in his earthly ministry, and Pilate, his partner in dialogue, rejects the possibility of truth and the revelation of God in Jesus. Nonetheless, Pilate seeks to hold a neutral position by acting as if the challenge of Jesus has nothing to do with him.

Pilate moves outside again to "the Jews" to launch Scene 3 and makes his initial ruling. He emphasizes his own judicial authority over his audience by stating, "I find no case against him." He may not be open to the truth of Jesus, but he is also unwilling to give in to the demands of Jesus's accusers. In this second "outside" exchange, he uses this wording as a basis for his next move: an attempt to release Jesus. But in doing so, Pilate uses the title of the very charge the accusers brought before him, "Do you want me to release to you the King of the Jews?" The mockery inherent in Pilate's title for Jesus, whom he has just determined is no pretender to the throne in any political sense, serves to intensify the irony interweaving this entire passage. They ask instead, now shouting, for Barabbas. On the edge of the "slippery slope" he introduced himself, Pilate must once again deal with matters inside the praetorium.

Of the seven core scenes of the Roman trial and their narrative frame, only Scene 4 contains no verb of motion for Pilate and no dialogue. Here, inside the praetorium, Jesus is crowned with thorns and dressed in purple as a king, while his captors strike him and ironically proclaim the truth that he is "the King of the Jews." This is the scene around which the entire Roman trial narrative turns. The narrator does recount that Pilate took Jesus and flogged him. This interlude between the offer of the Passover amnesty and Jesus's presentation to "the Jews" is Pilate's second attempt at political astuteness to save himself from the necessity of leaving his position of neutrality. However, the effect of his decision is all the more active and powerful as he sends Jesus forward to meet his accusers dressed as a king. This action colors the rest of the proceedings.

Pilate goes outside again to confront Jesus's accusers with the flogged king. Scene 5 opens as he calls their attention and asserts for the second time his judgment of the threat Jesus poses, "I find no case against him" (v. 4). Pilate remains intent on not deciding against Jesus, even as he has refused to decide for the truth of Jesus's identity. Jesus then makes his own entrance, not led out as Pilate claimed, but exiting by his own volition. Thus the three parties come together at center stage, each brought to this place by their choices of roles in God's plan. As a result of Pilate's attempt to ridicule the charge that he is "King of the Jews," Jesus faces his accusers, ironically wearing the crown of thorns and the purple cloak of royalty. Pilate nonetheless takes his position of authority and presents Jesus to his accusers with his now famous proclamation, "Behold, the man." Pilate thus demonstrates Jesus to be no threat to Rome as a royal claimant of "the Jews." Audiences of the Gospel thus far, however, may surmise that he points beyond his own ken to Jesus as the Son of Man, who will be lifted up and glorified by God, despite any and all human machinations. When Jesus's

Ecce Homo
by Hieronymus Bosch

accusers see and hear this, they begin to make their demand for crucifixion. Pilate, however, will not be pressed into their service by simple rage. He counters with an imperative of his own and concludes with the third iteration of his position, "I find no case against him" (v. 6). Pilate's presentation of "the man" (v. 5) is thus framed by declarations of Jesus's innocence (vv. 4, 6). Pilate's saying is true: Jesus will die, but he will die an innocent man.

Jesus's accusers have a response of their own to Pilate's challenge. This is the second time that Pilate has attempted to shift responsibility to them. Their initial response was based on Roman law (18:31b). They now turn to Jewish law to articulate their desire for capital punishment once again. The charge of blasphemy, which has arisen in the course of Jesus's public ministry, comes to the fore: "because he made himself the Son of God." This gives Pilate pause since it is consonant with Jesus's self-identification as one who has come into the world to bear witness to the truth. Thus Pilate becomes "very afraid," because it is becoming clearer and clearer that he will not be able to escape making a decision about truth. This fear sends Pilate back inside with Jesus.

Pilate enters the praetorium again for Scene 6 and asks Jesus where he is from. He has come to understand that this is the real charge against Jesus, and thus Jesus's identity is a more profound issue than what he may have done. Jesus offered Pilate the truth of his identity in their previous encounter, but that gift was dismissed. Accordingly, Jesus now offers only silence. Pilate indignantly reminds Jesus of his power and that Jesus's life is at stake, but Jesus responds that Pilate would have no power over him if it had not been given from above. The double meaning incorporates both Pilate's worldly superior, the emperor, and God who is "above" them all. Jesus not only indicates what little power Pilate really has over him; he asserts his own agency in accepting his role in the divine plan. He then concludes by making the outcome clear: "Therefore, the one who handed me over to you has the greater sin" (v. 11). There is only one sin in the Johannine story of Jesus, namely, encountering the truth of Jesus and refusing to receive him. Pilate exits the praetorium for the final time.

Scene 7 begins with the narrator breaking in to explain that Pilate therefore sought to release Jesus. The accusers will not have it and threaten Pilate with his potential political vulnerability. They shout that if Pilate releases Jesus then he is "not a friend of Caesar," which would be politically disastrous for him. "The Jews" have turned the tables on Pilate, who tried to make them choose between Jesus and Barabbas, as they now put the choice to Pilate: Jesus or Caesar? Since their charge of blasphemy has backfired, they return to their initial charge of sedition and refer to Jesus as one who "makes himself a king." This time it will work. Pilate's hand is forced. He has sought to negotiate with Jesus and bargain with the accusers to no avail. His attempts at neutrality have failed and now must end. He brings Jesus outside for the last time and sits on the judge's bench.

The narrator then provides the first temporal marker since the trial began. The entire proceedings have been taking place on the **Day of Preparation** for Passover. Further, the trial has taken up the morning, and now the hour is "about noon." These final moments of the Roman trial are taking place during the very hour that the priests in the temple are slaughtering the lambs for the Passover meal to be eaten that evening. Jesus, who has already been portrayed and proclaimed as the true king, is therefore also the Lamb of God who will be sentenced to death at the very hour when the lambs for the Passover begin to be killed (see 1:29, 36). Jesus is the new **Passover Lamb**. Pilate clarifies his contempt for Jesus's accusers as the bearers of responsibility by echoing his earlier declaration and pronouncing the claim for which Jesus will be convicted: "Behold, your king!" He finally, however ironically, proclaims the truth about Jesus before his accusers. For their part, the accusers continue shouting and gesturing their responses. Pilate spells out the responsibility as the trial reaches its culminating point, "Shall I crucify your king?" (v. 15), thereby forcing Jesus's accusers to confess the full

The Day of Preparation and the Passover Lamb

The Gospel of John does not dedicate great attention to the traditional Christian interpretation of the death of Jesus as expiation for sins. However, the author is aware of this tradition and does not neglect it entirely. Early in the Gospel, John the Baptist points to Jesus and describes him as "the Lamb of God who takes away the sin of the world" (1:29, 36). Now in the Passion, we encounter the relationship between Lamb of God and the slain Passover Lamb, clearly associated with the death of Jesus in 19:14, as he is handed over to death: "Now it was the day of preparation for the Passover, and it was about noon." This is the time for the preparation for Passover by slaying the Passover Lamb. Whatever the background was in Jewish thought, John associated the death of Jesus with the taking away of sins, and he makes a link between the Lamb of God and the slaying of the lambs at Passover.

implications of their decision. The chief priests answer with finality, "We have no king but Caesar!" With these words they seal Jesus's fate as well as their own. In their fervor to reject and condemn Jesus, they renounce God as their one true king. The irony of the scene reaches its pinnacle as "the Jews" utter the ultimate blasphemy with the same breath they use to reject Jesus, whom they have accused of the same. And with that they have the last word of the Roman trial.

Now that Jesus's accusers have completed their self-condemnation, Pilate's turn arrives to complete his. He articulates his final response to both Jesus and "the Jews" by his action as he hands him over to them to be crucified. With the onset of the Roman trial, "the Jews" have taken on the role of handing Jesus over alongside Judas "the betrayer." Now Pilate too becomes one who hands Jesus over to his enemies in this world. Although it is certainly the Roman soldiers who actually implement the sentence of capital punishment, Pilate does hand Jesus over—insofar as he completes his own self-condemnation by betraying one he knows to be innocent—to the desires of those who perceive his threat and wish him dead. Despite the intentions of both parties, the audience knows that what Pilate and "the Jews" have really facilitated is the lifting up of the Son of Man in fulfillment of his mission to the world.

B′ 19:16b–37 Jesus is Crucified before "the Jews": Completion

Act Four sends audiences directly to the cross with Jesus. This is a powerful component of the narrative, possibly the most powerful on the narrative level. Jesus resolutely sees his mission to its fulfillment. Likewise several disciples remain with Jesus at the foot of the cross and beyond, and audiences learn more about abiding with Jesus. We nonetheless understand the Roman trial to be the crux of the chiasm here because of the question of truth. That act confirms Jesus to be the gift of truth, given by God to the world, who must be sacrificed to fulfill his mission. This act presents the completion of that mission, which results from that revelation of truth and Pilate's inability to stand on its behalf. The **crucifixion** of Jesus is therefore presented in five scenes, framed by typical introductory verses of character and setting (19:16b–17) and concluding verses of reflection upon the consequences of the action (19:35–37). The central scenes narrate the inscription (vv. 18–22), the seamless tunic (vv. 23–24), Jesus's interaction with his mother and the Beloved Disciple (vv. 25–27), the death of Jesus and the gift of the Spirit (vv. 28–30), and the piercing of Jesus's side (vv. 31–34).

Unlike the Synoptic Gospels, which narrate Simon, from the North African region of Cyrene, being conscripted to carry the cross for the faltering Jesus, John is careful to assert in the introduction that Jesus still has the wherewithal to carry the cross himself to the designated location identified as Golgotha, the Place of the Skull. Little is said about this journey as the new location, and the crucifixion itself, is the focus.

The first scene indicates that like the Synoptics, however, Jesus is crucified between two others. Nonetheless, he remains the focus and has no interaction with them. The nailing of Jesus to the cross is not described in detail, but depicting Pilate's sign and its inscription is. "Jesus of Nazareth, King of the Jews" is posted in Hebrew, Latin, and Greek for all who might pass to see. In protest, the Jewish leadership ask that he qualify the title to indicate that kingship was a claim and not a reality, but Pilate is finished and declares that this writing will indeed be his final, however ironic, proclamation of Jesus as King. This is followed by a brief second scene of fulfillment as even the soldiers take part in God's plan by not dividing Jesus's tunic. Rather, they cast lots so that instead of dividing the fabric, one might get the entire garment.

In a moment of profound dramatic irony, the third scene shows how Jesus's last breaths on the cross establish the **church**, as symbolized by that garment that cannot be torn apart. Jesus is not alone with his enemies but is still surrounded by some of his own, including his mother, his mother's sister, Mary Magdalene, and the Beloved Disciple. The mother of Jesus and the Beloved Disciple in particular come together "because of that hour" (v. 27). The gift of mother and son at the foot of the cross, therefore, stands at the center of this act. The first to believe (Jesus's mother at the wedding feast in Cana) and the beloved model disciple are given to each other by Jesus to establish a new community in faith and love. Even on the cross, Jesus's primary concern is for his own, as he gives them to each other as a new mother and son to form a family to nurture the children of God.

The earthly life and ministry of Jesus the Son of Man ends in the fourth scene when he declares, "it is finished"—the affirmation that all has been brought to completion and perfection. The fulfillment language of the entire passion narrative reaches its peak here. Only after the acknowledgment of his glorification and the completion of his mission, but still in full knowledge of God's plan, can he go. Jesus finally bowed his head and "handed over the spirit" (v. 30). As the fifth scene commences, Jesus's side is pierced to confirm his death on the Day of Preparation, the day of the sacrifice of the Passover Lamb (vv. 31–34; see 19:14), and a flow of mingled blood and water is witnessed from his side. From the beginnings of Christian reflection upon this scene, interpreters have seen the symbolic "gifts" that Jesus hands over to the church in his "lifting up" and his death. A new community is founded (vv. 25–27), made up of loving disciples and the believing mother. In the handing down of the Spirit, Jesus gives the Spirit to this nascent church (see 7:37–39), and in the blood and the water, the church symbolically reads the gifts of the Eucharist and baptism.

The intensifying fulfillment language across the passion narrative comes to its climax in the concluding reflection of this act. The Beloved Disciple, now given into the family of the new community of God, testifies to all that he has seen. The narrator affirms that, like Jesus before him, this disciple's testimony is true. The truth of his testimony is necessary so that all future audiences may believe that these things took place so that the Scripture might be fulfilled. The new community of the children of God (see 1:12) immediately begins its own mission of faith and witness through the testimony of the Beloved Disciple who is joined in family with the mother of Jesus. The belief of the Johannine churches, which have not "seen and yet believe" (20:29), is based upon the authority of an eyewitness who did "see and believe" (19:35; 20:8)

Jewish Burial Customs

Due to the climate of the Mediterranean basin and the belief that a corpse was ritually impure, burial typically took place as soon after death as possible. Allowing a body to succumb to the elements was not only understood to be a health hazard but also dishonorable. During the period of the Second Temple, Jews of the region developed both first and secondary burial customs. They built room-sized tombs underground or in rocky cliffs with shafts or ledges for individual corpses. The dead would be covered and anointed, and the tomb would often be sealed with a movable stone. About one year later the family would return to collect the bones and place them in stone boxes called ossuaries. These ossuaries could contain multiple family members. They were marked or engraved according to the family's means or status.

A′ 19:38–42 Jesus Is Buried by His Friends in a Garden

Act Five brings the passion narrative full circle as Jesus comes once again into a garden, this time brought by friends to rest in a new tomb. To say that John 18–19 has a chiastic structure in five acts is to claim that the final two acts revisit the themes of the first two acts, as determined by the narrative and discourse of the central act. The nature of this passion drama presented by the evangelist turns on Pilate's failure to recognize the truth of the revelation of God when it stands before him; therefore, now in this final act we experience a garden in all its symbolism once again, but now as a place of **burial** and friendship instead of confrontation and animosity. Nicodemus finally finishes his journey as he comes forward with spices to anoint Jesus for his burial. The narrator is careful to remind audiences of Nicodemus's first furtive visit by night, now countered by his weighty participation in Jesus's burial in the full light of day. Joseph of Arimathea, otherwise unknown in the Johannine narrative, fulfills his role of providing the burial place. He is present in this role in all four of the Gospels, thus reflecting a strong historical memory. Together they lay Jesus in a nearby new tomb before the close of the Day of Preparation. The scene is thus set for what was destroyed in a garden (18:1; see also Gen 1–3) to be restored in a garden (John 20).

What Have We Learned So Far?
The Passion of Christ and Completion of His Mission

Everything that happens in the passion narrative of John 18–19 first moves Jesus and those around him through a process that leads to the cross (18:1–27) and then, after the Roman trial that concludes with the accomplishment of that end (18:28–19:16a), emanates from Jesus's being sent to his lifting up on the cross (19:16b–42). The Roman trial was, therefore, the focus of our interpretation, especially around the question of truth and the correlating question of kingship and the nature of Jesus as the Christ and Son of God. Although Jesus is fully in control of his destiny throughout the passion account, the reality that he *is* the Christ and Son of God by *being* the Son of Man who is lifted up on a cross to die for others is affirmed. Therefore, we can say that Christology is a primary teaching of this narrative unit.

The culminating "hour" of Jesus's mission shows Jesus going forward to his destiny of crucifixion and glorification—or paradoxically, glorification through crucifixion—caring for the disciples God has given him. He ensures their safety before speaking openly about his identity in front of both the Jewish and Roman authorities. He stands accused of insurrection, of making himself a king. Indeed he is, but his kingship is that of the heavenly realm, not this world. He is the Son of God, who, like God the Father, is the Good Shepherd who cares for his flock and who will even lay down his life for his own. This is the new definition of the messiah that Jesus has been teaching across the Gospel, which comes to fullness during his passion.

The other key theological components that emerge from this narrative unit are ecclesiology and soteriology. In the final moments of his life, Jesus gazes upon his mother at the foot of the cross. Jesus's mother, the first to believe in relationship with him, and the disciple whom Jesus loved stand before him. Jesus gives to his mother, the model disciple before "the hour," a new son in the Beloved Disciple, the one who emerged as the model disciple during "the hour" of Jesus's glory. Jesus then completes the family formation by giving to the Beloved Disciple his mother in this same kinship. By using performative language, Jesus's pronouncement accomplishes the new relationship that it declares. By his declaration, Jesus constitutes a new family. The theological and dramatic significance of "the hour" of Jesus is affirmed when the narrator explains that "because of that hour" the Beloved Disciple takes his new mother into his home. From the beginning, the evangelist has employed the language of kinship to characterize the believer's new relationship to God (see 1:12; 11:52). Here at the foot of the cross, the formation of this new family provides a nucleus for the new community of believers that will become the church. In terms of salvation, the redemptive significance of the cross in John is, therefore, not merely individual but corporate. John has an underlying ecclesiology of the cross, insofar as a community of family that lives beyond the earthly life of Jesus is born and emanates from the cross, culminating in Jesus's last words, "It is finished." The gift of the Spirit, Eucharist, and baptism ensures the ongoing presence of Jesus and his mission in the community founded at the cross. His mission is perfected, not ended, and we now turn to the evangelist's presentation of the next chapter in the story: the resurrection.

Key Terms and Concepts

burial	narrative gap
church	passion
crucifixion	passion narrative
Day of Preparation	Passover lamb
fulfillment	Pontius Pilate
garden	praetorium
kingship	truth

Questions for Review

1. In the passion narrative, John 18–19, how is Jesus portrayed throughout these events? Why might we understand this narrative unit to be presented as a chiasm?

2. What happens to Peter across these scenes? How might he be presented as traveling on a journey of self-discovery and faith?

3. What is the significance of the Roman trial and Pilate's query on the nature of *truth*?

4. What happens at the foot of the cross on both the narrative and discourse levels of the Gospel? What are the roles of the mother of Jesus and the Beloved Disciple?

5. In this vein, what is the significance of Jesus's final word on the cross: "it is finished" (which could also be translated, "it is completed" or "it is perfected")?

6. Reflect upon the suggestion that has been made for many centuries, that at the
   cross Jesus also gives the Spirit, Eucharist, and baptism? Does it ring true?

7. In the Gospel of John, who is Nicodemus, on both the narrative level and the
   teaching levels of story? Why must we not overlook his story within this narrative
   of good news?

Bibliography and Further Reading

Brown, Raymond E. *The Death of the Messiah: From Gethsemane to the Grave.
    A Commentary on the Passion Narratives in the Four Gospels.* 2 vols. Anchor
    Bible Reference Library. New York: Doubleday, 1994.

Brown, Sherri. *Gift upon Gift: Covenant through Word in the Gospel of John.* Prince-
    ton Theological Manuscript Series. Eugene, OR: Pickwick, 2010.

————. "What Is Truth? Jesus, Pilate, and the Staging of the Dialogue of the Cross
    in John 18:28–19:16a." *Catholic Biblical Quarterly* 77 (2015): 69–86.

Culpepper, R. Alan. "The Theology of the Johannine Passion Narrative: John
    19:16b–30." *Neotestamentica* 31 (1997): 21–37.

Moloney, Francis J. *Glory not Dishonor: Reading John 13–21.* Minneapolis: Fortress,
    1998.

————. "John 18:15–27: A Johannine View of the Church." *Downside Review* 112
    (1994): 231–48.

Schnelle, Udo. "Recent Views of John's Gospel." *Word & World* 21 (2001): 352–59.

The Resurrection of Jesus:
The Promise of John 20

PURPOSE Chapter fourteen discusses the first post-resurrection narratives of the Fourth Gospel (John 20) with a particular emphasis on the evangelist's purpose in writing and the call to believe without seeing.

ASSIGNMENT Reread John 20 before proceeding with this chapter.

In this chapter we come to the final two narrative units of the Book of Glory, which we introduced in chapter twelve: The Resurrection (20:1–29) and the First Conclusion to the Gospel (20:30–31). Chapter 20 of John's Gospel, therefore, begins to bring his story to a close with several accounts of appearances of the resurrected Jesus. Scholars often call these **post-resurrection accounts** or encounters. Across the Gospel, the evangelist has depicted his understanding of the crucifixion of Jesus as his "lifting up" (3:14; 8:28; 12:32), the "hour" that is "not yet" (2:4; 7:6–8; 7:30; 8:20), until the story turns to the Book of Glory upon its arrival at 12:23. From then on, "the hour has come" (see 13:1; 17:1; 19:27). The cross is the ultimate glorification that "finishes" Jesus's mission in the world (19:30). One might therefore wonder at the necessity for explicit post-resurrection encounters; but the evangelist is concerned to continue to fulfill the word that Jesus spoke during his earthly ministry. There have been hints of his **resurrection**, his return to life after his death (see 2:22; 10:18; 12:16). Even more, through his interactions with the disciples in 20:1–29, Jesus fulfills his promises to return to them (14:18–19; 16:16); and they are able to begin to understand the Scripture of the word of Jesus about the raising of the temple of his body (2:19–22). As the journey of the disciples begins to reach its *telos*, or goal, the evangelist can then turn to the audience to bring them to their own moment of a faith decision based upon this his telling of his particular story of Jesus.

The vast majority of scholars posit John 20:30–31 as the **conclusion to the body of the Gospel**, with John 21 following as an epilogue. We accept that view, but with certain modification, which we will develop in the next chapter, in our study of John 21. For the moment it is sufficient to know that there has never been a "text" of the Gospel of John *without* chapter 21. All the manuscripts that we have of the ending of the Gospel of John finish with John 21. It must be there for a reason that maintains a connection with the rest of the Gospel. For that reason, we will call John 21 an "epilogue" and not (as some do) an "addendum." The former means that it brings something to an end, while the latter suggests that it is a mere "addition." The concluding sounds of John 20:30–31, therefore, must be interpreted not as an end to the whole story, but to what began with Jesus coming into his ministry, culminating now with post-resurrection encounters.

The Narrative Flow and Structure of John 20

The post-resurrection narratives begin at John 20. These episodes can be broadly divided according to the location of the actions: at the empty tomb (vv. 1–18) and in the upper room (vv. 19–29). The activity at these locations is structured in two additional scenes each. At the tomb in the garden, the action centers first around Mary Magdalene (vv. 1–2), then Peter and the Beloved Disciple (vv. 3–9), then back to Mary Magdalene (vv. 10–18). Mary's commission leads her to the disciples to give her message (v. 18). The following scenes take up the action in the disciples' room, first without the presence of Thomas (vv. 19–23), then later with the presence of Thomas (vv. 24–29). The final verses of John 20 conclude both these post-resurrection narratives and the body of the Gospel (vv. 30–31).

While this presentation of the narrative flow and structure represents what is found in 20:1–31, it is perhaps better to read it according to the unfolding experience of faith of the respective characters in vv. 1–29. Following the flow of the narrative in this fashion leads very strongly into the words of the author, directed to the audience in vv. 30–31. The book has been written that they might believe (vv. 30–31). These encounters present the evangelist's story of the resurrection of the Word of God through the lens of his concern for the members of the early Christian community. Therefore, on the basis of the faith experience of the characters in the story, and eventually of the appeal to the faith of the audience of the story, John 20 can be diagrammed as follows:

Part Three: The Resurrection   20:1–29

20:1–2	Mary Magdalene at the Tomb and with Simon Peter and the Beloved Disciple
20:3–10	Simon Peter and the Beloved Disciple's Journey of Faith at the Empty Tomb
20:11–18	Mary Magdalene's Encounter with the Risen Jesus and Her Journey of Faith

Part Four: The First Conclusion to the Gospel   20:30–31

Moving seamlessly from the disciples' encounters with the risen Christ, through Jesus's words to Thomas about his faith in the one he can see, the evangelist addresses his audience, telling them that he has written a book so that, even though they do not see Jesus, they will believe.

Interpreting John 20:1–29: Part Three—The Resurrection

The post-resurrection encounters narrated in John 20 are marked by journeys. Several disciples begin, continue, or conclude **journeys of faith**. Through their stories, the evangelist provides models for his audiences. This is what everyone goes through as they pursue life in the name of Jesus.

20:1–2 Mary Magdalene at the Tomb with Simon Peter and the Beloved Disciple

Consistent with the other Gospels, John reports that **Mary Magdalene** came to the tomb "on the first day of the week." The Christian celebration of Sunday as the Lord's Day is based in this tradition. However, in this Gospel, Mary Magdalene is alone, not with a group of women, and the audience is told "it was still dark." For John, **darkness** is an indication of a lack of faith, and that is exactly the case with Mary Magdalene. She will come into the **light** but has a journey to travel. She sees that the stone had been removed (v. 1), and she rushes to Simon Peter and the other disciple, whom Jesus loves, to report to them that the tomb has been emptied by someone, and none of them knew where they had placed the executed Jesus. She associated the two disciples ("we do not know") with her own complete absence of any Easter hope or faith. A dead body has been taken from the tomb (v. 2). The use of a passive verb ("the stone had been removed" and the phrase "where they have laid him") indicates that someone else has entered the drama. The audience suspects that God may be the one involved, but there is no hint of such belief in the situation of Mary Magdalene, Simon Peter, and the other disciple, whom Jesus loved.

Mary Magdalene and the Risen Jesus. *Noli me tangere* by Jerónimo Cósida.

20:3–10 Simon Peter and the Beloved Disciple's Journey of Faith at the Empty Tomb

Mary Magdalene has run away from the tomb; Simon Peter and the other disciple reverse that flight. They run *to* the tomb (v. 3). This is already a sign that the disciples are responding more positively. Peter leads, but the other disciple passes him, sees that the signs of death, the linen wrappings, are empty, and waits at the entry to the tomb to give first access to Peter (vv. 4–7). To this point nothing has been said about the faith of the two disciples, but the signs are good. The audience can also reflect on the difference between what the disciples witness here, the burial cloths rolled to one side, and what they witnessed when Jesus raised Lazarus, still bound in them. What is unfolding here is distinctive. Following Simon Peter into the empty tomb, the disciple then sees further evidence of the signs of death overcome by the action of God. The burial cloths are now folded and lie at differing ends of the tomb. The other disciple, whom we have been told in v. 2 was the Beloved Disciple, sees the victory of God over death and believes (v. 8). Peter's response is not recorded, so we must not judge him one way or the other. He seems to have further to travel on his journey. As we will see later, the evangelist's concern is to present the figure of the Beloved Disciple as a disciple who did not see the risen Jesus, but believed. Peter's journey of faith needs more time.

The audience is informed that Simon Peter and the Beloved Disciple return home (v. 10), as yet unaware that the **Scripture** told of Jesus's resurrection (v. 9). The Scripture is the Gospel of John, and the audience will later be told how blessed they are to have it (vv. 30–31). The evangelist is **writing Scripture**, and the audience is receiving it. Such an understanding was not possible for the two disciples at the tomb, as they are characters within the Gospel story: "as yet they did not understand" (v. 9). An audience that has the Gospel of John will understand and will be summoned to believe on the basis of this "Scripture."

> **The Divine Passive Voice**
>
> In constructing sentences, authors use either the active or the passive voice; that is "Peter denied Jesus" or "Jesus was denied by Peter." When authors use the divine passive voice, no agent of the action is identified. In the biblical stories, this unidentified agent is typically understood to be God; thus, the "divine passive." In John 20:1–2, the evangelist employs both the divine passive voice and irony, since Mary Magdalene does not know who the agent of the action she describes is, but the audience, who have read the prologue and paid careful attention to the story thus far, are well aware that God has entered the scene.

20:11–18 Mary Magdalene's Encounter with the Risen Jesus and Her Journey of Faith

Without any indication of how and when she arrived there, Mary Magdalene is again at the tomb, weeping (v. 11). Her sorrow continues to show her lack of faith, and it takes three spectacular encounters to bring her to recognize Jesus and to profess her faith in him. In the first place, like the disciples, she bent over and looked into the tomb, but her experience is unique. She sees two angels, messengers of God, instead of the body of Jesus. The angels ask why she is weeping, but she can only repeat what she has said to the disciples in v. 2: someone has taken away the body of Jesus, and she does not know where they have put it (v. 13). Turning, she finds that the risen Jesus is standing behind her, but again she manifests no faith. Thinking he is the gardener, she insists that the body has been carried away and continues her search for a dead body. In a moment of intimacy, Jesus calls her by her Hebrew/Aramaic name: "Mariam." She responds by using the Hebrew/Aramaic "**Rabbouni.**" The evangelist translates that it means teacher (v. 16). In fact, it is more intimate. It means "my teacher." She has obviously embraced her former friend and teacher, and Jesus asks her not to cling to him. The days of human intimacy between Jesus and Mary are over. He must now continue to respond to God, and that means returning to his God and Father, who, because of the cross and resurrection, is now also the God and Father of his disciples, who are now called Jesus's "brothers" (v. 17). Without a word, Mary Magdalene, who has taken so long to arrive at true faith, does as Jesus has instructed her: she goes to the disciples, describes what has happened to her, and makes a wonderful confession of faith: "I have seen the Lord" (v. 18).

To this point in John's account of the resurrection, the audience has met two people who have made a journey of faith. The Beloved Disciple began sharing the unfaith of Mary Magdalene (v. 2), but he comes to belief *without seeing the physical presence of the risen Jesus* (v. 8). Mary takes a long time to move away from unfaith (vv. 1–2, 11–16) but eventually confesses faith in her risen Lord (v. 18). There is also "proleptic" hint in the narrative that there will eventually be a time when those who know the Scriptures will come to believe in the resurrection of Jesus (v. 9).

The Tradition of Women at the Empty Tomb

All four Gospels report that female disciples of Jesus discovered the empty tomb. Only in the Gospel of John is Mary Magdalene alone. John singles out Mary Magdalene's journey of faith. Her presence alone at the tomb may reflect the earliest tradition. As the witness of one woman would not be accepted, the number of witnesses to the empty tomb likely increased as the story was told in the early church.

Like many responses of faith in the Gospel (see the section from Cana to Cana of the Gospel [2:1–4:54]), Mary Magdalene begins convinced that Jesus's body has been taken away, but without any faith in the risen Christ (20:2, 11–15). On meeting Jesus, her Rabbi, she attempts to restore the partial faith that she once had in her personal affection for him, as she tries to cling to him (vv. 16–17). Finally, responding to the command of the Risen Jesus, she proclaims to the disciples: "I have seen the Lord" (v. 18). She journeys from no faith, through partial faith, to full faith.

20:19–23 *Jesus Commissions the Disciples and Confers the Holy Spirit*

On the evening of the same day, the first day of the week (our Sunday), Jesus comes to his frightened disciples with his greeting of "**peace**" (v. 19). This greeting from Jesus could represent a simple Jewish greeting (**shalōm**), but for John there is more to it. Across the last discourse, Jesus has promised a peace to his disciples that only he can give (see 14:27; 16:33). This is the peace that the risen Jesus bestows upon his disciples, contrasting sharply with the fear that has driven them behind locked doors (v. 19). Typical of post-resurrection accounts, the evangelist makes it clear in v. 20 that the Jesus who was crucified is among them: he showed them his pierced hands and sides, and they rejoiced to see their Lord. There is no doubt about who Jesus is. Yet, there is something "unworldly": he comes to the fear-stricken disciples, even though everything is locked down (v. 19). The risen Jesus is the same—but different! Once with them, he again grants them his peace and then associates them with his God-directed mission. Jesus is the sent one of God (see, among many places where this is said: 3:17, 34; 5:36; 6:57; 8:42; 10:36; 11:42; 17:3, 18, 23), and he now formally sends them (20:21), as he had promised he would (see 13:20). Their commission is guaranteed by a creative act on the part of Jesus, breathing the Spirit upon them, just as the Spirit hovered over creation in Gen 1:2. Full of the **Holy Spirit**, they have two tasks: they are to forgive the sins of any who seek forgiveness and bring the ongoing presence of Jesus's judgment into the world (see 3:16–17; 9:39; 5:27–29). People will be called to decision in the light of the ongoing presence of God's missionaries, down through the ages.

The audience has now met a third group of people who encounter the risen Jesus (the Beloved Disciple, Mary Magdalene, and the disciples). Because of his greeting of "peace," their **fear** turns into **joy** at the sight of the risen Lord (vv. 19–20). Notice, however, that (like Mary Magdalene) they have a *physical* experience: they see his hands and his side. To this point, only the Beloved Disciple has come to faith in the risen Jesus without seeing him.

Prolepsis Reprise

Recall from chapter eleven that **prolepsis** is a storytelling technique that is used to represent an event as happening before it actually does. It serves to alert readers of the impending occurrence by raising questions about plot sequence and the storyteller's integrity. It also maintains the audience's curiosity, as they look for the eventual acting out of what has been promised earlier—the reprise.

20:24–29 Jesus Appears to the Disciples and Thomas's Journey of Faith

The final scene opens with the information that **Thomas**, one of the Twelve, was not with the other disciples for the events told in vv. 19–23. He is not yet part of the believing community (v. 24). He will not accept the confession "We have seen the Lord" (v. 25), unless he has a physical encounter with the Risen Jesus during which he can test the reality of the wounds in Jesus's hands and side. Thomas puts severe limitations upon his willingness to make an act of faith: "Unless I see . . . I will not believe" (v. 25).

Again on a Sunday ("a week later," v. 26) an experience identical to the one experienced by all the other disciples in v. 19 takes place: the doors are shut, and the disciples are frightened. But this time Thomas is with them when Jesus appears and greets them with his "peace." He challenges Thomas to place his finger into his wounded hands and his hand in his side, asking him to stop his unfaith and become a believer (v. 27). Again we find an encounter with the physical reality of the risen Jesus at the heart of resurrection faith. There is no indication that Thomas touched Jesus. He makes a wonderful confession of faith

The Resurrected Jesus

A principle of "same yet different" applies to the presence of Jesus in the resurrection stories. Jesus speaks to the disciples, recalling relationships (20:16), using familiar language (vv. 19–21), showing his pierced body (vv. 20, 27), and eating with them (21:9–13). However, he also transcends human limitations (20:4–8, 17, 19), he gives the Spirit (vv. 22–23), works miracles (21:6–8), and establishes leadership in the future church (21:15–24).

that in many ways sums up what Johannine faith requires: "My Lord and my God" (v. 28). Jesus, as risen Lord, is the revelation of the presence of God among humankind.

Partly turning away from Thomas's journey of faith, Jesus makes an important comment for the audience. Thomas (and Mary Magdalene and the disciples in the upper room) have come to faith because they have seen Jesus. There will be generations of believers who will come to faith without ever having had that experience. No doubt all the people who encounter the risen Jesus in John 20 are blessed, but there is an even greater blessing in store for "those who have not seen and yet have come to believe" (v. 29). Jesus's first words to potential disciples and his first words of the Gospel, "What do you seek?" (1:38) and "Come and you will see" (1:39), are balanced by his blessing, his final words in the body of the Gospel to all disciples who live beyond his earthly ministry in his new covenantal community of believers: "Blessed are those who have not seen and yet have come to believe" (20:29).

Interpreting John 20:30–31: Part Four—The First Conclusion to the Gospel

The narrative of John 20:1–29 has prepared the way for the powerful conclusion of John 20:30–31, directed to the audience. In these verses the evangelist provides his philosophy of writing. As we know from the other Gospels, there were many signs and stories of Jesus that could have been gathered into the document that we know as the Gospel of John. But the author has made a choice from among those many possibilities, and he has *written them* (v. 30). Looking back to the "Scripture" that Peter and the Beloved Disciple "did not yet know" (v. 9), the author is explaining to his audience why they are specially blessed. They may not have seen Jesus (v. 29), but they have a *Scripture* (v. 30). Why has the author provided them with this "writing"? He tells them without hesitation in v. 31 why he has written in this way: so that they may continue to believe that Jesus is the Messiah, the Son of God, and that through believing they may have life in his name (v. 31).

The author of this Gospel, therefore, writes an account to bring the narrative tradition of the Bible to a culmination in Jesus. The indication is that the next generation, believing without seeing, is better off. He begins by sharing with audiences that the telling of the activity that signifies who Jesus is was not exhausted by his story. Rather, he has chosen from the wealth of traditions about Jesus in crafting his narrative. Here he uses his preferred term for Jesus's miraculous activity, *sēmeia*, "signs." The choice of this term indicates the signifying role this activity carries throughout the Gospel. He then confirms that this was done not only for literary but also for theological purposes.

By way of two final purpose clauses, the evangelist affirms his intention behind what he has written for his community of readers. As we introduced in chapter two, a famous textual difficulty initiates the telling of this purpose: "that you may believe." There is the difference of only one letter (what we would call an "s"), the Greek for "that you may go on believing" (indicating that the book is written for people who already are on a journey of faith) and the Greek for "that you may come to belief." The second possibility would suggest that it is written to introduce people to Christian faith. For many reasons, some of which we have seen in the "journey" of faith of the characters in John 20, we prefer the former meaning: "that you may **go on believing**." First, therefore, he explains that he is writing so that his community of believers, who are making their own journeys of faith, which include facing doubt, opposition, and rejection, "may go on believing." The second clause provides both the content ("that Jesus is the Christ, the Son of God") and the result ("life in his name") of that ongoing action of believing. Regardless of the mainstream social, cultural, and theological categories of the world that may have expelled them, the Johannine community of readers has chosen the path that fulfills Scripture and gives the true gift of life. This same **life in his name** is also possible for all future audiences.

In terms of discipleship and the discourse level of John 20, this ending to the body of the Gospel of John opens the door for its audiences to situate themselves as Jesus's disciples, whose belief is affirmed and reaffirmed as they journey through "life in his name" (20:31). In fact, as we have pointed out several times, among the characters in John 20, only the Beloved Disciple believes without seeing the physical Jesus. The audience is in the same situation, and the author wants them all to be, in their own time, "Beloved Disciples." The epilogue, John 21, is certainly a portrait of how that can happen. This first ending to the Gospel's main narrative makes sense because it returns to the faith articulated at the beginning: Jesus is the Word, the revelation of God, made flesh in the person of Jesus Christ, Son of God (1:1–18, see 20:30–31).

Thomas's Journey of Faith

When Jesus first appears to the disciples in the upper room, Thomas is absent. On hearing that Jesus has been raised, he sets conditions for belief: only if he experiences the physical body of the crucified Jesus. When Jesus comes to him, a week later, he falls before him and confesses: "My Lord and my God" (20:28). Like Mary Magdalene, and many others in the Gospel, Thomas experiences a journey of faith, moving from no faith, to a conditioned faith, to full faith.

What Have We Learned So Far?
The Promise of the New Community of Christ

The body of the Gospel comes to a close with the post-resurrection accounts that send this community forward with the memory of their encounters with Jesus, now the risen Christ (John 20). Jesus sends Mary Magdalene forth, as the apostle with the message of his rising, to his "brothers," the new family of his own. She fulfills her mission in going to the disciples. They have also had their encounters. The final words in direct speech of the body of the Gospel come first from a witness to Jesus, as Thomas proclaims the truth he sees before him, "My Lord and my God!" Christologically this is the clearest expression in the Gospel of John's understanding of the divinity of Jesus. Thomas's witness is true, but Jesus's response points beyond the first generation to the Johannine community and the community of audiences who take faith in and relationship with Jesus into the future, "Have you believed because you have seen me? Blessed are those who have not seen and yet believe" (v. 29). With these words the narrator can then conclude the body of the Gospel with the proclamation that this Scripture has indeed been written so that the community of audiences may be affirmed in their belief and may go forward into the world of their future as the community of Christ (20:30–31). **Believing without seeing**, they become a community that matches the faith of the Beloved Disciple who believed without seeing the risen Jesus.

The Importance of the Audience

The final words of Jesus in John 20 are directed to the audience, those who read, hear, or see performed this Gospel. They are blessed because they do not see the physical Jesus, and yet they believe (v. 29). The prologue to the Gospel (1:1–18) was also directed to the audience. The people in the story do not know the prologue. The Gospel of John was not written to tell about the characters who played a role in the life of Jesus, but to bring the audience to a deeper experience of faith. As John tells them: "These things have been written so that you may go on believing that Jesus is the Christ, the Son of God, and that believing you may have life in his name" (AT: 20:31).

Key Terms and Concepts

believing without seeing
conclusion to the body of the Gospel
darkness/light
fear/joy
go on believing
Holy Spirit
journeys of faith
life in his name

Mary Magdalene
post-resurrection accounts
rabbouni/my teacher
resurrection
Scripture
shalom/peace
telos
Thomas

Questions for Review

1. Describe the two "places" where the resurrection events take place. Are they important?
2. Who are the major characters? How does each of them respond to the Risen Jesus?
3. Is there a difference between the faith of the Beloved Disciple (v. 8), the faith of Mary Magdalene (v. 18), and the faith of Thomas (v. 28). If so, what is the difference?
4. How does this story point outside itself to the audience hearing or reading it? In other words, what is the discourse level of John 20?
5. What is the meaning of "go on believing," and why is this an important question for understanding the purpose of the Gospel of John?
6. What is the significance of the words the evangelist uses to describe Jesus in this purpose statement: the Christ, the Son of God?
7. How is the first "ending" of the Gospel (20:30–31) related to the "beginning" (1:1–18)?
8. Is there a deliberate relationship set up by the author between the Beloved Disciple and the audience of the Gospel story? How might it be described?

Bibliography and Further Reading

Byrne, Brendan. "The Faith of the Beloved Disciple and the Community in John 20." *Journal for the Study of the New Testament* 23 (1985): 83–97.

de la Potterie, Ignace. *The Passion and Resurrection of Jesus according to John: Text and Spirit.* London: Slough, UK: St Paul Publications, 1989.

Moloney, Francis J. "'For as Yet They Did Not Know the Scripture' (John 20:9): A Study in Narrative Time." *Irish Theological Quarterly* 79 (2014): 97–111.

———. *The Resurrection of the Messiah. A Narrative Commentary on the Resurrection Accounts in the Four Gospels.* New York: Paulist, 2013.

Schneiders, Sandra M. *Jesus Risen in Our Midst: Essays on the Resurrection of Jesus in the Fourth Gospel.* Collegeville, MN: Liturgical, 2013.

The Epilogue and Call to the Community in John 21

PURPOSE Chapter fifteen explores the final chapter of the Gospel, typically understood as an epilogue to the body of the narrative that presents the ongoing community of the church and its leadership (John 21).

ASSIGNMENT Reread John 21 before proceeding with this chapter.

We now come to the final chapter of the Gospel of John. Biblical scholars often ponder the intent—and even the origin and role—of John 21, given the concluding tone of 20:30–31. Nonetheless ancient manuscripts always conclude with the scenes of this chapter as the final act of the Gospel. Many of these same scholars also agree that the Gospel was likely composed in stages over a period of time. This final chapter could, therefore, have been added late in the composition history of the Gospel to respond to the changing needs and circumstances of the Johannine community. Although some commentators reduce the chapter to an "addendum" or "appendix" and even exclude it from their narrative overviews; others have increasingly understood John 21 as a seamless final component of the narrative whole. In this vein, understanding John 21 as an **epilogue** indicates that it brings the Gospel story beyond its conclusion into the time of its early audiences and clarifies the form and mission of the community it creates.

An epilogue, as a literary and storytelling device, *carries forward* some aspect of the narrative by describing the consequences resulting from its climax, solution, or outcome. Epilogues are typically set anywhere from a few hours after the climax of the narrative to far into the future, but the function is to allow the author to speak to audiences either directly or indirectly through the point of view of a character or characters in the story. For example, the performance of ancient Greek stage plays would often conclude when an actor stepped forward, spoke directly to the audience, and offered gratitude to the members for watching the play. In tragedies, the actor, in character, would describe the lesson or moral the audience should have learned from the story. Although not intended for the stage in the same way as the dramas of the day, we see the influence of that medium in the Gospel of John's more intimate and informal environment of a story told for the community of believers.

Broadly speaking, the relationship made possible by Jesus in John 1–20 leaves its community with two commands: *to love* and *to believe* (see 1:12; 3:16; 6:29; 12:36; 13:19, 34–35; 14:1, 11, 15, 21–24, 29; 15:9–13, 17, 19; 20:27–31). However completely these truths are revealed, living through them as a community can become problematic over time when members struggle to understand whom and what exactly to love and to believe. Therefore, with the development of John 21, the storyteller actualizes the new commandments given by Jesus into the lived experience of the audience.

The Narrative Flow and Structure of John 21

Chapter 20 of John's Gospel begins to bring the story to a close with several accounts of appearances of the resurrected Jesus. Through his interactions with the disciples in 20:1–29, Jesus fulfills his promises to return to them (14:18–19; 16:16), and they are able to begin to understand words of Jesus about the raising of the temple of his body (2:19–22). As the journey of the disciples begins to reach its completion, the author, as storyteller, can then turn to the audience to bring it to its own crucial moment of faith decision. The vast majority of scholars, therefore, posit John 20:30–31 as the conclusion to the body of the Gospel.

This ending to the body of the Gospel of John thus opens the door for its audience to situate themselves as Jesus's disciples, whose belief is affirmed and reaffirmed as they journey through "life in his name" (20:31). The epilogue, John 21, is, at the very least then, a portrait of how that can happen. But what if it is more than just an example in afterthought? What if the earliest telling of this story, possibly concluding at 20:31, raised more questions from audiences? As profound and provocative as this ending is, several threads of the narrative have been left hanging, including the fate and ongoing roles of Peter and the Beloved Disciple. The community the Gospel engendered may have needed something more to understand and sustain their new life, and early audiences may have clamored for answers.

If the Beloved Disciple bestowed upon the community a new covenant relationship with two commands, **to love** and **to believe**, the resulting struggles can be summarized as an **ecclesial**, or church-oriented, **problem** (whom and how do we love?) and a **ministerial**, or authority, **problem** (whom and what do we believe?). After a brief introduction that presents the new setting (v. 1), the former is handled in the first scene of John 21 (vv. 2–14), and the latter in the second scene (vv. 15–23). This final act can then conclude, providing a second ending of the Gospel now in the world of the audience (vv. 24–25). When the story of this chapter is told as an epilogue, with some sort of pause or fade to black, reflecting the history of its development, then the corresponding shift of the spotlight is made from the life of the first generation to the life of those who have not seen and yet have the courage to believe (20:29), that is, the ongoing community—the audience seated before storytellers of all time.

Therefore, the structure of John 21 can be diagrammed as follows:

Church and Authority in the New Community of the Gospel   21:1–25
> 21:1   Introduction and Setting
>> 21:2–14 Jesus, His Disciples, and the Catch: Whom Do We Love?
>>   Ecclesiology and Inclusion
>> 21:15–23 Jesus, Peter, and the Beloved Disciple: What Do We Believe?
>>   Authority, Dialogue, and Distinction
> 21:24–25   The (Second) Conclusion to the Gospel

Our interpretation of the epilogue to John's Gospel will follow this guide.

Interpreting John 21:1–25: Church and Authority in the New Community of the Gospel

The narrative of John 21 can be contextualized in terms of problems emerging as the community of the Gospel encountered both the Judaism of its past and the Greco-Roman world of its future. We will see how this problem progresses when we study the Johannine letters. We have suggested that the world behind the text of the Gospel reflects an ethnically Jewish Christian community facing alienation and possible expulsion from the synagogue for their profession of Jesus as the Messiah (see John 9). Scholars then posit that John 21 may have been composed as the community moves on attempting to live in the context of a larger developing "Peter-oriented" Christianity, as reflected in the Synoptic Gospels, with the Beloved Disciple as *their* model. If we accept the largely oral/aural culture of the first century, then it is likely that the interactive environment between storytellers and audiences facilitated an atmosphere of give and take. As audiences continued to ask questions, the final author of the Gospel cultivated a response in narrative form from the wealth of his traditions. The result is John 21, the epilogue.

21:1 Introduction and Setting

John 21:1 serves as an introduction to the epilogue and a reintroduction to the Gospel story in a new, later, time and place. The evangelist's favorite temporal marker to designate the passing of extended time, "after this," coupled with the somewhat awkward repetition of "manifested," accentuates the raising of the curtain in this new setting: "After these things, Jesus manifested himself again to his disciples at the Sea of Tiberias. He manifested like this." The construc-

"Peter-Oriented Christianity"

Simon Peter appears as a significant character in all the Gospels. In both the Synoptic Gospels and in the Gospel of John he is portrayed as someone who represents the disciples and speaks in their name, but also as someone with a warm heart and a rather foolhardy and imprudent tendency to rush into situations, ask the wrong questions, and do the wrong things—especially denying knowledge of Jesus. The strong presence of Peter across the Gospel traditions suggests that historically he was a very important figure in early Christianity. This is also clear in the early chapters of the Acts of the Apostles. Maybe not everyone in the early church followed the leadership of Peter, but it is clear that many did. They formed what we have called a "Peter-Oriented Christianity." For John, Peter is clearly a flawed shepherd, and Jesus asks him to confess his love three times, before he then tells him that one day he will glorify God by martyrdom (21:15–19).

tion of this verse immediately following 20:31 leads a storyteller to pause, even withdraw perceptibly, then begin again, articulating a later time, a new place by the sea in Galilee, with the disciples at the forefront of the receiving end of the revelation. Further, the double use of "to manifest" provides the interpretive key to understanding the story as a **theophany**, or manifestation of God's presence, among the disciples. Far from sloppy editing, the evangelist has embedded this reintroduction to alert, even surprise, audiences that the story is not ended. Indeed, the journey of faith may never "end" as such. As this final act proceeds in the two scenes of the fishing expedition (vv. 2–14) and the post-meal dialogue (vv. 15–23), audience members participate in the ongoing experiential education of the disciples and can place themselves in the "class."

21:2–14 Jesus, His Disciples, and the Catch: Whom Do We Love? Ecclesiology and Inclusion

The intricacy of the narrative is revealed in the introduction of the primary characters of the second scene in the setting and action of the first scene. Seven of Jesus's disciples are gathered by the shore (vv. 2–3). Simon Peter, a primary character whose journey of faith has been left at a loose end, is identified, as well as Thomas and Nathanael. The naming of Thomas connects the epilogue narrative with the closing scenes of the body of the Gospel, while naming Nathanael and his hometown of Cana alongside Simon Peter echoes the first gathering of the disciples in John 1 and the initial revelation of Jesus at Cana in John 2. Grouping the remaining four disciples somewhat ambiguously as "the sons of Zebedee and two others" allows for the presence of the Beloved Disciple as well as for audience members to place themselves in the scene. However, not identifying the Beloved

Disciple at the outset also allows for the "surprise" that could be generated by suddenly having him recognize Jesus as "the Lord" in v. 7 when he has not been an explicit part of the scene thus far. These disciples and the audience follow the lead of Peter, who last spoke in the Gospel while warming himself by a charcoal fire with the enemies of Jesus in the court of the high priest (18:18–27). There Peter denied Jesus three times as Jesus predicted he would (18:17, 25, 27; see 13:38). Peter had sworn that he would lay down his life for Jesus (13:37), but Jesus prevented him from doing so when Peter tried to defend him in the garden (18:10–11). Peter, the earnest, aggressive spokesman for the disciples (see 6:68–69; 13:6–10, 24, 36–37), was so thrown from his former self-understanding he found himself denying all knowledge of and relationship with Jesus.

In the present scene, Peter says, "I'm going fishing" (v. 3). The response from the audience at this point in the story, given Jesus's charge to Peter and the disciples and their acceptance in John 13–17, must be something to the effect of "Oh no!" Peter, who was meant to lead others to life in the new community, has returned to the occupation of fishing, the role and relationship he accepted from Jesus now possibly dropped. Believing without seeing Jesus has been established across the Gospel as the primary challenge for the fledgling community. Peter's journey of faith began when he could not follow his nature and fight for Jesus the way he envisioned. Although the shock of Peter's decision is palpable, audiences may well identify with this natural tendency and wonder now where their own places might be. Will the new covenant community accept them for who they are in the midst of all their imperfections and humanity? A primary focus of the remainder of the chapter is, therefore, to reconstitute the relationship between Jesus and Peter and set Peter in his role of pastoral authority over the community of Jesus's flock. Before that happens the nature of the ecclesial community is affirmed to answer questions of whom they are to love and how they are to love one another.

The seemingly ill-advised fishing trip commences in the Gospel's typical imagery of darkness. After a long night of failure, morning breaks to reveal Jesus standing on the shore. Again in the evangelist's symbolic sense of the light of day, Jesus comes even to actively failing disciples to guide them on their way. He greets them by calling them "children" (v. 5). These are the same sentiments for the disciples expressed in the last discourse, where the disciples were characterized as "his own" (13:1) and Jesus called them "children" (13:33). This Greek term *paidia* might be more commonly used of students, but the disciples are, in fact, still learning and about to receive another lesson. Jesus's greeting for his disciples thus recalls the identity of the community as "children of God" (1:12; 11:52) and sets the stage for the wondrous catch and renewal to come.

The Beloved Disciple, in keeping with his character established in chapters 13–20 as the one who witnesses and gives access to the other disciples, is the first to recognize Jesus: "It is the Lord!" (v. 7). Peter, likewise in keeping with the earnest zeal of his character presented across these same chapters, gets

Christ at the Sea of Galilee by Tintoretto

dressed and jumps into the sea in an effort to get to Jesus (v. 7). As they all reach land, Peter returns to the boat on Jesus's command to haul ashore the wondrous catch of fish in the unbroken net. The abundance of fish, 153 in total, reminds audiences of the abundance of wine (2:1–12) and the abundance of food (6:1–14) provided by Jesus, echoing these earlier encounters and indicating the fullness and inclusiveness of the church. Many scholars have tried to interpret the meaning of this number. The ancient church leader Jerome suggested its inclusive symbolism based upon ancient zoological identification of 153 species of fish. Other scholars have focused on mathematical symbolism and suggested that 153 is a perfect number since it is the sum of the numbers 1–17. Again, the idea is that 153 represents the perfect number to include; that is, everyone. In the end, the evangelist seems to be teaching that the universal character of the mission of the community consists of bringing into one the scattered children of God (see 11:52). The unbroken net further reflects this unity of the community in the new life given by Jesus, previously indicated by the garment of Jesus that could not be torn apart at his crucifixion (19:23–25). The abundance motif of completion and unity, therefore, punctuates the presence of the messianic era and signals the actualization of the new messianic covenant community.

The ecclesial issue at stake is thus addressed by the coming of Jesus to struggling disciples and signifying the inclusive nature of the church and its mission. Any audience member struggling with the "who" of loving in the new covenant, questioning their own inclusion or that of any other, is sated by the telling of this miraculous haul and its universal implications: all those who profess Jesus as Messiah are welcome regardless of ethnic identity.

21:15–23 Jesus, Peter, and the Beloved Disciple: What Do We Believe? Authority, Dialogue, and Distinction

The second part of John 21 properly situates authority in this inclusive church (vv. 15–23) in an effort to answer questions of whom and how to believe. Peter is designated the leader, the head of the church; the Beloved Disciple is the witness, the model disciple in the church. Jesus has brought Peter and the disciples around a new charcoal fire and provided a meal of bread and fish. The charcoal fire is a narrative marker that calls to mind Peter's last scene of breach with Jesus. The meal calls to mind their final meal together before Jesus's passion, which itself echoed both the ritual meals of the OT (John 13:1–11; see Gen 26:26–30; 31:43–54; Exod 24:5–11; Deut 27:6–7) and the sign and subsequent teaching of John 6. Although all seven disciples are involved in the meal and its aftermath, the narrator places a steady focus on Peter, and the reconciliation of Peter's relationship with Jesus will take center stage in the following verses. Jesus confronts Peter time and again in the narrative, continuing to upset his equilibrium and challenge him to make decisions and take new action.

In the context of this meal, the evangelist presents the central dialogue of the epilogue. Jesus asks Peter three times whether he loves him (*agapas me*; vv. 15, 16; *phileis me*; v. 17), reconstituting Peter's three-time denial by that earlier charcoal fire into a binding relationship with the consequences of mission and leadership. Jesus addresses Peter with the formal appellation, "Simon, son of John," (v. 15), repeating his initial call of Peter to discipleship (1:42), and preparing the audience for Peter's restoration. He initiates the dialogue with the comparative "do you love me more than these?" Translators and interpreters have struggled to determine to what Jesus wants Peter to compare his love, since there does not seem to be a direct referent to the pronoun "these." Since Jesus carefully directs attention to himself and Peter's love, audiences should focus not on the subject of Peter and how well he loves, but on the object of Peter's love. Understanding Jesus's question of Peter's love for him as a comparison to Peter's love for other things, including his former way of life symbolized by "these" freshly caught fish in front of them, calls to mind the absolute claim for love and commitment that God makes on those who enter into covenant in the OT as well as the challenge Jesus has made to those he has encountered across this narrative. Emphasizing Jesus's *me* of "Simon, son of John, do you love *me* more than these?" would accentuate this distinction as well as provide both a challenge to Peter's seeking solace in his former occupation and a knowing nod to audiences who may have been shocked by his return to fishing.

The articulation of Jesus's threefold question and Peter's threefold response has also garnered much discussion regarding the apposition of the two different words for **love**. Peter always responds to Jesus's question regarding his love by saying yes, but he uses a form of **phileō**, while Jesus uses **agapaō** the first two times he asks and then shifts to Peter's *phileō* the third time. The question is whether there is any difference in meaning between the two terms or whether the usage is just part of the evangelist's internal thesaurus. Regardless of whether there was a semantic distinction between the words in the larger milieu, the evangelist seems to make a distinction across the Gospel as Jesus tends to use *agapaō* in his calls to love, especially in the last discourse. This would make Jesus's shift in wording a distinctive move toward Peter, something an audience would hear and possibly appreciate. Peter's "anguish" at this third query could then be the result of his realization that Jesus is reconstituting his earlier three-part denial. But Jesus is also meeting Peter where he is, in all his imperfection and desire to chuck it all and go fishing; and this is a powerful lesson of hope for struggling believers of all time.

This dialogue thus reconciles their earlier breach and renews their relationship. Jesus's commands that are integral to this reconstitution articulate Peter's mission as action in service of the new community. He is to "feed" and "tend" the flock (vv. 15, 16, 17). Peter's leadership is clarified pastorally as he is mandated to be the new shepherd of the burgeoning flock of the children of God. Peter indicated at the foot-washing that he wanted to follow Jesus, but he was not ready. Jesus said then that Peter would indeed follow him, but later. Now that he has been reconstituted, Peter's journey thus comes to an end *in* the story even as it begins anew *beyond* the story's boundaries. In a final poignant moment, Jesus demands Peter's obedience, suggests his role in authority, and implicates his eventual crucifixion in parallel to Jesus's own: "Follow me" (vv. 18–19, 22).

Then what of the Beloved Disciple? The narrator indicates there have been some queries about the destiny of the disciple Jesus loved who has journeyed alongside Jesus throughout the Gospel story. Peter gives voice to those questions, and the scene closes with Jesus describing the unique mandate of the Beloved Disciple (vv. 20–23). He is the ideal model of a disciple and witness. The relationship between Peter and the Beloved Disciple has come to the forefront across the second half of the Gospel as they have worked in tandem to understand their experience of Jesus. Already in the first century of the church, the story seems to reflect, there is a concern for the recognition of the pastoral role in authority and the testimonial role in discipleship. These roles do not have to be incorporated in one person. They can be, but they usually are not. The best disciple is not necessarily the shepherd of the community, and the best leader is not always the model disciple. Therefore, in this Gospel these roles are embodied in two separate characters, Peter and the Beloved Disciple.

Jesus's instruction to Peter that the Beloved Disciple's role is of no consequence for his following confirms their distinctive but mutual roles. Peter is the one who must learn to follow so that he can lead, even to martyrdom (vv. 18–19; see 16:1–4), and the Beloved Disciple is the consummate follower who becomes the witness to this good news (v. 24; see also 19:35). Audience questions about believing and authority are resolved with the affirmation that Peter is their shepherd and they are part of the larger burgeoning church. Nonetheless, the Beloved Disciple remains their model for faith and witness, ever more so now that they must believe without seeing the physical signs and presence of Christ (see John 20:8, 29).

21:24–25 The (Second) Conclusion to the Gospel

The narrator concludes his story by attesting to its limitless nature (vv. 24–25). He turns to the audience and speaks directly in the first person in the testimonial tradition of the Beloved Disciple. His final words send his audience into the world and their shared future as the new children of God living in the love and faith of Jesus.

What Have We Learned So Far?
Epilogue and Outreach to the Future

Storytelling has transformation as its primary aim. The force of telling and retelling a story may be to confirm the identity of the community or, and more likely as well as, to evoke within the audience both the desire and capacity to change. By telling his story, the Fourth Evangelist is articulating for his community the continuation of God's work in creation through the new community founded on truth and belief in the revelation of the Word of God. He wants his audiences, who may already be in this community, to *become* children of God who are steadfast in love and unity in the face of a challenging world. This is how social memory functions in forming communal identity.

The Gospel, therefore, becomes the lifeline for fledgling Johannine audiences to find their genealogy in the story of Israel and God's saving relationship with that chosen people of God. At the same time, they are able to perceive their future in a story where the revelation of God in Jesus, God's gift of truth as articulated in the prologue (1:1–18), has set all humankind free to receive and believe in the Word of God. This is what we have called the new vertical commandment of the Gospel. It is a theological and christological summons to a journey of believing that never ends. Now, they must also live in community with that Word and *each other* as the true children of God. This is what we have called the new horizontal commandment that is oriented toward ethical action among all humankind. The epilogue is composed to send audiences out into this world as part of this newly formed and still forming community with two models shaping their identity and interaction. It is important that the recipients of this Jesus-story accept that Peter, and especially the Disciple whom Jesus loved, provide the foundational experiences of shepherd and witness for further disciples who are to make known the love of Jesus and the love of God. But the proof of their "blessedness," the result of their access to Jesus given to them in this Gospel (20:30–31), can be found and tested only in the quality of the lives of people whose story is found outside the confines of the Johannine narrative.

Although the world may not be big enough to contain all the books that could have been written about Jesus, it is precisely the place for transformed audiences of the Gospel of John to live their lives and do their work. Again, the function of an epilogue is to carry forward the outcome of the narrative into the world beyond its boundaries by allowing the author to speak to audiences indirectly through characters in the story. John 21, which likely developed in this interactive storytelling culture, facilitates this transformation and sends its audiences out there as a new community on their own journeys, maybe as witnessing disciples or as shepherding leaders, but always as steadfast children of God. This is the theological, christological and ethical summons of the Gospel of John.

Key Terms and Concepts

ecclesial problem	ministerial problem
epilogue	theophany
love/*agapaō*	to believe
love/*phileō*	to love

Questions for Review

1. What is an epilogue? What difference might it make to interpret John 21 as an epilogue as opposed to an "addendum" or "appendix"?
2. What are the two commandments presented across this Gospel story, and how do they play out in the narrative of John 21?
3. What is the effect of Jesus's brief but crucial dialogue with Peter by the charcoal fire? What is the evangelist teaching about love in these verses?
4. Why is it important to differentiate the models presented in the characters of Peter and the Beloved Disciple? How might these models encourage and support believers?

Bibliography and Further Reading

Brown, Raymond E. *The Gospel according to John*. 2 vols. Anchor Bible 29–29a. New York: Doubleday, 1966–1970.

Brown, Sherri. *God's Promise: Covenant Relationship in John*. New York: Paulist, 2014.

————. "What's in an Ending? John 21 and the Performative Force of an Epilogue." *Perspectives in Religious Studies* 42 (2015): 29–42.

Culpepper, R. Alan. *Anatomy of the Fourth Gospel: A Study in Literary Design.* New Testament Foundations and Facets. Philadelphia: Fortress, 1983.

Moloney, Francis J. *Love in the Gospel of John.* Grand Rapids: Baker, 2013.

————. *The Resurrection of the Messiah. A Narrative Commentary on the Resurrection Accounts in the Four Gospels.* New York: Paulist, 2013.

Smith, D. Moody. *The Composition and Order of the Fourth Gospel.* New Haven: Yale University, 1965.

The Letters of John

PURPOSE Chapter sixteen studies the three Letters of John as the canonical extension of the community of the Beloved Disciple and the challenges they faced as Christianity grew and developed in an ever-changing world.

ASSIGNMENT Read 1, 2, and 3 John before proceeding with this chapter.

We encounter the three Letters of John at the end of the course for two major reasons. First, they are among the latest documents of the NT. More importantly, it is largely through the association of 1 John with the Gospel of John, and then the description of 1 John as a "Catholic Epistle," that the Gospel of John gained its place in the canon, and the seven Catholic Epistles became a unique collection in the NT. As well as the role that these letters played in the formation of the Christian canon, they contain important teaching that calls for the attention of those who regard the Bible as Scripture. Thus, we now turn our attention to the interpretation of 1, 2, and 3 John.

The Community and Letters in Context

The three **Letters of John** are sometimes called, more formally, the **Johannine Epistles**. The two terms are synonyms and either may be used to refer to these three texts. A determining factor for interpreting the three Letters of John is their historical relationship to the Gospel of John and the community that produced it. Scholars take various positions in this regard in terms of whether the letters come from the same hand as the Gospel and whether they were written before or after the work of the Fourth Evangelist. The Gospel itself likely underwent several drafts and refinements over the years until it reached its final form that has been preserved in the New Testament. It is truly the product of a community's experience of God's activity in the world. Therefore, even if the letters did not come from the same first hand as the Gospel, they certainly arose from the same community of believers and reflect the ongoing life of that community as it sought to come to terms with its particular understanding of the good news of Christ and God's new covenant in a larger socio-cultural environment. Further, they reflect a slightly different and slightly later theological context where the author(s) thought that the message of the Gospel needed further clarification and adaptation. Indeed, the content of the Letters is best understood as arising from the community after the crisis with post-war Judaism has faded. The crisis then fades and transitions into a focus upon the life and belief of the community itself. As we discussed in some detail in chapter five, the Gospel was likely written ca. 90–100 CE in a community that is defining itself over against the rest of the world, including the mainstream Judaism of its past. The Letters, then, were likely written in the following decade at the end of the first century, ca. 100–110, in a community of churches that now found it necessary to define itself against schism *from within*. The ideals of the new Christian community were proving difficult to live out in the larger Greco-Roman world, with its variety of beliefs and ideals. The author writes from a position of authority to stem the tide of discord and dissolution in a possibly last ditch effort to strengthen and unify his people into a community.

In chapter five, we have already discussed in some detail the world behind these texts, alongside the Gospel. Therefore, in this chapter we will focus the discussion of historical context on the development of these letters in general and how they came to be part of the New Testament more particularly. We will then turn our attention to the literary world in the texts, and finally to how they might be received and interpreted by audiences in front of the texts both in the first century and in our own time.

The World behind the Texts

As we discussed in the Introduction, several documents in the New Testament have been regarded by the Christian tradition as originating in a single person named "**John**." In addition to the Gospel of John, three Letters of John and the book of Revelation are an important part of that tradition. Only the book of Revelation refers to its author by the name "John," and he identifies himself as an **Elder** or "Presbyter" (**presbyteros**) writing from the island of Patmos (Rev 1:9). No historically verifiable evidence links John the Elder at Patmos with any of the disciples, but a long tradition associates all five of these documents with the disciple of Jesus, John the son of Zebedee. Similar to the anonymity of the Gospel, there is no address or salutation at all in 1 John. The author of 2 and 3 John describes himself as "the Elder" (v. 1 in each), but this expression was widely used in the early church and can be found in many Christian documents. Thus, on the basis of the documents alone, it is not clear that "the Elder" of Revelation and "the Elder" of 2 and 3 John are the same or that one person named "John" was the "Elder" John of Revelation, the "Elder" of 2 and 3 John, the author of 1 John and the Beloved Disciple of the Gospel. But the second-century church was quick to make such associations, and "John the elder" of Revelation was quickly associated with "the elder" of 2–3 John. Once that was in place, "John" was seen as the author of all three letters, and the name "John" was then associated with the Gospel alongside the letters.

As early as 180 CE, the church leader Irenaeus became a vital advocate of this literature and made the link between John, the son of Zebedee, and the Beloved Disciple. A large number of Christians had been attracted to a form of Christianity called Gnosticism, which was strongly influenced by speculative Greco-Roman religions. One of Gnosticism's many features was the way in which it minimized the importance of the physical life and death of Jesus—even denying that there ever was a real human life or a real experience of death. The Gnostics were very fond of John's Gospel, which provided them with a story of Jesus that was more spiritual and less down-to-earth than that of Matthew, Mark, and Luke. Irenaeus fought hard against Gnosticism and strove to show that John's Gospel was deeply embedded in the life and death of the man Jesus of Nazareth, and not just an extraordinary speculation. One of the major elements that enabled Irenaeus to rescue the Gospel of John for the Christian community and its canon of Scripture was the identification of the author of the letter we now call 1 John with the author of the Fourth Gospel. In that letter, so many of the same theological, christological, and ethical issues found in the Gospel were stated in a more grounded, "orthodox" fashion. Irenaeus went on to be the first to identify the Beloved Disciple, and thus the author of both works, as John the son of Zebedee, one of the founding apostles of the Christian church. This position has been held down to our own time. There are good scholars who claim that Irenaeus was correct: John the apostle, the son of Zebedee, was the Beloved Disciple. But this once universally held position is not widely held today. Nonetheless, no modern scholar denies the close relationship between 1 John and the Fourth Gospel.

If the Gospel and 1 John were established very early as coming from the same author and this assured the place of both in the canon, what of 2 and 3 John? The history of their reception is complex, as one would imagine. It is

---

Gnosticism

In the second Christian century a very speculative form of Christianity emerged, influenced by Eastern religions. Although it had many forms, scholars refer to it generally as "Gnosticism." The physical reality of the human Jesus and the bloody event of Jesus's death—followed by God's action in the resurrection—were not deemed "salvific." People were saved by "knowledge" (Greek: *gnōsis*), not by Jesus's life, teaching, death, and resurrection. Throughout the Letters of John, and especially 1 John, the author insists on the humanity of Jesus as the Christ. It is as the human Jesus Christ that Jesus is the Son of God, and his self-giving death in love saves. These letters may have been written early in the second century CE. They are written to help early Christians overcome false opinions about Jesus Christ as Son of God, and the saving act of his death and resurrection. The Letters of John may offer early evidence for the emergence of gnostic tendencies in the early Christian church.

John the Evangelist in Silence. Wood panel by Nectarius Kulyuksin (1679).

not surprising that during the second century CE, 1 John became well known as "the letter of John." It is equally unsurprising, given the brevity of the two other letters attached to the name "John," that they are not used by the church in the second century or even into the third century. Finally, first 2 John then eventually 3 John did begin to circulate more widely, and a connection began to be made between 1 and 2 John. Once 2 John began to gain acceptance, however, it brought into play the possibility that 3 John should be accepted as part of the canon of Scripture as well. The similarity between their messages and the occurrence of the title "the Elder" in both letters led the early church leaders eventually to regard 1, 2, and 3 John as Johannine letters alongside the Gospel, and all four texts as part of the NT Canon.

It was also the role of 1 John that led to the development of a group of **Catholic Epistles**. These seven books located toward the end of the New Testament are sometimes called the **General Letters**. These two terms are synonyms: the former is derived from the original Greek words, while the latter provides a more common English translation. Therefore, both terms can be used interchangeably. Toward the end of the second century CE, the term "catholic" was first used to describe an individual letter when Clement, Bishop of Alexandria (who died in 215 CE), called the letter arising from the Jerusalem Council, mentioned in Acts 15:22–29, a "catholic epistle." With this identification he was indicating that it was written by all the apostles to the church in general. The prominent church leader Origen, writing in the first half of the third century, seemed to be the initiator of a trend to call 1 John the "catholic epistle." He also refers to 1 Peter by the same term. Thus, it seems that the term began to be used to identify certain formal letters that were written to the universal church, as distinct from those addressed to a local congregation. In other words, they were written to a wider, more general, audience.

By the fourth century, the expression "Catholic Epistles" was used to identify seven NT documents as a collection: James, 1 and 2 Peter, 1, 2, and 3 John, and Jude. A number of letters had already been gathered in the name of Paul, and they were always identified in terms of their destination audience. These remaining letters cannot be identified by their destinations, so each one is known by its author. The general nature of these Catholic Epistles was one of the determining factors leading to the collection, with the Letters of John a key component.

The World in the Texts

We will briefly address the literary characteristics and structures of the three Johannine Epistles in order to get a sense of their overall flow and content. The First Letter of John shares much in common with the Gospel, including language, themes, and style. The second two letters are far briefer and, although they share some similarities with the Gospel, show more commonality with each other. Therefore, we will discuss their literary flow and structures together.

The First Letter of John

The formal, treatise-like tone of 1 John is evident even in a first encounter with it. We can see why early church leaders referred to it as a catholic epistle, because there is no personal address or distinctive audience. It seems to be written to a general group. Further, the relationship between 1 John and the Gospel of John becomes evident even across the first verses of the letter. Indeed, the celebrated interpreter of the Johannine literature, Raymond Brown, sees a link between the literary structure of 1 John and the structure of the Gospel, with its prologue, Book of Signs in which Jesus publicly reveals light and life, Book of Glory, where love is a major theme, and an epilogue. The author uses the same language and imagery in this more grounded and direct plea for the community. The evangelist's language of love, knowledge, and the gift of truth for the children of God continues to permeate these pages. Further exploration of the epistle's structure reveals a prologue that mirrors the prologue of the Gospel (1:1–4); while the final verses likewise echo the concluding sounds of the Gospel (5:13–21). Within this theological frame the author makes three resounding appeals to the new community in terms of the characteristics of God that form the heart and soul of God's children: light (1:5–2:27), justice (2:28–4:6), and love (4:7–5:12). The content of these appeals warns the community of the dangers of the world, while instructing it on the power of faith to conquer all for those who abide in Christ and thus remain in the new covenant community.

The letter can thus be outlined as follows:

1 John

1:1–4	Prologue: The Word of Life for the Community
1:5–2:27	Opening Appeal to the New Community: God Is Light
1:5–2:2	The Experience of the Light: The Word of God in Jesus
2:3–11	The Message of the Light: Knowledge of God Is Fellowship in God
2:12–27	The Crisis of the Light: The Dangers of the World
2:28–4:6	Central Appeal to the New Community: God Is Just
2:28–3:10	The Mark of the True Children of God
3:11–24	The New Covenant Commandment
4:1–6	The Call for Discernment and the Testing of Spirits
4:7–5:12	Closing Appeal to the New Community: God Is Love
4:7–21	The Presence of God in Relationship: Love for God and One Another
5:1–12	The Foundation of Love: Faith That Conquers the World
5:13–21	Epilogue: Prayer for the Faithful Community

We can use this outline as a roadmap to further interpretation of 1 John in the next section.

The Second and Third Letters of John

The brevity of the final two epistles neither diminishes their power nor the insight they give into the challenges faced by this early Christian community that would have appealed to accept all humankind into their family. By this stage the faithful are struggling, and the community is falling prey to the contentiousness of human nature and the pressures of the larger world. The two letters offer direct appeals that address the real-life situations of early Christian communities. Second John counsels a particular church within the larger Johannine community to remain in the Gospel commandment of love and to guard against deceivers. Third John offers specific praise for the fidelity of Gaius and Demetrius while warning against the betrayal of Diotrephes. The Elder thus makes his final pleas for fellowship in truth. The letters can therefore be outlined as follows:

2 John

vv. 1–3 The Elder's Address: Life Lived Walking in the Truth
vv. 4–6 Love Is the Fulfillment of the Gospel Commandment
vv. 7–11 Believers Are to Guard against Deceivers of the Gospel
vv. 12–13 Farewell: Appeal to Joy as the Mark of Fellowship

3 John

vv. 1–4 The Elder's Address: Encouragement in Love and Truth
vv. 5–8 Praise for Hospitality—Gaius
vv. 9–10 The Politics of Ecclesial Power—Diotrephes
vv. 11–12 Faithfulness to the Community—Demetrius
vv. 13–15 Farewell: Desire for Fellowship and Appeal to Friendship

We will return to these outlines in the next section as we interpret the letters more closely.

The World in Front of the Texts

When we introduced the methods of biblical interpretation in chapter two, we discussed the world in front of the text in terms of particular critical approaches that ask questions about how a biblical book or passage affects its audiences, be they readers of the text or audiences of biblical performances. The three Letters of John are direct appeals to the community at large and individuals within the community to stand fast in the Gospel traditions. The author is offering (possibly final) pleas for unity in faith and love in the manner of the Beloved Disciple in the hopes of responses in action on the part of his recipients. Therefore, we can use the rubric of the world in front of the text more generally to interpret how he makes these powerful entreaties.

First John

Just as we saw with the Gospel, the best method of interpreting the Letters is to begin at their beginning and exegete our way through each Letter, following the structure we establish through our exploration of the world in the text.

1:1–4 Prologue: The Word of Life for the Community

The author states his purpose in the prologue with intentional echoes of both Genesis and the new "beginning" of the Gospel prologue (1:1–4; see Gen 1 and John 1:1–18). But "the word of life" he declares is only that which the community has collectively perceived through the senses—what they have "heard," "seen," "looked at," and "touched." Therefore, he can "testify" to that which has been "revealed." This is the mark of the true fellowship he wishes for the community grounded in the complete joy of union with God the Father and Jesus Christ the Son. The ensuing appeals are all written toward that goal.

1:5–2:27 Opening Appeal to the New Community: God Is Light

The opening appeal is the proclamation that God is light in terms of the community's experience of the Light (1:5–2:2), the message of the light itself (2:3–11), and the crisis the light faces in this world (2:12–27). On the basis of their own experience of the light in their lives, the community is called to acknowledge the Word of God in Jesus. Here the author gives insight into the conflict that has arisen in the community. In a series of conditional statements he asserts that the claim to be without sin lies outside of the truth. To claim such is to make a liar of Jesus and his blood that cleanses this sin (referring to his death on the cross) a lie. Further, just as Jesus spoke of the Holy Spirit as the Paraclete, or Advocate, for humankind in the last discourse (John 13–17), the author speaks of Jesus as the Advocate for humankind and its sinful nature before the Father. Indeed, the indwelling of the word in truth leads to his claim that Jesus "is the atoning sacrifice for our sins, and not for ours only but also for the sins of the whole world" (2:2). This experience is affirmed in Christ, the light of God and of all humankind, and his central message that knowledge of God leads to fellowship in God. This is a further reference to what we have called the vertical and horizontal commandments of the Gospel: to believe in God and to love one another. The author teaches that ongoing faith in God leads to ethical living in community with each other.

The core of this first appeal is made up of the language of obedience and knowledge of God that are affirmed by keeping the new covenant commandments of believing in Christ and loving one another. This is how the community will abide in the light. The language of family is emphasized in the final section of this appeal as the author warns of the dangers of the world. As he did in 2:1, he again echoes the call of the Gospel to be **children of God** (see John 1:12; 11:52) as he warns them against those who "went out from us" (2:18–19). Here we have the strongest indication of the fragmentation the community is experiencing. Those who left are somehow denying that Jesus is the Christ, rendering them **antichrists**. It is very important to notice here that this term "antichrist" refers to all people who are anti-Christ in the sense that they do not believe that the person Jesus is both the incarnation of God and a fully human Christ. The term does not identify some sort of supernatural embodiment of evil, but people who are in conflict with the core teachings of this community. By contrast, the author teaches that knowledge of the truth of Christ will keep the true children of God safe. That said, the author is uncompromising in his insistence on the right way to live in this knowledge and belief. Those who "went out" from the community are in the wrong. This **polemic** reflected in the letter indicates the strong conflict going on behind it. For the author, who understands unity to be integral to the community, this leads to the heart of the first appeal: "Let what you heard from the beginning abide in you . . . . Then you will abide in the Son and in the Father" (2:24).

2:28–4:6 Central Appeal to the New Community: God Is Just

The central appeal to the new community emphasizes that God is just in terms of the mark of the true children of God (2:28–3:10) who are known by their keeping of the new commandment given by Jesus Christ (3:11–24) and their ability to discern and test spirits (4:1–6). The justice, or righteousness, of God will manifest in the children of God as a strong sense of ethics. Indeed, the hope of the children of God is union with God in his image and likeness. This ethic is once again based in the commandments of the new covenant to believe in the name Jesus Christ and to love one another—and be known by this way of life (3:23). This abiding reality is expressed in the heart of this central appeal, "Little children, let us love, not in word or speech, but in truth and action" (3:18). Abiding by this ethic brings the Spirit of God into the fellowship of the community and both empowers and emboldens the community to stand fast against the spirits of the world. Finally he addresses them as "Beloved," resonating with their founding figure, the Beloved Disciple of the Gospel (4:1). They are called to think critically and carefully about "the spirits" of the world, those who teach new ideas and values. They must make their decisions with the traditions of the community at the forefront of that process. The uncompromising polemic begins to ease at this point in the letter. The author can thus conclude this appeal with the consoling security of eternal relationship with God: "Little children, you are from God, and have conquered them; for the one who is in you is greater than the one who is in the world" (4:4).

4:7–5:12 Closing Appeal to the New Community: God Is Love

The author's closing appeal to his new community focuses on the attribute of God that embodies all other characteristics—that God is love. This is revealed in their love for one another when God is present in their relationships with each other and with God (4:7–21), as well as in the foundation of all love: a faith that conquers the world (5:1–12). Indeed, he begins his final appeal with the imperative for his "beloved," another strong reflection back to the Beloved Disciple of the Gospel as their model of faith and love. He commands, "let us love one another, because love is from God." The author follows this command with his characteristic formulation of the children of God: "everyone who loves is born of God and knows God" (4:7). God's love is witnessed by the gift of the atoning sacrifice of his Son and is perfected in the ongoing mutual indwelling love of the community. The language of being and abiding in God and love comes to the fore in these verses as he demands the presence of God in their relationships. The heart of this closing appeal is therefore: "The commandment we have from him is this: those who love God must love their brothers and sisters also" (4:21). The result of this love is the victory of faith, and this faith conquers the world (5:4–5). The author has already affirmed the atoning sacrifice of Christ; now he upholds the incarnation of Jesus as God's testimony, through the Spirit of truth, that the one who believes that Jesus is the Son of God has life, and this life in faith conquers all the dangers of this world (5:6–12).

5:13–21 Epilogue: Prayer for the Faithful Community

Echoing John 20:30–31, 1 John concludes with a purpose statement, through which the author shares his desire for the children of God to go on believing in the name of the Son of God and thereby have knowledge of eternal life (5:13–21). He affirms their boldness in prayer as fundamental communication in this relationship, for "we know that we are God's children" (v. 19). The strong summons of the letter culminates in the closing thoughts of the epilogue:

> And we know that the Son of God has come and has given us understanding so that we may know him who is true; and we are in him who is true, in his Son Jesus Christ. He is the true God and eternal life. (1 John 5:20)

Second John

The Second Letter of John is addressed to "the **elect lady** and her children," likely a metaphor for one of the local house churches within the extended Johannine community (v. 1). Referring to the church as a woman with children once again uses the language of family to describe the community. These churches could have been some distance from each other, and communication would have been maintained through letters delivered by personal couriers. In the address the Elder affirms his love for this sister church in the new gift of truth, which is Jesus Christ, the Father's Son who abides in them both (vv. 1–3). In the body of the letter he first appeals to the church to continue to keep the commandment of the new covenant and to love one another (vv. 4–6). Then he warns her to guard against those who have split with the larger community (vv. 7–11). There may be a link here between these divisive elements and the ones who had "gone out" from the original community in 1 John 2:19.

The Elder has rejoiced to learn that the fellow children of God of this church are walking in truth and sharing in the love of their Gospel traditions. He seems to hope that this affirmation and appeal to continue in love will buttress them against those he calls "deceivers," who apparently not only broke with the community but seem to be actively spreading their alternative theological teaching. The one indication that the Elder gives of the content of this theology is that the deceivers "do not acknowledge Jesus Christ as coming in the flesh" (v. 7). As we indicated above, the notion that Jesus as Christ was not really human may be early evidence of a movement that developed into the form of Christianity known as Gnosticism, which was popular in the second century CE. These beliefs have already fractured the Johannine community, and the Elder hopes to stop the spread before this sister church falls prey as well. He counsels her to abide in the Johannine teaching of the incarnation that she has heard from the beginning and thereby abide in the new covenant of Christ (v. 9). The children of God are to receive and believe in Christ (see John 1:12), and they are not to receive these deceivers (v. 10). The unity and foundation of the Christian community is at stake. The Elder closes with hopes of a future visit to continue the conversation and solidify their relationship as children of elect sisters (v. 13).

Greco-Roman Letters and 2-3 John

There are many documents in the New Testament that we call "Letters," but very few of them are typical first-century letters. Like contemporary letters (beginning with "Dear . . ." greetings, body of the letter, conclusion, and signing off with "Sincerely . . ."), Greco-Roman letters also had a fixed form. The best examples of such letters in the New Testament are 2–3 John. They are both about the same length, matching a single piece of papyrus, and they have the following format:

Opening formula: Sender (the Elder), to whom the letter is sent (the Elect Lady, Gaius), Greeting (grace, mercy, peace, health, etc.).

Body of the Letter: The issues that the Elder wishes to discuss, his concerns, and his desire to be with them again.

Conclusion: Greetings of peace, prosperity, or good health.

Third John

The Third Letter of John is addressed to Gaius, a Christian who is otherwise unknown in the New Testament literature. These letters are increasingly more specific. The third letter is essentially a personal note indicating the splintering of the community and a final appeal for unity from the Elder to a trusted friend. He praises the prospering of Gaius's soul as he walks in truth, thereby indicating that Gaius is abiding in the Gospel commandments of love and belief in the incarnate Christ. This faithfulness has brought joy and encouragement to the Elder (vv. 1–4). In the body of the letter he first gives attention to the reflection of truth in hospitality, which has characterized Gaius's leadership (vv. 5–8), and then turns to the politics of ecclesial power in terms of a warning against Diotrephes, who does not seem to accept the Elder's authority (vv. 9–10). Here the theological disputes of the previous letters have deteriorated into more personal conflicts with hints of factions, a decided lack of hospitality, and even expulsions from the community. In 2 John we saw the recommendation that people who do not share the community's faith are not to be made welcome. In 3 John we see that a possible leader in another Johannine community is now practicing this "exclusion" of the Elder himself. The hopes for a universal egalitarian Christian community based in love and belief seem to be fading in the wake of the contentiousness of human nature.

This brief letter begins to close with a commendation of Demetrius, who may well be the letter carrier and who has proven himself to be one who walks in truth, love, and faithfulness to the community (vv. 11–12). As in 2 John, the Elder closes with a desire for a personal visit to continue the conversation. He offers a final greeting to Gaius as a "friend" instead of his more typical "child." This could indicate—in keeping with John 15:12–17 where Jesus begins to call his disciples "friends," as new leaders who keep the new commandments— that Gaius is a faithful fellow leader of the community who is striving for the unity for which the Elder hopes. The Elder closes his testimony, and indeed, the entirety of his correspondence preserved in the NT, with a final appeal for peace (v. 15).

What Have We Learned So Far?
The Community of the Beloved Disciple

The collective summons of the three Letters of John revolves around theology, Christology, and ethics. They punctuate the Gospel's teaching on believing in God as revealed through Jesus, the human Christ who is also God incarnate, and on loving one another as the ethic that naturally follows from living as authentic children of God. One's vertical relationship with God through believing in Jesus Christ empowers, enlivens, and sets parameters for the ensuing horizontal relationship with other people who are likewise struggling to live in an often difficult world. These Letters give testament both to the powerful, self-giving love of God through Christ in relationship with humankind, as well as to the profound frailty of the nature of that same humankind. The open call for a community to live in equal fellowship through believing in Jesus as the Christ and Son of God and love of both God and one another is a vocation that every Christian can agree upon. This summons to relationship is never in question. The ability of humankind to live in this ideal, if unstructured, relationship in an imperfect world is in question. This is the ongoing challenge of living in community as children of God.

The preservation of these letters alongside the Gospel of John in the Scripture of Christianity gives voice to the beauty of God's love and the fire of conviction that love sparks in humankind. Jesus and the disciples of every sort, including the Elder, speak to that truth. But these four books also reveal the journeys of faith and sometimes failure human beings are destined to travel in this world. The Letters indicate the beginnings of the tragic collapse of the Johannine community, but this is not the end of their story. This literature also teaches that God and God's plan succeed even when humans fail. These Christians are eventually integrated into the larger developing faith tradition of the church, and their writings live on to continue to give witness to the new life in Christ to which all human beings are called.

Key Terms and Concepts

antichrists

Catholic Epistles

children of God

elder/*presbyteros*

elect lady

General Letters

Johannine epistles

John

letters of John

polemic

Questions for Review

1. What are the distinctive terms, concepts, characteristics, and themes shared by the Gospel and Letters of John?

2. What are the similarities among these three letters? In responding, be sure to note also how the letters are addressed, how the author characterizes himself, and how the author characterizes the recipients.

3. What does the occasion of each letter seem to be (i.e., what situation or events may have prompted the letter on the basis of what issues the writer discusses)?

4. What characteristics of the author's opponents can be reconstructed from these three letters?

5. Can you get a sense of the flow of thought of this correspondence? If you had to articulate themes for each letter, what would they be?

6. How might the Letters shed light on the Gospel and on the community of the evangelist? What is happening to this community at the end of the first and the beginning of the second centuries CE?

7. What might be important about the inclusion of this common literature, that is, the Gospel and Letters of John, in the NT canon?

Bibliography and Further Reading

Brown, Raymond E. *The Community of the Beloved Disciple. The Life, Loves, and Hates of an Individual Church in New Testament Times.* New York: Paulist, 1979.
————. *The Epistles of John.* Anchor Bible 30. New York: Doubleday, 1982.
Brown, Sherri. *God's Promise: Covenant Relationship in John.* New York: Paulist, 2014.
Culpepper, R. Alan. *The Gospel and Letters of John.* Interpreting Biblical Texts. Nashville: Abingdon, 1998.
Lieu, Judith. *The Theology of the Johannine Epistles.* New Testament Theology. Cambridge: Cambridge University Press, 1991.
Malatesta, E. *Interiority and Covenant: A Study of εἶναι ἐν and μένειν ἐν in the First Letter of Saint John.* Analecta Biblica 69. Rome: Biblical Institute Press, 1978.
Parsenios, George L. *First, Second, and Third John.* Paideia. Grand Rapids: Baker Academic, 2014.

The Good News of the Community of the Beloved Disciple

PURPOSE This brief conclusion draws together the themes of the texts and the textbook by discussing the challenge of the first-century Johannine community for our present world.

ASSIGNMENT Review and reflect upon the Gospel and Letters of John

We have come to the end of a long journey through several worlds. In the first place, we have had the opportunity to travel through the historical world that produced the Bible, the New Testament, and especially the Gospel and Letters of John. We called this "the world behind the text." We then looked at the many literary techniques that can be found in the Gospel, and we called that "the world in the text." We also decided on the approach that we wanted to adopt in reading through the Johannine Gospel and Letters. We did not ignore the historical and literary questions, but we continually asked the question of the ongoing meaning of these texts, sacred to many, for those who read it, hear it, or see it performed. We called this "the world in front of the text."

Once we had our "worlds" in place, we followed the unfolding story from John 1 to John 21, and then the later teaching from the same "world" that can be traced in 1–3 John. We trust that this has been an interesting experience for all who have used this textbook. Of course, not everyone who uses this book comes from a Christian tradition. Nonetheless, the portrait of Jesus of Nazareth that John has handed down to the church continues to speak to us. There is much in the Christian faith that depends upon this story, especially the way Christians understand Jesus as the incarnate *logos* who became flesh and dwelt among us (John 1:14), whose name was "Jesus." Very early in the life of the church he came to be known as "the Christ," and thus, already in 1:17, John tells his audience that his name is "Jesus Christ." For this Gospel, Jesus Christ is further described as the Son of Man, who is lifted up on a cross, and the Son of God who came from God, made God known, and returns to God, whom he always calls his Father. The Johannine Jesus tells us God's story, how

God acts lovingly in offering life and light to humankind, providing a unique way to God (see 14:6: "I am the way, the truth, and the light"). This man who made God known was truly one of us, and 1 John was written largely to insist that the community never forget that (see 1 John 1:1–4). The challenge to love as Jesus loved was a difficult one, and we can see in 2 and 3 John that tensions arose among the various Johannine communities.

We have also seen John's emphasis on events in Jesus's ministry that foreshadow the sacramental life of the church. He speaks to a Christian audience that depends upon baptism and Eucharist for that life. You will recall especially our study of John 3, John 6, John 13, and John 19, where this emphasis is most clear. John does not mention these institutions formally as baptism and Eucharist, but he presupposes them through references to living water and rebirth, as well as living bread and the wine of the new dispensation. Behind this is a living community, continuing to celebrate the presence of Jesus Christ, even in his absence. As we have seen, the fishing trip with its unbroken net containing many fish, and the discussion of the roles of Peter and the Beloved Disciple in John 21, point to a church where this celebration takes place.

The Gospel was written for people who were feeling the loss of Jesus's presence among them. John has developed the figure of the Beloved Disciple as the model disciple. A person from the earliest church, and the bearer of the Johannine story (see 21:24), he is close to Jesus, especially in intensely sacramental moments (see 13:23; 19:25–27). At the empty tomb, he did not *see* the risen Jesus, but he *believed* (20:3–10). The final words of the risen Jesus in John 20 are: "Blessed are those who do not *see*, yet *believe*" (20:29). John expresses his hope that all who come to know Jesus and confess him as the Christ will become Beloved Disciples of Jesus, and have life in him (20:30–31). We join the author of the Gospel of John in that same hope, aware that even after years of reflection, and attempting to live Jesus's command to love (see 13:34–35; 15:12, 17; 17:21–26), we still have a way to go, like the Johannine disciples in 1–3 John!

But even if the Christian tradition is not your "home," we trust that this introduction to the Bible, study of how one should approach it, and then your experience of this unique story from Christianity's earliest years have been helpful. The Gospel of John is one of the most treasured pieces of literature in Western society. We have been honored to lead our readers through it and congratulate you all for coming to these final words, remembering the words of the author of John 21:25: "the world itself could not contain the books" that could be written about Jesus. You have made a solid start on those "books." May it stand you in good stead, no matter what your faith background and what future you will create. John would ask you, however, to create that future *with others*, in contexts of genuine love and care.

Bibliography and Further Reading

Commentaries

What follows is a list of the major commentaries on the Gospel and Letters of John in English. These are the fundamental building blocks for any serious study of the Johannine Literature in academia today. The Gospel of John is one of the most commented upon books of the New Testament. The following list provides not only a *number* of interpreters, but also a *number* of differing *interpretations*.

A commentary upon the Gospel of John works through the whole text, verse by verse, and offers a general introduction to its time and place of writing, the author, and why he or she wrote it. Commentaries are especially important. Other studies focus upon one or other issue in the Gospel that calls for further investigation.

Barrett, C. K. *The Gospel according to St John*. 2nd ed. London: SPCK, 1978.

Beasley-Murray, George R. *John*. 2nd ed. Word Biblical Commentary 36. Nashville: Thomas Nelson, 1999.

Brant, Jo-Ann A. *John*. Paideia. Grand Rapids: Baker, 2011.

Brown, Raymond E. *The Epistles of John*. Anchor Bible 30. New York: Doubleday, 1982.

———. *The Death of the Messiah: From Gethsemane to the Grave. A Commentary on the Passion Narratives in the Four Gospels*. 2 vols. Anchor Bible Reference Library. New York: Doubleday, 1994.

———. *The Gospel according to John*. 2 vols. Anchor Bible 29–29a. New York: Doubleday, 1966–70.

Bultmann, Rudolph. *The Gospel of John: A Commentary*. Oxford: Blackwell, 1971.

Byrne, Brendan, SJ. *Life Abounding: A Reading of John's Gospel*. Collegeville, MN: Liturgical, 2014.

Culpepper, R. Alan. *The Gospel and Letters of John*. Interpreting Biblical Texts. Nashville: Abingdon, 1998.

Hoskyns, Edwyn C. *The Fourth Gospel.* Edited by F. N. Davey. London: Faber & Faber, 1947.

Kysar, Robert. *John.* Augsburg Commentary on the New Testament. Minneapolis: Augsburg Publishing, 1986.

Lightfoot, Robert H. *St. John's Gospel.* Edited by C. F. Evans. Oxford: University Press, 1956.

Lincoln, Andrew T. *The Gospel According to Saint John.* Black's New Testament Commentary. Edited by M. Hooker. London: Continuum, 2005.

Lindars, Barnabas. *The Gospel of John.* New Century Bible. London: Oliphants, 1972.

Malina, Bruce J., and R. L. Rohrbaugh. *Social-Science Commentary on the Gospel of John.* Minneapolis: Fortress, 1998.

Moloney, Francis J. *Belief in the Word: Reading John 1–4.* Minneapolis: Fortress, 1993.

———. *Glory not Dishonor: Reading John 13–21.* Minneapolis: Fortress, 1998.

———. *The Gospel of John.* Sacra Pagina 4. Collegeville, MN: Liturgical, 1998.

———. *The Resurrection of the Messiah. A Narrative Commentary on the Resurrection Accounts in the Four Gospels.* New York: Paulist, 2013.

———. *Signs and Shadows: Reading John 5–12.* Minneapolis: Fortress, 1996.

Newsom, Carol A., Sharon H. Ringe, and Jacqueline E. Lapsley. *Women's Bible Commentary.* 3rd ed. Louisville: Westminster John Know, 2012.

O'Day, Gail R., and Susan E. Hylen. *John.* Westminster Bible Companion. Lousiville: Westminster John Knox, 2006.

Painter, John. *1, 2, and 3 John.* Sacra Pagina 18. Collegeville, MN: Liturgical, 2002.

Parsenios, George L. *First, Second, and Third John.* Paideia. Grand Rapids: Baker Academic, 2014.

Schnackenburg, Rudolf. *The Gospel according to St John.* 3 vols. Herder's Theological Commentary on the New Testament 4.1–3. London: Burns & Oates/New York: Crossroad, 1968–82.

Smith, D. Moody. *John.* Abingdon New Testament Commentaries. Nashville: Abingdon, 1999.

Stibbe, Mark W. G. *John.* Readings: A New Biblical Commentary. Sheffield: JSOT Press, 1993.

Talbert, Charles H. *Reading John: A Literary and Theological Commentary on the Fourth Gospel and the Johannine Epistles.* London: SPCK, 1992.

Thompson, Marianne Meye. *John: A Commentary.* The News Testament Library. Louisville: Westminster John Knox, 2015.

General Books and Articles

The books and articles mentioned at the conclusion of each chapter are listed below. This is by no means a complete bibliography for the Gospel and Letters of John. In some cases we have listed them because they have guided our interpretation, and in others because they can serve an advanced student for reading beyond what is provided in this book. Students who are interested in further study are encouraged to consult their libraries for these and other works by these authors as well as authors mentioned in the bibliographies of their works.

Alter, Robert. *The Art of Biblical Narrative*. New York: Basic Books, 1981.

Anderson, Bernard W., Steven Bishop, and Judith H. Newman. *Understanding the Old Testament.* 5th ed. Upper Saddle River: Pearson, 2002.

Asiedu-Peprah, Martin. *Johannine Sabbath Conflicts as Juridical Controversy*. Wissenschaftliche Untersuchungen zum Neuen Testament 2.132. Tübingen: Mohr Siebeck, 2001.

Attridge, Harold W. "Genre Bending in the Fourth Gospel." *Journal for Biblical Literature* 121 (2002): 3–21.

Barrett, C. K. *The Prologue of St John's Gospel*. London: Athlone, 1971.

Brown, Raymond E. *The Community of the Beloved Disciple: The Life, Loves, and Hates of an Individual Church in New Testament Times*. New York: Paulist, 1979.

———. *An Introduction to the Gospel of John*. Edited by Francis J. Moloney. Anchor Bible Reference Library. New York: Doubleday, 2003.

Brown, Sherri. *Gift upon Gift: Covenant through Word in the Gospel of John*. Princeton Theological Monograph Series. Eugene: Pickwick, 2010.

———. *God's Promise: Covenant Relationship in John*. New York: Paulist, 2014.

———. "John the Baptist: Witness and Embodiment of the Prologue in the Gospel of John." Pages 145–62 in *Characters and Characterization in the Gospel of John*. Edited by Christopher W. Skinner. Library of New Testament Studies 461. London: T&T Clark, 2013.

———. "What Is Truth? Jesus, Pilate, and the Staging of the Dialogue of the Cross in John 18:28–19:16a." *Catholic Biblical Quarterly* 77 (2015): 69–86.

———. "What's in an Ending? John 21 and the Performative Force of an Epilogue." *Perspectives in Religious Studies* 42 (2015): 29–42.

Bultmann, Rudolf. *Geschichte der synoptischen Tradition*, 1921. English edition: *The History of the Synoptic Tradition*. 3rd ed. New York: Harper & Row, 1972.

Byrne, Brendan. "The Faith of the Beloved Disciple and the Community in John 20." *Journal for the Study of the New Testament* 23 (1985): 83–97.

Carvalho, Corrine. *Encountering Ancient Voices: A Guide to Reading the Old Testament*. Winona, MN: Anselm Academic, 2006.

———. *Primer on Biblical Methods*. Winona, MN: Anselm Academic, 2009.

Chatman, Seymour. *Story and Discourse: Narrative Structure in Fiction and Film*. Ithaca: Cornell University Press, 1978.

Chennattu, Rekha M. *Johannine Discipleship as a Covenant Relationship*. Peabody, MA: Hendrickson, 2006.

Collins, Raymond F. "The Representative Figures in the Fourth Gospel." *Downside Review* 94 (1976): 26–46, 118–32.

Conzelmann, Hans. *Die Mitte der Zeit*. Tübingen: Mohr Siebeck, 1954. English edition: *The Theology of St. Luke*. Minneapolis: Fortress, 1982.

Culpepper, R. Alan. *The Anatomy of the Fourth Gospel: A Study in Literary Design*. Foundations and Facets. Philadelphia: Fortress, 1985.

———. "The Pivot of John's Prologue." *New Testament Studies* 27 (1980): 1–31.

———. "The Theology of the Johannine Passion Narrative: John 19:16b–30." *Neotestamentica* 31 (1997): 21–37.

Dawes, Gregory. *Introduction to the Bible*. New Collegeville Bible Commentary: Old Testament. Vol. 1. Collegeville, MA: Liturgical, 2007.

de la Potterie, Ignace. *The Passion and Resurrection of Jesus according to John: Text and Spirit*. London: Slough, UK: St Paul Publications, 1989.

Fitzmyer, Joseph A. *Scripture, the Soul of Theology*. New York: Paulist, 1994.

Frigge, Marielle. *Beginning Biblical Studies*. Rev. ed. Winona: Anselm Academic, 2013.

Green, Barbara. *From Earth's Creation to John's Revelation: The INTERFACES Biblical Storyline Companion*. Collegeville, MN: Liturgical, 2003.

Hooker, Morna D. *Beginnings: Keys That Open the Gospels*. Harrisburg: Trinity, 1997.

———. "John the Baptist and the Johannine Prologue." *New Testament Studies* 16 (1970): 354–58.

Hunt, Steven A., D. Francois Talmie, and Ruben Zimmerman, eds. *Character Studies in the Fourth Gospel*. Wissenschaftliche Untersuchungen zum Neuen Testament 314. Tübingen: Mohr Siebeck, 2013.

Hurtado, Larry. *How on Earth Did Jesus Become a God? Historical Questions about Earliest Devotion to Jesus*. Grand Rapids: Eerdmans, 2005.

Johnson, Luke Timothy. *The Writings of the New Testament: An Interpretation*. 3rd ed. Minneapolis: Fortress, 2010.

Kelber, Werner H. "The Birth of a Beginning: John 1:1–18." *Semeia* 52 (1990): 121–44.

Knight, Douglas A., and Amy-Jill Levine. *The Meaning of the Bible: What the Jewish Scriptures and Christian Old Testament Can Teach Us*. New York: Harper One, 2011.

Kurz, William S. *Farewell Addresses in the New Testament*. Zaccheus Studies: New Testament. Collegeville, MN: Liturgical, 1990.

LeDonne, Anthony, and Tom Thatcher, eds. *The Fourth Gospel in First Century Media Culture*. Library of New Testament Studies. London: T&T Clark, 2013.

Lee, Dorothy A. *Flesh and Glory: Symbolism, Gender and Theology in the Gospel of John*. New York: Crossroad, 2002.

Lennan, Richard. *An Introduction to Catholic Theology*. Mahwah, NJ: Paulist, 1998.

Lieu, Judith. *The Theology of the Johannine Epistles*. New Testament Theology. Cambridge: Cambridge University Press, 1991.

Lincoln, Andrew T. "The Lazarus Story: A Literary Perspective." Pages 211–32 in *The Gospel of John and Christian Theology*. Edited by Richard Bauckham and Carl Mosser. Grand Rapids: Eerdmans, 2008.

Malatesta, Edward. *Interiority and Covenant: A Study of εἶναι ἐν and μένειν ἐν in the*

First Letter of Saint John. Analecta Biblica 69. Rome: Biblical Institute Press, 1978.

Martyn, J. Louis. *History and Theology in the Fourth Gospel*. 3rd ed. Louisville: Westminster John Knox, 2003.

Miller, John W. *How the Bible Came to Be: Exploring the Narrative and Message*. Mahwah, NJ: Paulist, 2004.

Moloney, Francis J. "Can Everyone Be Wrong? A Reading of John 11.1–12.8." *New Testament Studies* 49 (2003): 505–27.

———. "'For as Yet They Did Not Know the Scripture' (John 20:9): A Study in Narrative Time." *Irish Theological Quarterly* 79 (2014): 97–111.

———. "The Function of John 13–17 within the Johannine Narrative." Pages 43–66 in *"What Is John?" Volume II. Literary and Social Readings of the Fourth Gospel*. Edited by Fernando F. Segovia. Symposium Series 7. Atlanta: Scholars Press, 1998.

———. "John 18:15–27: A Johannine View of the Church." *Downside Review* 112 (1994): 231–48.

———. *Love in the Gospel of John: An Exegetical, Theological, and Literary Study*. Grand Rapids: Baker Academic, 2013.

———. "Narrative and Discourse in the Feast of Tabernacles." Pages 155–72 in *Word, Theology, and Community in John*. Edited by John Painter, R. Alan Culpepper, and Fernando Segovia. St. Louis: Chalice, 2002.

———. *Reading the New Testament in the Church: A Primer for Pastors, Religious Educators, and Believers*. Grand Rapids: Baker Academic, 2015.

Neirynck, Frans. "The Anonymous Disciple in John 1." *Ephemerides Theologicae Lovanienses* 66 (1990): 5–37.

Neyrey, Jerome. "The Jacob Allusions in John 1:51." *Catholic Biblical Quarterly* 44 (1982): 586–605.

Nickle, Keith F. *The Synoptic Gospels: An Introduction*. Revised and expanded edition. Louisville: Westminster John Knox, 2001.

Powell, Mark Allan. *Fortress Introduction to the Gospels*. 6th ed. Minneapolis: Fortress, 1998.

———. *Introducing the New Testament: A Historical, Literary, and Theological Survey*. Ada, MI: Baker Academic, 2009.

———. *What Is Narrative Criticism?* Guides to Biblical Scholarship: New Testament Series. Minneapolis: Fortress, 1990.

Powell, Mark Allan, ed. *Harper Collins Bible Dictionary*. 3rd ed. New York: HarperOne, 2011.

Rhoads, David. "Performance Criticism: An Emerging Methodology in Second Testament Studies." *Biblical Theological Bulletin* 36 (2006): 118–40, 164–88.

Schneiders, Sandra M. *Jesus Risen in Our Midst: Essays on the Resurrection of Jesus in the Fourth Gospel*. Collegeville, MN: Liturgical, 2013.

———. *Written That You May Believe: Encountering Jesus in the Fourth Gospel*. Revised and expanded ed. New York: Crossroad, 2003.

Schnelle, Udo. "Recent Views of John's Gospel." *Word & World* 21 (2001): 352–59.

Skinner, Christopher W., ed. *Characters and Characterization in the Gospel of John.* Library of New Testament Studies 461. London: T&T Clark, 2013.

———. *Reading John.* Eugene, OR: Cascade Books 2015.

Smith, D. Moody. *The Composition and Order of the Fourth Gospel.* New Haven: Yale University, 1965.

Steggemann, Ekkehard W., and Wolfgang Steggemann. *The Jesus Movement: A Social History of Its First Century.* Translated by O. C. Dean. Minneapolis: Fortress, 1999.

Thatcher, Tom. *Why John Wrote a Gospel: Jesus-Memory-History.* Eugene, OR: Wipf & Stock, 2012.

Thompson, Marianne M. "The Raising of Lazarus in John 11: A Theological Reading." Pages 233–44 in *The Gospel of John and Christian Theology.* Edited by Richard Bauckham and Carl Mosser. Grand Rapids: Eerdmans, 2008.

Yee, Gale. *Jewish Feasts and the Gospel of John.* Eugene, OR: Wipf & Stock, 2007.

Index of Authors

Index of Subjects

Index of Scripture